The Many Panics of 1837
People, Politics, and the Creation of a Transatlantic Financial Crisis

In the spring of 1837, people panicked as financial and economic uncertainty spread within and between New York, New Orleans, and London. Although the period of panic would dramatically influence political, cultural, and social history, those who panicked sought to erase from history their experiences of one of America's worst early financial crises. *The Many Panics of 1837* reconstructs the period between March and May 1837 in order to make arguments about the national boundaries of history, the role of information in the economy, the personal and local nature of national and international events, the origins and dissemination of economic ideas, and most importantly, what actually happened in 1837. This riveting transatlantic cultural history, based on archival research on two continents, reveals how people transformed their experiences of financial crisis into the "Panic of 1837," a single event that would serve as a turning point in American history and an early inspiration for business cycle theory.

Jessica M. Lepler is an assistant professor of history at the University of New Hampshire. The Society of American Historians awarded her Brandeis University doctoral dissertation, "1837: Anatomy of a Panic," the 2008 Allan Nevins Prize. She has been the recipient of a Hench Post-Dissertation Fellowship from the American Antiquarian Society, a Dissertation Fellowship from the Library Company of Philadelphia's Program in Early American Economy and Society, a John E. Rovensky Dissertation Fellowship in Business History, and a Jacob K. Javits Fellowship from the U.S. Department of Education.

The Many Panics of 1837

People, Politics, and the Creation of
a Transatlantic Financial Crisis

JESSICA M. LEPLER
University of New Hampshire

CAMBRIDGE
UNIVERSITY PRESS

CAMBRIDGE
UNIVERSITY PRESS

32 Avenue of the Americas, New York NY 10013-2473, USA

Cambridge University Press is part of the University of Cambridge.

It furthers the University's mission by disseminating knowledge in the pursuit of education, learning and research at the highest international levels of excellence.

www.cambridge.org
Information on this title: www.cambridge.org/9781107640863

First published 2013

A catalogue record for this publication is available from the British Library

Library of Congress Cataloguing in Publication data
Lepler, Jessica M.
The many panics of 1837 : people, politics, and the creation of
a transatlantic financial crisis / Jessica M. Lepler, University of New Hampshire.
pages cm
ISBN 978-0-521-11653-4 (hardback)
1. Depressions – 1837.   2. Financial crises – United States – History – 19th
century.   3. United States – Economic conditions – To 1865.   I. Title.
HB37171837 .L47   2013
330.973'057–dc23   2013015877

ISBN 978-0-521-11653-4 Hardback
ISBN 978-1-107-64086-3 Paperback

To
Michelle and Allan Lepler

It became evident that a dark cloud hung over the business atmosphere. Unexpected failures every day took place. Some attributed the thick-coming evils to the removal of the deposits, others to interrupted currency; some to overtrading, and some to extravagance. Whatever was the cause, the distress was real. Mr. Draper's cotton became a drug in the market; manufactories stopped, or gave no dividends. Eastern lands lost their nominal value, and western towns became bankrupt. Ships stood in the harbor, with their sails unbent and masts dismantled. Day laborers looked aghast, not knowing where to earn food for their families. The whirlwind came; it made no distinction of persons. 'It smote the four corners of the house,' and the high-minded and the honorable fell indiscriminately with the rest. Well may it be asked, Whence came this desolation upon the community? No pestilence visited our land; it was not the plague; it was not the yellow fever, or cholera. Health was borne on every breeze; the earth yielded her produce, and Peace still dwelt among us.

– Hannah Farnham Sawyer Lee, *Rich Enough: A Tale of the Times* (Boston: Whipple & Damrell, 1837), 70–71.

Contents

List of Figures

Acknowledgments

The failures of this book are entirely self-made; the successes are the product of the support I have received from many individuals and institutions. Permit me to attempt to express my gratitude to some of those who have made this book possible.

Without Jane Kamensky's trenchant questions and unwavering support, I would never have found the many panics of 1837. She led a superb doctoral committee that included David Engerman and Dan Dupre. Milton Kornfeld, Jacqueline Jones, David Hackett Fischer, Michael Willrich, Joyce Antler, and many others at Brandeis University provided me with the tools of a professional historian. Outside of my graduate institution, my mentors and close friends Cathy Kelly and Cathy Matson have helped me navigate my academic life. My excellent teachers and professors, especially John Hewlett, Gloria Sesso, Wilfred McClay, Christian Brady, and the late Philip Stuart and Jean Danielson, inspired me to pursue a career in history.

As we prepared for our comprehensive examinations more than a decade ago, Emily Straus asked me to explain the Panic of 1837; this book would not exist without her question and the many other insightful queries of my graduate school cohort, especially Kim Frederick, Denise Damico, Eric Schlereth, Will Walker, Gabe Loiacono, Jason Opal, Hilary Moss, Alexis Antracoli, Alexis Messing Tinsley, Maria Noth, Lindsay Silver Cohen, and Lynda Yankaskas.

One day in the spring of 2007, two literary scholars – Yvette Piggush and Hunt Howell – informed me that bills of exchange were texts; in 2009, historian of science Emily Pawley taught me that these same financial instruments were paper technology. I could not have written this book without their insights. Other fellows who opened my eyes to new ways of seeing include April Haynes, Meredith Neuman, Lloyd Pratt, Ezra Greenspan, Mary Beth Sievens, Michael Winship, Sean Kelley, Adam Nelson, Marla Miller, Rose Beiler, Candice Harrison, and Jenna Gibbs. I owe similar unpayable debts to people too numerous to mention by name. Fellows at the American Antiquarian Society and the Library Company of Philadelphia shaped my work in ways big and small. Although I was not an official fellow at the McNeil Center for Early American Studies, Daniel Richter always made me feel like one. During my year as a visiting assistant professor at Case Western Reserve University, Jonathan Sadowsky, Renee Sentilles, John Broich, and their outstanding colleagues welcomed me as a full member of their community and assisted me in finding my own academic home. Since I arrived at the University of New Hampshire in 2008, all of my colleagues have been generous with both their time and their confidence. Dean Ken Fuld and the several chairs of the History Department – Jan Golinski, Bill Harris, and Lige Gould – have consistently supported my work. Everywhere that I have taught, my students have been a font of provocative questions and insightful comments. In particular, Cory McKenzie's meticulous editing of my footnotes deserves special recognition.

I am incredibly fortunate that the American Antiquarian Society brought together Scott Sandage, Adam Rothman, Bruce Mann, Caroline Sloat, and Paul Erickson to discuss my dissertation. So many other scholars have answered my questions, suggested sources, or read versions of this manuscript that it would be impossible to thank them all by name. I owe particular debts to John Larson, David Green, Michael Zakim, Mary Poovey, Robert Lee, Richard John, David Nord, Steven Bullock, Roderick McDonald, Michael Zuckerman, Mary Templin, Brian Murphy, Edward Balleisen, Jeffrey Pasley, Joshua Greenberg, Margot Finn, Sven Beckert, Lesley Doig, Stephen Mihm, Daniele Besomi, Nancy Davison, Christopher Clark, Brian Luskey, Richard Latner, George Bernstein, Peter Temin, Stanley Engerman, Seth Rockman, Andrew Shankman, Robert Wright, Scott Reynolds Nelson, Naomi Lamoreaux, Emma Rothschild, Walter Johnson, Ann Fabian, Larry Schweikart, Alice O'Connor, Steve Fraser, Mary Fuhrer, and Wayne Bodle.

Commentators, fellow panelists, and participants at conferences, seminars, and colloquia have provided me with indispensible feedback. I was fortunate to present my work to the Organization of American Historians, the American Historical Association, the American Studies Association, the Society for Historians of the Early American Republic, the History of

Economics Society, the American Antiquarian Society, the Program in Early American Economy and Society at the Library Company of Philadelphia, The Historic New Orleans Collection, the Hagley Library, the McNeil Center, the Center for History and Economics at Harvard University, the University of Georgia, the Culture of the Market Network at the University of Oxford, the University of Liverpool, the University Seminar on Early American History and Culture at Columbia University, the UNH History Faculty Seminar, and the Kompactseminar of Brandeis University and Universität Augsburg.

The libraries and librarians at UNH, Brandeis, Case Western, and the affiliated institutions of the Boston Library Consortium have provided me with extraordinary research capabilities. For enabling me to access digital and print sources when I was far from my home institutions, I would like to thank the King's College London Department of Geography; the British Library; and the libraries of the University of Pittsburgh, the University of Pennsylvania, George Washington University, and Tulane University. I am grateful to all of the institutions that granted me image and manuscript permissions. I owe a heartfelt thanks to the staff at the Rothschild Archive, the Bank of England Archive, the Baring Archive, the British Library Newspaper Reading Room, the National Archives at Kew, the Manuscript and Newspaper Reading Rooms of the Library of Congress, the Louisiana Research Collection at Tulane University, the Williams Research Center of The Historic New Orleans Collection, the City Archives and Louisiana Division of the New Orleans Public Library, the New Orleans Notarial Archives, the Earl K. Long Library at the University of New Orleans, the Hermann-Grima Historic House, the New-York Historical Society, the Manuscripts and Archives Division of The New York Public Library, the National Archives at New York City, the Library Company of Philadelphia, the Historical Society of Pennsylvania, the American Antiquarian Society, the Baker Library of the Harvard Business School, the Boston Public Library, the Massachusetts Historical Society, and the Boston Athenaeum. Some of the people who make these institutions such delightful workplaces include Melanie Aspey, Moira Lovegrove, Clara Harrow, Sarah Millard, Melissa Smith, Ken Owen, Lee Miller, Irene Wainwright, Priscilla Lawrence, John Lawrence, Jessica Dorman, Mary Lou Eichhorn, Gigi Barnhill, Vince Golden, Lauren Hewes, Elizabeth Pope, Laura Wasowicz, Andrew Bourque, Jackie Penny, Diann Benti, Jim Green, Wendy Woloson, and Connie King.

I am grateful to *Common-place*, *Journal of Cultural Economy*, and Ashgate Publishing for granting me permission to include in this monograph material originally published as "Pictures of Panic: Constructing Hard Times in Words and Images," *Common-place* 10, no. 3 (Spring 2010); "'The News Flew Like Lightning': Spreading Panic in 1837," *Journal of Cultural Economy* 5, no. 2 (May 2012): 179–95; and "'To Save the Commercial Community of New York': Panicked Business Elites in 1837," in *Commerce and Culture: Nineteenth-Century Business Elites*, edited by Robert Lee (London: Ashgate, 2011), 117–38.

My work has benefited from the financial support of a Hench Post-Dissertation Fellowship from the American Antiquarian Society; a Dissertation Fellowship from the Program in Early American Economy and Society at the Library Company of Philadelphia; a John E. Rovensky Fellowship in U.S. Business or Economic History; an Irving and Rose Crown Fellowship and a Sachar International Travel Award from Brandeis University; a Jacob K. Javits Fellowship from the U.S. Department of Education; a Dianne Woest Fellowship from The Historic New Orleans Collection; an Annette K. Baxter Travel Grant from the American Studies Association; a travel grant from the University of Liverpool; a Research Bursary from the Rothschild Archive; a Dean's Honor Scholarship from Newcomb College of Tulane University; and funds from the UNH College of Liberal Arts, the UNH History Department, and the Signal and Dunfey Funds.

In 2008, the Society of American Historians awarded my dissertation the Allan Nevins Prize. I will forever be grateful to Mark Carnes, Robert Cowley, and Susan Hartmann for this honor. At Cambridge University Press, I have had the pleasure of working with Eric Crahan, Lew Bateman, Deborah Gershenowitz, Abigail Zorbaugh, Alison Daltroy, and Dana Bricken, and Sumitha Nithyanandan and her team at Integra Software Services. David Lyons made good sense of the manuscript in his index.

I could not have performed the far-ranging research for this book without a wide network of wonderful friends who hosted me on my travels. I would especially like to thank Vanita Neelakanta, Rachel Kapelle, Becky Olson, Jeremy Colson, Vicki and Ryan Wepler, Royden Tull, Eric Olson, Stefan Friedl, Lars Lierow, Wolfgang and Barbara Siegert, Stephane Saal, Connie Siedler, Vincent Webb, Ken Damico, Brian Kinney, Cindy Chen, Louise and Lawrence Francis, Jennifer Cricenti Rheder, Tania Playhay, Kathryn Davies, William Danny, Hilary Guite, Petr Barta, Jo Collins, Leena Pradhan-Nabzdyk, Christoph Nabzdyk, Lisa Singleton, Nezahualcoyotl Xiuhtecutli, Margarita Vargas, Michael Joyce, James McAllister, Jeannie Sowers, Ben Chandran, Riki Greenspan, and the Jakobs sisters.

Finally, Spencer Lepler; Reginald Waters; Marcia Dube; Sheila Feingold; and the Lepler, Gratz, and Rodden families have allayed my many personal panics. Several of my biggest supporters did not live to see the end product of all my years of work: my maternal grandparents Estelle and Max Feingold, my paternal grandparents Gertrude and Louis Lepler, and my "Nana Dog" Zak. This book is dedicated to my parents, Michelle Feingold Lepler and Allan Lepler. Michael Dube, my bashert, you will always be my lawyer (and songwriter) perfect.

Abbreviations

NARA   Entry 117, Bankruptcy Records, Act of 1841, United States
         District Court for the Southern Federal District of New
         York, National Archives at New York City
NOCA   Louisiana Division/City Archives, New Orleans Public
         Library, New Orleans, LA
NONA   Clerk of Civil District Court, Notarial Archives Division,
         New Orleans, LA
NYPL   Manuscripts and Archives Division, The New York Public
         Library, Astor, Lenox, and Tilden Foundations, New York
RAL   The Rothschild Archive, London, United Kingdom
UNO   Historical Archives of the Supreme Court of Louisiana
         (Mss 106), Earl K. Long Library, University of New Orleans,
         New Orleans, LA

PERIODICALS

NI3   *National Intelligencer* (Washington, D.C.) [Thrice-Weekly
         Edition]
NOTA   *The True American* (New Orleans)
NYH   *New York Herald*
PIC   *Picayune* (New Orleans)

NAMES OF FIRMS, BANKS, AND OTHER INSTITUTIONS

BOE   Bank of England
BUS   Second Bank of the United States
JLSJ   J. L. & S. Joseph & Co.
NBER   National Bureau of Economic Research
NMRS   Nathan Mayer Rothschild & Sons

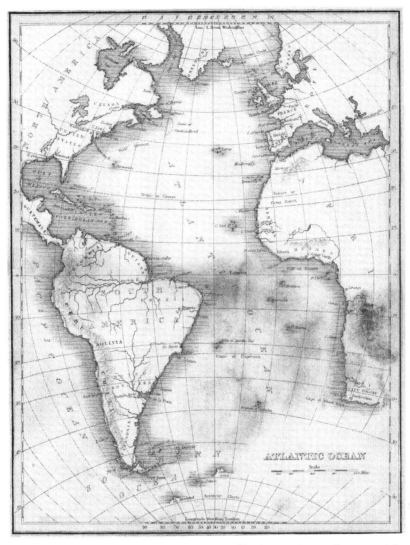

FIGURE 1. "Atlantic Ocean," T.G. Bradford, *A Comprehensive Atlas Geographical, Historical & Commercial* (1837), 80.

The Many Panics of 1837

On the morning of May 2, 1837, Théodore Nicolet, Swiss consul, founder of New Orleans's first Francophone Evangelical Church, and international financier, woke up in his mahogany bed.[1] He was probably alone. He was a bachelor in his mid-forties who owned two slaves in their twenties, a cook named Nancy and a servant named Billy.

We can guess that while Nancy prepared his breakfast, Billy helped him perform his morning ablutions. Nicolet washed his face in the bowl of his mahogany washstand and dried it on his towel that hung on his mahogany towel stand. He picked out his clothes from his mahogany armoire and sat on his mahogany sofa or his mahogany armchair. Perhaps he stole a glance at himself in one of his bedroom's two mahogany-framed looking glasses. He got dressed in a crisp linen shirt, a wool suit, and a flannel waistcoat. He picked out one of his more than forty pocket-handkerchiefs and tied a cravat or perhaps a silk foulard around his neck. He put on his shoes and, after his morning meal eaten at his mahogany table, he walked out of his home on Bourbon Street and to his counting house on Royal Street.[2]

And there he worked through the day and the night of May 2. At some point, he sat on a mahogany armchair and scribbled a note in pencil to an old friend. He left it on his mahogany bureau for his clerk. In the early morning of May 3, still dressed from the day before, he walked to a friend's property below the city limits. Shortly after noon, as a French letter recounted, Nicolet "*s'est brulé la cervelle*," or as a newspaper reported later that day, "he committed suicide by blowing his brains out with a pistol."[3]

* * *

Why did Théodore Nicolet kill himself? Or perhaps more to the point, what caused his death? The newspapers would editorialize on the morality of Nicolet's actions. Their columns and the letters of New Orleanians reporting on the death of this leading merchant banker all blamed the same cause: "*le dérangement des affaires commerciales.*"[4] His mind may not have been stable, but neither were the times. They were deranged, crazy, a whirlwind, an earthquake, a tempest. Nicolet was one among many casualties of one of America's first worst financial crises.

This all seems to make sense. It sounds like a familiar story: wealthy financier takes his life when the ravages of a financial crisis take his fortune. But the story has a problem: the timing is off. The Panic of 1837, according to many history books, started on May 10, 1837. Why would the panicked merchant kill himself before the crisis began? To solve this question, I traveled to more than a dozen manuscript archives on two continents, piecing together the path of information that spread panic in 1837. I discovered that Nicolet killed himself during what I call the panic in 1837: the period between approximately March 4, 1837, and approximately May 10, 1837, when people experienced acute financial uncertainty and, yes, panicked. Historians had gotten the chronology wrong. I thought I had solved the mystery.

Then something happened. As I began writing this book, investment banks crumbled and the financial system wobbled on its subprime foundation. I faced a historical conundrum. How could I write a history book about a similar but not identical moment nearly two centuries earlier without imposing the interpretive frameworks of my own time on my subjects? How could I avoid turning the panic in 1837 into the panic of 2007?

I realized there was a second problem with my story of the mahogany lover's suicide: I did not really know why Nicolet killed himself. I had assumed that I knew what it meant to panic in 1837, but what if people thought about the economy differently? After all, they had no unemployment benefits; no national bankruptcy laws; and most importantly no conceptualization of the business cycle, capitalism, or "the economy."[5] To avoid anachronism, I would have to figure out the economic frameworks of my subjects. To do so, I stopped reading the morning's newspaper and started reading the newspapers of 1837. I read novels, phrenology textbooks, political economy treatises, domestic economy manuals, songs, plays, sermons, and even jokes. I read more than two thousand sources printed in 1837 to try to imagine how troubling financial information might have been interpreted in that particular context.

These sources suggested that I had not solved the real mystery of 1837: why did historians get the chronology wrong? The print sources taught me that during the panic in 1837, people experienced not only uncertainty about their solvency (financial uncertainty) but also uncertainty about the causes of failure (economic uncertainty). By May, people calmed their troubled minds by blaming the crisis on systems larger than any individual. Ironically, these new ideas caused the actual period of panic to be forgotten. The change in economic thinking caused historians and economists to tell stories of a panic-less Panic of 1837.

* * *

We can hear this powerful economic uncertainty in the language used to describe events in the spring of 1837. "In one word, excitement, anxiety, terror, panic, pervades all classes and ranks," a correspondent from New Orleans wrote to a New York newspaper in April 1837 in an article that would be reprinted in papers throughout the United States.[6] With these four words, the author attempted to describe for distant readers his experience of a financial crisis. Such efforts at communication enabled the long-distance exchange of goods in a time before telegraphs, telephones, text messages, or tweets. Economic survival depended on the successful interpretation of such information; thus, writing the right word mattered. Despite his best intentions, this author could not choose just "one word" to explain the financial uncertainty caused by enormous business failures and contracting credit markets. He was not alone.

The substitution of four words for one reflected a broader trend during the panic in 1837. Between the first failures in March and the suspension of payment in specie (gold and silver coin) by banks throughout the United States in mid-May, American authors suffered from linguistic imprecision. No single term had come to define the event unfolding before their eyes. In fact, no single event could yet be identified as occurring within New Orleans or the other hardest hit cities, New York and London, let alone across the municipal, state, and national boundaries that separated these interrelated markets.[7] As the list of failures lengthened, Americans who had prided themselves on their self-made success began to doubt their faith in individual economic agency. This economic uncertainty mingled with financial uncertainty until the banks suspended specie payments. At nearly the same moment, American writers of newspaper columns, letters, novels, songs, poems, and diary entries began to describe a single event defined by a single term: panic.

The meaning of the word "panic" had been evolving for a decade. In 1828, Noah Webster defined panic as "A sudden fright; particularly, a sudden fright without real cause, or terror inspired by a trifling cause or misapprehension of danger."[8] Webster's definition emphasized sudden and causeless fear. But the word had also developed an additional meaning. As President Andrew Jackson and the Second Bank of the United States (BUS) waged war during the 1830s, Americans expanded the definition of panic to refer to a financial crisis with an illegitimate, politically inspired cause. In 1833, this new meaning gained prominence when the twenty-third session of Congress met on the heels of a financial crisis and became known as "The Panic Session."[9] Panic remained sudden but was no longer generally causeless. If panic had political causes, it implied individual innocence. By turning to the term panic in May 1837, rather than revulsion, crash, or the times, American authors blamed their troubles on collective forces beyond the control of all but political elites. Whigs and Democrats blamed their opponents within the political system.

While Americans turned to the word panic, a different word described events across the Atlantic. To British writers, events in the spring of 1837 were a "crisis." According to Webster's 1828 dictionary, this word signaled a "decisive state of things, or the point of time when an affair is arrived to its highth, and must soon terminate or suffer a material change."[10] Armed with a more generic term, British writers blamed a different system: the financial system.[11] In May 1837, writers on both sides of the Atlantic reduced their "excitement, anxiety, [and] terror" to single terms that implied systemic causes.[12]

The language choices made by people during the panic in 1837 mattered. The single terms employed by both American and British writers suggested single events; these linguistic choices undermined the plurality of personal and local experiences in the spring of 1837. Moreover, the two different terms suggested two different events with two different causes: a panic caused by the political system in America and a crisis caused by the financial system in Britain. These two explanations have influenced both historical accounts of 1837 and economic theories about financial crises.

* * *

We can see the results of the linguistic choices made during the panic in 1837 by turning to two American history textbooks that appeared a few years before I began studying the panic. Published in 1999, the brief fifth edition of *A People and A Nation* explained the panic by writing, "Van

Buren took office just weeks before the American credit system collapsed. In response to the impact of the Specie Circular, New York banks stopped redeeming paper currency with gold in mid-1837 ... Hard times persisted until 1843." By mentioning President Van Buren and the "Specie Circular," an economic policy instituted by Van Buren's predecessor, these sentences suggest a political cause. They also provide a chronology of the panic, which began "just weeks" after President Van Buren took office in "mid-1837" and ended years later in 1843. The textbook confirms the chronology of the panic on the next page where, in a list of sources of Anglo-American tension, the authors reference "the default of state governments," which occurred beginning in 1839, as happening "during the Panic of 1837."[13] So from this textbook, we learn that the Panic of 1837 started in New York City, was caused by national politics, and spanned roughly seven years from mid-1837 until 1843.

The second textbook provides an entirely different account of the Panic of 1837. According to the first edition of *The American Journey*, which was published in 1998, the panic began "in late 1836" in London when "the Bank of England tightened its credit policies." This textbook reports, "The shock waves hit New Orleans in March 1837 and spread to the major New York banks by May." It divides the events between 1836 and 1843 into two "round[s] of credit contraction" and "a depression."[14] So according to this textbook, we learn that the Panic of 1837 reached New York City after London and New Orleans, was produced by international financial causes, and lasted from late 1836 through mid-1837.

How could the same event be the product of two different causes, start in two different places, and vary in length by six years? Furthermore, where is the experience of panic in either of these accounts? To answer these questions, we need to think about the sources employed by these textbook authors.[15]

The first explanation was derived from the work of political historians who saw the Panic of 1837 as a national event caused by federal policy that resulted in a turning point in the contest between Democrats and Whigs. Historians relied on politicized sources emphasizing events that happened long after people stopped describing themselves and their neighbors as panicked. As a result, many history books replaced the actual experience of panic with a longer and later Panic of 1837, one that began with the suspension of specie payments in May and ended sometime in the 1840s.[16] The redefined Panic of 1837 became a tool for presentist agendas. To *laissez-faire* advocates, proponents of regulation, central bank supporters, and monetarists, the story of partisanship and policy making was more useful than the history of people actually panicking.

The second textbook explanation was the product of economic historians who saw America's Panic of 1837 as part of an international crisis based not on politics but on global monetary flows. These accounts were based on both banking records from 1837 and later economic theories that had, in part, been inspired by events occurring during 1837. British pamphlets published early in 1837 contributed to a slowly growing interest in cycles of crises among writers of political economy treatises. Later, economists would claim these texts as the first theories of the business cycle. Eventually, business cycle theorists promoted their work as providing policy makers with the ability to cure the economy of financial crises. This vision of a panic-free future, at first a motivating force behind economic research, ultimately made the study of crises seem unnecessary. As economists' thinking about panics and crises changed, accounts of the Panic of 1837 lost sight of the panic in 1837.

No student could be expected to provide a standard definition of the event when the textbooks can offer such little consensus. Nevertheless, as this book seeks to illustrate, this lack of consensus may not be the fault of textbook authors, historians, or economists, who trusted their sources. The divergent accounts of the Panic of 1837 were, in great part, the product of cultural constructions that occurred during the panic in 1837. When we peel back the prior generations of scholarship and broaden the source base, the various experiences of panic explain the disagreement between the textbooks' accounts of chronology, geography, and causation. We can find a new consensus by recognizing panic's plurality.

As the following chapters illustrate, panic was more complicated than past explanations have conveyed. Individuals, communities, and even nations experienced different versions of the panic in 1837 colored by cultural, political, and economic contexts. There were many panics in 1837 as individuals channeled their uncertainty into action that spring. With transatlantic news stranded at sea, the business communities of New York, New Orleans, and London faced parallel crises that forced each city to reevaluate its local and national structures of political economy.

***

This book makes arguments about the origin, progress, and resolution of these many panics and parallel crises. These arguments challenge our conceptions of the national boundaries of history, the role of information in the economy, the personal and local nature of national and international events, the origins and dissemination of economic ideas, and most importantly what actually happened in 1837. The seven chapters that follow demonstrate how the parallel crises and many panics in 1837 led to the invention of a single, national event that would become known as the Panic of 1837. The epilogue traces the evolution of this event into competing versions of the Panic of 1837 that all lost sight of the experience of panic. But this tale of panic's disappearance is the end and not the beginning of our subject. The process of restoring the panic in 1837 to the history of 1837 begins with a survey of the early to mid-1830s, when transatlantic bank wars raged and individuals constructed a financial system held together through confidence in a prosperous future.

CHAPTER I

A Very "Gamblous" Affair

Strivers in the 1830s coined a new phrase to describe their boom-time decisions: "to go ahead."[1] Going ahead was no joke; it produced calculable economic change. Economists estimate that the U.S. gross domestic product (GDP) increased by as much as 38 percent between 1820 and 1829 and by approximately 36 percent more between 1830 and 1836.[2] Although these statistics demonstrate remarkable growth between the Panic of 1819 and the Panic of 1837, they hide the real story of economic change: a nearly infinite number of individual choices.[3]

Going ahead required difficult calculations. In "The Dollars," a comic song of the time, thirty-six lines describing bad gambles caused enough chuckles to sustain two long encores. Performers lampooned wives who tried to buy status through expensive imports: "French clocks, French lamps, and French quelque chose / Each day her taste more costly grows / And that's the way the money goes." Dilettantes choosing to risk their fortunes against professional gamblers shared in the ridicule. The song assured, "All lottery tickets turn up blanks / And those who play at pharo banks / At poko, brag, or loo, or bluff / Must all be sure to lose enough."[4] The song's humor depended on the hazy moral line between illegitimate gambles and legitimate investments such as city real estate, bank bonds, and stock shares. Buying slaves and farming the lands of dispossessed indigenous peoples could easily have been added to the song's list of dubious dealings that contributed to the economic prosperity of the times.[5] Slavery and Indian removal, however, provoked serious debate. Religious revivals, which preached that the nation's future depended on the morality of individuals, burned through the United States.[6] The same individualism that motivated Americans to reform what they saw as their sinful behavior encouraged them to go ahead, to make the financial choices that revolutionized their lives one market transaction at a time.

Despite the fast pace of economic growth, America was still a nation of farmers in the 1830s.[7] Warnings about shavers, speculators, gamblers, and monopolists taught readers to distinguish the "keen sharp features, rapid eye, and general attitude of the gamester intent upon his play" from the necessary work of auctioneers, bankers, bookkeepers, brokers, cashiers, clerks, dealers, directors, factors, jobbers, merchants, and tradesmen.[8] As one scholar has noted, in the 1830s, the ambition that drove sons and daughters from the countryside to cities became "more feasible and less threatening."[9] Nevertheless, new dangers lurked inside the brains of the driven. "Over stimulated Acquisitiveness," phrenologists explained, was a "cerebral disease" that proved widespread "particularly in a mercantile country like our own, where every one is pressing hard on the heels of another in the pursuit of gain, where changes of fortune are not less sudden in occurrence than extreme in amount, and where, consequently, those who are remarkable for devotedness to selfish objects, live in a state of continual anxiety."[10]

Anxiety was not an exclusively American emotion. After fifty years of political independence, Americans remained dependent on English credit. To English capitalists, even America's most respected financiers looked like speculators gambling with insufficient resources. Foreign capitalists, especially in England, sought the highest available interest rates, and many invested in the high-yielding bonds, stocks, and other paper promises offered by cash-poor Americans. The decision to invest depended on trust in distant trade partners, what contemporaries called "confidence." Historian John Larson has described confidence as "that mysterious, invisible energy that keeps all financial bodies snug in their proper orbits."[11] Confidence had the power to transform economic backwaters into bustling cities because it generated credit – the ability to use money before earning it. Those who sought credit believed in a bright future. By cultivating confidence through correspondence, would-be debtors convinced their creditors to share this view. Individual Americans were not trying to increase the GDP or make the United States a more powerful nation; they wanted British credit to build their businesses.

National economic development was an illusion. The boom of the 1830s was actually the product of individuals forging local ties to transnational finance for personal profit. The development of cities and their hinterlands depended on bankers and merchants who established personal relationships with other mercantile men in distant places for their own profits. The particular urban geographies of three of the most important cities in the trade of the 1830s – New Orleans, New York, and London – shaped the possibilities of their residents. These communities, however, were divided politically into nations, and, in the 1830s, the national governments of both the United States and Great Britain engaged in sweeping reforms.[12] On both sides of the Atlantic, politicians saw policies of decentralizing and democratizing banking as good for their entrepreneurial constituents who needed credit for farms, factories, trade, and infrastructure, commonly called "internal improvements." Their opponents represented not only the already successful elites who benefited from limited competition and the stability of centralized control but also the financial Luddites who dreamed of eliminating credit entirely.[13] Public figures waged what Americans called a "bank war." This term, however, should be applied to the policy making that reshaped both nations' financial systems. Although the outcomes of these "bank wars" would be different in England and in the United States, the "flush times" of the early 1830s depended on institutions, politics, correspondence, confidence, and the choices of individuals.[14]

* * *

Without indicators such as the GDP, how did individuals weigh the risks of going ahead? Earlier generations of merchants developed intricate thumb scales for literally balancing payments on the road. Gold and silver coins replaced pure barter before the rise of the Roman Republic.[15] By the 1830s, cumbersome and valuable metal coins, the specie that served as official currency in every nation, traveled mostly between bank vaults, if at all. Financiers tried to avoid the risks and costs of transporting precious metals by expanding the use of millennia-old technology: paper and ink.

A merchant, banker, or broker's office was a menagerie of ruled and unruly paper. In a list of the "Vocabulary of Terms used in Book-Keeping," an 1830 self-help book taught future clerks to distinguish between the operation of a day book, ledger, journal, cash-book, invoice-book, sales-book, commission sales-book, account-sales-book, letter-book, account-current book, bill-book, receipt-book, check-book, waste-book, book of expenses, bill of exchange, bill of lading, draft, order, acceptance, advice, protest, debenture, bond, inventory, balance-sheet, and cash.[16] All of this paper allowed the exchange of large sums of money to occur symbolically – through math rather than metal.

To be able to depend on paper, however, people had to travel. In 1830, a New Orleanian *négociant* or merchant named Edmond Jean Forstall left his home in pursuit of a larger number at the end of his line of credit in the books of English bankers.[17] He needed these bankers' deeper purses to finance his growing business: shipping U.S. cotton to Liverpool and Mexican silver to China. Most of all, Forstall needed the correspondence of well-connected men situated at the center of global finance. Newspaper editors, merchants, financiers, and clerks learned through their practical training something that theorists of political economy had not yet recognized: the most valuable commodity in the world was reliable news. Before credit reports or telegraph tickers, trustworthy information could not be bought; it had to be earned.[18]

To earn the trust of two men whom he met on their tour of America, Forstall traveled to London. One of these men, Francis Baring, was born into a family at the center of British private banking. The other, Joshua Bates, was a New Englander whose acumen for interpreting financial information had elevated him to partner in the Barings' family firm. In New Orleans, Baring and Bates explored the results of a financial transaction their bank had facilitated a quarter century earlier, the Louisiana Purchase. Barings did not want to hire an agent in New Orleans because as Bates wrote to another mercantile firm in London, "people are perfectly sick of the name of agents" who often did "injury" to their employers. Rather, Bates proposed to "open a correspondence with some active good house that will use all proper exertion to increase your American connexions."[19]

Bates and Baring chose Forstall. When they left New Orleans, Forstall "enter[ed] into correspondence" with them and promised to provide them "with such information as we think may be of interest."[20] After a year of correspondence, the Barings thanked Forstall and his partners by offering "new marks of confidence" in the form of a small amount of credit and "recommendations" to key financiers on the European continent. Forstall traveled to London to thank them and to negotiate terms. On July 28, 1830, before the big meeting, Forstall received a letter of advice from his Liverpool-based partner Alexander Gordon. The "new marks of confidence" offered by the Barings made Gordon "more than ever anxious that all that we do with these gentlemen be done entirely to their satisfaction." "I leave it entirely to you to make such arrangements and stipulations with these gentlemen as they & you may deem right," wrote Gordon, conveying his confidence in Forstall.[21]

Baring Brothers also confided in Forstall. By 1835, the Barings had bought the bonds of several New Orleanian banks based on Forstall's recommendation.[22] Forstall played an essential role in directing three "property banks," a new species of state-chartered bank that based its assets on mortgages of real estate and slaves.[23] This structure suggested just how valuable land and slaves had become in the hinterlands of New Orleans.

Located at the mouth of the Mississippi, the port of New Orleans received produce from throughout the South and West to be sold and shipped around the world. Cotton, the most valuable export, was sent to the world's textile manufacturing centers; some went to New England, some to France, but most went to northern England.[24] Since the late eighteenth-century transformation of the cotton gin and its efficient production of short staple cotton, this fiber had claimed increasingly more American land, labor, and financial resources.[25] The expansion of cotton cultivation in the American South paralleled a rising demand for cotton by textile manufacturers in northern England.[26] During the 1820s, cotton became the lynchpin in the transatlantic trade as the southern cotton fields in the United States would grow to supply 80 percent of the raw materials for England's Lancashire factories. More than half of all American exports traveled to Great Britain.[27]

The high prices British manufacturers paid for American cotton created incentive for western migration within the United States and the cultivation of more cotton.[28] By 1830, the population of the trans-Appalachian West was greater than that of the entire United States in 1790.[29] Public land sales in the five largest cotton-producing states – Arkansas, Alabama, Louisiana, Mississippi, and Florida – produced more than $20 million, enough to pay off the federal debt.[30] "Between 1831 and 1836, the value of cotton exports almost trebled" to reach $71 million and grew to more than half the value of America's total exports.[31] A diplomatic easing of Anglo-American trade relations in 1830 facilitated the importation of manufactured goods as well. Growing American demand for imports and the tariffs paid by merchants who fulfilled these desires resulted in even more revenues for the federal government than land sales.[32] Approximately 30 percent of American imports came from Great Britain.[33] These imports as well as English demand for foreign grain to feed its increasingly industrialized population generally helped balance the Atlantic trade, but the United States was often Britain's debtor.[34]

Cotton was not the only agricultural commodity traded in New Orleans and not the only interest of British investors. The value of produce shipped to New Orleans doubled between 1831 and 1837 to provide for the swelling plantation populations who devoted their acreage to cotton. This demand and the resulting high prices for sugar, corn, pork, wheat, and other produce encouraged the emigration of northerners into the areas surrounding tributaries of the Mississippi.[35] Steamboats on the rivers changed the direction of trade so that farmers not only sent their goods to New Orleans but also purchased goods shipped upriver from that emporium of imported and domestic manufactured products. Following the model used to build the Erie Canal, directors of new state-chartered corporations marketed securities through their English correspondents to finance new canals and railways to previously remote areas.[36] This tie to Britain connected the American interior to the transatlantic financial system and funded the expansion of commercial agriculture.[37]

Although British demand for cotton incentivized London bankers to invest in the American South, British firms like Baring Brothers needed correspondents in New Orleans like Forstall to channel their capital into specific investments. The six thousand miles and difficult ocean travel that separated New Orleans and London contributed to the desire for dependable informants. In addition to geographical distance, the pace of change in New Orleans gave local knowledge a short shelf life. Bates and Baring visited New Orleans in 1828; less than two years later, they had already made significant additional investments based on Forstall's advice.[38]

* * *

The decision of British firms such as Baring Brothers to invest in New Orleans shaped the urban geography of the city to reflect international trade. In the first eleven months of 1835, about 2,300 steamboats arrived in the port – a more than tenfold increase over the entire number of vessels to enter the port when the city became part of the United States in 1803. This large number of steamers did not include the thousands of river-bound flat boats and ocean-bound ships that competed for dock space.[39] The spectacle of such a large number of boats struck a visiting British doctor who wrote, "Here are those gigantic steamers, which communicate with the whole of the great western country ... here are trading vessels from every civilized country under heaven – and here arks, which bring down the produce of the interior, from the very sources of this great vein of the Western world, to its termination in the Gulf of Mexico."[40] In 1835, during this golden age of river traffic, before year-round northern railroad routes to the Atlantic, the Mississippi River accelerated New Orleans past its northern rival New York as the nation's leading export city based on the value of its produce.[41]

New Orleans was the fastest-growing American city in the decade of the 1830s, trailing only New York and Philadelphia in terms of population. In the three decades since the Louisiana Purchase, the population had increased from 8,000 in 1803 to 100,000 in 1836.[42] The number of slaves in the city in 1835 was larger than the entire population in 1806. Even more enslaved people lived in New Orleans temporarily as they waited, imprisoned in slave markets, to be sold to serve as laborers, as markers of status, and as collateral for their new owners who would often buy them on credit.[43]

Mirroring the flow of slaves from the upper South to the Cotton Belt, most free New Orleanians were also newcomers. Americans from farther north, who sought profits amid the cotton boom, brought such linguistic, ethnic, and religious tension to the formerly French city that in 1836, the New Orleans city government was split into three municipalities.[44] Anglophone and Francophone theaters, museums, hotels, newspapers, and churches competed for patrons.

Despite the competition between and within linguistic communities, New Orleanians speaking any language shared a passion for making money. One visitor described the city as "a spot exclusively dedicated to worship of Mammon."[45] The god of greed smiled on Creole and American businessmen alike as the city's trade expanded.[46] This go-ahead atmosphere, although not unique to New Orleans, infused the city's culture. In taverns, restaurants, and hotels, the city's men of business, clerks, and laborers spread commercial news.[47]

Newspapers converted the rumors circulating in these local networks into transportable news through ink and paper. Editors sold financial information to people occupying all ranks in the commercial community and exchanged this information with other editors elsewhere. On the national and international levels, newspapermen created a network to trade financial information between the presses of different cities that relied domestically on the postal service. The U.S. government heavily subsidized the circulation of newspapers. In 1832, newspapers generated only 15 percent of the revenue of the post office but 95 percent of the weight transmitted by horse and stagecoach. By the 1840s, every newspaper published in the United States received free copies of an annual average of 4,300 exchange papers, and editors sent through the mail almost 40 million newspapers to subscribers. Capitalism developed not only in the cotton fields and banking houses but also through the gossip spread under tavern roofs, between the plates of printing presses, and in postal bags.[48]

The commercial environment in New Orleans inspired more than spoken and printed words. Along the boundary between the American and

French sections of the city, New Orleanians built Greek-inspired temples to house their mammon worship. Bankers built structures that incorporated national and international tastes for neo-Classicism with local touches. In 1820, the Louisiana State Bank board hired Benjamin Latrobe, architect of the nation's largest bank, to design its building. In 1827, the Bank of Louisiana literally incorporated transnational commerce into its structure by importing a London-style fence manufactured by a New York firm.[49]

As these examples suggest, New Orleanians constructed many new banks. In 1831, there were four banks in New Orleans with a total capitalization of $9 million. By 1837, Louisiana had chartered sixteen banks with a total capital of $46 million. Between Creole cottages and French townhouses that captured the Mississippi's breezes, the city's new banks erected sparsely windowed, stone edifices designed to evoke security, cosmopolitanism, and permanence.[50] They were the visible symbols of the confidence and the credit generated by Forstall and others.

* * *

The construction of so many bank buildings in the 1830s was a result of changing financial organization throughout the United States. Although states had always chartered their own banks, between 1816 and 1833, the federal government invested all of its funds in one institution – the Second Bank of the United States (BUS). Headquartered in Philadelphia, the BUS was the only bank in the nation permitted to open branches in multiple states. It was, thus, national rather than local.

Throughout the nation, state-chartered banks printed paper money that was exchangeable for the only currency produced or authorized by the U.S. government: gold and silver coins known as specie.[51] Bank notes were in essence small, interest-free loans by note holders to the bank.[52] Not all the paper money printed by banks, however, could be redeemed for specie at the same time because banks printed much more money than the coins they held in their vaults. This was the magic of banks; they could multiply the currency because holders of their bank notes trusted the promise printed on the paper. Despite the fact that banks could not redeem all their paper at once, they convinced the people who took their paper to trust that the note would be exchangeable for specie and that the bank was worthy of this credit.[53] In essence, bank paper demonstrated the force of confidence on a small scale.

Bank directors acted as the guardians of that confidence. They built buildings that conveyed security. They printed images on their bank notes that reminded holders of sources of local or national pride – George Washington, Fulton's steamboat, or Lady Liberty in a toga.[54] And most importantly, they bore the responsibility of determining the "reserve ratio" – the relationship between the bank's paper and its assets. The specie that banks raised through deposits, collecting interest on loans, and stock and bond sales existed primarily in ledgers rather than in vaults. Coins were too valuable to be locked away. Instead, banks' real assets consisted primarily of illiquid investments that promoted local economic growth: promissory notes, mortgages, commercial loans, railroads, canals, and even gas-lit streets. Banks may have looked like secure structures designed to protect valuable coins, but their most valuable assets were actually symbolic – the paper that accounted for debts and credits and the ability to inspire confidence.

Because banks could not afford to redeem all of their notes at any given time, bank paper was a gamble. Within the local community, the reputation of the bank and its directors generated trust in its notes. As people brought notes from one location to another, however, fewer people knew the local background of the bank or its directors.[55] For example, most people in New Orleans would trust a $10 New Orleans Canal Bank note as if it were the gold eagle coin it represented, but few people in New York knew the credentials of the bank's board or the holdings of the bank's securities, and thus, the paper was worth considerably less there. New Yorkers' doubts about the ability of the New Orleans Canal Bank to keep its promise resulted in the deduction of a discount rate from the note's face value. The discount rate also reflected the cost of physically transporting the piece of paper back to the New Orleans Canal Bank's counter for redemption in specie.[56] So bank notes lost a significant amount of their value the farther they traveled, making trade within the geographically expanding nation expensive.

The BUS ingeniously solved this problem.[57] Because its branches in New York and New Orleans could communicate their local knowledge of bank reputations to one another and efficiently return notes to their banks of origin, the BUS simplified the process of exchanging local currencies. This kept bank directors everywhere from printing more paper than they could expect to redeem.[58] The BUS nationalized local currency.

Bank notes, however, were a small part of the BUS's business and were not involved in the largest transactions. As the depository for federal funds, the BUS received the proceeds of import duties and federal western land sales.[59] It held these funds for the federal government, but more importantly it could move the specie and paper money generated by these sources of revenue to and from its branches around the country. When merchants in New York City owed money to England, the BUS could send specie to this commercial port. This was important because the largest transactions in the United States were calculated not in dollars but in pounds sterling. The debts owed to England could not be paid in American bank notes. They had to be paid either in specie, which could be melted down and minted in the king of England's image, or in paper promises of specie located in London banks. These paper promises of pounds sterling, called "foreign bills of exchange," made up the majority of the BUS's earning assets and financed most of the nation's trade.[60]

Bank notes were nationally bounded, but foreign bills of exchange facilitated global trade.[61] Bills of exchange allowed the growers of American cotton to receive payment on the Liverpool auction blocks. They allowed the American importers of English manufactured goods to pay for their wares. Most importantly, bills of exchange allowed both of these halves of the transatlantic trade to occur without coins moving across the Atlantic Ocean. And their successful operation was entirely dependent on confidence.

How did a bill of exchange work? American merchants like Forstall established lines of credit in banks like Baring Brothers. When a merchant wanted to make a purchase, instead of handing a seller coins, he filled out a simple form. The form was a contract promising to pay the seller with money located in a bank. The seller could bring this form to the specified bank and receive payment in coins. In essence, bills of exchange were promises of payment and operated like modern-day personal checks drawn on bank accounts.

Very few bills of exchange, however, actually traveled along this simple route from purchase to payment. Instead, bills of exchange traveled from hand to hand as payment not for one purchase but for many. Rather than travel to London to claim his specie, the original seller who was paid for his wares with a bill of exchange generally sold the bill to a bank or a bill broker. Banks and bill brokers would give the original seller specie, bank notes, or other paper promises worth slightly less than the face value of the bill. This process was called "discounting." Like the exchange rate charged by banks dealing in long-distance bank notes, banks and bill brokers charged a "discount rate" that covered the cost of shipping the bill to London, reflected the demand for bills of exchange in the local money market, and assessed the likelihood the bill would actually be converted to specie in London. Once a bill had been sold to a bank or bill broker, its journey had only begun.

After discounting the bill, the bank or bill broker would seek to resell it for slightly more than face value. In other words, from sellers of bills, they subtracted their discount, and from buyers of bills, they demanded more than the bill's face value. Their profit was the difference between these prices. Sometimes, they would sell the bill of exchange to another bank or broker in a distant market where bills of exchange were in demand because merchants needed to make payments in England. One of these merchants would buy the bill and send it to a correspondent in London. The correspondent would present the bill to the specified bank and receive the original face value in pounds sterling. This correspondent would then use the money received from the bill to pay the merchant's debts. When the bill reached the London bank, its travels were complete. Redeemed bills were destroyed to prevent fraud; as a result, few examples of these bills survive in the historical record. Nevertheless, we can see how they worked from other paper records of their existence, such as letters, ledgers, and lawsuits.

This evidence of bills of exchange is not only helpful to historians but also proof that bills of exchange passed through many hands on their journeys. The more people traded a bill, the more complicated its journey and the less it retained its full value. Every stop between purchase and payment resulted in a deduction of a discount rate. Discounting was often necessary for merchants because it allowed them to get cash quickly, but selling a bill for less and buying a bill for more than its face value could be costly. Ideally, the merchant who needed to make a payment in London banked at the same London bank as the original merchant who wrote the bill. If so, this would result in an efficient transfer of funds. The bill's value would merely be added to one line of credit and subtracted from another, all within the same ledger. No extra brokers, correspondents, or merchants would charge their fees and discount rates; the bill would retain as much value as possible. In this most efficient of outcomes, money never moved (not even within London), just paper.

Despite the complexities of a bill's route from purchase to payment, paper made transatlantic trade simpler. Of course, this simplification of payments depended on a risky mental calculation. Everyone who bought and sold the bill had to trust that it would eventually be worth the value promised on its face. When everyone involved in the bill's journey had confidence, the system was incredibly efficient.

* * *

International trade could not function without discounters who moved the bills from one place and one pair of hands to another. In the early 1830s, the BUS conducted the largest discounting operation in the United States. It easily conveyed these important financial instruments from one part of the country to another because it enjoyed unparalleled access to capital thanks to the federal deposits and unparalleled efficiency thanks to its national system of branches. By the early 1830s, the BUS had become the largest corporation in the nation.

Not surprising given its size and significance, the BUS inspired both confidence in financial paper, including both notes and bills, as well as charges of corruption.[62] Disparaging the national paper currency, William Leggett, a New York newspaper editor who disliked banks and the economic changes they facilitated, warned that "[men] count, deluded creatures! on the continued liberality of the banks, whose persuasive entreaties seduced them into the slippery paths of speculation."[63] Leggett's idea, that trust in paper money encouraged speculation and that this behavior had corrupted America's citizenry, echoed the language of many who tried to stop the go-ahead spirit. Ironically, even such critics, called "croakers," relied on the infrastructure that economic growth enabled: cheaply distributed newspapers subsidized by a federal budget bloated with the revenue of import tariffs and land sales.[64] The issues of how to balance security and risk, morality and sin, independent democracy and national improvement congealed into a debate over banking that dominated American politics for much of the 1830s. Moreover, with nearly universal white male suffrage, the American electorate became so divided over the bank war that it helped build partisanship on a scale the world had never before known.[65]

President Andrew Jackson joined Leggett in his concern about banks' control over Americans' lives. Jackson's Democratic Party was divided between "hard-money" advocates who wanted to eliminate all banks and eager entrepreneurs who wanted to sever federal ties with the BUS to free the nation's capital for more local investments. Together, these two factions encouraged Jackson to wage "war" on the "monster" BUS. Jackson chose his words carefully and allowed his supporters to define the terms of the debate. By referring to the BUS as a monster, he suggested that the institution held titanic and unnatural power. Some of his supporters would extend this condemnation to all banks; meanwhile, others argued that state-chartered banks offered a favorable alternative to the BUS. By waging war on the BUS, the former general claimed his anti-bank policy making to be within his job description as commander in chief; his opponents in the Whig Party and even some Democratic legislators would come to see Jackson's war with the bank as executive imperialism.[66]

Due to expire in 1836, the charter of the BUS became a topic of congressional debate in Jackson's first term. In 1832, the president vetoed a bill to recharter the BUS, and with his veto message turned the bank war into a reelection campaign platform that attacked plutocracy and centralized power. Jackson viewed his electoral victory in 1832 as a mandate to destroy the bank; his exit strategy for the bank war, however, remained vague.

To remove the federal government's funds legally from the BUS, the secretary of the treasury had to provide evidence to Congress that the federal funds were unsafe. Jackson had to replace one and dismiss another secretary of the treasury before, in 1833, he finally appointed Roger Taney, who ignored the glowing reports from Congress's recent investigation of the BUS. Taney gradually depleted the federal deposits by withdrawing but not depositing funds in the BUS. Congress censured the president, but Jackson nevertheless directed Taney and his successor, Levi Woodbury, to deposit incoming federal tax revenue in hand-chosen state-chartered banks, derisively called "pet banks," located throughout the nation. The network of federal deposit banks was designed to democratize finance by providing nonelite, non-eastern white men access to banks. To some extent it succeeded, but it would be more accurate to say the pet bank system Democratized banking because it rewarded loyal Democratic Party–affiliated bank directors with federal capital. Accusations of demagoguery replaced accusations of plutocracy, but the bank war was far from over.

Jackson's democratization utterly failed to fulfill the demands of the hard-money men who wanted to eliminate all banks and paper money. The number of banks immediately began to multiply and some historians argue that the quantity of paper money also increased out of proportion to any sensible reserve ratio.[67] A political cartoon entitled "General Jackson Slaying the Many Headed Monster" (Figure 2) visualized the bank war by depicting the financial system as a hydra; Jackson decapitated one head only to release many more.

Banking had become decentralized but less regulated. Nicholas Biddle, president of the BUS, demonstrated the centralized power that would be lost when the BUS charter expired by directing his employees to redeem large quantities of notes at the nation's banks and by increasing the discount rate on bills of exchange. Biddle argued that these were necessary procedures for insuring the solvency and liquidity of the BUS after its loss of the federal government's funds, but he injured the BUS's reputation by causing trouble for merchants and financiers who relied on low rates to turn a profit on international trade. His opponents saw these actions as partisan retaliation and labeled the 1834 credit crisis "Biddle's Panic."[68]

GENERAL JACKSON SLAYING THE MANY HEADED MONSTER.

FIGURE 2. Henry R. Robinson's lithograph "General Jackson Slaying the Many Headed Monster" depicts the argument that Jackson's destruction of the BUS led to the creation of new state-chartered banks. (New York, 1836. Courtesy of the American Antiquarian Society.)

Between Biddle's Panic and the Panic Session, the word "panic" began to carry a political meaning as a crisis provoked unnecessarily by political partisanship.

Meanwhile, the Democrats promoted policies that would appease their disgruntled hard-money constituents. American specie was almost entirely composed of silver, the less valuable of the two officially sanctioned metals. Congress increased the value of gold relative to silver in American coins and, by so doing, lowered the price of silver coins in the United States below the going global market rate. This was meant to encourage international investors to send gold to the United States in order to buy cheap silver.[69] In addition, Jackson strong-armed the French government into making gold indemnity payments for American losses from the Napoleonic wars. These two supplies of gold enticed the Jackson administration to try to replace paper bank notes with a metallic money supply, placating those who distrusted banks and their paper money.

Unbeknownst to Jackson or any of his contemporaries, specie supplies in the United States also increased because of drug addiction in the globe's Eastern Hemisphere and political revolution in the Southern Hemisphere. By 1836, Chinese merchants began to prefer to trade their exports, principally tea, silk, and ceramics, for paper bills of exchange that could be used to purchase opium from India through English and American merchants.[70] At the same time, Spain's former colonies in Latin America, home to the world's most productive silver mines, stopped minting the colonial currency, which had become a global silver standard because of its uniform appearance and quality. The new coins proudly displayed icons of independence, but Chinese merchants doubted their value. This provided the Chinese with an additional reason to turn to bills of exchange. American merchants who bought silver in Mexico to sell in China redirected the flow of coins to the United States. Silver supplies in America grew. Few people in 1837 could have recognized such macroeconomic forces; indeed, the money supply of the 1830s remains a debated topic in the twenty-first century.[71]

At almost exactly the same time that the Chinese began to trade with London-based bills of exchange, the U.S. federal government's deposits in the nation's banks increased. Based on the large amount of import tariff collected and land sold, the federal government's revenue exceeded its expenditures. Americans had bought so many French lamps to decorate their new slave plantations built on confiscated Creek Indian lands that for the first and only time in American history, the federal government had not only paid off its debts but also amassed a surplus. These extra funds fueled the bank war as Whigs passed legislation to remove the money from Jackson's control by distributing most of the surplus to state legislatures. Congress required East Coast banks to send federal deposits to western banks selected by the states. Fearing that these new deposits would escalate speculation in land, Jackson countered with the "Specie Circular," a Treasury order that required all payments for federal lands to be made in coin. This order also decentralized American finance by further incentivizing the shipment of specie to the West.[72]

So by the summer of 1836, the bank war resulted in an unplanned bipartisan consensus; most Democrats and Whigs supported policies of decentralization and democratization of finance, just not the same ones. Whereas these national policies along with the cumulative choices of individual American and Chinese consumers influenced the new financial system, local financiers built it. To replace the services offered by the BUS, Forstall and others like him appealed to state legislatures for new bank charters. Nationwide, more than one hundred new banks opened their doors in 1836 alone, bringing the total number of banks in the United States to seven hundred.[73] With a new state charter from the Pennsylvania legislature, the BUS maintained its Philadelphia neoclassical headquarters and its prestige but lost its ability to police the financial system. No national institution would control America's exchange or discount rates. Banks and financial markets in different states became more isolated. Financial confederacy rather than union prevailed. Politics reshaped American banking.

* * *

These changes in the national financial system produced concrete changes in New Orleans. In addition to the construction of newly chartered banks, the financial confederacy was visible in the residence of one of New Orleans's wealthiest merchants, Samuel Hermann. In 1831, Hermann contracted to build a new house on his property just inside the French section of town. In stark contrast with the neighboring Spanish-style townhouses, Hermann's new home paid homage to his ties to American commerce. Although distinctly a New Orleanian home complete with a balcony, a courtyard, and slave quarters, the outside was cloaked in painted bricks to appear like a Philadelphia townhouse (Figure 3).

FIGURE 3. Samuel Hermann's house is currently a museum. It is located at 820 Saint Louis Street, New Orleans, LA. (Photograph by author.)

After the destruction of the BUS's federal authority, Hermann's house gained new meaning as it represented the adaptation of Philadelphian style to the local environment. Provincial banks and financiers no longer merely modeled themselves on Philadelphia's national institutions but, in fact, rivaled them as a new financial elite. From his writing desk looking out at the oldest section of the city, Hermann, like Forstall, put pen to paper to build a future for his family, for his city, and for his country.[74] His home was a showcase of American promise. One guest remembered a "most magnificent soirée" thrown by Hermann there in 1833. "Wretchedly bad" weather prevented him from "illuminating his court, and showing his Fireworks." Nevertheless, Hermann's nearly 350 guests enjoyed "the finest party that had ever been given here, his commodious house, splendid furniture, and Mr. Hermann's own good [knack] giving him every facility of making it as agreeable as it could possibly have been made."[75] Like the new banks, Hermann's showcase home may have been composed of plaster, wood, and stone, but it was built on credit.

To raise the funds to construct the city's new urban landscape, stock sales, bond issues, and personal promissory notes floated around New Orleans. Some of these financial instruments made their way to the nation's largest money market in New York. Others traveled even farther to the center of credit for global trade – London. For example, in 1832, Forstall, acting as president of the Union Bank of Louisiana, negotiated a bond sale with Baring Brothers. To its customers, Baring Brothers would sell sheets of paper signed by the directors of the Union Bank that not only promised to pay interest but also physically represented these interest payments through coupons printed along the margins of the sheet. The coupons would be redeemable for specie at specified future dates. Thus, this single sheet of paper was worth a great deal of money over time; it could be traded again and again in money markets anywhere. By selling the bonds, Baring Brothers channeled specie from English investors to the Union Bank, allowing the bank to loan money to planters, merchants, and urban developers – like Hermann.[76]

Beyond financing internal improvements such as new buildings or New Orleans's infant railroads, credit was necessary for the city's life-blood – cotton. In 1836, New Orleans shipped nearly a third of U.S. cotton exports overseas.[77] Before they sold their first cotton crop, would-be planters needed to buy land, seed, food for their workers, and the workers themselves. Every year, they would reinvest in seed, food, and slaves long before they knew what price their cotton would fetch. At least nine months

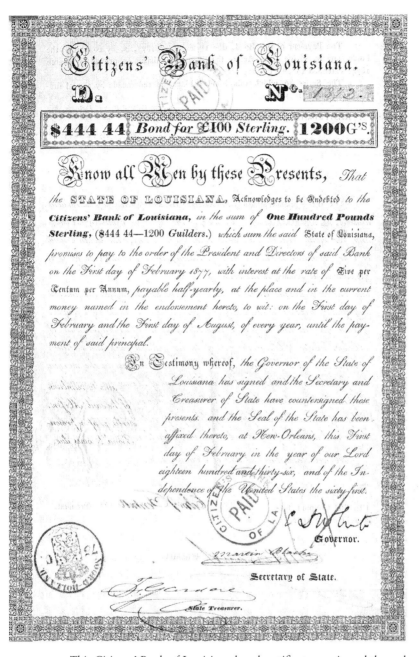

FIGURE 4. This Citizens' Bank of Louisiana bond certificate was issued through the State of Louisiana in 1836 and promised 5 percent annual interest on a £100 investment. Coupons or "dividend warrants" bordered the document visible here. The holder redeemed these small pieces of paper twice a year at the Counting-House of Messrs. Hope & Co. in Amsterdam in order to receive the interest payments. Originally due to mature in 1877, this date was renegotiated in 1874. As the stamps on both sides of the document indicate, Citizens' Bank paid the principal to this bondholder in 1902. (Courtesy of the Louisiana Research Collection, Tulane University.)

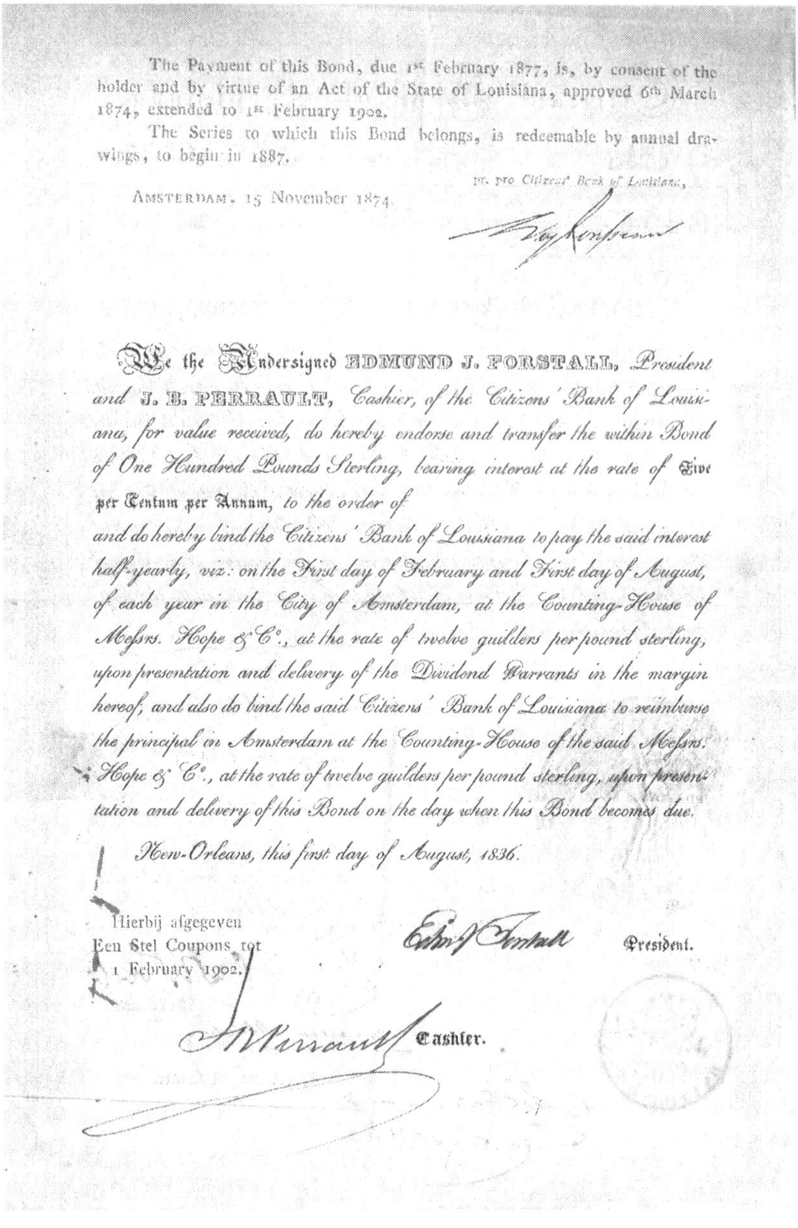

The Payment of this Bond, due 1ˢᵗ February 1877, is, by consent of the holder and by virtue of an Act of the State of Louisiana, approved 6ᵗʰ March 1874, extended to 1ˢᵗ February 1902.

The Series to which this Bond belongs, is redeemable by annual drawings, to begin in 1887.

pr. pro *Citizens' Bank of Louisiana,*

AMSTERDAM, 15 November 1874.

We the Undersigned EDMOND J. FORSTALL, *President and* J. B. PERRAULT, *Cashier, of the Citizens' Bank of Louisiana, for value received, do hereby endorse and transfer the within Bond of One Hundred Pounds Sterling, bearing interest at the rate of Five per Centum per Annum, to the order of and do hereby bind the Citizens' Bank of Louisiana to pay the said interest half-yearly, viz: on the First day of February and First day of August, of each year in the City of Amsterdam, at the Counting-House of Messrs. Hope & Cᵒ., at the rate of twelve guilders per pound sterling, upon presentation and delivery of the Dividend Warrants in the margin hereof, and also do bind the said Citizens' Bank of Louisiana to reimburse the principal in Amsterdam at the Counting-House of the said Messrs. Hope & Cᵒ., at the rate of twelve guilders per pound sterling, upon presentation and delivery of this Bond on the day when this Bond becomes due.*

New-Orleans, this first day of August, 1836.

Hierbij afgegeven Een Stel Coupons tot 1 February 1902.

President.

Cashier.

FIGURE 5. The reverse side of the Citizens' Bank of Louisiana bond certificate of 1836 includes the signature of Edmond Forstall as the bank's president as well as the original and revised terms of payment. Note the wide variety of fonts employed in the document. (Courtesy of the Louisiana Research Collection, Tulane University.)

passed between planting a crop in the early spring and shipping the baled cotton in the late fall and early winter.[78]

Baled cotton could be sold to local merchants in the small ports that dotted the Mississippi River or to export merchants in New Orleans. The merchants who bought and sold cotton calculated the cost of shipping the crop, their own profit, and the likely selling price of the cotton in England. Regardless of where the sale took place, the price per pound of cotton was based on an estimation of the price in Liverpool because, ultimately, most U.S. cotton would end its journey on these auction blocks across the Atlantic.[79] The actual proceeds of the sale of any particular bale of cotton would not reenter the New Orleanian market for more than a year after the seed entered the ground. Thus, all cotton transactions were gambles based on predictions of future profits.

To mitigate the annual cotton cycle, merchants called "cotton factors" specialized in extending credit to planters and selling cotton in New Orleans or elsewhere.[80] They sold planters' crops and used the proceeds to provide planters with what they needed, such as food and clothes for their slaves, and everything they wanted, such as French furniture, English ceramics, or Chinese silk. Cotton factors made their living by charging either a flat rate or a percentage on every transaction made on behalf of planters. Many planters never actually received cash from their factors. Instead, planters lived in a cycle of indebtedness to them. In this way, factors enabled planters to continue growing cotton without the hindrance of a shortage of capital or long treks for manufactured goods.

By the late 1830s, large networks of cotton factors based in New Orleans bought and sold much of the cotton that made its way down the Mississippi. Cotton factors connected the import and export businesses in New Orleans and thus personally tied the trade partners of New Orleans to the transnational economy. To extend credit to planters, cotton factors solicited credit from merchants and bankers. Despite the opulence of Samuel Hermann's home, the majority of his wealth was tied up in the credit of his business. Hermann wrote letters to correspondents in New York and London to facilitate the sale of cotton and the purchase of imported manufactured goods. In exchange for providing these correspondents with accurate news about his local financial and commodity markets, Hermann sometimes received a "letter of credit" that entitled him to buy and sell goods and financial instruments on behalf of distant merchants. With these accounts, Hermann could write bills of exchange. And he pushed the system of credit these financial instruments facilitated to its maximum.

Hermann used the credit of Londoners to buy cotton often with the intention of paying back the loan with some of the profits he earned from selling the same cotton in Liverpool. In other words, Hermann knew that the bill of exchange would take a long time to reach London and require payment, so he used this time to his advantage. As a cotton factor, Hermann's bills of exchange allowed even more time than most between purchase and payment. Bills of exchange generated by the cotton trade added an additional step designed to compensate for the hazards of transatlantic travel. Cotton bills were called "sixty-day sight bills" because the bill would not be exchanged immediately for specie when it was presented to the London bank. Instead, the London bank would check its records to make sure that the bill was legitimate, label the bill "accepted," and require the holder to return in sixty days to collect the money promised on its face. This process transformed the bill into an "acceptance" that could be traded in money markets at low discount rates. The two-month window when a bill circulated as an acceptance was designed to give the cotton factor time to make sure that he was not overdrawn on his line of credit and to allow the London bank time to manage its liquidity to make the payment.[81]

So Hermann's bills of exchange would change hands for an indeterminate amount of time within the United States, travel across the Atlantic Ocean for approximately a month, and then circulate for two months after arriving in London. This allowed Hermann more than a season before he had to pay for his loans. During these months, Hermann wrote letters to his London bankers informing them of his bills of exchange. He also hoped to sell his cotton for a bill of exchange that would replenish the credit in his account. Meanwhile, every person involved with one of Hermann's bills of exchange depended on the health of his account in London. All the merchants and bankers on both sides of the Atlantic who used the bill to transact business trusted that the London bank would honor the promise on the paper.

Confidence performed the alchemy of transforming paper into gold. Without confidence, the paper would remain paper. Or worse yet, if confidence turned to doubt while the bill was in progress, paper that had been trusted as if it was worth gold would turn out to be worth significantly less. This was the case with a bill of exchange written by Hermann on January 4, 1837 (Figure 6 and Figure 7). The bill traveled far, but when it reached its destination, Hermann did not have enough credit in his account for the London bankers to honor the promise on its face. The words on this rare document are jargon that only someone fluent in

FIGURE 6. Samuel Hermann signed this bill of exchange on January 4, 1837, in New Orleans. Tiny print on the left side of the bill reveals that it was printed in London, England. It was preserved as evidence in a court file. (Courtesy of the Louisiana Division/City Archives, New Orleans Public Library.)

FIGURE 7. The reverse of Hermann's bill of exchange reveals the endorsers who transported the bill from New Orleans to London. (Courtesy of the Louisiana Division/City Archives, New Orleans Public Library.)

nineteenth-century finance would understand: "*Sixty* Days after sight of this First of Exchange, (second, third & ~~fourth~~ unpaid) pay to *R. Greene, Esqre.*, or order *Eight Thousand Pounds Sterling*, Value received & charge the same to account as advised by Saml. Hermann & Son. To *Messrs. T. W. Smith & Co., London.*"[82] This meant that Greene could present this bill of exchange to T. W. Smith & Co. in London and receive £8,000 in gold sixty days later. On the back of the bill, the signatures of several endorsers fill out the story of the bill's journey: a New Orleans factor

(Hermann) paid an Alabama merchant (Greene) who sent the bill as a payment to New York merchants who sent the bill as a payment to London merchants who brought the bill to the bank (T. W. Smith & Co.) for payment. This means that at least five people trusted that this piece of paper would ultimately be worth gold. Although in this particular instance they were wrong, the fact that the bill traveled so far and through so many different hands attests to the power of confidence to facilitate transatlantic trade.

Whereas the words on the bill demonstrate the interconnectedness of southern, northern, and English trade, the bill itself provides a cultural artifact of the geographical circulation of the period. Composed of cotton rag paper, its material origins lie in southern slave labor. As its tiniest print attested, the company filigree and blank form had been printed in London. The handwritten details were added to the bill in New Orleans. On the reverse side, the handwriting bears witness to the different hands it passed through between Louisiana, New York, and London. As a material culture object, it embodies the nineteenth-century system of transatlantic trade from cotton to confidence.

The story of this slip of paper, however, does not end in London. Additional handwritten notes indicate the bill's reverse journey back to New Orleans where this piece of paper still resides in the records of that city's First Judicial Court along with a London notary's "protest for non-payment," a summons, a settlement petition, a mortgage, a writ for a sheriff's sale, a stay of proceedings, and ultimately a judgment that would cost Hermann two brick stores in the American part of town. Thus, Hermann's bill may not have been worth gold in London, but it was ultimately worth real estate in New Orleans. Even when a bill was protested, the paper was still worth more than paper.

Nevertheless, the confidence of all those involved with Hermann's protested bill would be shaken by this experience. Their letters to correspondents about the protest would raise doubts in the minds of others. And just as the bill passed from hand to hand, the news of these doubts would travel. A single failed bill could not destroy the transatlantic financial system, but many unfulfilled promises could. Confidence was valuable in part because it was vulnerable.

* * *

As with this bill of exchange, which traveled through many hands in many places, the circulation of information connected the local economy of New Orleans to its two most important financial partners – New York and

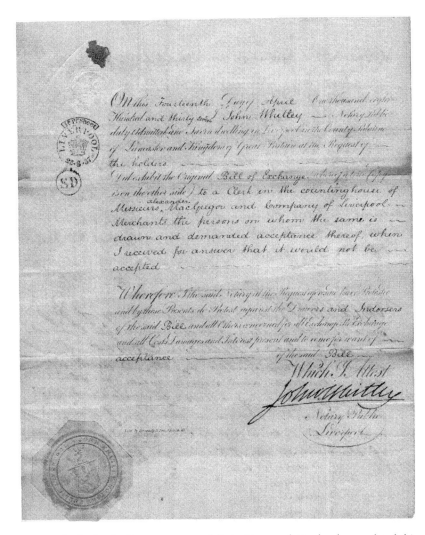

FIGURE 8. In April 1837, a notary public in Liverpool, England, completed this form, commonly called a "protest," to officially document the nonpayment of an accepted bill of exchange. The interior pages of this document trace the path of the bill of exchange. Parties who handled the bill include J. L. & S. Joseph & Co., Thomas Barrett & Co. (a member of the Hermann cotton factoring network), and F. de Lizardi & Co. (a firm affiliated with Edmond Forstall). (Private collection.)

London. Merchants, bankers, and brokers like Hermann and Forstall sent financial information to their correspondents in several forms. Bills of exchange represented transactions in their most abstracted form. Letters conveyed the same details but added paragraphs of analysis of local

market conditions – personal and often more accurate accounts of similar
content published in newspapers. Over land and across the sea, all of these
forms of financial information brought intelligence about New Orleans to
readers elsewhere. While inventors developed telegraphs that would eliminate the need to physically transport information, people making investment choices in the 1830s struggled with an information asymmetry that
resulted from geographically expanding and ever more interconnected
markets as well as slow (at least in hindsight) and unreliable information
technology.

Wind, steam, hoof, and lung power transported information to distant
places, but not every city connected to transnational commerce had the
same access to that information.[83] Compared to New York and London,
New Orleans was the last place to receive news about changes in transnational credit or Liverpool cotton prices.[84] The post office delivered mail to
New Orleans via several routes with varying regularity. According to an
1838 New Orleans guidebook, the "Northern" route arrived daily, and
the "Coast" and "Lake" routes arrived twice each week. The "River"
route, however, was less dependable as it could only be expected "every
time it gets here."[85] This same irregularity plagued the regularly sailing
packet ships that connected New Orleans to New York and elsewhere.
These privately owned vessels averaged eighteen days to make the roughly
1,700-mile trip between New York and New Orleans, but travel times
varied widely, if the vessels arrived at all. Because of the difficulties of
navigating the adverse currents, shallow reefs, and narrow passages
between the Atlantic Ocean and the Gulf of Mexico, marine insurers
considered the routes between these American cities to be riskier than the
international voyage between New York and Liverpool.[86]

Although packet ships arrived from and departed for several Atlantic
ports on a biweekly basis, by 1837, the fastest way to send information
between New Orleans and New York or London was through the post
office's express mail service. In 1836, the federal government established
an express mail route between New York and New Orleans to ensure that
northern speculators could not delay financial information and profit at
southerners' expense. Express mail riders made the trip between New York
and New Orleans in as few as seven days, although they often took
considerably longer. To provide this speed, the post office issued very strict
regulations. As the guidebook explained, "the Express Mail between this
city and New York closes at half-past 10 o'clock A.M. All letters sent by
this Mail *must be paid for in advance*, and marked '*Express Mail*.'" Only
letters weighing less than half an ounce and newspaper columns

transcribed onto tissue paper would be accepted. Although newspaper columns exchanged by editors traveled for free, correspondents paid dearly for the privilege of fast communication. As the guidebook continued, "letters will be charged with triple postage." The cost to send each page of a letter along one of the four regular mail routes was between six and twenty-five cents depending on the distance traveled. Thus, the cheapest letter in the express mail cost almost as much as a workingman's pay for a day's labor. This meant that few people sent letters, especially by the express mail. Historian Richard John found that in 1830, the total number of letters sent by the mail was 14 million, which roughly equated to one letter per person per year. An enclosed bill of exchange or envelope would count as an additional page. To save money, letter writers performed intricate folds to dispense with envelopes while preserving confidentiality.[87]

Bill brokers sent many of the bills of exchange written in New Orleans through the express mail to New York City. Although people throughout the United States traded financial instruments, millions of bills, bonds, bank notes, and stocks accumulated in the Wall Street money market because New York City offered America's fastest and most regular communication with Great Britain. Not only did Wall Street's bill brokers and banks trade paper between cities within the United States, but these financial intermediaries also handled a huge trade of international paper, especially after the destruction of the BUS. The national nature of American finance was more obvious in New York than anywhere else in the financial confederacy because the paper bank notes that circulated within the United States could not retain their value across international lines. New Yorkers translated between national currencies; bills promising to pay in American dollars were traded daily for bills promising to pay in British pounds sterling. In New York City, nations mattered.

* * *

Aside from the lack of slaves and humidity, in the 1830s, the biggest difference between New York and New Orleans was scale. In 1835, New York was the largest city in America with three to four times the population of New Orleans.[88] Merchants in New York were by far the largest importers of foreign goods into the United States.[89] New York's Wall Street and Pearl Street financial districts swelled with banks, mercantile houses, and bill brokerage firms. Merchants, bankers, and other financiers in New York performed the same functions as their Louisiana counterparts, but New Yorkers handled a greater quantity and diversity of financial instruments, imports, and exports. For example, one New York City broker enticed a potential English investor by explaining that he had "been honored with the Confidence of the States of Indiana, Missouri, and Michigan, to negotiate in Europe, portions of the Loans authorised [sic] by those states for Internal Improvements."[90] New York's development was the product of exactly the same confidence-inspiring strategies of men like Forstall and Hermann except that it made money by channeling transnational capital to more remote American locales rather than just the immediate community. This was a result in part of experience. Brokers in New York began marketing Erie Canal stocks to English investors in the 1820s.[91] By the 1830s, New York brokers, dealers, merchants, and bankers sold to their correspondents not only local bank bonds, internal improvement stocks, and bills of exchange but also financial instruments from investments throughout the nation.

After December 1835, the inflow of foreign funds became physically visible when a fire destroyed at least $20 million in property across thirteen acres of New York City's commercial district.[92] The conflagration consumed 674 buildings, including many of the new wharves, hotels, shops, auction houses, banks, restaurants, and mercantile firm headquarters that had opened up for business in the late 1820s and early 1830s.[93] When news of the destruction of New York's commercial neighborhood reached London, Joshua Bates confessed to his diary, "it remains to be seen what effect this awful calamity will have on the commercial prospects of New York."[94] He would not wait long to see the result; English investors immediately extended credit to New Yorkers to finance the rebuilding.[95]

The fire prompted landlords to raise rents; changed the physical layout of the city; and consolidated commercial operations as weaker, less insured firms were forced into bankruptcy. Four thousand clerks lost their jobs, thousands of porters suddenly became unemployed, and twenty-three of the city's twenty-six fire insurance companies went bankrupt.[96] Nevertheless, as Philip Hone boasted in his diary, "the indomitable spirit of the merchants was recovered from the loss and although they bent severely under the burthen of their affliction they were too proud and too honest to break."[97]

Invigorated rather than encumbered with these difficulties and new debts, New York's financiers built a bigger, grander, and brighter city. New Yorkers transformed their city by widening the streets, laying gaslight pipelines, building large Greek Revival buildings to evoke the city's commercial solidity, and renegotiating the urban geography to segregate elite residential areas from the financial district and the poor. Retail shops moved out of the crowded Wall Street to Pearl Street financial center and up the Broadway thoroughfare.[98] All of this movement encouraged speculation in New York's real estate. London merchant bankers and local developers bought swaths of city land as investments promising large returns.[99] Wall Street and its environs became an increasingly male, specialized, and frenetic neighborhood responsible for the exchange of local, national, and international financial information.

Correspondents from places as distant as New Orleans, London, Havana, and Canton courted New Yorkers, who could provide detailed information about the latest foreign transactions, prices, and exchange rates. For example, in 1836, Hermann established correspondent and credit relationships with one of the largest bill brokering houses in New York, J. L. & S. Joseph & Co.[100]

Bill brokering, like all commerce, was a gamble. To make educated bets, brokers needed information about the names on a bill – the merchant who had signed the bill, the endorsers who had traded the bill, and the banking house in London that promised to pay the gold. To learn these local details, bill brokers traded credit for trustworthy financial information. Letter by letter and bill by bill, brokers linked individuals who did not know one another in a precariously balanced financial circuit that powered global trade through the force of confidence.

More than anyone else involved in international trade, bill brokers had to pay attention to hints that confidence might be misplaced because their financial success depended on tiny changes in discount rates. So access to information and skillful interpretation were the tools of the trade. They dedicated their time to building their roster of correspondents and spinning their correspondence to suit their interests.[101] Despite attempts to democratize the spread of domestic news through the post office, New Yorkers were almost always the first Americans to learn of European news and could therefore influence the tone and interpretation of its reporting.

For more than a hundred years, New York City had competed with Boston and Philadelphia for control over the nation's domestic and foreign financial markets. In addition to its fairly central geography, navigable harbor, and growing canal system that stretched deep into the interior of the countryside, the establishment of regularly scheduled voyages to specific destinations ensured the central role of the city at Manhattan's tip in the transatlantic trade. Because no American city built a rival packet ship network, New York controlled the flow of international information. Newspaper editors nationwide copied verbatim foreign news from the New York papers. With ten ships operating on a circuit between New

York and London; fourteen heading to Le Havre, France; twelve to New
Orleans; eight to Savannah; six to Mobile; and at least three to Belfast,
Cartagena, Vera Cruz, Havana, and the New England ports, New York
was an undeniable hub of the Atlantic world.[102]

Among all of the packets' destinations, New Yorkers invested the most
capital, ships, and labor in their Liverpool lines. By 1835, sixteen ships on
three competing lines journeyed between New York and Liverpool each
week. The eastbound crossing was calculated at 3,086 miles, whereas the
westbound crossing averaged 3,483 miles because captains had to chart a
more roundabout southern course to avoid the Gulf Stream and icebergs.
The exclusive reliance on wind-powered technology made the westbound
crossing, as sailors joked, an uphill journey. Winter winds slowed the
crossing down to a crawl. In the 1830s, the eastbound journey averaged
twenty-one days. The westbound journey most commonly spanned thirty
days but frequently lasted forty-five days and could take as long as seventy-
three days.[103]

For the sailors and passengers on westbound vessels, the voyage could
be a harrowing experience of failed attempts to catch a breeze and tedious
waiting; for investors on either side of the Atlantic, the irregularity of the
westward voyage translated into weeks of anxiety. So much drama surrounded the arrival of the news that novelists employed this experience to
intensify their plots. As one fictional Pearl Street merchant in an 1834
novel explained:

Never shall I forget the anxiety we endured, from the time of our cotton purchase to
the time of our cotton sale. We were constantly on the look out for news from
Liverpool. The packet seemed too slow in coming. The winds were contrary. They
did not bring arrivals soon enough. Indeed, as if to ruin us cotton speculators, there
were no arrivals for a whole month. In that time what a mighty change in the cotton
market might take place! How prodigiously the article might rise! Or, again, how
shockingly it might fall! Ah, there was the rub. Had we been certain of its rising, we
might have gone to bed and slept comfortably. But the uncertainty kept us awake.[104]

Merchants invented tools to manage their financial uncertainty.
Commercial clerks penned many duplicate copies of letters and bills of
exchange to be sent on competing vessels to maximize their chance of a
speedy arrival. For example, the form Hermann filled out to pay Greene
informed anyone who handled the bill that three copies were in
circulation.[105]

Although only one copy of a bill of exchange would be traded for coin,
a duplicate letter pressed onto tissue paper while the ink on the original
was still wet retained its value. Letters were called "favors," "advices," or

"respects" – all of which connoted the importance placed on correspondent networks for transmitting information. Moses Taylor, a New York-based merchant who traded primarily with Havana, wrote letters for every vessel, even when his report was that "we have nothing new here."[106] The Rothschilds, an unrivaled family of merchant bankers on the European continent, sent at least three letters on every ship – one for each of their correspondents in New York, Baltimore, and Philadelphia. When their New York correspondents failed to send a letter via an eastbound packet ship, the London partners admonished, "you will always avail of these opportunities of affording us desirable information, especially when you have intelligence of importance to communicate."[107] For those engaged in transatlantic trade, every packet ship contained "desirable information" vital to business.

Anxiety about the arrival of news traveled in both directions. London merchant banking firms that specialized in trade with the United States, commonly called "American houses," eagerly awaited the arrival of New York's packet ships with news from their correspondents located throughout the United States.[108] English investors, after all, risked a great deal of capital in America.

* * *

Within a day of arriving in Liverpool, American news reached London. London was, in the words of geographer David Green, "a demographic colossus"; the population in London was more than double the population of the next five biggest cities in England combined. Built on the ruins of a Roman city, the oldest district within London, the City of London or the City for short, controlled a vast empire of trade. In this square mile of banks, coffee houses, and taverns surrounding the Bank of England, the world's most well-connected financiers traded paper linking trade in China with trade in the United States and everywhere in between. Despite the construction of formal structures such as the Royal Stock Exchange, commonly called the 'Change, much of London's business took place in informal settings. Business deals were conducted throughout the labyrinthine, narrow back alleys and along the broad avenues that linked this capital of global finance to the political capital of the British Empire – a neighborhood to the west called Westminster.[109]

While their clerks discussed the day's labor in basement taverns, financiers might mingle with scholars and politicians at the Political Economy Club, where in terms of "the excellence of its monthly dinners," one member joked, "the club does not seem to study economy."[110] Despite the difference in refinement, the men in both of these homosocial environments traded ideas about the workings of trade. Whereas clerks gossiped about the practical business of their employers, the thirty-five elected members of the Political Economy Club proposed and debated theoretical questions like Thomas Malthus's 1834 question, "Is there any valid apology for the American Tariff?"[111] This query like many others suggested the dominant issue of the decade: the relationship between government policy and the world of trade. And while the members built the ideological foundations for belief in an "economy" as a system independent of politics, they hired architects to design new purpose-built banks to house the work of transnational investment.[112] Built on the model of aristocratic townhouses, these buildings evoked an aura of confidence in the wealth and status of the bankers. Most of these buildings included a parlor for discrete negotiations with genteel customers and a long mahogany counter in the center of the ground floor for regular banking functions.[113]

Eight merchant banking houses financed the majority of trade with the United States and became known as the American houses; seven of them built headquarters in the City.[114] The men who ran these private banks corresponded with brokers, merchants, and bankers in locations throughout the United States and provided these distant correspondents with letters of credit that would allow them to write bills of exchange. Just like their correspondents in New York and New Orleans, London financiers sought personal profits and local development. In the capital of the British Empire, however, local prosperity generally implied national prosperity. This was most visible in material form in the centerpiece of the City's architecture: the Bank of England (BOE), a private bank that was explicitly charged by the government with the responsibility of protecting the British currency.

The BOE was formed in the seventeenth century as a private company that would raise money for the government's war chest. By the early nineteenth century, it not only controlled government funds but also had a monopoly on minting coins and printing paper money. Other private banks extended long-term credit to wealthy individuals and merchants but could neither print money nor form a joint-stock company, a business owned by a potentially infinite number of shareholders who contributed an expansive capital base.

After a financial crisis in 1825, a bank war began in England. Advocates of competition in banking and the politicians they elected chipped away at the BOE's monopoly through policies of democratization and decentralization. When the BOE was rechartered in 1833, it gained the right to open branches outside of London but lost its special position as the only London joint-stock bank. Some private banks merged with new joint-stock companies that were less conservative in their lending practices. Even more experimental in their strategies were the new banks formed by manufacturers in the industrial regions and investors involved in promoting railroads who seized the opportunity to create their own banks and finance their businesses.[115]

By 1836, more than two hundred new joint-stock banks had formed. Those located outside of London could print their own bank notes.[116] Nevertheless, the BOE remained responsible for making sure that its vaults contained enough gold to support the currency. Despite their central control over the nation's gold, the BOE directors received little information from joint-stock banks about how much money they circulated. The BOE directors disliked their predicament of trying to regulate the currency with insufficient information and distrusted the new bankers' incentives to print excess paper money.

Employing the shocking number of banks as ammunition, supporters of the BOE attacked the new banks in newspapers, Parliament, and pamphlets. By debating what they called "the currency question," old and new money battled for the right to print paper because they all wanted credit. Credit, however, came in many forms; bank notes were the most obvious. Although large quantities of ink and paper were devoted to solving the currency question, the discount markets for bills of exchange posed a greater challenge to the solvency of banks, merchants, and even nations on both sides of the Atlantic.

While currency debates took place in Parliament and in the press, the BOE directors debated a variety of ideas about how to accomplish the daunting task of protecting the currency while still generating profits for the shareholders. Advocates fell into two schools of thought: the Currency School emphasized protecting the currency despite the needs of trade, and the Bank School emphasized access of the commercial community to the BOE's capital. In 1832, John Horsley Palmer, then the governor of the BOE and a member of the Political Economy Club, proposed a compromise of these principles. The Palmer Rule defined a relationship between the gold supplies in the bank, the circulation of the bank's notes, and the discount rate that the bank would offer for buying bills of exchange.[117] The purpose of this rule was to ensure that when the balance of trade with foreign countries was not in Britain's favor, in other words when British merchants had to send gold to pay for their imports, the credit available in the money market would become more expensive. This increased cost for credit would, the directors believed, influence the balance of trade to swing back to Britain's favor and return gold to the bank. The BOE directors carefully monitored the flow of gold coins in and out of the BOE's vaults, but they did not always follow their rule precisely.[118] In general, the BOE directors tried to prevent crises in the currency and in the credit markets. Opponents invested in both halves of this financial balance heavily scrutinized their decisions.

Interested only in the safest of investments, the BOE primarily discounted acceptances. By doing so, the BOE not only offered accommodation to the bankers who needed to manage their cash flows but also made money for its shareholders. The directors raised or lowered the discount rate loosely based on the equation of the Palmer Rule. A large supply of specie called for low discount rates to encourage investment. When the vaults emptied, the BOE raised discount rates to protect the specie reserved for the currency.[119] Thus, protection of the national currency and transnational trade competed for the specie inside the vaults of the BOE. It was not, however, a fair contest. Because of its public duty, the BOE was obliged to protect the national currency at the expense of transnational trade.

In an era of debates over protectionism and free trade, the BOE was a quasi-laboratory of political economy. Every time the BOE directors faced the choice to discount a bill, they were actually deciding whether the nation should favor financial stability within British territory or private profit irrespective of political boundaries. Although there were many sources of merchant banking capital in London, the BOE's overwhelming specie supply and public duties made it the nation's largest and most powerful bank. Although the role of a central bank had not been formally defined, the BOE had already acted as a lender of last resort for the government, ensuring that the British Empire remained solvent. As a lender to private merchant banks, the BOE's responsibility in a crisis was less clear. Financiers had come to recognize a difference between an external drain of specie that required a tightening of credit markets to protect the currency and an internal drain of specie that resulted when investors lost confidence in instruments of credit and sought security in the BOE's gold. If the BOE raised interest rates during internal drains, the increased cost of credit could cause businesses that were solvent but illiquid to fail. The BOE dealt with this dilemma by limiting which acceptances it chose to discount and discriminating among the firms seeking accommodation. During crises, the directors had to make tough choices, especially because most of this group of elected shareholders were, themselves, involved in commerce or merchant banking. The effects of decisions made within the courts, halls, and rotundas of the BOE could be felt in markets around the world.

When London merchant bankers extended credit to their correspondents in New York or New Orleans, they loaned British specie to America. Although not all London brokers, bankers, and merchants understood the implicit national undercurrent to their transnational investments, their American counterparts showed little awareness that nation-states were involved in local development at all. By 1836, American specie was diffused to hundreds of state-chartered banks throughout the nation without central regulation. No institution monitored the nation's finances. Men like Forstall did not think about their credit in national terms or local investments as relevant to national or international specie flows. Busy developing their local markets, Americans dismantled their closest approximation to the BOE – the BUS. This lack of national regulation in America enabled entrepreneurs to channel capital into local investments. Nevertheless, without an institution overseeing the nation's finances, America could not offer a unified response to Britain's national currency policies. As a nation, the United States could not create financial foreign policy because Americans thought locally.

A national market, so obvious in British institutions, was barely discernible in New York's financial market and nonexistent in New Orleans. Thus, in 1836, as investors prospered on both sides of the Atlantic and intelligence circulated on private and public paper, Americans and Britons interpreted financial information within different political frameworks. And especially in the United States, politics paraded in the streets, filled the print of the newspapers, and pervaded the lives of ordinary Americans, whereas the transnational financial system and its dependence on confidence was barely visible – hidden in the paper of trade.[120]

* * *

In 1835, after five years of developing his banking, sugar refining, and cotton factoring businesses, Edmond Forstall returned to London. He was shocked to discover that Baring Brothers declined to buy his latest Louisiana bank bonds. Forstall blamed this disinterest in his stable 5 percent interest rates on "the gambling propensities of the times"; American investments, he suggested, were no longer risky enough for English capitalists. Forstall sought more conservative investors elsewhere.[121] But he misunderstood why Bates rejected his bonds.

The two men had different perspectives. Since their last meeting, Forstall had become a partner in M. de Lizardi & Co., an American house that shipped specie, financial instruments, and commodities across national borders with associated firms in Liverpool; London; Paris; Tampico, Mexico; and, of course, New Orleans.[122] As an agent of this firm, Forstall wielded considerable financial power in developing New Orleans's economic infrastructure. As evidenced by his marketing of the bonds, Forstall believed that New Orleans's trade would continue to grow.

In refusing to buy Forstall's bonds, Bates expressed the opposite view.[123] Over the course of the next year, he would increasingly believe that investing in American paper, whether or not the interest was guaranteed, was too great a gamble.[124] Rather than ponder the optimistic financial information from New Orleans or New York, Bates recorded in his diary his somber thoughts on "Advices from the U.S.," "American affairs," and "News from America."[125]

At the time of Forstall's visit, Bates was in the process of negotiating a loan to compensate slave owners on the emancipation of the British Empire's West Indian slaves. He decided ultimately that the credit required was too large for the London money market, which was already stretched to provide credit for the American trade. He was concerned about the stability of the financial system in America and confessed to his diary that the opposition between Jackson and the BUS would result in disastrous losses throughout the United States.[126] "Business is very brisk every thing is rising and looks prosperous throughout the world," he observed with a skeptic's eye, "too much so to last."[127] His concerns about, in Forstall's words, "the gambling propensities of the times" left him doubtful about continued prosperity. The problem with Forstall's bonds was not that they were safe but that they were risky.

Bates was left with a choice. He could continue to invest in America and risk his bank's fortune. Or he could express his doubts by refusing to buy American paper and risk destroying the confidence that supported the entire financial system. Either way, the market was, as he put it, "a very Gamblous affair."[128] In the course of the next year, the gambles would get even more risky.

CHAPTER 2

The Pressure of 1836

Some stories start with a crash. Others, like this one, end with one. Instead of a crash, this story starts with the gentle landing of a very tired pigeon.

Rumor has it that on August 2, 1836, a pigeon landed south of London. Although few birds play significant roles in history, this particular pigeon, whose existence has never been irrefutably confirmed but whose legend endures, carried a note under its wing that was quite valuable to those who could interpret it.[1] With three short words, "*il est mort*," the message on the thin scrap of paper set off "the variations of all stocks & their wild fluctuations," according to a prominent financier.[2] Within six months, markets in the United States and Great Britain faced a financial crisis that would ultimately lead to a global economic depression, the worst of many in the nineteenth century.

Was the pigeon a portent? Many Londoners seemed to think so. The little bird's cargo, the message "he is dead," dashed their hopes that the world's most skillful financial interpreter, Nathan Mayer Rothschild, would return to the City. Over the previous three decades, Rothschild had become the world's wealthiest man by profitably interpreting the latest intelligence. While he attended his son's wedding in Hamburg, news from across the Atlantic had created a "pressure," what one political economist defined as "a difficulty of borrowing money and the necessity of paying a high price for it."[3] The pigeon's note intensified the tight credit market because it confirmed that the bankers in London were left with only their own gloomy predictions of what the news from the American bank war would mean for their own battle-worn financial system. Without Rothschild's potentially positive reinterpretation, no semiotic rescue would avoid the financial crisis many Londoners predicted.

Not all merchants and bankers, however, recognized the same signs. While the bird glided on the air currents over the English Channel, transatlantic winds propelled Samuel Hermann toward London. When he arrived in the City, the New Orleanian cotton factor saw only potential. His cotton, growing in fields throughout the American southwest, would soon flow down the Mississippi and across the Atlantic to be converted into cash. High prices and abundant crops signaled a successful future, if he could find enough credit to finance the growing trade in this commodity. He was not alone in this prediction; he carried with him letters from other Americans so convinced of a bright future that they were willing to "guarantee" his business.[4] Confident in his interpretation, he paid no attention to prophesy of panic. London's bankers, however, were loath to extend credit lines when they saw signs of trouble. And the more they looked for warnings of eminent disaster, the more they found.

Is there any difference between an omen and an economic indicator besides the expertise of the prophet? Even today, markets rely on interpreters who through experience, technology, or luck claim the ability to predict the future. In 1836, authority for economic predictions had not yet become the province of professional economists employing statistical models. Instead, financiers tried to predict the economic future from a wide variety of intelligence that was itself the product of interpretation. Decisions to buy or sell, to extend credit or demand payment, to increase production or leave fields fallow are all the product of minds translating interpretations of intelligence into policy.

Economic theorists have only recently begun to challenge the principle that all participants in a market have the same information and that they use this information to reach the same rational conclusions.[5] But in 1836, Londoners knew that not all interpretations were created equal; more to the point, not all interpreters reached the same conclusions. Employing intelligence about the American bank war as evidence for their own political conflict over their national financial system, English investors interpreted American political diatribe as signs of a coming crisis. They initiated conservative policies designed to protect against a panic. These policies started the pressure of 1836, a transatlantic contraction of credit. The effects of this credit crisis convinced Americans that their balance sheets might not be strong enough to sustain the pressure of British doubt. By the end of the year, English pessimism had defeated American optimism, but it was too late for businesses that had already gambled on continued flush times. A crisis of interpretation set the stage for a financial crisis. By 1837, the precautious policies of investors created the panic they were designed to prevent.

***

On May 12, 1836, members of Parliament turned the "earnest attention of the Legislature" to the "system of joint-stock banking [that] has grown up already of great magnitude, which is daily extending its ramifications, and which promises very shortly to comprehend every portion of the kingdom, and every class of its population within the sphere of its operation." Supporters of joint-stock banks encouraged the inquiry because this "time of prosperity" could validate their theoretical model of bank competition.[6] "The commerce of the country was now proceeding with a flowing tide and a favourable wind," agreed one opponent of joint-stock banks who, perhaps inadvertently, expressed his conservatism through his metaphor of sail rather than steam power. He continued, "but the legislature ought to bear in mind that from the commercial history of the country, it was clear her commerce was liable to vicissitudes and changes." Warning that "prosperity might not be permanent," he too invited an investigation into the new banks.[7]

Whether in favor of competition or monopoly, the real debate focused on whether the inquiry should be public. Joint-stock bank supporters argued among themselves about whether a committee sworn to secrecy ought to perform the investigation for fear that "matters might be incautiously divulged which ought not to be published," or whether "the public were entitled to know every thing respecting these banks." In the end, a private committee would gather confidential information from the banks, but newspapers throughout Britain, and eventually even in the United States, reprinted the Parliamentary record. As this discussion referenced the "sinister objects" and "bad consequences arising from improper speculation" by the joint-stock banks, the BOE had won the Parliamentary skirmish regardless of the committee's findings.[8] The public would read of these threats to the British economy and then starve for information.

Without access to official facts, writers searched for information whether they wanted to present joint-stock banks as responsible for "the great works which enrich and adorn our country," or as the backers of an "absurd *mania*" for "romantic and outrageous" companies.[9] One pamphleteer bemoaned, "the public have no data from which they can form any probable conjecture." He bristled, "they are left totally in the dark."[10]

On the cheaply printed pages of pamphlets and periodicals, theories of political economy developed. "The paucity of facts is one cause why we have so many theories," suggested James W. Gilbart, the head of the first joint-stock bank in London. Inspired to write a guide to the theoretical debate, he suggested, "Had we more ample information there would be less room for speculations, and we should arrive at certain knowledge instead of being wafted about by fluctuating theories." Curious English readers in the summer of 1836 found themselves not only adrift on the hot air of rumor and opinion but also lacking skills to process the available "data." Gilbart explained: "the science of statistics has received till lately but little attention in this country, and perhaps, the statistics of banking have received less attention than any other portion of that science. It is only since 1833 that we have periodical publications of the circulation of the Bank of England, and of the country banks, and even these are imperfect."[11] "Imperfect" information not only left the public in the dark but also kept bankers from accurately assessing one another.

Unable to acquire perfect information about their financial system, English writers turned to the next best thing, evidence of a similar system. Voluminous accounts of American banking arrived on weekly packet ships from the United States. Throughout the American bank war, the London *Times*, a pro-BOE newspaper that even a joint-stock banker recognized as "the leading and influential press," published brief summaries of American financial issues.[12] But during May 1836, it reinterpreted these accounts as evidence of a general failure of decentralized finance.

The editor of the *Times* marketed his paper by vowing "to put capitalists and men of business in other places as nearly as possible on the same footing with them in the knowledge of what is actually going on in the City."[13] With this agenda in mind, the *Times* employed the American example of bank competition to frighten readers, near and far, who might be in a position to sway English policy in favor of the BOE. Ten days before Parliament turned to the currency question, the *Times* discussed the "very serious mischief" of the joint-stock banks, and referencing Biddle's Panic, pointed to the "close resemblance to the situation of the United States two years ago, when a panic was brought on by the sudden contraction of their issues by the United States Bank."[14] Panic was a horrifying prospect for all financiers because it suggested that an otherwise stable financial system would be subjected to the doubts of politically motivated or irrational actors who might cause real harm to honestly operated businesses. The most recent English panic, in 1825, resulted in the end of the BOE's monopoly and many business failures.

The *Times* published this analogy, and papers throughout Great Britain reprinted the article to encourage an investigation into English joint-stock banks; it was not intended as a report on American financial instability.[15]

After the Parliamentary debate, allusions to American banking as evidence of the deleterious effects of joint-stock banking increased. For weeks, the *Times* reprinted articles from both sides of America's partisan press that shared a condemnation of the American banking system. Critiquing President Jackson's policies, one column argued that "the country is turned into a gambling-house for the benefit of legislative favourites" and that the American people were "delivered up, fettered and weaponless, to the tender mercies of a set of incorporated banks."[16] In thinly veiled allusions to English joint-stock banks, the *Times* printed articles about hard money that described the American "paper mania"; banks that ought to face "a destructive run upon them in consequence of their extravagant issues"; and a comparison of the "power of coining paper money" to "lotteries, gambling, and forgery," or in other words, "the greatest evil of modern times."[17] Likening competition in currency to an infection, the *Times* referred to a "currency distemper which rages so violently all over the United States."[18] Another article in the *Times* hinted at the remedy: Jacksonian aspirations to return to the "safe constitutional metallic currency."[19] Gold would heal banks bleeding paper money.

At first, the discussion in the London press of the stability of gold, like the instability of paper, was intended to influence British banking regulation. Within a few weeks, the practical implications of American desire for gold transformed from example in an internal British policy debate to a new threat to the British system. On May 23, 1836, the *Times* reprinted a report from a New York paper that "A large house of brokers, connected particularly with foreign business, yesterday made insurance on a heavy amount of specie soon to arrive from England."[20] The *Newcastle Courant* reprinted two short articles. One announced that "a very considerable quantity of gold has been exported within the last three or four weeks, and the exportation is going on." The other suggested a potential destination for the gold by republishing figures from the Jacksonian *Washington Globe* indicating that the U.S. Mint had "issued upwards of six millions of dollars of new gold coin."[21] The *Brighton Patriot* reported that "Gold continues to leave the country; the government of the United States . . . use our sovereigns as if it were their own."[22] Gold, of course, was not the only commodity traveling westward.

Liverpool newspapers reported that only a quarter of the exports bound for the United States could fit on the usual packet ships. The

Derby Mercury, Hull Packet, and *Newcastle Courant* reprinted this news, which suggested to English readers that "overtrading," or an imbalance of trade, could be added to the list of troubles with America.[23] As manufacturers and merchants relied on country banks for financing, all of these indictments of American excess reaffirmed the charge of "speculation" by joint-stock banks. Readers who believed that America's financial chaos merely justified an inquiry into Britain's own banking experiments now envisioned more material concerns.

By printing accounts of American banking in order to fight their own bank war, supporters of the BOE brought the instability of the American financial system to the attention of its investors. As one letter to the editor attested, "The statements in your paper [have] excited much alarm in the minds of persons holding American stocks and engaged in the American trade."[24] While Americans read the newspaper accounts of fiscal policy debates through partisan eyes, Londoners saw primarily the potential risks of American commerce.

Had too much British specie been traded to America in exchange for paper that promised high interest rates but would not retain its value? Given the flawed statistical record, even economic historians with modern technology have not produced a clear answer.[25] Regardless of whether the Specie Circular, Deposit Act, or any other policy actually spawned an unsafe expansion of American banking and commerce, this possibility haunted London investors. By mid-June, the *Times* reported, "Great interest seems to be raised in the City by the discussions on American affairs, but many affect to doubt whether trading and banking have been carried on to the extent described, and ask for further evidence on the subject."[26] A *Times* reader alerted the press that it had "derived [its] facts, as well as the colouring of them, from a source much to be distrusted, being tainted with party politics." Rather than turning to "the authority of the best private letters" as an alternative to the press, the *Times* turned to the U.S. Congress, the pulpit of American party politics, for more "facts."[27]

The *Times* made an awkward choice. On April 27, 1836, New York Congressman C. C. Cambreleng, a former merchant and hard-money Democrat who chaired the House Ways and Means Committee, had delivered a speech in Congress designed to forestall Whig plans to distribute the federal surplus.[28] Although the bill's stated goal was buttressing the American military defenses, the congressman, like everyone who debated the bill, used only a fraction of his time to discuss the possibilities of war with Native Americans, France, Great Britain, or Mexico. Instead, he launched a volley of numerical artillery against the nation's banks.

Predicting that the "wild and uncalculating spirit of speculation" that had produced the federal government's surplus could not continue in perpetuity, he cited shocking statistics as "evidences of sudden and extraordinary overtrading" and of "the vast and sudden expansion of the business of all the banks in the Union." Cambreleng's adjectives conveyed his true fear: the reach of international trade was accelerating too fast over too vast a territory. Nevertheless, his speech was designed to frighten his fellow legislators and the wider audience of national voters into fearing only the distribution of the surplus. It was not designed for London.[29]

Americans ignored Cambreleng's speech. The numbers he supplied should have been frightening to anyone who understood trade. But in 1836, the "science" of political economy had not yet focused on data and models.[30] Besides, even if Americans wanted to use the numbers, those numbers were probably wrong.[31] For example, the New York *Journal of Commerce*, from one day to the next, misprinted one of Cambreleng's statistics; the difference between the two figures was more than a million dollars.[32] Errors notwithstanding, Americans were fascinated with numeracy but far from expert in manipulating statistics.[33] In American colleges, the discipline of political economy, if it was taught at all, was the province of experts in moral philosophy, theologians or other thinkers with little contact with the realities of trade.[34] Opposite to idealist political economists, American merchants and bankers who had practical experience with finance were often too busy managing their daily enterprises to spend time theorizing. Although officials marshaled numbers in support of policy, members of Congress tailored their speeches to economically uneducated voters who would read them in the nation's partisan presses.[35] If the politicians did not edit out the numbers, newspapers did. After listening to Cambreleng's hour-long speech, the correspondent of the New York *Journal of Commerce* provided the newspaper with only the most general of figures; this paper's readers would not learn the specific data the congressman cited for overtrading or banking because the press printed only the numbers for military expenditures.[36] Besides all of these practical problems, the country was not receptive to Cambreleng's gloom. In flush times, who paid attention to a croaker predicting the end was nigh? For all these reasons, Cambreleng's speech faded into the debate that would ultimately be decided not by economic calculations but along party lines. After years of the bank war, American readers were inured to the politically motivated, dire predictions for the American financial system published by Whigs and Democrats alike.[37]

Cambreleng's speech, however, found an eager audience in Britain. Ignoring the partisan motives of the text, the editor of the *Times* asserted that Cambreleng's words and numbers had "greater importance" in London because they demanded a reevaluation of the security of the entire American financial system rather than just the policy of surplus distribution. In statistic-starved England, Cambreleng's data provided evidence that democratized banking and decentralized control of the currency had brought this important trade partner and potential test case of the joint-stock system to the brink of crisis. Given the sums British investors had risked on American ventures, the *Times* editor believed that the figures cited by Cambreleng needed "to be made known and carefully watched in this country." He expressed the hope that the "utility" of publishing Cambreleng's statistics would not be to cause "very extensive mischief" but rather "that it may possibly, by exciting similar caution on the other side, avert altogether the otherwise inevitable consequences."[38] By mid-June, the *Times* concluded that "the rate at which the increase of bank capital is going on in the United States is quite portentous, and must accelerate the crisis in that country for which all reflecting men are now prepared."[39] News of American financial instability generated by the American bank war was no longer merely ammunition in the English bank war; negative interpretations of American finance began to influence investors' confidence in the financial system itself.[40]

* * *

Thanks to the *Times* articles and news from "the best private letters," the City's most important financiers began to express concerns about their investment in America. Joshua Bates penned his doubts in his diary.[41] These writings, unlike newspapers and letters, were not meant to circulate but to relieve the pressure in the mind of a man at the center of transatlantic trade; few financiers found time for this kind of reflection. In May 1836, he had already heard "a good deal of talk about gold going out and a sentiment of money matters in the City." Although Bates believed that inquiry into American specie flows would "probably do good," he was concerned that "if carried too far it must end in panic."[42]

As the summer wore on, the talk in the City spread to networks of investors outside the square mile. Having recently agreed to sell a bond issue for the Citizens' Bank of Louisiana, Bates's correspondents in Amsterdam, Hope & Co., complained that "the paragraphs in the *Times* respecting the unparalleled extension of Banking and Paper issues in the United States are not calculated to strengthen the confidence in trans

Atlantic loans."[43] On the day after the *Times* published Cambreleng's speech, Bates recorded in his diary that "the Newspaper contains accounts of the great increase of Banks in the United States and expressed fears that seem were founded that a crisis may happen in consequence." Echoing the *Times*'s opinion that "reflecting men" recognized a coming crisis, he wrote to himself, "we must prepare for consequence."[44]

Bates immediately strengthened the conservative strategy for the American trade that he had begun formulating in 1835. Baring Brothers supplied American merchants and banks with credit in the form of exchange accounts that allowed these clients to write bills of exchange. He immediately sent a letter to his Boston agent, Thomas Wren Ward, ordering him not "to have any more exchange accounts at present," to withdraw credit from several American state banks, and to "be cautious in granting credits in New York to houses having other accounts open in London." With this last request, Bates evidenced his loss of confidence not only in the profitability of American paper but also in his fellow London bankers. He feared that if Americans failed to pay their bills of exchange, English bill brokers who had extended credit across the Atlantic and tied up their capital in this paper would not be able to pay their debts. By refusing credit to New Yorkers with other London accounts, Bates sought to prevent his firm's ensnarement in this web of dubious credit.[45] By reacting early to the news, Bates anticipated a shift in confidence that extended far beyond his personal doubts. But he did not broadcast his concerns.[46] He did not need to; the *Times* had made American banking important British news.

Into these swirling currents of doubt about American and British banking flew the carrier pigeon with news of Rothschild's death. Transacting international negotiations while leaning on the same column of the 'Change for more than thirty years, Rothschild had been characterized as a "pillar" of the exchange – a component of the architecture of the Empire's currency.[47] Attending his son's wedding in the German city of Frankfurt am Main, the fifty-nine-year-old Rothschild died of an infection that spread from, as his son described it, "a most terrible boil on his bottom."[48] The financial world grieved with memorabilia such as mourning rings and silk scarves, which provided a balance sheet of his profits and philanthropy.[49] A funeral procession of seventy-five carriages attracted a crowd "so great that many of the shops were shut to protect the windows from the pressure."[50] Nevertheless, pressure built in the streets and in money markets. Several months later, one financier referred to Rothschild's death as "an event of some importance in the derangement of the circulation of the country." He argued, "I attribute much of the late embarrassment to the loss of that activity, zeal, and enterprise, which he always displayed in times of financial difficulty."[51] Without Rothschild's creativity, few imagined a cure for the credit contraction. Confronted with daily accounts of evil portents, most just wanted to survive.

Rothschild's survivors were no exception. "We shall be glad to learn what effect the death of Mr. Rothschild is likely to have in London and what measures will be taken for the continuation of his establishment," wrote Hope & Co. to Bates.[52] Less than two weeks after the funeral, Samuel Hermann would learn the "measures" Rothschild's widow and sons intended to take as they faced the daunting task of continuing his global business.[53] After months of travel, first from New Orleans to New York and then across the Atlantic to London, Hermann learned of Rothschild's death. Undaunted, he continued with his mission to establish a line of credit for his expanding business; he may even have thought Rothschild's death worked in his favor.

In 1834, Hermann had written to Nathan Mayer Rothschild proposing that his firm "may be in many instances useful to you – for this place [New Orleans] offers yet great chances for stock & exchange business." He argued "the rising condition of this city requires a large capital – & money may be placed at any time with perfect security either for a series of years or for a short period." He offered references from firms in Paris, Hamburg, and even Baring Brothers, but his letters failed to convince Rothschild to invest in his firm.[54] The next summer, the ebullient Hermann decided to make his case to Rothschild in person. They were, after all, both successful German-Jewish expats from Frankfurt. Just before the two men met, a newspaper in Hermann's native district, the *Stadtteil* of Roedelheim, recounted his rags-to-riches story and described him as the "head of the first commercial firm in New Orleans."[55] Similarly, shortly after Rothschild's death, newspapers eulogized him as a "self made man," and a playwright described him as "the Honest Jew of Frankfort."[56] Similar biographies, however, did not translate into trust. In 1835, Rothschild chose not to invest in Hermann.[57]

The indefatigable New Orleanian planned a return trip in 1836. High prices in Liverpool combined with an anticipated bumper crop suggested a very profitable future to Hermann. Armed with a letter from the extensive bill brokers, J. L. & S. Joseph & Co., who also served as Rothschild's New York agents, Hermann again sought credit from the world's wealthiest banker. The Josephs assured that Hermann "enjoy[s] unreservedly our perfect confidence and therefore [we] recommend him to you." In case their trust was not enough, the Josephs were willing to back up their claims with a "guarantee" of their own credit and capital.[58] Had Rothschild lived to read this letter, he may have reconsidered his faith in Hermann and signaled a different prediction for America's financial future.

In his absence, Rothschild's sons met with Hermann and converted the general gloom about American business into policy. They declined to "open a Banker's account" for Hermann. In a letter to the Josephs acknowledging the New Yorkers' "very favorable observations" about Hermann, the Rothschilds cited "the unfortunate event which has lately taken place" as a reason "not to have more bills out than we can avoid." Presumably, the "unfortunate event" referred to their father's death.[59] The vague phrase, however, could be interpreted differently. Across a busy intersection from their office, another "unfortunate event" was unfolding within the BOE.

After the financial crisis in 1825, the BOE mapped a survival strategy for the currency based on the directors' belief in the Palmer Rule, which required evaluating the BOE's discounting business. James Pattison, governor of the BOE, saw in the numbers recorded in his ledgers evidence of approaching danger. Gold was vanishing, but no thief had penetrated the vaults. The discount rate at the BOE had been low for several years, encouraging trade, circulating the bank's gold supply, and producing shareholder profits; in July, the directors voted for a half of a percent increase in the rate.[60] This increase suggested a subtle shift in the priorities of the BOE from private profits and free trade to national security and protectionism.

After Rothschild's death, Pattison examined the books of the BOE to determine the effect of the rate increase on the currency. He found in the ledgers that over several months leading up to August, the BOE's bullion diminished by several million pounds sterling.[61] This large drop in the bank's supply of gold left Pattison concerned that the BOE had not achieved the desired ratio between gold and paper currency. Connecting the *Times* articles with the ledger's data, Pattison became convinced that his institution was losing specie because London investors sent it to America to supply capital for America's many new banks. As Bates warned Ward in early July, "the Governor of the Bank pretends to be or really is most alarmed about the gold going to America and the amount of American bills in circulation."[62] For Pattison, the *Times*'s reporting on the American bank war was no longer evidence to support his bank's answer to the currency question but a direct threat to his nation's financial security.

Unable to constrain the paper circulation of American banks and satisfied that he had done all he could to diminish the paper circulation of British banks, Pattison devised a strategy for defending the BOE's gold. Although he could have prevented the discounting of bills of merchants who traded with any corner of the globe, he would specifically target the English firms that offered commercial credit to American merchants and sold American bonds and stocks to British investors. During the week prior to the August 24 meeting of the Committee of the Treasury, Pattison and the directors informally decided to stop discounting the paper of seven American houses.[63]

Although the directors must have debated whether these American houses had exceeded the bounds of safe banking and were now threatening the currency of Britain, they left no paper evidence in the BOE's official records. Instead, the clerk's pristine handwriting recorded that toward the end of the very long Committee of the Treasury meeting, Pattison "laid before the committee an account of the acceptances of certain Mercantile Houses in the hands of the Bank at stated periods."[64] The Committee of the Treasury "resolved that the said account be laid before the Court of Directors."[65] The next morning, August 25, 1836, the Court of Directors, the world's most powerful collection of financiers, officially began to reconsider their confidence in America. Turning intelligence into policy, the directors of the BOE set in motion the crisis they were trying to avoid.

Governor Pattison's presentation of the American houses' accounts suggests that he blamed the American trade for the BOE's specie shortage. More than a century later, economic historians argue that this may have been an erroneous assumption on Pattison's part. The doctrinal belief of nearly all bankers of the nineteenth century that adequate specie reserves prevented crises is now believed false; many other factors, including information asymmetry and the velocity of money, complicate more modern models.[66] But assuming that the specie ratio was a valid indicator, the BOE directors did not adequately monitor their supply. Troubled about specie levels when the vaults emptied, the directors examined the forces withdrawing gold from the vaults more carefully than those that had deposited gold before 1836. The coffers of the BOE may have been artificially swollen from the end of the East India Company's monopoly on trade with China as well as the 1835 sale of the loan to compensate West Indian slave owners that troubled Bates during Forstall's visit to London.[67] Perhaps this capital had been loaned to the American houses, but economic historians have demonstrated that the specie supplies in America were composed primarily of Mexican silver, not English gold; thus, the BOE's coins had not physically crossed the Atlantic.[68] If large quantities of European gold sailed across the ocean, the money was French indemnity payments not British specie shipments.[69] Finally, as the BOE "lost" about $17 million in gold and the United States imported only $7 million in the twelve months before September 1836, some economists argue that those involved in the market wrongly associated the BOE's specie with the American trade.[70] Of course, it is possible that Pattison had evidence that has not survived in the paper records. At more than a century's remove, the destination of the BOE's gold remains a mystery to scholars. But in some ways it does not matter, because Pattison's interpretation – that American loans threatened British specie – fueled the BOE's policies.

By August 1836, the English directors of both private financial institutions, like Bates and the Rothschilds, and quasi-public institutions, like Pattison, put in motion policies designed to protect themselves from the financial crisis they predicted based on intelligence interpreted out of context.

* * *

If the directors meant to keep their decision to stop discounting American bills of exchange a secret, they failed. Even before the directors recorded their official concerns in the BOE minute books, "an active intelligent director of the Bank of England" informed one of the seven merchant banks, T. Wiggin & Co., that "more British capital has been absorbed by American and continental houses than can be spared." T. Wiggin & Co. immediately wrote to its agent in New York that the new policy threatened the reputations of individual firms, "however high may be their standing or credit," as well as investors' confidence in the larger Anglo-American trade. "This decision places all houses in jeopardy that do business with American dealers in British merchandise," the letter warned. In response to the BOE's policy, T. Wiggin & Co. announced that it would contract the credit it offered to American merchants.[71]

Shortly after T. Wiggin & Co. sent this letter, the BOE directors changed their minds. Bates explained to Ward, "We are indebted to the interest of the Liverpool cashier [of the BOE branch] for the first information of these foolish proceedings of the Bank, for he notified all the Banks at Liverpool which excited such alarm that a deputation came immediately to London which procured the recall of the obnoxious edict at once." In this single sentence, Bates combined two distinct stages of BOE policy making. The directors first decided to stop discounting the bills of the American houses and then retracted this decision.[72]

As Bates summarized, the Treasury Committee members met with William Brown, Liverpool-based and American-born head of a large bill brokerage. As a trader in the Anglo-American exchange business for more than thirty years, Brown recognized that the BOE's decision not to discount bills would be disastrous for the American trade. England's Liverpool-based cotton merchants had extended millions of pounds of credit to American cotton factors. They expected the year's harvest to be large enough to cover their debts and leave a profit, but the cotton had not yet arrived. While they waited for shipments from New Orleans and elsewhere, they would be ruined if they could not continue to discount their bills. To the BOE directors, Brown offered "my calculations which I hope will convince you that the Bank has not at present any cause to apprehend a further drain of Gold" to the United States. Brown blamed the specie drain of the previous months on the "measures of the President," arguing "to guard themselves against a run from their opponents . . . [the banks] deemed it advisable to have more specie in their vaults than usual." Brown believed that politically motivated policies from Washington had threatened financial security but American banks acted wisely. Contrary to the arguments in the *Times* article, Brown asserted that American banks were drawing specie not for speculation but out of caution. They, too, were trying to prevent a panic. Thus, Brown reinterpreted the external drain of British specie as a reason for increased confidence in American banking rather than doubt.[73]

Brown's interview brought the American bank war to the heart of British finance; he forced the directors to recognize that their interference in another nation's partisan dispute had global ramifications. The directors' distaste for Jackson's domestic agenda had already begun to reverberate far beyond the BOE's parlors in the form of policies that could cripple America's system of credit. Brown informed the directors that in the week following their decision to stop discounting the bills of exchange drawn on American houses, textile factors dealing in the Manchester market "suspended their orders as far as practical and apprised their correspondents in America of the measures taken by the Bank of England." Liverpool cotton prices fell but rebounded after traders learned that the BOE had listened to Brown and agreed to continue discounting American paper. Merchants wondered whether "it would be safe to go on with the purchase of goods on American accounts." With large amounts of credit extended and the long wait for both goods and news, the American trade grew more dangerous daily.[74]

By the time Brown returned to Liverpool, ships carrying news of the BOE's decision to refuse to discount American bills had already left port.

A second set of departed vessels carried accounts of the extreme reaction in Liverpool. The falling price of cotton, an unintended consequence of the BOE's policy, might indicate to Americans that Britain's central bank was attacking America's most important cash crop. Undoubtedly wishing he could replace this old information with news of his successful meeting with the directors and the restoration of cotton prices, Brown regretted, "the mischief is done." As this news traveled to America where it too would be subject to interpretation, the "mischief" had only begun.[75]

* * *

On September 27, 1836, or perhaps a day earlier, news of the BOE's decision reached New York. That day, James Gordon Bennett, editor of the *New York Herald*, reported "IMPORTANT. – The Directors of Bank of England, in consequence of the amount of British capital absorbed by American and Continental houses, have refused to discount their Bills of Exchange, however high their standing. They say it cannot be done without injuring the commercial and manufacturing interests of England."[76] The next day Bennett revealed his source for this shocking news. He wrote that a mercantile house had "received intelligence from the banking house of Messrs. Wiggons [sic] of London, stating that the Bank of England intends to check the further investment of capital in American securities. This purpose is to be effected by refusing to discount bills of exchange, and thus impede the trade between England and the United States." Despite his capitalized headline, Bennett downplayed this news, describing the BOE's "measure" as "temporary."[77] He was, of course, correct. In early October, news arrived in New York that the Bank of England reversed its policies and, instead, raised interest rates on bills of exchange.[78]

Stock markets did not respond to any of this news; money markets, already strained, continued to charge high rates for loans. "The imports of foreign goods are greater than in any antecedent year, but so are our exports of cotton, rice, tobacco, &c," Bennett reported, suggesting that exports would balance imports.[79] To many, the balance of trade seemed to be in America's favor. Americans were too busy worrying about the Specie Circular, local bank scandals, and the presidential election to worry about how these events were interpreted in London.[80] New York confidence seemed impervious even to personal warnings from London financiers. The Josephs ignored calls for restraint from the Rothschilds. Attesting to their confidence, the Josephs opened an account for Hermann and claimed additional credit from London in direct disobedience of the Rothschilds' wishes.[81] They risked their livelihood on their faith in future prosperity.

Other Americans similarly disregarded the news of the BOE's doubts about America. Nearly two months after the Court of Directors decided to stop discounting American bills, news of the BOE's policy change reached New Orleans. On October 15, 1836, that city's newspapers printed sparse references to this information, instead filling their columns with calls for political rallies and details of a treaty with Native Americans in Michigan.[82] Oblivious to the clues of London doubt, New Orleanians shared Hermann's optimism.

While Hermann was still on his mission to recruit credit for the cotton trade, other New Orleanians translated predictions of future flush times into local policy.[83] After a victorious battle in the Louisiana state legislature to increase the capital supply of the Citizens' Bank of Louisiana, Forstall negotiated a sale of new bonds in Europe in early 1836.[84] (See Figure 4 and Figure 5 in Chapter 1.) Hope & Co. purchased the majority of the loan to sell in Amsterdam. The bank's directors would channel the proceeds of the sale through the American house of F. de Lizardi & Co., the London associates of Forstall's firm.[85] In August, as Forstall inked his signature across each individual slip of paper that promised in ten ornate fonts to pay in dollars, pounds sterling, and guilders, he expressed his confidence in the continued prosperity of their market. When the bonds arrived in Amsterdam ready to be turned into gold, Hope & Co. had already grown skeptical.[86] New Orleanians ignored the BOE's policy changes because cotton prices remained high; soon they would start to recognize signs of impending doom.

* * *

On November 2, 1836, news from London arrived in the middle of the day, and it rattled New Yorkers. "'What is the news?' 'How is the money market?' 'What say the Rothschilds?' burst from every quarter," reported Bennett. New York's financiers crowded around the Josephs, who "speedily stated that the London market was tighter – that all American securities were flat and depreciated – that the rates of interest were high and likely to advance." Bennett continued, "The cotton market had indeed sustained itself, and some sorts had advanced, but the money market was tighter towards this country. The effect of this news on the stock market was instantaneous." Bennett noted that the market reversed its morning advances. The pressure increased, and there was "a complete stagnation in general business." Predictions of panic, failure, and dire consequences circulated. Bennett, however, concluded that "the present crisis is wholly financial." He distinguished between finance and trade. American trade was fine, he reasoned, because "production, distribution, and consumption don't stop for a moment."[87] But as the first clues arrived that the financial system was freezing, this continued making, shipping, and buying of things would leave Americans even more in debt with no way to make the payments.

Two days later, Bennett reported, "The course of the Bank of England has caused a deep sensation on both sides of the water."[88] Americans earnestly questioned the BOE's agenda. Rumors circulated that a coterie of British capitalists, including the BOE directors, had been manipulating American credit to lower the price of cotton. Without historical hindsight, the fall in cotton prices looked like the intentional result of the BOE's attempt to decrease the supply of bank paper on both sides of the Atlantic. It looked like economic war. The cosmopolitan notion promoted by Bennett only weeks earlier that the United States and Britain were "but as one country" was replaced by the interpretation that the BOE was actively pursuing a sinister plan to shift the balance of trade so that American merchants would be forced to send gold back to England.[89]

Bates shared this skepticism about the BOE directors' intentions. He confessed to his diary that the BOE had been "playing some shabby tricks" and predicted that this would cause "a crisis in the U. States."[90] "The Bank seem [sic] incompetent and unqualified to comprehend what they are about," he confided.[91] Having acted quickly by contacting Ward after the *Times* articles in June, Bates hoped that Baring Brothers would lose "not much probably."[92] Bates strictly defined the script for withdrawing credit from American accounts so that it would not upset the overall money market. He instructed Ward to "manage cleverly so as not to let slip any word of hostility towards any one."[93] By challenging the trust between only certain correspondents, Bates hoped to avoid contributing to any additional pressure in the already tight American money markets while carefully screening his clients for trustworthiness. He directed, "to good people say we make no change, to those that have too much credit use the circumstances as an excuse to cut them down." Although he worried that his firm's actions would increase existing problems, he acknowledged that "you cannot prevent a crisis on the U. States."[94]

As of mid-October 1836, the directors of the BOE had no idea whether "a crisis on the U. States" had happened. Even with the fastest boats and the most favorable wind, the news of the effects of the previous two rounds of BOE policy making would not have reached London by that time.[95] On October 13, with the BOE's vaults having lost an additional million pounds sterling of gold, the BOE directors passed another secret measure designed to squeeze gold from the American houses.[96] They would communicate to these merchant banks that "the extensive credits hitherto given to the Bankers of the United States & others ... are objectionable so far as the Bank of England is concerned" and request that the American houses agree to "checking that system, which they deem to be prejudicial to the currency of the country."[97]

The merchant bankers tried to persuade the BOE directors to reconsider. Motivated by "anxious desire," F. de Lizardi explained that the volume and the value of the trade financed by the banks in New Orleans was "rapidly augmenting." He had already shown how firmly he believed in the future of New Orleans banks with his involvement in the Citizens' Bank bond issue. Lizardi feared the repercussions for what he saw as otherwise stable institutions that prevented "the most ruinous fluctuations" caused by a lopsided annual trade cycle. As the BOE's first round of policies came midway through the cycle, merchants and bankers would be stretched to their credit limits as they awaited news that large and expensive cotton crops had sold in Liverpool. Further credit contractions by the BOE would cause extensive failures.[98]

Bates agreed that the BOE should stop interfering in commerce. He argued that the BOE's initial policy changes "produced a shock" that might prove beneficial:

Ten years of prosperous trade has naturally created a very extended confidence & with it facilities have been extended probably too far; all persons have now an excuse for reforming their system in this respect, & by making people abroad pay up & use more [of] their own means a very great influence will be produced on the balance of trade, & things will come right much sooner than the ordinary favorable balance of commercial operations would lead one to expect.[99]

But further actions against the "perfectly legitimate" business of using credit "in anticipation of cotton bills" would not return gold to their vaults. He insisted, "It is useless for the Bank to make war on Bills of exchange." Rather, the BOE should "destroy the market for foreign stocks" through its increased interest rates. Bates believed emancipation payments to former British slave owners had increased the amount of money available for investment in the global economy, but low interest rates in Britain had pushed investors to find foreign markets, like high-yielding American stocks. Eventually, trade would return the gold to the BOE's coffers. He argued, "any further action on the money market would only tend to check exports of Merchandise & thus increase in place of diminishing the evil." In sum, he argued for patience.[100]

The BOE refused to slow the speed of its policy making to allow either for transatlantic transportation of news or for the balance of payments to readjust. The directors were too scared by the diminishing gold supplies. One English periodical's editor admonished, "In a matter so momentous as that of commercial confidence and the circulation of credit, one would have expected to see the most unequivocal manifestations of anxiety exhibited by the Directors of the Bank of England on the first symptom of approaching danger."[101] Blind to the larger economic hazards of their policies, the directors inadvertently set an international financial crisis in motion by trying to prevent the devaluation of the currency.

In his diary, Bates fumed, "the Bank has been on very bad principles for the last 18 months and it will be difficult to get matters righted."[102] The larger market followed the BOE's defensive principles. The *Times* reported that the latest pressure at the Stock Exchange "may be traced to the precautions which the more cautious class of men are taking against what they conceive to be the coming difficulties."[103] Predictions of the credit market crashing began to produce a crash.

* * *

Meanwhile, as a result of adverse winds, Americans knew little about the crisis brewing in England. News of the first round of BOE policy changes, William Brown's rebuttal, and the brief shock to Liverpool cotton prices had recently reached New Orleans when Samuel Hermann arrived home on December 2, 1836.[104] The next day, the New Orleans *Commercial Bulletin* reprinted a report from Liverpool dated October 25, 1836, that hinted at trouble for those, like Hermann, who expected record profits based on large quantities of cotton sold at high prices. "The pressure on the money market still continues and has injurious influence on our cotton market in which the business has been limited," it reported. Beyond a sign that demand for cotton might not be as high as the New Orleanians had anticipated, the next sentence of this report indicated that prices had been overestimated because "Confidence is a good deal shaken and holders [of cotton] generally are anxious to reduce their stocks." Merchants wanted to get rid of their cotton, even at lower prices, and manufacturers "purchase[d] with reluctance and only such parcels as they consider decided bargains and such only as suit their immediate wants."[105] As this account indicated, financial "pressure" weighed down the price of commodities. British pessimism began to sink American optimism. Of course, New Orleanians might interpret all of this as temporary; they had not yet learned of the next round of policies instituted by the BOE.

For Hermann, however, prices and optimism were not the only things sinking in early December 1836. A dark and stormy night, the cliché sign of brewing trouble, portended a personal disaster that combined with the changing predictions for cotton prices and the pressure in the credit market suggested Hermann's financial doom. From the deck of his New Orleans–bound Mississippi River steamboat, on December 8, 1836, the captain of the *Fort Adams* observed, "the wind and swell increasing and the night setting in dark with every appearance of a storm."[106] For months, the river suffered from low water levels, exposing ships to the dangers of the Mississippi's shallow bottom.[107] Just after sunrise the next morning, the ship's steam engine struggled against the wind, the river, the weight of a thousand bales of cotton, and the added burden of a brig in tow. Although invisible and weightless to the engine, thousands of dollars of paper signed by Louis Florian Hermann and endorsed by his father, Samuel, could be added to the burden of the boat.

Discovering "that the hold was rapidly filling," the crew attempted to save the valuable cargo but inadvertently lodged the ship on a bar of Mississippi mud. Immediately, they tried to "land the cargo from the deck" and prevent a total loss of ship and contents. Crew members were sent to find other ships to transport the load; carpenters and engineers set to work trying to assess the damage and save the cotton flooded in the hold. By the next day, the *Fort Adams* was "full of water" with "17 feet water amidships." The captain decided that his ship was "in peril every instant of breaking up" and personally departed to seek assistance in New Orleans from his backers, the mercantile firm of Hermann, Briggs & Co.[108]

Louis Florian Hermann sent laborers, bank notes, and scarce specie to the scene in order to help salvage the boat and the cotton. His clerk visited the insurers of the vessel, Western Marine & Fire Insurance, which previously counted among its board one of Hermann's brothers. Nepotism proved worthless. The president of the insurance company informed the clerk that the captain ought "to act as if there were no insurance effected at all." The insurance company refused to pay because the *Fort Adams* had been towing the brig; the Hermanns and their partners would be forced to absorb the losses.[109]

Hermann, Briggs began hemorrhaging money. Despite attempts to save the sodden cotton, more than half of the bales were damaged or "totally lost supposed to have floated off." As cotton factors, Hermann, Briggs had already paid the planters advances for their crops. Now, it had to pay additional money to transport the salvaged cotton to New Orleans for shipment to England and to acquire additional bales to meet its consignments for Liverpool merchants. The captain found "little hope could be entertained of saving" the $60,000 *Fort Adams*. Despite years of litigation in Louisiana's courts, the insurance company would never provide the firm with a penny toward its damages – especially not in the crucial few weeks after the disaster when the Hermann family tapped whatever credit it had not tied up in the cotton crop.[110]

Fortunately for the Hermanns, however, the news from England of the BOE's next round of policies and resulting lower cotton prices and high interest rates remained stranded mid-Atlantic. Despite the sinking of the *Fort Adams*, northern newspapers reported in mid-December that in New Orleans "the money market [was] easier – interest and exchanges lower."[111] Samuel Hermann could believe with slightly more confidence that his business would survive any crash.

Hermann was not the only optimistic New Orleanian. As news of even tighter credit and lower cotton prices remained at sea, local newspapers reported that prominent merchants (including Hermann) had developed a new speculative venture – a line of transatlantic packets that would create a direct connection between New Orleans and Liverpool.[112] Without New York as an intermediary, the merchants of New Orleans hoped to eliminate the information asymmetry of their communication network. Some investors suggested that the new fleet be powered by steam in order to avoid dependency on good weather for reliable communication, but no steam ship had successfully traversed the Atlantic.

Steam power attracted interest outside of New Orleans as well. Predicting that "a complete revolution will be made in our intercourse with Europe," Bennett believed that steam packets would cut the time for transatlantic communication by two-thirds and eliminate the irregularities of wind power. "A month will be sufficient to go and return," he estimated hopefully, "we shall have all the European news regularly every 10 or 12 days."[113] In November, announcements appeared that the Glasgow-based British and American Steam Navigation Company had contracted for the building of the world's first steam packet ship to run the Liverpool to New York route by March 1838. At five times the cost of the *Fort Adams*, this new vessel embodied the value ascribed to fast information.[114]

Meanwhile, without wind, New Yorkers knew as little as New Orleanians about the crisis brewing in England. "We are now a long time without advices from Europe," wrote New Yorker Moses Taylor to his correspondents in New Orleans. The packet ships were more than two weeks late, leaving Americans in the dark concerning the BOE's latest dealings and unaware of the latest Liverpool cotton prices. He assured, "as soon as I see how the staple [cotton] is going on the other side [I] will give you my views more fully in relation to the article."[115] Without news, Americans experienced a "pause" from the wild fluctuations of stocks and the pressure of the money market.[116] Commerce waited for the winds, literally.

During the pause, national politicians brokered confidence at the end of the congressional session in Washington, D.C. As one spectator observed of the only senator who brought Adam Smith's theories on banking into the congressional debates on the Specie Circular, "he stood as an oracle dispensing knowledge on a very complicated & ill understood subject."[117] Of course, not everyone agreed with Smith. The BOE was hardly practicing free trade; this was protectionism's moment. From his office at the now Pennsylvania-chartered BUS, Nicholas Biddle wrote a letter on the subject to former President John Quincy Adams. When this document was published in New York's papers, it "infused a species of confidence into the public mind, that operates exactly like a strike of galvanism." Magnetized by the optimism, Wall Street rallied.[118] Merchants sent accounts to their London creditors reporting that "our money market is easier." "The early and large shipments of our produce abroad," assured a New York correspondent of Bates, "gives confidence to banks and their dealers." New Yorkers would "fain believe that our chief difficulties are passing." Interpreting improved conditions as reasons for renewed optimism, he continued, "we hope our letters will continue to give you better & better news as to the state of affairs here."[119]

The term "better news," however, veiled the conundrum of interpretation. Would the news be "better" if it signaled future prosperity to New Yorkers or if it demonstrated an awareness of the dire predictions of Londoners? The continued optimism of New Yorkers read as naïve or, worse yet, duplicitous to Londoners who believed that a crisis was approaching. News of confidence might inspire both higher prices and an increase in trade – two conditions that would worsen the crisis predicted across the Atlantic – but it might also seem like a ploy designed to increase English investment. Intelligence about improved market conditions might, above all, convince Londoners that Americans could not be trusted.

* * *

On December 23, "long-looked-for" news from London arrived, and the pressure returned. As Bennett reported to his readers, "London, Liverpool and the manufacturing districts have felt the effects of the recent conduct of the Bank of England as much, if not more, than Wall Street or New

Orleans." Bennett's sources attributed the problem to a lack of confidence caused by the British bank war: "These events in the commercial affairs of England, are attributed to the general derangement of the joint stock banking system, and the want of confidence between these establishments and the Bank of England." Parliament's banking investigation produced effects in New York, Bennett reported: "In consequence of this news from England, the market in Wall Street opened yesterday in a depressed state of feeling."[120]

But not everyone attributed increasing pressure in the money market to the arrival of news from London. Hard-money advocate William Leggett insisted in his newspaper that *"the pernicious bank system of our country is the cause!"* He assured his readers that his pro-banking opponents in either party could no longer "lay all the difficulties of the money market to the account of certain orders of the Treasury Department" or "ascribe the evils to the necessary operation of the distribution law." He was convinced that the appeals of merchants and bankers to relieve the pressure ought to be ignored because they "have to learn that there is but one relief for an overtrading nation, and it must wait for that to be applied by the slow hand of time."[121]

Although Leggett wanted the nation to wait for a slow contraction of commerce, the invisible hand formed a fist. Newspapers reported on "people losing their senses."[122] After the New Year, alternating favorable and unfavorable reports from England triggered continuing fluctuation in American markets. Stocks returned to America unable to be sold in London.[123] As ship after ship brought "a heavy arrival" of cotton from the American South, the market in Liverpool remained "very dull and flat."[124] In New Orleans, cotton prices declined and sales diminished because of "unfavorable reports from Europe."[125] The city's boosters nevertheless continued to "behold the erection of new and splendid buildings – the paving of streets – the opening of stores and hotels – and every thing that promises wealth, prosperity, and happiness."[126] Some correspondents recognized that fulfillment of these promises depended on good news from Europe. New York's newspapers reported that many Americans "look with great anxiety to the next arrival from England"; meanwhile, most found the cause of their distress much closer to home.[127]

* * *

Desperate bankers and future bankrupts looked to the government for a form of relief that would sustain existing businesses. Washington refused to keep them afloat. During Jackson's final annual address to Congress,

he congratulated the nation on "the high state of prosperity which our
beloved country has attained with no causes at home or abroad to lessen
the confidence with which we look to the future."[128] This did not prevent
voters from glaring at Washington as the election for Jackson's successor
continued. A Philadelphian correspondent of the frontrunner, Vice
President Martin Van Buren, confirmed that "the amazing scarcity and
high price of money" was "attributed, as all things always are, to the
operations of the government."[129] This statement confirmed not only
that many Americans perceived both their anxiety and the difficult market
conditions as deriving from national economic policies but also that
this correspondent disagreed with this attribution of blame. Partisan
policy making was one interpretation of the cause of the crisis, but it was
not the only means of understanding why the flush times seemed to be
coming to an end.

During the pressure of 1836, politicization allowed those most
immediately affected by the credit crisis to absolve themselves from
blame for constructing and then overestimating the system of confidence.
For example, the Josephs concluded, "our money market is still suffering
under pressure owing entirely to the Circular of the Government."[130]
Partisan policy, like the Specie Circular, offered a convenient excuse for
the credit contraction; indeed, political explanations would win widespread support over the coming months. Nevertheless, these explanations
were not irrefutable fact but interpretation. Those who believed the battles
of the American bank war caused the pressure stopped their search for
causes at the nation's boundaries. Given the intelligence motivating
the BOE's policies, a broader, transnational perspective would have,
ironically, proven they were partially right. The American bank war
deployed as evidence in the British bank war diminished British confidence
in American financial security; these doubts translated into policies that
launched a transatlantic bank war to see which nation's paper money
would win its metallic reinforcement. The war's biggest losers, however,
would be people who had never calculated an exchange rate.

CHAPTER 3

Practical Economists

A fine white powder coated New York City's streets on the frigid morning of February 14, 1837, but it was not snow.[1] The evening before, rioters had broken into several dry goods warehouses and had heaved hundreds of barrels of flour and a thousand bags of wheat through windows as high as five stories above the pavement. The knee-deep mix of glass, splinters, wheat, and flour on the city's streets offered material proof that by early 1837, the pressure of 1836 had spread to people who had never discounted a bill of exchange; speculated on cotton; or, perhaps, even heard of the Bank of England.

Why was there a riot? The simple answer is that in just a few months, the price of flour had jumped from $7 to $12 per barrel. Few working people could afford bread. It takes more than hunger, however, to create a riot. Aware of the political potential of starving workers, several candidates from the Equal Rights Party, a splinter group of Democrats derisively dubbed the Loco-Focos by mainstream Democrats and Whigs, planned a rally to "inquire into the Cause of the present unexampled Distress, and to devise a suitable Remedy." On placards, handbills, and newspaper advertisements, they announced: "Bread, Meat, Rent, Fuel – Their prices must come down." On the afternoon of February 13, as "the wind blew a Hurricane," nearly twenty thousand New Yorkers gathered in the park in front of City Hall for a rally.[2]

The speakers wanted votes, not violence. True to their political platform, the Loco-Focos blamed banks for extending credit to greedy merchants and for printing depreciating paper money. They resolved that "the true remedy for the people, which will reduce the price of all the necessaries of life is, that every workingman refuse paper money in payment for his services, or demand specie of the banks for all notes paid to him."[3] When an unidentified speaker suggested that "Mr. Hart had several thousand barrels of flour in his store, let us go and offer him $8 a barrel," the Loco-Focos silenced him.[4] The political speakers supplied suggestions for radical but legal choices; the crowd, however, demanded immediate change.

Approximately a thousand people forsook banks or ballots for barrels. They rammed in the doors of brimming warehouses, strew grain in the streets, broke counting house desks to pieces, and tore apart the papers of the commission merchants who sold flour as agents of country millers. The rioters did not steal the thousands of dollars worth of flour they handled (even though a few accounts noted that Swiss or Irish immigrant women filled small bags); they destroyed it.[5] They overwhelmed a "posse of police officers" and "pelted" the mayor with "balls of flour."[6] The bitter cold, the arrival of soldiers, and an offer from one of the commission merchants to distribute his stock to the poor brought the riot to an end. Fifty-four New Yorkers "of all sizes, ages, sexes and colours, and conditions" were arrested, and thirty men were indicted.[7] Philip Hone, who assisted in the investigation of the rioters, noted in his diary, "the big fish break through the nets which catch the little ones, or rather they drive or entice them to go in, but have sagacity enough to keep out themselves."[8] Never identified, the riot's leaders did not explain the reason behind their actions.

Who was to blame for the riot? The press tried to answer this question. Whigs blamed Democrats. Democrats blamed the Equal Rights Party, which argued that none of the arrested rioters were members of their organization. Most condemned the inadequate police force. And everyone blamed the rioters, who lacked a newspaper to explain their motivations. All the papers just assumed they were hungry; none wondered why starving men destroyed food.

Searching for a source of the poor's hunger, all of the newspapers blamed their particular hobbyhorses. Some argued that wheat was scarce because the frozen canals prevented the replenishment of supplies. Others blamed the scarcity on ambitious agricultural laborers who had moved to the cities and, therefore, had not grown enough wheat for the cities. One paper blamed the predilection for wheat flour over other grains among the poorest consumers who, many newspapers argued, were mostly foreign immigrants willing to violate the nation's legal protection of property rights to obtain their preferred food. Others blamed the flour dealers, labeling them greedy monopolists who had hoarded flour for profit. Eli

Hart & Co., the mercantile firm that sustained the most damage, wrote to several papers assuring that "There is no shadow of combination or speculation in the article of flour; the price is, as always, the effect of supply and demand."[9] All of the papers were shocked that this principle could be so misunderstood by the rioters.

Although hurling barrels out of a five-story building may have relieved some stress, the destruction of the flour made no sense from the perspective of political economy. Exposing the barrels to gravity would not cause prices to "come down" as well; the diminished supply would only increase the price. How could Americans so engaged in economic pursuits and so opinionated regarding banking policies ignore the laws of supply and demand? Like most Americans, the rioters were not thinking about textbook principles of political economy; in fact, the first college-level American political economy textbook had only reached bookstores one month earlier. The rioters attacked the warehouse to make a point: poor people would not starve for merchants' profits. Rather than blaming the London bankers who had contracted credit or the politicians who had restructured the nation's financial system, these New Yorkers targeted local merchants.

By destroying property, the rioters unleashed the idea of revolution that would lurk in the minds of the powerful and act as a stimulus to economic change. As historian E. P. Thompson demonstrated for similar eighteenth-century English events, the ideas of political economy were invented in part to counteract this system of price adjustment.[10] By 1837, elites who benefited from an economic system devoid of regulatory intervention ensured that principles of political economy informed English policy in the BOE and in Parliament. In the United States, however, politicians wooed a broader citizenry whose economic ideas derived from a wider source base. The religious views presented in sermons and the reforms advocated by advice manuals and novels competed with the theories of political economy as explanations of the market. All of these texts, however, cited a common cause for economic change: individual choice. Even phrenologists argued that economic change happened, literally, inside individual minds.

Why did flour and not flowers fill New York City's streets on Valentine's Day in 1837? To answer this question, the following pages provide what economist Mark Blaug has labeled a "historical reconstruction" of the wide range of American economic thought on the eve of panic.[11] Nearly every print genre that reached American bookstores in the first days of 1837 preached that individuals bore responsibility for their economic fates.

These texts congratulated self-made men; for the failing and the starving, the lesson stung.

* * *

Portland, Maine, was bitter cold on New Year's Day in 1837, and like its harbor, its credit market was frozen. Many New Englanders had speculated in Maine real estate hoping that the nation's construction boom would make lumber scarce and increase the value of wooded property. Later critics snidely called this a lumber mania, but at the start of the new year, the pressure of 1836 had just begun to squeeze the bubble.[12] Portlanders felt the pressure, including Jason Whitman, the pastor of the city's newly constructed Second Unitarian Church.[13]

Following the new trend in Unitarianism of preaching about timely subjects, Whitman's New Year's sermon took as its biblical text a question that could easily be applied to current events: "can ye not discern the signs of the times"?[14] He knew his qualifications for answering this question were suspect. "I have never made either the subject of party politics or the science of political economy my study," admitted the minister, adding "nor am I about to speak of these causes as a matter of finance. For in this view of the subject also, and for the same reasons, I am an incompetent judge." Instead, he "would speak of the subject, as viewed in its relation to moral character and religious improvement." He required no political or financial education because "The care-clouded countenance and the anxiously hurried step, of almost every man of business you may meet, proclaim in language, which, if not audible, is perfectly intelligible, that the times are hard, that money is scarce."[15] Enunciating the troubles of the commercial world through the vocabulary of the church, he conceived of the pressure one "care-clouded" soul at a time.

Whitman was not the first minister to explain the economy in terms of individual morality. In fact, two published sermons, one Unitarian and one Congregationalist, took their titles from the same text in March and May 1836.[16] The Unitarian version praised the nation's "zeal for commercial adventure," painting a "canvass prefiguring the moral history of the coming prosperous year" with sketches of the blessings of "good times" as well as "some most melancholy images" of individuals who acted immorally.[17] A Presbyterian sermon entitled "A Rebuke to the Worldly Ambitions of the Present Age," also published in 1836, attempted to calm the "rage to be rich" with the threat that "they who will seek supremely the great things of earth for themselves, must calculate with infallible certainty upon a ruined immortality."[18] Whether as a heaven or a hell, the boom was conceptualized by these sermons as the product of individual choice.

Unlike these earlier ministers who argued for moderation in the midst of a period of prosperity, Whitman gave voice to the all-too-present troubles of his congregation. He explained, "the pressure is actually upon us. We all feel it, we all mourn over its trials and anxieties and distress." Although Whitman claimed to be interested in "the causes of the present severe distress," he advocated disregarding most of them: "The question, to which I would direct your attention, is not, whether 'the removal of the deposites [sic],' or 'the management of the Bank,' the 'issuing of the treasury order,' or 'the curtailment of the loans' have caused the general pressure which is felt." The only cause he cared about could be answered by the following question: "what particulars in our own conduct have caused this pressure to bear more heavily upon us, than it otherwise would have done"? By sidelining the issue of how the larger pressure came to exist, he focused the "heart-searching, the all penetrating eye of God" on the central target of the nation's Great Awakening: the individual.[19]

Whitman asked his parishioners to reflect on their recent behavior. He suggested, "we have lived ... as though we were already rich." In addition, "we have made haste to get rich" rather than "gradually amassing wealth." Both of these behaviors suggested to Whitman that Americans lacked foresight; they harbored "the unreasonable expectation that the times will always continue good." Clearly, the answer to the question that he took as his biblical text was negative; his parishioners could not "discern the signs of the times." They suffered from semiotic illiteracy; yet, they listened to one another. "Reports of success" fed "the dangerous current of speculation," he argued. When "the change comes," Whitman continued, "All feel it. But he, who has made haste to get rich, finds his liabilities greater than he can meet." He assured that "whatever then may have been the cause of the general pressure, such an individual suffers, more than he otherwise would have done."[20]

But suffering "more" does not explain why individuals suffered at all. To Whitman, "the cause of the general pressure" was not political or financial; in fact, it was not even entirely human. He explained, "All the trials and perplexities of business, all changes in the times, and all prosperity and all pressures in pecuniary matters, we have reason to believe, are ordered or permitted by an overruling providence – and are ordered or permitted for our highest and best good." Here is the simplest statement of Whitman's causation: God created crises or, at least, permitted them to provide humans with "moral instruction." Just as dangerous ocean currents were part of divinely created nature, so the "current of speculation" was part of God's plan. Individuals needed to learn to steer clear of both.[21]

Whitman avoided the obvious lessons of hard times – "the study of economy and the retrenchment of expenses" – to teach four more obscure principles, or "duties," of correct economic behavior. The first was to "pause and reflect, to examine carefully the signs of the times, with the prayer that we may be enabled to read and understand them aright." Clearly, the people of Portland had failed at this. But what would have happened if they had predicted the pressure? Whitman's second duty taught economic neophytes how to make sense of bad news without panicking: "carefully cherish calmness and composure of mind under our trials." He cautioned,

If there be a season in our lives, when we need all our mental energy, all our moral courage, all our self-possession, it is when we are involved in embarrassment, when we are in danger of being overwhelmed by perplexities and anxieties, by the agitating and enervating fear that we shall not be able to meet and fulfil [sic] engagements which we have made.

A placid mental state facilitated Whitman's third duty: "to hold fast our integrity." Even if you lose everything you own, Whitman assured his listeners, "in this land, where wealth and honor are open to honesty and enterprise, you need not fear" because these trials "will have served to strengthen your principles and establish more firmly your character." God could see through an "assumed confidence, or indifference, – with him, there can be no bravado."[22] Faith – in one's self, in God, and in America – was Whitman's cure for failure.

Failing, however, was painful. "Is one of your neighbors in such pecuniary embarrassment that he has fallen prostrate before the pressure of the times?" Whitman asked rhetorically. In his answer, the minister sketched the causal link between one individual's choices and those of the next:

If he has fallen before the pressure under which you stand firm, consider that it may be but an indication of the increasing weight of that pressure, and that it may soon become too burdensome even for you – that his fall may be but the precursor of your own. Consider too, that, in all probability, he is now suffering intense anguish of mind, not indeed at the loss of property, for that he could bear, but at the thought that those with whom he has dealt, those who have placed confidence in him and shown themselves his friends, must suffer loss from their connection with him – at the thought that he may be suspected of something dishonorable or dishonest, that, as he goes forth, the eye of every one may look upon him with scrutinizing suspicion, and the heart of every one be turned coldly away from him.

God might allow a crisis, but human relationships spread it. Thus, Whitman argued, individuals could change economic history through a final duty that was counterintuitive for people in the midst of a credit crisis: "to bear and forbear."[23] This solution sounded so appealing; individuals could choose to forgive debts or extend time. But this simplicity reflected naïvety. The chains of trade were so long and so tangled that few could afford such leniency when their own creditors did not do the same.

Whitman, however, was tied into his own chains of friends and correspondents.[24] His sermon would not stay in Portland, Maine. By publishing it, he hoped to teach by example and spread the message of his pulpit: agency could cure economic anguish. He surely hoped that his own choice to preach about pressure might help alleviate it.

Just as Whitman was not the first to exhort the power of individual choice, he would not be the last. In 1837, Whitman's sermon would be followed by at least ten sermons on "the times," including "The Duties of Hard Times," "The Temptations of the Times," "Views of Duty Adapted to the Times," "These Bad Times the Product of Bad Morals," and simply, "The Times." These vague references to the changing economic climate joined sermons with more specific assessments of the crisis, such as "Moral Tendencies of Our Present Pecuniary Distress," "The Duties Connected with the Present Commercial Distress," "Babylon Is Falling," and "God Our Only Hope."[25] Preached in New England, New York, and even New Orleans; distributed in print; and reviewed in periodicals with nationwide circulations, sermons spread religious interpretations of economic responsibility far beyond New England's pews.[26] Despite geographical and doctrinal diversity, the words of America's spiritual leaders emphasized economic choice as a test of human sin conducted by God. For the faithful, the source of the crisis was not in the BOE's discount rate or partisan policies; it could only be found in their own souls.

* * *

Ministers, however, were not the only authors explaining the economy through individual morality. The lessons of frugality and retrenchment, passed over by Whitman, inspired a wide variety of texts published to instruct individuals on how to live economically. Often written by and for women, these books explained the economy as manageable, one household at a time.

Published just after the flour riot, Frances Green's *The Housekeeper's Book* offered advice for preserving furniture, bedding, and provisions through her "complete collection of receipts for economical domestic cookery." A woman needed to be efficient with her expenditures, starting with the physical structure that defined her role: the house. Choose a smaller house, the book suggested, because it "might be fitted up at less cost than a larger one, and would certainly present a better appearance than a house that is rather too large for the quantity or for the style of its furniture." The author exhorted, "When I see showy furniture in the houses of people of small fortunes, I cannot help suspecting that it has been purchased without being paid for; the long upholsterer's bill rises like a phantom before the couches, the ottomans, and the ottoman sofas, which are crowded into small drawing rooms." The ghosts of faulty calculations of future prosperity romanticized Whitman's admonishment of living "as though we were already rich," but Green was not against appearing rich. She advocated hiring servants and warned, "nothing gives the appearance of stinginess, as over carefulness of fuel."[27] Without the minister's evocation of divine condemnation, Green acknowledged the value of appearance to Americans trying to be economical while going ahead.

The responsibility for keeping a family solvent, according to Green, fell on the wife's shoulders or, more accurately, on her ability to calculate the family's cash flow. "The first care of a young married woman," she asserted, "should be to ascertain, as precisely as possible, the sum of money which may be required annually towards the maintenance of her establishment; and then to form a determination to confine her expenses *within that sum*."[28] Clerks learned numerical skills on the job, in schools, at lyceum lectures, in study groups, or by buying how-to manuals such as *The Book-Keeper's Diploma* or the popular *Science of Double-Entry Book-Keeping, Simplified*. The tabulations and calculations of trained bookkeepers eased the anxieties of those engaged in global trade by claiming to offer the scientific truth of their solvency, an indisputable "bottom line."[29] Applying these techniques of the mercantile world to the "establishment" of a home required women to possess not only an ability to predict future expenses but also to calculate arithmetically the family's budget. Unlike Whitman's religious view of individual economic behavior, Green's domestic economy relied on individuals making sense of numbers.

Clerks' bookkeeping involved operating a nearly endless list of paper technology. For the "mistress of a house," Green aimed to make "keep[ing] an account of the expenditure of her family … as simple an affair as possible." "By keeping a very strict account of every article, for the first two months," she suggested, "she may calculate how much she is to allow, each month, for meat, bread, groceries, washing, &c. &c." Like the book-keeper's accounts, this "estimate for the year" would work if prices were constant. Of course, this was not the case when this housekeeping manual reached bookstores in early 1837, as commodity prices were rapidly increasing. So housekeepers would not enjoy, as Green promised, the "satisfaction, independent of the pecuniary benefit, for the head of the family to be able, at the end of the year, to account to herself for what she has done with her money."[30] Unlike the bookkeeping men performed for a wage, the accounting of female "head[s] of the family" was unpaid labor with its only compensation in intellectual satisfaction.[31] Clerks were fired for miscalculations; women could either blame the merchants who charged high prices or internalize their failure.

Not all domestic economy manuals advocated this sort of women's introspective examination. In 1837, Lydia Maria Child was working on the twenty-first edition of her famous *The American Frugal Housewife: Dedicated to Those Who Are Not Ashamed of Economy*, which suggested an external record of success. She counseled, "keep an exact account of all you expend – even of a paper of pins. This answers two purposes: it makes you more careful in spending money, and it enables your husband to judge precisely whether his family live within his income."[32] For Child, women might spend money, but men judged the economy of their expenditures.

Unlike Green, Child ascribed no economic value to appearing affluent. She disparaged the "false and wicked parade" of trying to project wealth. "No false pride, or foolish ambition to appear as well as others, should ever induce a person to live one cent beyond the income of which he is certain," she argued.[33] Certainty of income, however, would join predictable prices as inconvenient fictions in the uncertain times of 1837.

Child's real target, however, was not miscalculation but extravagance. "Living beyond [one's] income" was, according to Child, unproductive because "it does not in fact procure a man valuable friends, or extensive interests." "More than that," she shouted from the page, "it is wrong – morally wrong, so far as the individual is concerned; and injurious beyond calculation to the interests of our country."[34] Child extrapolated from individual behavior:

Nations do not plunge *at once* into ruin – governments do not change *suddenly* – the causes which bring about the final blow, are scarcely perceptible in the beginning; but they increase in numbers, and in power; they press harder and harder upon the energies and virtue of a people; and the last steps only are alarmingly hurried and irregular. A republic without industry, economy, and integrity, is Samson shorn of his locks. A luxurious and idle *republic!* Look at the phrase! – The words were never made to be married together; every body sees it would be death to one of them.[35]

National prosperity and national poverty, she argued, resulted from an infinite number of individual choices. Especially in a republic, a nation governed by the people, individual economic behavior mattered; individuals controlled the life and death of the nation.

Child's view of those responsible for the nation's success or failure expanded beyond the limits of its citizenry – white, male voters. "Let women do their share towards reformation," she argued, assigning economic if not political responsibility to women.[36] Her "cheap little book of economical hints" instructed women to save money and to save souls. "True economy is a careful treasurer in the service of benevolence; and where they are united, respectability, prosperity, and peace will follow," she assured.[37] Like many writers of the reform movements that accompanied the religious revival of the 1830s, Child argued that individual choices, in this case frugality, served the higher purpose of national salvation.

Child's frugal advice would haunt her. In her preface to *The Family Nurse, or Companion to the Frugal Housewife*, a home remedy guide published in 1837, she complained, "I should take undue credit to myself if I professed that the usefulness of such a book was my strongest motive." She confessed that she wrote the book for profit. Even more damning, the former novelist continued, "If any other than very practical works would sell extensively, I fear I should still be lingering in more poetic regions."[38] Child's best-selling advice stressed efficient use of money; "poetic" and fictional books were hardly the kind of expenditures a frugal housewife would want to justify to her husband. "Poetic" publications, however, could also be "practical works," especially if their titles sounded less like fiction and more like domestic economy manuals that offered practical guides to "the management, regulation and government of a family or the concerns of a household."[39]

* * *

On Christmas Eve, 1836, one week before Jason Whitman's sermon, William S. Damrell, a Boston publisher, prepared his presses to print the first edition of a "little volume" that would sell through more than twenty thousand copies in the first two months and twenty printings in 1837, achieving, according to one reviewer, "a popularity unparalleled in so short a period since its first appearance."[40] Over the next few years, the book would be reprinted more than thirty times in the United States and ten times in England. Proclaiming itself part of a "revolution" of cheap, pocket-sized printed texts, the book bore a title that could be confused with a domestic economy manual, looked like a temperance tract – small, unadorned, and printed quickly on cheap paper – and taught its readers about economic responsibility through a story.[41]

Some periodicals confused the novel with a reform tract, advertising it on a list of "works on health and economy."[42] This confusion suggests that Damrell and Hannah Farnham Sawyer Lee, the middle-aged widow who wrote the novel, understood their financially strapped market.[43] People who bought *Three Experiments of Living: Living Within the Means, Living Up To the Means, Living Beyond the Means* were eager for the novel's moral instruction in domestic economy, eager enough to spend a scarce twenty-five cents for paper or thirty-seven and a half cents for a version "neatly bound in cloth."[44]

Three Experiments of Living offered its readers a morality tale of the seduction of an honest family by credit, property, and status. The novel narrates the rise and fall of the well-intentioned but flawed Dr. Frank Fulton, his wife Jane, and their children. The first section, *Living Within the Means*, describes the couple's efforts to build a medical practice by offering free services to the poor. The couple learns lessons about moral economic choices from the "richly dressed" people who spend their money on extravagance and fail to pay the poor for their labor. Counseled by Jane's pious Uncle Joshua, they profess their "modest desires and simple habits" and vow "never to exceed our means."[45] Frank and Jane's sentimental concern eventually attracts wealthy patients who, in turn, entice the couple with invitations into high society.

By the opening of the second section, *Living Up To the Means*, Frank and Jane have yielded moderately to temptation. They rent a house in a better neighborhood and purchase furnishings, clothing, and education for their children to display their ascending status. "As the *appearance* of property had become necessary," the narrator explains, "economy must be practiced somewhere." They choose to hire low-cost help. The result brings the scorn of Uncle Joshua who asserts that "it is very well for people to live in what is called style ... if they can afford to have the best attendance, of cooks, &c.; but there is no gentility in doing things by halves." Concerned, Jane proposes that "they should retrench in their expenses." The narrator continues, "But, after various calculations, there seemed to be nothing they could give up, except what was too *trifling* to make any difference. As if domestic economy did not consist in trifles!" Unable to hear the narrator's advice, the couple searches for a way to make more money. Jane had already admitted that she had "a horror of getting into debt" and Frank agreed, adding "it is *possible* embarrassment, not actual, that troubles me, and makes me sometimes a little petulant."[46] Nevertheless, with "the little capital, which they had been, all their married life, accumulating," the couple decides to put her fears and his irritability aside and speculate.[47]

Business failure and overindulged children dominate the third section, *Living Beyond the Means*. They move "to a very fine house" next to affluent neighbors, but instead of renting the house, they mortgage it. Although Jane does not understand this transaction, Frank convinces her that the house's value "*must rise*" and they will profit by the purchase. The subject of whether the house is "paid for" undermines Jane's relationship with her dying uncle. When Jane asks Frank to explain whether or not they own the house, he declares "women never understand these things, and, therefore, should not talk about them." Uncle Joshua's will leaves money to the Fulton children and prepares, in modest ways, for "any change of circumstances" in his niece's monetary affairs but places the money under the guardianship of a "respectable mechanic," or artisan. Their eldest daughter, Elinor, befriends the pious invalid son of the mechanic, preferring his company to preparations for her own debutante ball. Meanwhile, we learn "Frank had wholly ceased his communications to Jane, with regard to his pecuniary affairs." As a result, "[Jane] saw no restraints laid on anything, she presumed, very naturally, that, as long as his business was so flourishing, it was of little consequence what they expended."[48]

The story reaches its climax on the night of Elinor's ball when Frank is forced to confess to Jane that "We are ruined!" At first he resists her questions, asserting "that is my affair." "Are not your affairs and mine the same?" she retorts.[49] The family fails, falling from prosperity and falling apart. As rumors circulate through the city, Frank decides to "disappear from the scene of action." Abandoned by her husband and by the wealthy, Jane seeks assistance from the poor yet pious guardians of her inheritance. Guilt-stricken over the family's inability to pay its debts, Jane assures herself that "our creditors are rich men who will not feel it in reality." The mechanic's wife, however, implores Jane that she be certain that "there are no butchers' or bakers' bills unpaid; – no carpenters, masons, or tradesmen of any kind; – no mantua-makers or milliners; – no women who go out to daily labor, and who have families of children depending upon them for bread."[50] Jane realizes that she needs to return to the behaviors that governed her life when she was "free from debt, and had not a family of children, brought up in indulgence." The story ends with a letter from a revitalized Frank, whose move "to the western country" has brought him a similar moral reawakening. He describes his plan to "convince my creditors, that, however wide I have traveled from the right course, it is not irrecoverable." In the final pages, Lee's narrator clearly enunciates the three lessons embodied in the story: that although a man and a woman have different economic roles, they are jointly responsible for their family's economic behavior; that uncertain finances and aristocratic pretensions lead to failure; and that "real independence consists in *living within our means*."[51]

Avoiding financial terms, Lee used the language of Protestant reform to explain economic relationships, but her compelling narrative was, as one reviewer noted, "of far greater power and effect than lectures or essays, or even sermons."[52] This incredibly popular book taught people to find the cause of hard times in the collective behavior of families. All of Frank's business and his speculations happen outside the pages of Lee's texts. The really important unit of economic behavior, according to Lee, was neither Whitman's individual businessman nor political economists' emphasis on nations; the balance of global trade was based on the union between husband and wife.

Although Lee carefully points out that the Fultons "had not lost any large amount, by the sudden changes to which mercantile speculations are subject," her readers applied her lessons to the pressure and the panic that would follow.[53] In March, a reviewer noted that "there have been several editions sold in the course of a few weeks and the demand for it is increasing."[54] The New York *Knickerbocker* called it "the best work of the kind which it has ever been our good fortune to read." Aimed originally at women, reviewers recommended the book for "every intelligent American family throughout the union" as it "cannot but have a great effect upon almost every reader."[55] One military journal recommended the book, especially for sailors.[56] Although it was a northern publication, southern magazines such as Charleston's *Southern Rose* advertised it, and *The Southern Literary Messenger* praised its messages, arguing "they are not the mere speculations of a theorizer, but emanate from the pens of those practical economists, the wives and mothers of the land."[57]

Such positive reviews increased sales. Its only negative review was a response to its success. The *Boston Medical and Surgical Journal* cited the Fultons' advertisement of free medical services for the poor as unprofessional and argued "we ought not to let [the novel] have so wide a circulation as it now has, without, in the name of all that is respectable in our profession, uttering this disclaimer of the moral principles of Dr. Fulton."[58] Few could doubt, as *Godey's Lady's Book* reported, "this little book is one of the most successful *experiments* of popularizing domestic economy which has ever been made."[59] The book was so overwhelmingly popular that Lee wrote four related novels before the year's end, all of which drew on the economy as inspiration.

More than economic theory for the masses, Lee's novels provided financial security for her own family. By 1844, she had published eight novels featuring morality, family, and finance. Attesting to the profitability of Lee's panic fiction, Horatio Weld wrote *The Fourth Experiment of Living: Living Without Means* shortly after the publication of Lee's *Three Experiments*. It sold through fifteen editions in 1837. In his diary entry for March 19, 1837, Ralph Waldo Emerson noted that ten thousand copies were sold in less than ten days; this champion of the individual saw the commercial success of the original *Three Experiments* and this *Fourth Experiment* as "a good problem." Countering Child's remark about the impracticality of poetry with a quotation from Goethe, he wrote, "lively feeling of the circumstance, and faculty to express it makes the poet."[60] The poetry of Lee and her imitators who wrote about the circumstances of their time would never find the acclaim of the classic writers of the American Renaissance, such as Poe, Hawthorne, and Melville. Nevertheless, these now-famous writers struggled to find publishers and readers during hard times, whereas Lee and her imitators found eager audiences.[61]

As the preface to Lee's next book accused, Weld and other writers imitated the "name and external appearance" of *Three Experiments*.[62] Weld could not deny this but defended his unauthorized sequel by arguing that there had been "no theft of subject matter – no infringement of privilege – no want of courtesy" because his book would describe scenes that "it is hardly possible that a lady can have witnessed." Focusing on the economic activities that took place outside of the home, he portrayed dunning creditors, an alcoholic lawyer, cheating financiers, a failure-hungry notary, extravagant clerks, and a suicidal forger. Opposing Lee's vision of the possibilities of understanding the economy through familial choices, this darker story insinuated that businessmen, the real unit of the economy, were predisposed to sin. If preventing economic crises depended on moral behavior, Weld implied that the results would be disastrous.[63]

Weld was far from alone in jumping on the "experiments" bandwagon. In a "fifth experiment" entitled *New Experiments: Means Without Living*, an anonymous author exposed the frauds of "Quackery" and "Ultraism," defining the latter as "extensive edifices of theory upon true premises, though all too narrow for the superstructure erected upon them." Following Lee's narrative structure of a family ruined in three acts, this text illustrates the impossibilities of living according to any "*science* of living." It ridiculed fields as diverse as diet reform, domestic economy, temperance, phrenology, and animal magnetism, as well as the concept of division of labor advocated by political economists.[64] The largest target, however, was Dr. William Alcott's *Ways of Living on Small Means*, a spin-off of Lee's novel that replaced narrative with extreme recommendations for economical living. For example, Alcott argued against underwear, saying "we wear *too many* clothes," and scorned eating hot, diverse meals, insisting that "nothing is more common, I may say again, – nothing is more universal – than slavery to this bad practice." Americans, Alcott argued, were enslaved to more than just their stomachs; they were in "everlasting slavery" to "modern toilets," "modern kitchens," and "modern bed-chambers."[65]

But what if Americans were enslaved by their minds? "Sudden changes of fortune, whether good or bad, are known to excite cerebral disease and insanity," explained one of the world's leading phrenologists.[66] How exactly this happened was open for debate because, as the same author suggested in a different book, "the structure of the brain is so complicated, that less is known of its true nature than of that of almost any other organ."[67] Dissection manuals for medical students included lithographic plates of the brain's anatomy but guided readers to phrenology for explanation of the brain's functions.[68] Famous for measuring heads and "reading" the bumps on scalps, phrenology looked at these external physical properties to explain how the inside of the skull worked. By assigning different psychological "faculties" to different "cerebral" or "mental organs" in the brain, phrenologists anatomized economic behavior.

Many organs contributed to economic choices.[69] From its position above the left ear, Acquisitiveness starred, but Cautiousness, Sympathy, Self-Esteem, Individuality, Eventuality, Firmness, Imitation, Combativeness, and even Conscientiousness all played supporting roles.[70] Through the proper exercise of mental organs, an individual could be "the master of his own mind."[71] But without proper care, the relationship between organs could become imbalanced: "the organs of Acquisitiveness, Self-Esteem, &c. from excessive stimulus, become permanently and uncontrollably excited, and assume the master. The suggestions of the other faculties become proportionally feeble, and are not listened to." Diseased brains were responsible when "the shortest, though most dangerous road, to the point desired, is alone looked at, and speculations are entered upon with a rashness, and defiance of sense and obstacles."[72] By choosing to be undisciplined, Free Americans could become senseless slaves to their own greed.

But what about actual slaves? Eager to write about the bonds of extravagance, the *Three Experiments* genre, written by New Englanders and New Yorkers, entirely ignored the issue of chattel slavery. These books avoided this subject not only to appeal to a national market but also because slavery challenged their underlying economic argument that all Americans were responsible for their own economic choices. To buy a slave was a choice; to be a slave was not. Slaves could not be held responsible for economic failure.

Everyone else could. Even the pro-agrarian spin-off *Living on Other People's Means* blamed the high price of food during the pressure on farm laborers who chose to join "the constant emigration which is flowing from the agricultural to the commercial towns." Simon Silver, the main character in this tale, chooses to take advantage of naïve farmers. Silver uses his false corporation, the "Drumstick Manufacturing Company," and his puppet "Bubbleville bank" to profit from hard times because, as the author indicates, "pressures of late years, are much more common than formerly." He continues, "so many men live up to their means, beyond their means, without means, and upon other people's means, that a scarcity of money is a very common occurrence."[73] In the *Three Experiments* genre, free men, even those on the bottom of the social ladder, failed because of bad choices.

The novels inspired by the success of *Three Experiments of Living*, written by Lee and by other authors, filled out her explanation of the economy, but few matched the original's eloquence. As one book review of *Three Experiments in Drinking*, a pro-temperance spin-off, attested, "like all the 'experiments' which have succeeded the 'Three Experiments of Living', it lacks the force, spirit, and *vraisemblance*, of its excellent archetype."[74] Lee triumphed over her male successors. Her emulators were criticized for "sucking sustenance though their goose quills," whereas periodicals such as the *Ladies' Companion* praised Lee as one of the "writers who devote themselves to benefit their fellow-creatures." She was, however, also making money by selling her readers the ideas they wanted to hear – that "by the exercise of domestic virtues of patience, frugality and content ... every privation may be borne, and every difficulty be surmounted." Unlike the darker sequels written in a more sensational and less hopeful style, Lee's first book was empowering for middle-class men and women who felt powerless amid the uncertainty of the times. With unprecedented book sales, Lee was "amply rewarded" for making financial crisis seem preventable, survivable, and understandable.[75]

The readers of Lee's novels learned the same lesson as Whitman's churchgoers: individuals bore responsibility for their economic fates. The

texts of ministers, phrenologists, handbook authors, and novelists rein-
forced a common instruction in economic causation.

* * *

Francis Wayland, author of America's first political economy textbook,
shared Lee's goal of making the vicissitudes of economic life understandable. A Baptist minister, he also shared Jason Whitman's theological view
of individual sin. As the president of Brown University, Wayland based his
textbook, *The Elements of Political Economy*, on a course of lectures he
offered annually to the university's senior class. This book, in both its
original and abridged versions, became the classic mid-nineteenth-century
American textbook for courses on political economy in colleges and academies; during the next three decades, students purchased more than sixty
thousand copies.[76] By the time the seventh and final edition of the book
was printed in 1886, its concepts were outdated; experts with mathemat-
ical and scientific backgrounds had transformed political economy into
economics, a field that sought separation from both politics and religion.[77]
But in January 1837, when *The Elements of Political Economy* first
reached bookstores, Wayland synthesized nearly a century of conflicting
and confusing treatises full of explicit partisanship.[78] To this, he added his
own unabashed Christian doctrine. The text's readers would learn that
"God intended that men should live together in friendship and harmony."
As a means of promoting human harmony, trade was therefore "intended
by the Creator" and anything that enabled trade to occur more efficiently,
such as merchants, banks, and paper money, were fulfillments of divine
will. Finance never seemed so holy.

Wayland knew more about writing discourses than about righting
accounts. He admitted in his preface that he had "no experience in mercantile business."[79] Fortunately, political economy was not the study of
business practices; it was a theoretical subject devoted to "Judicial and
frugal management of public affairs."[80] The discipline's critics described it
as full of "Paradoxes, palpable untruths, and overwrought metaphysical
theories"; "forbidding" because of the "abstract and repulsive nature of
the reasoning employed"; and worthy of "no right to the appellation of a
science."[81] The editor of *Three Experiments of Living* condemned individuals who applied its theories to their moral choices: "They repeat, like
parrots, the maxim of the political economists, – '*Laissez-nous faire* – let us
alone,' – morals will take care of themselves; just as they tell us, to let alone
the prices and qualities of the physical subjects of trade, and they will take
care of themselves."[82] Had Wayland's book preceded Lee's, the subject

might have seemed less bird-brained to the editor because the textbook merged piety and prices.

Structurally, Wayland's book placed greater emphasis on finance than did his sources. He divided political economy into four parts: production, exchange, distribution, and consumption. As one of the book's reviewers pointed out, "most preceding writers have made but three divisions, – Production, Distribution and Consumption." The reviewer continued: "We think it a decided improvement in an elementary treatise that the doctrines of *Exchange* receive distinct and prominent attention. This part of the work before us is peculiarly valuable."[83] Wayland's emphasis on banking was itself an example of supply and demand. His book provided a readable explanation of the complicated and all-consuming subject of political debate. More than political demand, however, motivated Wayland to add a section on exchange to the traditional triumvirate of political economy subjects. By increasing the efficiency of exchange, banks represented to Wayland the pinnacle of the progress "by experiment" from "rude beginnings to greater and greater perfection."[84] Wayland saw divinity in discount rates.

Attacking prejudice against paper money, he turned the Jacksonian era financial system into a general law. His book extolled the efficient virtues of democratized banking by building, step by step, from a single local exchange to a complex international financial system based on paper instruments of credit. He explained methodically how "merely writing a few words in a bank ledger" on receipt of slips of paper sent through the postal service enabled the exchange of enormous quantities of goods between nations separated by vast distances. He marveled, "It is hardly possible to find a case, in which, by the division of labor, a greater increase of productiveness is given to human industry."[85] Beyond apology, Wayland's account of exchange describes the credit system as an apotheosis of economy.

He justified America's use of financial paper by assuring his readers that bank notes "possess some considerable advantages over specie; that is … they are lighter, occupy less bulk, and are equal in exchangeable value to specie." Even though he recognized that the "exchangeable value" of paper money depended on "the confidence of the community," he dismissed this concern in his list of advantages.[86] Wayland's confidence in paper money derived from his confidence in bankers. If bank directors found the right "ratio between the issues of the bank, and the capital in its vaults, such a bank would be of undoubted security," he argued.[87] Banking, in other words, depended on human choice. And Wayland believed that bad decisions were motivated by sin, not uncertainty. As he explained, bank directors who knowingly defied this ratio performed "nothing more than a fraudulent arrangement for picking the pockets of the public, on an extensive scale. It is nothing more nor less, than downright swindling."[88] Bank failures, then, were not the product of a bad financial system, but the result of moral failings.

He did, however, find problems with the existing system. As much as Wayland approved of banks, he was no proponent of decentralization. "It would be much better, to have several banks nearly connected, as the branches of a large bank; than to have them isolated, and independent of each other" because, he argued, in a decentralized system, "each is naturally fearful of the solvency of the rest." This was clearly veiled praise of the BUS. Although he rued the destruction of the national bank, he justified the post-BUS financial system by recognizing that a multiplication of banks could increase American access to credit. Local banks, he assured, served as "an inducement for the investment of *foreign* capital." "If money can be borrowed in London, at four per cent., and be loaned here, for six per cent.," he explained through an example that mirrored the precise state of affairs when he wrote the book, "we have the benefit of the use of the money, and of two per cent. in addition. In this manner, money is constantly borrowed by a new country from an old, with great advantage to both, but specially to the new country."[89] Of course, this general law created out of the experiences of the early to mid-1830s assumed that the "new country" could afford to pay back the "old country" when its debts became due, a certainty Wayland did not question.

Beyond faith in the nation's credit, his text expressed a naïve confidence in individual economic actors. Bankers would correctly determine the reserve ratio, unless they were immoral. Similarly, bill brokers should be trusted:

He, whose only business it is to loan money will keep himself, at all times, acquainted with the state of the money market; he will ascertain the character and responsibility of the individuals who are requesting loans; he will be the first to ascertain the indications of their failure, either in skill or in fidelity; and will, therefore, be the best prepared to decide whether it be necessary to withdraw capital from a debtor.[90]

Bill brokers would perfectly size up not only the money market but also potential debtors, who could only fail based on personal flaws "either in skill or in fidelity." Nothing was beyond the power of the individual to control through practical and moral behavior. His faith in these individuals undergirded his entire explanation of the system of exchange.

In addition to financiers, merchants bore a great deal of the burden of keeping trade in good shape. "*The Merchant* will succeed," he argued, "in proportion as he is able to select the most profitable places and times for exchange, to foresee probable changes of the market, and to avail himself of the fluctuations of capital which are always taking place, in various parts of the civilized world."[91] Of course, if success required nearly perfect information, instantaneous transportation, and omniscience, readers should have expected failure.

Wayland, writing in the midst of the boom, was an optimist.[92] Nevertheless, the book arrived just in time to offer explanations of the pressure that was in the process of freezing both credit markets and the poor, who could afford neither bread nor fuel for heat. And as one reviewer noted, "at a time like this, the teachings of a great intellect . . . are listened to as the responses of an oracle." Readers looked to Wayland's "luminous chapters" as a source of "a vast amount of practical wisdom."[93]

Despite Wayland's practical inexperience, they had good reason to read his work. Without predicting the panic, he wrote a nearly perfect description of what would come: "Sometimes the pressure for money is so great, that those who have purchased products with borrowed capital, cannot sell them fast enough to make their payments. These are obliged to stop payment, or become bankrupts, and assign their effects to their creditors." To Wayland, however, the effects of the pressure did not stop with these first failures: "But these were debtors to many others who were depending on the payment to be received from them, to pay their own debts. These, being disappointed in this expectation, also fail. Their failure leads again to the failure of others, and the panic becomes general." By the time pressure transformed into general panic, "No one dares to trust their neighbor, and the banks dare not trust any one. An universal crash of mercantile credit succeeds, and none are able to withstand the shock, save those of the heaviest capital, and of the greatest financial ability."[94] Given the flaws in his explanation of the system of exchange, it is hard to believe that Wayland could predict, so pitch-perfectly, its collapse.

His language, nevertheless, reveals that he missed one key component of the coming crisis: the question of blame. Panic, in this description, was not a political process. Wayland anticipated that banks, not partisanship, would be the target of animosity. "The blame, when such a state of things as has been described, exists, is always laid upon the banks. This is manifestly unjust," he argued. "It belongs to the borrower, just as much as it does to the lender. Men are very willing to borrow, but they very commonly call upon the community for great commiseration, when they are obliged to pay," he concluded.[95] Wayland did not blame partisan policy for panic; he found fault in individuals not as citizens but as borrowers.

Moreover, Wayland praised financial institutions during crises. "The bank, by enforcing payments in a time of pressure, is really doing a great service to the community," he assured readers, continuing "if, by their exacting punctuality, some persons fail, it is better that a few should lose, than that the whole community should be ruined." Banks, then, saved communities at the expense of failed individuals who, in Wayland's view, bore responsibility for their own failure because they had borrowed more than they should have. Confirming this moral judgment, Wayland wrote, "The only remedy for the evils manifestly is, for both parties to be willing to grow rich more slowly, and thus to assume less formidable risks. When a whole community has run its transactions beyond its means, and has become embarrassed, there is very little gained by the abuse of banks and of bank directors." A community's failure, then, was the result of individual evils; no system or institutions were responsible. All of this – pressure, bankruptcy, failure, panic, universal crash, and ruin – was the result, according to Wayland, not of partisan policies or financial institutions but of "the hopes, wishes, and anticipations of men."[96] Individuals should shoulder blame for failure on any scale.

Wayland did not want to see panic as political because he clearly wanted his readers to separate the two halves of his field: the political from the economic. As he explained in his preface, "It has been to the author a source of regret, that the course of discussion in the following pages, has unavoidably led him over ground which has frequently been the arena of political controversy."[97] In nearly five hundred pages, he argued for industrialization, free trade, and democratized banking. Wayland's views on these highly contentious topics, however, placed the book's proposals outside the typical partisan divide. His justification for mechanization placed his book in opposition to many of the workingmen's groups within the Democratic Party, but his anti-tariff stance placed him in opposition to Whig protectionism. This politically split agenda earned the book praise from critics as "far above the foul atmosphere of political rancour" even though it had an explicit agenda: to foster faith in banks.[98]

Neither labor nor tariffs captivated readers' attention like Wayland's ideas about finance. One reviewer praised, "Of the several works on banking which we have seen, none can be compared with this." Wayland wrote about the most complicated and most contentious topic of his day, and he did it with ease. "For perspicuity and simplicity of language and arrangement; for soundness of thought; and, we may add, for candor in his statements;" the reviewer concluded, "we think Dr. Wayland has no rival in this point."[99] Wayland, however, did have rivals.

Richard Hildreth's *The History of Banks* also appeared in bookstores in January 1837. Hildreth traced the development of banking from twelfth-century Venice to the post-BUS decentralized banking system that he saw as nearing the pinnacle of financial progress through its democratization of the printing of paper money. The pressure, in his view, was "mistaken by many practical men, whose experience does not extend beyond the panic of 1818–19, if so far, for a sign of commercial distress; and they have been sighing over the ruin of the country, at the very moment of its highest prosperity." Hildreth advocated a positive interpretation of the pressure. Accordingly, his book's purpose was to stop the "fear and trembling" of the nation's merchants and bankers by providing the memory these "practical" men lacked, however colored by his fierce pro-Jackson partisanship. He criticized those who blamed the credit crisis on "'speculation,' 'over-issue of bank-notes,' 'overtrading,' or some other of those verbal reasons by which practical men account for things they do not understand." Rather than emphasize these particular "verbal reasons" for the pressure of 1836, Hildreth reminded his readers about previous periods of "commercial distrust" and "scarcity of capital."[100] Complete with chronology and argument, *The History of Banks* provided exactly what its title promised: a history. It urged using the past as a guide for the present, but it did not try to explain how banking worked within a system of trade. This task was left to political economists and their synthesizer, Wayland.

But what if "practical men" had written texts describing their understanding of economic responsibility? Wayland justified his authorship of the textbook because "there seemed very little hope that this subject would be undertaken by men engaged in active business."[101] True, few businessmen wrote textbooks, but even the most formulaic of commercial letters revealed lessons about economic relationships. For example, the New Orleanian firm of Smith H. & Co. wrote to its correspondents in Hartford, Connecticut, on February 15, 1837, that "Business continues very dull & we have more goods than we can take care of. We do not want to see anything more in the shape of a box for two months to come . . . You must not think of sending the work you are now making to us." This letter expressed the law of supply and demand in concise and colloquial language. The clerk who wrote this message and the university student reading Wayland's text would both learn that prices declined when supply exceeded demand.

The next part of the letter, however, instructed the clerk in a different conceptualization of markets than that offered to the student of political economy: "Mr. L. N. Clarke, one of our old customers has commenced business again – has just bought 800 of us & promises to give you an order to fill next summer. Mr. Goodrich from Middletown is within 14 miles of Clarke & has made a good beginning (Mr. C. says). You had better send us some of your cards."[102] Millions of letters like these expressed a mercantile perception of the economy as a web of local markets peopled with identifiable individuals who held business cards in their hands as they balanced buying and selling. Clerks learned to think in terms of specific people and prices in particular places whereas political economy's students learned to think in terms of national policy making.

A student of political economy need only pick up a newspaper to get a whiff of the practical ways merchants thought about trade. Regardless of a paper's political orientation, most numbers contained a heading entitled "Commercial" that included snapshots of local business that provided estimates, in words and numbers, of the extent of sales, the terms of payment, the cost of credit, the predictions of future market conditions, and the prices paid for wholesale commodities (from anchors to zinc). In grids such as that of the *New Orleans Prices Current and Shipping List*, merchants read and interpreted terms such as "limited demand" or "dull" and "moderate supply" or "scarce," in reference to specific goods such as "cotton, La. & Miss. Choice"; "drugs, Ginseng"; and "lard."[103] This shorthand condensed a great deal of local knowledge into a form that could be sent cheaply through the postal service to markets located around the globe, where similar reports were compiled, printed, and distributed. Public reports, "carefully revised and corrected," as the *Shipping and Commercial List and New-York Price Current* advertised, enabled merchants to make sense of the economy in terms of discrete markets.[104]

Unlike columns that focused on politics, the terms "imports" and "exports" provided the only references to nations in commercial sections of newspapers. In the New Orleans *Commercial Bulletin*, accounts from Wall Street, the Charleston Market, and Liverpool appeared one after the next with no national or sectional designation because, in practice, merchants thought locally and globally.[105] Although merchants employed the terms of political economy, such as supply and demand, Wayland was right to argue that there was little hope that his subject, theories of national policy based on generalized laws, "would be undertaken by men engaged in active business" because their subject was the opposite – practical trade between a world of individuals.[106]

Written by men with little practical experience, *"the Science of Wealth"* lingered on the edges of science, more peripheral than phrenology.[107] In 1837, Wayland's book was no exception. Some hoped that numbers might convince Americans to take political economy more seriously. "The science of statistics has hardly an existence in this country," decried Francis Bowen, a reviewer of Wayland's book, who pointed to deficiencies he would later try to fill with his own book, *American Political Economy*, published in 1870.[108] The title was significant. Bowen and others criticized Wayland for not adapting the theories of English and French political economists to the American environment. Indeed, unlike the BOE directors or English members of Parliament who were responsible only to other elites, American politicians could not use political economy for policy making without their constituents' support. One reviewer lamented, "our truly competent statesmen so often feel themselves compelled to truckle to popular prejudice and clamour, and enact laws at variance with the true interests of the nation, because the people will have them."[109] And more than just numbers or facts prevented Americans from voting according to theory. Formulated for foreign contexts, political economy did not conform to the most important force in American elections of the 1830s: political parties.

"We want an American treatise of Political Economy, one that shall contain not merely the higher truths, that are strictly universal, and which no circumstances can limit or disprove," Bowen wrote, "but the less general maxims founded on … a careful observation of facts, that may form a text book for legislators and senators." Americans needed a specifically adapted, factually or numerically based, and easily understood explanation of the economy because, he argued, "in this country we are all legislators." "The humblest individual, who puts in a vote at town-meeting, exerts an influence on the laws, and does his part in determining vexed, political questions," he asserted, continuing, "In recommending the study of Political Economy, then, we merely advise, that such knowledge may be obtained, as may fit a citizen for the proper exercise of his functions."[110] According to Bowen, white, male Americans needed an education in political economy because their choices determined the nation's economic success.

Whether as Wayland's lenders and borrowers or as Bowen's citizens, Americans were taught that their individual choices determined their economic fates. Ultimately, then, for all of political economy's claims to general theory designed to influence national policy, it made the same argument as ministers, domestic economy manuals, and Lee's novels:

individual choice controlled the economy. As one reviewer of Wayland's book noted, "the inductions of Political Economy, and the teachings of Christianity, though proceeding by different routes, arrive eventually at the same end."[111] Wayland and even the flour rioters agreed on economic principles, at the most fundamental level, because they blamed the same source for financial trouble: the poor choices of individuals with free will.

* * *

The difference between the ideas of the president of Brown University and the men throwing flour out of New York City's warehouse windows was not in the cause but in the effect. Wayland argued, as did every political economist, that destroying the supply of flour would only raise prices, but this theory was based on the notion that all participants in the economy acted according to their own rational, profit-maximizing self-interest. Perhaps it was in the rioters' best interest to scare the merchants; in the short term, the riot did provoke the merchants to provide the poor with free flour. The riot suggests a more fundamental difference between adherents of political economy and the rioters. The rioters' actions reflected the idea that rational choices involved more than calculations of monetary profit.[112] Self-interest for some might be generating wealth, but for others it might be the preservation of a family's economic independence or the protection of individual souls from sinful temptation.

Who decides what choice is rational? This debate was just beginning to be formulated by Emerson and other Romantic thinkers in the 1830s; the existing literature, nevertheless, suggested that reason was debatable.[113] According to phrenological arguments about brain function, choice had more to do with properly sized mental organs than intellectual prowess. The explanation of the economy provided by political economy was not necessarily more "true" than its competitors, but it was more convenient for those who prioritized money and power, the same people who won offices and crafted policies.[114] Moreover, the generalizations based on simplified motivations created simple "laws," like supply and demand, that were easier to theorize than the messy systems based on more complex calculations of individual choice.[115]

Political economy might prove useful, but it won few believers. In his review of Wayland's textbook, Francis Bowen wrote,

It is mournful to reflect, that, in a country where so much depends on the correctness of the opinions held by the people at large, hardly any progress has been made in defining and limiting the maxims of Political Economy for our own use, or in diffusing that degree of elementary knowledge, which is requisite for the security and wellbeing of the state.[116]

He drew on a specific example of how the "elementary knowledge" offered by Wayland's textbook would have been useful: "the absurd prejudice against wholesale dealers in grain, which recently caused an alarming riot in New York, cannot exist in a mind imbued with the simplest and most evident maxims of the science."[117]

Bowen was not alone in pointing to the flour riot as evidence that Americans needed to learn political economy. Wayland's abridged version of *The Elements of Political Economy*, which went to press in October 1837, posed the following discussion question to his student readers: "a few days since, a mob, because flour was so dear, broke into a flour store in New York, and destroyed seven or eight hundred barrels. Is this calculated to make flour cheaper?"[118]

The flour riot had literally become a textbook example of American economic miscomprehension. But Wayland did not ask his pupils to understand the "mob's" perspective. The point of the textbook was to teach students to see beyond the nuance of individual choices to predict the outcome of policy; they did not need to sympathize with the starving children whose fathers rioted as a demand for immediate economic change. Instead, the question Wayland asked required a simple answer: no. Students would learn calculation rather than compassion. The actions of the rioters seemed entirely uncalculated and irrational – the cardinal sins of political economy. With time, Wayland taught, the market would correct itself; the Loco-Foco rally organizers preached that elections and bank runs offered the surest method to provoke economic change. This all required patience. But the rioters refused to wait. They rioted because, as all economic theories in early 1837 emphasized, they were responsible for their own fate.

Failure resulted from either uncontrollable physiological conditions or the wrong choices – whether made by men, women, businessmen, housewives, merchants, bankers, or citizens. If the rioters suffered from swollen mental organs that prevented patience, no awareness of political economy would teach them to obey the laws of supply and demand. But if they could control their brains, inaction was failure. And if they failed, they were responsible for their families' economic and moral demise. The burden of economic responsibility overwhelmed the workingmen of New York who could not wait for politics or laws of political economy to address their distress. Rather than a misunderstanding of economic principles, the riot was a practical application of the dominant economic belief of the time: individual responsibility.

* * *

After walking through the exorbitantly priced Fulton Market and considering both the rising prices of food and the growing unemployment, Philip Hone asked himself, "What is to become of the labouring classes?" He reported, "It is very cold now, if it continues so for a month there will be great and real suffering in all classes."[119] The weather, along with a long list of causes, increased the tension. No amount of rioting or political maneuvering could have prevented the shifts in specie flow, the spread of American news to Britain, or the winter cold. As greedy as the merchants probably were, they were unable to end the pressure in part because, like the rioters they condemned, they had no idea of its causes.

By the end of 1837, sermons, novels, and even Wayland's later editions of *The Elements of Political Economy* diminished the power of individual economic choice. Overwhelmed individuals demanded explanations of the economy that supplied larger entities to blame: God, science, or the political system. But in February, the flour on the streets of New York represented only the first in a series of acts of economic desperation by people who believed that on every scale – individual, familial, local, or national – they were responsible for the "hard times."

CHAPTER 4

Mysterious Whispers

On March 4, 1837, a bald man stood under a dome and quietly swore an oath. President Martin Van Buren was more accustomed to hushed innuendo than stentorian oratory. When he addressed the crowd gathered outside the U.S. Capital, he spoke in "a rather low voice." A correspondent wrote to a newspaper, "The inaugural of the new president was heard by very few."[1] People standing right in front of him on Washington's snow-covered streets wondered what the president said. Those involved in the pressurized financial markets of New York, New Orleans, and London shared their curiosity. But when the newspapers reprinted the inaugural address, readers quickly discovered that although the new president uttered the word "confidence" several times, his speech inspired none.

Meanwhile, nearly one thousand miles to the southwest and more than three thousand miles to the east, bankers attempted to accomplish what the president would not. They worked to revive confidence not only by bailing out failing firms but also by keeping the news of their financial maneuvers confidential. Although some of the bankers would succeed in extending credit, they all failed in preventing the spread of rumors. The reprinting of these whispers, unlike the publication of the president's soft-spoken address, changed history.

Rumor-filled letters and newspapers described the failures in imprecise terms: distress, mischief, embarrassment, derangement, madness, disease, evil, emergency, disaster, earthquake, tempest, crash, convulsion, confla-gration, revulsion, revolution, ruin, and panic. These words were not synonyms describing a single event; the language used to convey financial uncertainty caused and constituted crises in local communities and indi-vidual minds. Only precise calculations could provide relief, but accurate information was a chimera. Like the old joke, the news was bad and there was not enough of it. Writers manipulated news for their own profit; it traveled irregularly. Even a well-maintained ledger could not evaluate all the circulating goods and paper it documented because prices were in a state of flux. Incomplete and inaccurate information prevented nearly anyone from doing business because no accounts could be trusted, not even one's own. In this uncertain context, pressure transformed into both many personal panics and several local crises.

Despite his poor projection, Van Buren's inaugural address found permanency in print. American history textbooks of the mid-nineteenth century taught students that this address took place on March 4, 1837; they did not teach their young readers that March 4, 1837, was also the day that people began to panic. This is because the whispers that spread financial crisis in New Orleans, New York, and London evaporated nearly instantaneously after they were spoken. Their evidentiary ghosts nevertheless lingered, waiting for historians to reveal the paths of panic in 1837 and, even more importantly, the power of communication as a causative force in economic history.

* * *

For Thomas Fidoe Ormes, a trip to the "convenience" proved very inconvenient. In 1836, Ormes was employed as a junior clerk in the BOE, where he continued more than seventy years of service by his father, grandfather, and great-grandfather.[2] Like his fellow clerks in the Bill Office, Ormes spent his days processing the bills discounted by the bank. Although employed in mundane tasks, the junior clerks of the Bill Office like Ormes physically handled the proof of the reputations of mercantile houses responsible for international trade.[3] With their fingers on the pulse of the global economy, Ormes and his colleagues knew the information they processed was valuable. So valuable, in fact, that the BOE had developed a special Committee of Inspection to detect in-house sources of information leaks. Ormes's fateful trip to the toilet became the subject of an exceptionally well-documented investigation. The records of this case illuminate the vulnerability of the financial system to diminished confidence.

On the morning of Thursday, December 8, 1836, a colleague mentioned to Ormes that he had been ordered to pull the bills of exchange drawn on George Wildes & Co., one of the most extensive American houses in London. About twenty minutes later, when he "had occasion to go to the Public Drawing Office," Ormes walked through the labyrinthine BOE to the public-access section of the bank and stopped under the dome to use "a convenience in the corner." Walking back, Ormes met an old "school fellow," stockbroker James Woolley, who had "a seat in the Rotunda," a convenient spot for gathering gossip to employ across the street at the 'Change. Ormes asked his friend "if he had heard that George Wildes & Co. had failed." His friend said, "No." "I told him in confidence," Ormes confessed the next day, "I did not expect he would have told anybody, as I said to him I told him in confidence."[4]

Woolley immediately betrayed Ormes's trust. The London *Times* reported in its evening edition, "There have been rumors of failures about to-day, which at first created some degree of alarm, but they were ascertained, on inquiry, to be without foundation."[5] The initial "inquiry" received praise from the *Times* in the next day's paper. "With the view of preventing such practices in future, which do great mischief and often arise from stock-jobbing motives, or in some cases private malice," the newspaper sanctioned the investigation. "Such a practice as this, could it be followed upon similar occasions," the *Times* recommended, "would give great satisfaction to the trading and banking interest, who are often exposed to great inconvenience and even subject to much expense by false allegations, and would go far to check the rash and imprudent talking on matters of extreme delicacy, which is so common in the city."[6] The *Times* approved of the investigation not because rumors were wrong but because they came from the clumsy tongues of the City's white-collar laboring men capable of "rash and imprudent talking."[7]

Clerks may have gossiped, but print spread the reach of a rumor. The *Times* reported, "the rumours were traced to a party in the employ of the Bank of England against whom the evidence appeared to be so strong, that he was suspended by the order of the Directors." But the story did not end here: "Subsequent inquiry, however, satisfied them that his meaning had been misunderstood by those who followed up the spreading of the report, and he was this afternoon, as it is said, reinstated in his office."[8] In the process of condemning the spreading of one rumor (commercial failure), the *Times* spread another (the reinstatement of the misunderstood clerk). Both were wrong or, more precisely, mostly wrong. The kernel of truth at the center of some rumors made them dangerous, especially in times of financial pressure, and discovering the source of the information demanded detective work.

When the Committee of Inspection was charged by the BOE directors with uncovering "the circumstance connected with the origin, progress, and communication to the Public of the Report respecting the House of George Wildes & Co.," they discovered that the case of the leaky clerk was much more complex than the *Times* had described.⁹ By interviewing a number of men who worked in the Bill Office, the investigators revealed how gossip became rumor through the City's unofficial network of financial information.¹⁰

Formal buildings such as the 'Change were designed to remove transactions from taverns to more private settings.¹¹ The exclusivity of these new venues, however, allowed men with less certain information and socially isolating jobs to continue to gossip in the City's pubs. As the Committee of Inspection discovered, Ormes was the unfortunate mouthpiece of gossip that began the day before at the Windmill Tavern where a clerk ate his mid-day meal and overheard "two persons talking of an American house that had failed." When he returned to the BOE, this clerk asked John Smith, a clerk in the Bill Office, if he had heard of "the stoppage of an American house." Smith and two other clerks began to discuss this rumor first using addresses and initials and finally naming two possible suspects: Timothy Wiggin & Co. and George Wildes & Co. That night, at the Shades tavern, Smith became convinced of the failure of George Wildes & Co. as he overheard "a gentleman say, there was a report of a house beginning with a W in Coleman Street." The myopic Smith, whose eyesight had deteriorated over twenty-four years of service at the BOE, could not recognize the speaker but recognized the address as belonging to George Wildes & Co. The next morning, Smith asked several tellers if they had heard about the failure; one responded: "Good God, is it possible?" When later accused not of asking a question but of declaring a fact, the partly blind clerk insisted that the seemingly deaf teller "from indistinctness of hearing must have misunderstood me."

Shocked that such a reputable house that owed so much to the BOE could have failed, one of the tellers brought the news to the attention of Thomas Whitford, the "Principal of the Drawing Room." Believing that the message was presented not "as a report, but as a fact," Whitford urged two junior clerks to take out the bills of George Wildes & Co. for inspection. One of these clerks conveyed the instructions to his colleague Thomas Fidoe Ormes. A half an hour later, Ormes met his "friend" the stockbroker in the Rotunda, and the shocking office gossip became a terrifying public rumor.¹²

As the tavern chatter indicated, clerks could not be relied on to keep quiet either inside or outside the BOE. Whitford assured the committee that "I have 28 clerks in my office, I have never heard any conversation on the credit of any houses." Smith insisted, "It is not the habit of the

Gentlemen in the Office to talk of failures, they are too much engaged." Nevertheless, another clerk admitted, "at times the probability of Bills we have in charge being paid is the subject of conversation as we look over them." Men who worked all day on confidential material were too enmeshed in the financial world to consistently feign their disinterest. And after the previous months of financial pressure, the bills they processed grew increasingly interesting as the clerks' chairs turned into ringside seats to financial crisis.[13]

The committee therefore blamed the principal, Whitford, for "imprudently" telling the clerks any nonessential information, especially without "having made due enquiry into the fact." In addition, it cited Smith for being "the first to name the House as having failed." Smith's misbehavior, however, paled in comparison to that of Ormes. The committee reported to the directors, "the conduct of Thomas Fidoe Ormes in giving information of what had occurred in the office involves a principle of great importance." This "principle of great importance" was the policy of confidentiality. When clerks publicized information from the office, they jeopardized the value of the bank's portfolio and destroyed what later economists would describe as the BOE's advantageous information asymmetry in the London money market. For this reason, Ormes was targeted for the most "severe punishment."[14]

The directors weighed the committee's findings against petitions for mercy written by the three men. Far from the compassion reported by the *Times*, the BOE did not reinstate its clerks. Instead, the Committee of Inspection recommended and the Court of Directors ordered the immediate suspension of Whitford, Smith, and Ormes. Whitford petitioned the directors. The increase in the BOE's discounting business during the previous months had already physically strained him, as he was suffering from "great nervous debility, palpitation of the Heart, and frequent pain in the side" brought on by the "great increase of business which has taken place." He argued that his suspension "tends greatly to increase the disease." After forty years of service at the BOE, he believed that only returning to work would restore "him to that tranquility of mind so necessary to the regaining of his health." Whitford was demoted but returned to the BOE.

Smith and Ormes were forced to resign. The Court of Directors granted the fifty-year-old Smith a slim pension because his long employ had left his "health seriously impaired and his sight defective." This man's sight had been harmed from processing transactions that made other men rich, and he had so internalized the financial world that he memorized the addresses of the seven American houses. In a stroke of sad irony, this knowledge ended his career.[15]

The youngest clerk received no such pity from the directors. The investigators believed that "it is evident he knew, he was not justified in making the communication public" because he "told Woolley that it was in confidence." Ormes swore in his "humble petition" that the meeting with Woolley was "entirely accidental and without the most distant expectation that it could lead to any injury whatever." Ormes presented himself as a financial neophyte who "had not the slightest intention of producing any mischief or ill consequence," but this is hard to believe given Ormes's background.[16] He knew what happened to wayward clerks; he also knew what happened to clerks who behaved. Six years earlier, his father had testified in a case that had led to the death sentence of a young clerk found guilty of forgery. Then, his father died.[17] The deteriorating health of his superiors suggested the hazards of a lifelong clerkship. The earliest news of a failure was a valuable commodity with the power to change a poor man's life. And it did. With shattered prospects and a widowed mother to support, Ormes suffered the dishonorable loss of the salaried job that had sustained four generations of his family.[18] Ormes's severe punishment reveals the power he wielded. The response of the BOE to the rumor indicates not only the general threat of employee agency to the institution's operation but also the directors' specific sensitivity to the reality that George Wildes & Co. might fail.

On the same day as Ormes's meeting with Woolley, the governor of the BOE proposed to inform Wildes and four other American houses that the directors wanted them to satisfy their debts and reduce the amount of their discounted bills. The BOE directors were uncomfortable with the "magnitude of these accounts."[19] Wildes owed the BOE in excess of half a million pounds, a huge amount of money. As security for the loan, the BOE held a great deal of Wildes's paper – bills of exchange, mortgages, stocks, and bonds. The pressure in the money market had already reduced both the likelihood of Wildes repaying its loan and the value of the securities held by the BOE.

These financial considerations were both the reason for the investigation into the clerks' rumor and its most likely source. With the governor and directors talking about Wildes under the domes of the BOE, clerks certainly could have overheard whisperings of failure. Although in mid-December, Wildes and the other American houses continued to redeem their bills of exchange for specie with the help of the BOE, a few more months of pressure would transform Ormes's rumor into reality. These early hints about Wildes's failure set the stage for later communication that would lead to crisis.

* * *

Shortly after the New Year, falling cotton prices and diminished confidence in American paper triggered several failures in Liverpool and London. By early February, the London *Times* reported on the "gloomy" state of the City's money market as the "natural consequence of recent failures and the depression in price which all articles of import and foreign produce have undergone." The newspaper explained that this increased pressure in the money market "led to various reports of other failures, but as far as could be ascertained, and certainly as regards any houses of eminence, they were wholly without foundation." Even rumors that seemed to be "wholly without foundation" influenced investments. Furthermore, just because a rumor's foundation could not be "ascertained" did not mean that it was groundless. As in early December, the public rumors in February were based on real negotiations within the BOE's most private parlors. Once again, Wildes was in trouble.[20]

In mid-February, as the BOE faced "unusually large" applications for discounts, the *Times* surmised that "money is never so scarce as when it is made so by doubts of commercial credits," based on "hints thrown out by journals understood in the city to speak the sentiments of the Bank directors." The directors knew that the scarcity of money was a sign of trouble. With the March 4 deadline for bill payment approaching, the BOE directors assessed the shrinking gold supply in the vaults to determine a safe amount of discounts. The *Times* commented that the directors "never had a more difficult part to play than at the moment, in reconciling their duty to the proprietors with the interests of the public."[21] In October and December of the previous year, the BOE had tried to pressure the American houses to collect specie.[22] But American correspondents sent paper – bills that required even more discounting.[23] "There has been no small attention towards the deliberations of the bank directors," reported the *Morning Chronicle*. Many looked to the BOE to "dissipate the terrors."[24]

Meanwhile, rumors buzzed around the City. "Mysterious whispers," the *Morning Chronicle* reported, "are now very freely sported in town and country, but on what they are founded remains to be discovered."[25] The *Times* reported on "gloomy anticipation and rumours, which have not, assumed any definite shape."[26] "A very critical state of things in the city," appraised Joshua Bates in his diary. He echoed the rumors of the past months: "George Wildes & Co. in difficulties and a sort of panic approaching." Employing a system of numerical codes to replace the names of firms, Bates calculated the consequences: "if 619 should fail, 617 & 999 would go also." No prying eyes could spread rumors based on Bates's reckoning because few had access to his key. But his prediction was simple and damning: if Wildes failed, the houses of Thomas Wilson & Co. and Timothy Wiggin & Co. would fail as well. These firms, later referred to as "the three Ws," were large traders in American commercial paper and securities, too large, according to Bates: "The overtrading of these firms is beyond all question and it seems indispensable that they reduce their business to a more reasonable state as soon as possible." If the three Ws failed, many merchants and bankers would struggle to remain solvent. "This is an awful state of things the Bank of England might stop," he suggested, "the Bank of England should know all about it and if any aid is given it should come from the Bank."[27]

Rather than give aid, the BOE collected information. On February 23, the directors of the BOE authorized the governor to "ascertain the extent and duration of support by Discount that may be required by the Houses trading with America."[28] The *Times* predicted, "From appearances we are disposed to anticipate that the next will be an uneasy week in higher commercial circles."[29] Five American houses wrote letters to the governor requesting support. On Thursday, March 2, the directors met to read and discuss the letters. The houses knew with certainty that they would require several hundred thousand pounds of discounting during each week of March and April. "For May," William Brown explained, "we cannot however *precisely*, ascertain, for the foreign 60 day Bills & many of the inland ones have not yet appeared." Wildes shared this sense of uncertainty but optimistically asserted, "if the Money Market improves, we shall receive more cash payments & require less discount." F. de Lizardi & Co. informed the directors that "our transactions being chiefly with New Orleans we require full five months to effect our object with our correspondents there." Transatlantic logistics necessitated two to five months of heavy discounting; this was more than the BOE directors expected. Brown anticipated their concern. He thanked the directors in advance: "your friendly aid is indispensably necessary to carry them through this crisis." But he laced his gratitude with a threat: "otherwise, I fear for the consequences, to the American interest first, & through them, to every manufacturing town in the kingdom." The BOE's leniency, he suggested, might prevent a more dangerous economic, political, or social revolution.[30]

The BOE directors were more intimidated by the sums under consideration than an uprising. They resolved that the BOE would not "pledge itself" for the full amounts requested by the American houses. Instead, they would accept applications from houses in "temporary difficulties" and raise their standards for discountable bills to conserve their resources.[31] The *Times* complained that "a very large class of persons" would now be "shut out" from "temporary accommodation at the Bank" because of the new narrow definition of "approved securities."[32] The *Morning Chronicle* approved of the limitation because "it renders aid where it is required and checks that unwholesome speculation in stocks and other things which has so materially tended to bring about the present embarrassments."[33] The BOE, however, mostly sought aid for itself. To assist the American houses, the directors requested "proposals for such arrangements with the Bankers and Money dealers as may tend to restore due confidence in the circulation of the regular Bills of the American trade."[34] Several private bankers agreed to provide some of the needed discounts. One assured the directors that this "course of proceeding" was expected to produce "a tone of renewed confidence."[35] Bates, however, felt coerced into helping the BOE do its job. He argued in his diary that if he did not work with the BOE, "12 to 15 millions of bills of exchange would have become useless as a security and the trade of the Country would have stopped."[36]

As the bankers negotiated, rumors evoked ghosts of financial crises past. Alluding to the events of 1825, the *Times* reprinted the City's gossip:

Much gossip has been current to-day in the city relative to supposed communications between the Bank of England and the Ministers, not strictly of an official nature, tending to settle the extent to which the Bank might go in assistance to the mercantile interest. The rumours assume that Ministers had become convinced of the necessity of such interference to prevent consequences of the most serious nature, but it is said that they are asked to give permission to suspend cash payments, in the event of a reaction on the Bank itself, in consequence of such interference. Of course, no sane men could for a moment entertain such a proposition. Without offering any conjecture on the truth of such statements, it requires no great power of observation to perceive that many transactions, connected with some of the largest mercantile engagements into which this country has even entered, are in a perplexed and anxious state, out of which, however, we see at present no reason for supposing that all parties may not pass safely. The Bank directors have credit up to this time for going to the full extent of assistance that is compatible with prudence.[37]

Would the BOE directors prove prudent enough? Given such rumors, the *Morning Chronicle* wondered whether the prevention of panic remained possible. The paper hoped that the BOE's "remedy may not now prove too late to revive confidence."[38]

It was a close call. Ultimately, Bates summarized, "the Bank directors agreed to do all that was proper."[39] After two full days of debate, on March 4, the directors of the BOE in conjunction with a group of private bankers agreed to bail out the American houses.[40] The bank would perform half the necessary discounting; private bankers who were not affiliated with the American trade would discount the other half. Bates along with a group of other financiers would provide security for the embarrassed firms. Through this coalition, the three Ws survived to continue business, at least until the next bill cycle.

The rumors were not entirely wrong; they were just early. March 4 passed without much panicked behavior in London. The arrangements made by the BOE temporarily shored up London's financial market, and newspapers reported that the public regained confidence. The *Times* assured its readers that "distrust is fast wearing away in the City, and even compared with yesterday there is a perceptible difference." Nevertheless, the newspaper cautioned its readers not "to decide in the dark" about the benefit of the bank's action; the effectiveness of the policy would only be illuminated with time.[41]

Bates congratulated himself that his house had been one of the few American houses to survive without assistance. He boasted that "our House has never discounted on a bill and never had aid from the Bank in any way, so that our skill and judgment has excited the admiration and astonishment of everybody." Bates blamed the crisis on bad business decisions of the partners of the embarrassed firms that had to beg the BOE and the rest of the commercial community to save them from failure.[42] The *Times* and other London newspapers, however, located the cause of the American houses' trouble not in the powers of individual human minds, but in the national mistake of allowing British gold to fund the development of a distant country. The *Times* argued, "the origin of our commercial difficulties was the sending money which was so cheap at home for employment in America and elsewhere." The paper commented that it was time for "calling that money back again, before ... our embarrassments [can] be finally put an end to." Rather than viewing the pressure in the London money markets as a local crisis, the *Times* considered this problem to be of national importance requiring an international resolution. "Now that matters are adjusted here seemingly at last," reported the *Times*, "the attention of the merchants is beginning to be turned towards the United States and other foreign parts, upon which the penalty of the late arrangements with the Bank must ultimately fall." The paper believed that "Every port will carry out, as it has done for some time past, pressing orders to foreign countries to realize and send home all assets belonging to English houses, and great distress and pressure will be the necessary consequences, particularly at New York, and in the large trading towns of the Union."

March 4 may have passed without panic in London, but Americans might not be so lucky. Londoners would have to wait to discover the effects of March 4 elsewhere. As the *Times* summarized: "the accounts from the United States must possess great interest for some time to come."[43]

* * *

One account from the United States would prove disappointingly uninteresting. While the BOE directors and private bankers decided to support the Anglo-American trade, more than twenty thousand Americans gathered in front of the East Portico of the U.S. Capital to hear President Van Buren offer "an avowal of the principles that will guide me."[44] The new president tried to evoke confidence, but he managed only a pronouncement of "principles" as dubious in their expression as in the message they conveyed.

In the 3,800-word speech, the term "confidence" appeared seven times. None of these usages referred directly to economic policy. As he pledged to "faithfully execute the office" of the presidency, Van Buren expressed confidence in the electorate, in the Constitution, in the military (twice), and in the balance between federal and state governments. He derived confidence from Americans' "present fortunate condition." By this, he meant not only that America enjoyed respect abroad but also that, domestically, Americans "present an aggregate of human prosperity surely not elsewhere to be found." He did not advocate government actions that might ease the pressure in credit markets in part because he saw only "prosperity perfectly secured" and in part because his economic ideas focused economic responsibility on the individual. He warned, "the obligation [is] imposed upon every citizen, in his own sphere of action, whether limited or extended, to exert himself in perpetuating a condition of things so singularly happy!" He cautioned, "To the hopes of the hostile, the fears of the timid, and the doubts of the anxious, actual experience has given the conclusive reply ... Present excitement will, at all times, magnify present dangers, but true philosophy must teach us that none more threatening than the past can remain to be overcome." History, then, taught Americans that "we ought to entertain an abiding confidence in the stability of our institutions."

The "institutions" of finance, however, had been far from stable during the previous decade. But Van Buren pronounced the nation's problems solved: "While the Federal Government has successfully performed its appropriate functions in relation to foreign affairs, and concerns evidently national, that of every State has remarkably improved in protecting and developing local interests and individual welfare." This statement implied that states would continue to control banking and internal improvements under his administration, but he neither confirmed nor denied his support of the pet banks or the distribution of the surplus. Similarly, his promise to follow "a strict adherence to the letter and spirit of the Constitution, as it was designed by those who framed it" suggested that he might stand behind the Specie Circular and would veto legislation to recharter the BUS.[45] But did this mean he would support the hard-money advocates of a "constitutional currency" who pointed to the U.S. Constitution, which enumerated: "No State shall ... emit Bills of Credit; make any Thing but gold and silver Coin a tender in Payment of Debts"?[46] In other words, would he end the state-chartered banking system? The ambiguity of these economic pronouncements was brought into sharp relief by his straight-forward vow to "resist the slightest interference with [slavery] in the States where it exists." Van Buren's abstruseness, except on slavery, was coupled with the obsequious language that had advanced him through the back-rooms of politics. "In receiving from the people the sacred trust twice confided to my illustrious predecessor," he concluded:

I know that I cannot expect to perform the arduous task with equal ability and success. But, united as I have been in his counsels, a daily witness of his exclusive and unsurpassed devotion to his country's welfare, agreeing with him in sentiments which his countrymen have warmly supported, and permitted to partake largely of his confidence, I may hope that somewhat of the same cheering approbation will be found to attend upon my path.[47]

In office for a few minutes, he was already suggesting his reelection. Hushed, vague, and smarmy, the new president's speech avowed his principles more in its style than in its substance.

"Wall Street was a little Bedlam," declared a New York correspondent of the *National Intelligencer* describing the arrival of Van Buren's address. The report continued, "all day after the message arrived in town, which was about 8 A. M., the crowds in and about the Wall street printing offices were immense. Ten thousand copies of the address were soon put in circulation. The interest of the address died with the reading of it. People are disappointed in it; his opponents agreeable, his partisans otherwise."[48]

To the Whigs at the *New-York Spectator*, the document was full of "non-committalism."[49] The defensive Democratic *Washington Globe* reprinted an article that assured "We would not spare a line or a letter" of the "masterly production" but only pointed to Van Buren's "one pledge" regarding slavery as a "declaration" of the "firmness with which he will administer the Government."[50] With slightly less enthusiasm for Van Buren's text, the *New York Herald* quoted Shakespeare, "it is 'words, words, words.' It tells nothing – reveals nothing – advises nothing – recommends nothing. It is the prettiest piece of nothing that ever came from a Talleyrand." If the *Herald* characterized Van Buren as a diplomatic "Talleyrand," the paper described Jackson as a "Napoleon," whose presidency was "like a career of a hero in a romance."[51] To Hone, Jackson was the villain rather than the hero and the one problem with Van Buren's "very good" inaugural address. "I should have said Hurrah! for Martin the first," he granted, "if he could only have kept himself quiet about the old Lion who is now about to drag his reluctant steps away from the Den."[52] Offering Americans a speech about which Democrats could find almost nothing to praise and Whigs could almost cheer, the new president did not need to commit to policies because he knew that the "old Lion" was about to let loose a final roar.

According to the *National Intelligencer*, a pamphlet arrived in the Whig newspaper's Washington office the same morning as the inauguration. The paper reported, "The Farewell Address makes four-fifths of the pamphlet; and the Inaugural Address is absolutely overlaid by the mass of it. It would have been at least more respectful to the new president, it appears to us, to have published his Address independently, and not as a sort of *rider*, merely to the address of the Ex-President."[53] As merely a "rider" rather than the main contract, Van Buren proved evasive even in his first act as president.

Both parties' newspapers printed Jackson's farewell. His detractors labeled the long tract "a stretch of vanity perfectly ludicrous, and a degree of self applause amounting to arrogance," whereas Democratic supporters praised "his last political legacy" and recommended "every American reader to peruse it again and again."[54] Even the *Globe* textually foregrounded Jackson as the five-column farewell pushed the inaugural's last half column onto a subsequent page. Before Jackson, the only president to issue a farewell address had been George Washington. That address guided American foreign policy for half a century; Jackson hoped for a similar immortality.

Although he discussed topics such as Indian removal, slavery, and nullification, Jackson devoted the largest section to currency and banking.

Siding with his hard-money supporters, Jackson claimed that history had illustrated "the mischiefs and dangers of a paper currency." He argued, "The paper system being founded on public confidence, and having of itself no intrinsic value, it is liable to great and sudden fluctuations." While praising the nation's "intimate commercial connections with every part of the civilized world" and its "general prosperity," Jackson heaped ignominy on the paper that facilitated America's global trade.[55]

Without the mobility of bills of exchange, the nation would be left "without commerce, without credit," two of Jackson's dystopian predictions for the end result of sectional tensions. Yet by decentralizing America's financial system, Jackson left the nation with no organized means of checking the "ebbs and flows in the currency." Even if the business elite were, as he pronounced, intending to use the paper money system "as an engine to undermine [citizens'] free institutions," Jackson's declaration of a Democratic war on paper was not going to save the nation from an external threat. Although Jackson saw the fact that the banks "are competitors in business, and no one of them exercise dominion over the rest" as a positive attribute of his financial democratization, this decentralization left American financial institutions unable to function nationally at a moment when their most significant foreign trade partner constructed adverse international financial policies.[56]

Jackson explicitly delegated the power of financial regulation to the people rather than to a government institution. He echoed the nearly universal belief in individual economic responsibility: "it is to yourselves that you must look for safety, and the means of guarding and perpetuating your free institutions. In your hands is rightfully placed the sovereignty of the country, and to you every one placed in authority is ultimately responsible." In stark contrast with the British government's delegation of the BOE as the guardian of the nation's currency, Jackson argued that the American people bore the responsibility of protecting their financial system. He insisted that the press provided the people with the possibility of making informed decisions that did not completely rely on the information conveyed by "the moneyed interest."[57]

Of all the individuals responsible for protecting the nation's financial system, Jackson most trusted himself. At the end of February, a bill to rescind the Specie Circular passed both houses of Congress, but Jackson refused to sign it. This was his true farewell message to the merchants, bankers, and brokers who hoped that this new bill would ease the pressure in American money markets. "True to his principles," Hone thundered in his diary, "[Jackson] has shown his disregard to the expressed will of [the people's] representatives by putting in his pocket an act rescinding the treasury order, which is the principal cause of our fiscal embarrassments." He concluded, "there is much speculation as to the course of the new president on this interesting subject."[58] The *National Intelligencer* asked, "Will not Mr. Van Buren repeal the odious Treasury order? Has he no mercy for the country? No feelings of independence? No wish to alleviate distress? Or is he still determined to walk in the footsteps of his predecessor, at the expense of hazarding the best interests of the country?"[59] By blaming the old and imploring the new president, these writers framed federal policy in individual terms. Moreover, communication about these political speeches fed Americans' financial uncertainty and mingled with the first whiffs of even more disturbing news.

* * *

On March 3, 1837, long before Jackson's address arrived in New Orleans, the newspapers reported on a local politician's attempt to regulate what the former president called the "ebbs and flows in the currency."[60] Louisiana State Representative and Chairman of the Committee of Finance Edmond Forstall proposed a bill that would, according to the *New Orleans Bee*, "place the circulating medium of this State on a footing of perfect safety from all fluctuation." The legislation sought to define a ratio between paper and specie for the state's banks. The *Bee* published its hope that Forstall's law would provide a "salutary influence upon the currency of the State."[61]

This was New Orleans's typical optimistic buzz. Self-interest motivated Forstall; the health of the state's finances would be a pleasant side effect. He had recently been elected president of the Citizens' Bank of Louisiana and proposed the law to protect the specie his bank anticipated receiving from the Dutch bond sales he had negotiated during the summer of 1836. His timing, however, was disastrous. At the same moment that he addressed the Louisiana legislature, F. de Lizardi & Co., his London-based associates and the intermediary for the Citizens' Bank loan, begged the BOE for assistance. This coincidence was not Forstall's fault; he could not know about events in London. But like his fellow New Orleanian boosters, he was counting his specie before it had been deposited.

After months of rosy-tinted views, New Orleans faced reality the next day. On Saturday, March 4, 1837, drenching rain doused the nearly finished Citizens' Bank building. Behind the columned edifice, Forstall informed his board of directors that he had been invited to an unprecedented meeting of the city's sixteen bank presidents to be held the next morning, a Sunday. The purpose of the meeting was "to take into consideration the state of the affairs of Messrs. Hermann, Briggs & Co."[62] The potential failure of any single firm could have waited until Monday. Hermann, Briggs, however, was part of a network of cotton factors that monopolized the region's exports. If this firm failed, it would bring down the network.

The partners of Hermann, Briggs also owned Briggs, Lacoste & Co. in Natchez, Mississippi. Throughout the fall and winter, Briggs, Lacoste had consigned cotton from southwestern planters and extended them credit for their fall purchases by writing bills of exchange drawn on Hermann, Briggs. Approximately $230,000 of these bills passed through just one bank in Natchez during the winter of 1836–37; several million dollars in this form was in circulation. The partners floated paper back and forth between their firms, paying for one promise to pay in Natchez with another promise to pay in New Orleans. Louis Florian Hermann also traded such "accommodation bills" or "kites" with his father and his brothers who were affiliated with other firms. The Hermann family also endorsed one another's bills of exchange. Bound through blood and paper, the Hermann family's firms were inextricably intertwined.[63]

Kites and endorsements had kept Hermann, Briggs afloat since the sinking of the *Fort Adams*. The firm counted on the proceeds of high-priced cotton sales in Liverpool to safely draw in their kites, but they needed more time. The partners appealed to the banks of New Orleans for greater discounting privileges and an extension of their existing loans.[64] Hermann, Briggs presented the bankers with an estimated debt of $3 million, although the partners later calculated that they owed $6 million.[65] This imprecise sum represented between 6 percent and 20 percent of the banking capital of the state of Louisiana.[66] This state of affairs could not wait until Monday. Indeed, by the next week, several firms located in Louisiana and Mississippi with principals surnamed Hermann, Reynolds, Marshall, Byrne, Barrett, and Nathan all asked the banks of New Orleans for extended time to repay their debts.[67] Despite the interstate implications of this network's failure, local banks offered the only source of institutional relief.

Inside the Sunday meetings, bankers endeavored to calculate the debts and assets of the firms. This was a Sisyphean task given the fluctuation in cotton prices, the instability of credit markets, and the unpredictability of intelligence arriving from elsewhere. Nevertheless, the bank presidents needed this information to decide whether or not to loan more money to the Hermann network. Armed with highly confidential uncertainties, the sixteen bank presidents left the Sunday meeting to report to their boards of directors. By Monday, at least one hundred men deliberated behind scattered neoclassical facades. The bankers and the partners of Hermann, Briggs surely aimed for secrecy to maintain the value of the firm's paper, but with more directors and less security, the banks of New Orleans suffered more than the BOE from the problem of information control.[68]

Although no Committee of Inspection left documentation of the pathways of rumor in New Orleans, whispered speculations were recorded on paper. Four days after the meeting of the banks, at half past ten a.m. on March 8, 1837, two important pieces of mail left New Orleans in the satchel of the express mail carrier headed to New York City. The first, a private letter, cost the sender at least seventy-five cents to send. The second, a newspaper column from the New Orleans *True American*, traveled for free. Just as the post office charged two rates, these messages were written for different purposes and dissimilar audiences. Despite these differences, the letter and the column created the same result: many panics and a local crisis.

* * *

During the evening of March 16, eight days after the mail left New Orleans, the letter, addressed to the bill brokerage firm of J. L. & S. Joseph & Co., arrived in New York.[69] In the letter, Thomas Barrett, the principal of a New Orleans firm that included members of the Hermann family, relayed news of the Hermann, Briggs failure and reported on the Sunday bankers' meeting. The letter was a private message from a trusted correspondent who offered an account of the firm's finances based on existing records.[70]

March 17 was, as one newspaper expressed, "the 'beginning of the end' in New York."[71] That morning, J. L. & S. Joseph & Co. immediately announced its failure and cited the Hermann, Briggs suspension as the direct cause of its embarrassment. The Joseph failure would eventually transcend the Hermann debacle in terms of the amount of debt and the geographical reach of its commercial entanglements. When J. L. Joseph filed for bankruptcy protection in 1842, his firm had failed to pay millions of dollars to creditors from Paris to Havana.[72] Nevertheless, the Josephs must have interpreted the letter announcing the Hermann failure as a windfall.

Although the Josephs, like every mercantile firm, traded on credit that far exceeded their liquid capital, they claimed to be in the black. Indeed, only two days earlier, the Josephs had reported to the Rothschilds, their London correspondents and creditors, without indicating any troubles.[73]

Despite their claims, the Josephs were not innocent bystanders doomed to failure by the news from New Orleans. As skillful brokers of confidence, they manipulated the news of their financial wreck and the opinions of the public in an attempt to salvage their fortunes.

Just as the financial pressure that pervaded Anglo-American money markets in the spring of 1837 had developed gradually, so too the Josephs' problems began in the minds of their creditors long before the mid-March arrival of the letter from New Orleans. In August 1836, after Samuel Hermann's interview, the Rothschilds informed the Josephs that they were "at present desirous of not extending our business." When the Josephs provided Hermann with credit anyway, the Londoners began to doubt the New Yorkers' fidelity. In letter after letter, the Rothschilds asked the Josephs "to be good enough to curtail your transactions with us." Finally, in early February 1837, after a rift over several hundred shares of New Orleans bank stock, the Rothschilds expressed their "decided disapprobation" in the New Yorkers, officially withdrew their credit, and required the repayment of significant advances. When the Josephs received this news a few days before March 15, 1837, they mirrored the response of the Rothschilds the previous summer and replied that a recent "death in the family" prevented them from acquiescing to the Londoners' demands.[74]

Indeed, the news from the Rothschilds was only one of several blows to the Josephs that week. At 1:00 a.m. on March 14, 1837, their already leased but not yet occupied brand new office building collapsed "with a crash like that of an earthquake." They lost $50,000 worth of marble, granite, brick, and labor. Hone noted that the Josephs were lucky: "at any time during six hours of the day the loss of many lives would have been nearly inevitable. Lenders and borrowers, shavers and shavees, would have been crushed *stone* dead."[75] For the Josephs, however, death had already struck much closer to home when it claimed J. L. Joseph's only son.[76] The Josephs dealt with all of these calamities privately. Death and disaster could certainly explain harried appearances for a little while. Financiers may have suspected the Josephs' woes, but as one newspaper reported, "To the public such a suspicion never entered their minds."[77] And the Josephs told no one that they had lost their London backers.

Without the Rothschilds' credit and deeply indebted to them, the Josephs were doomed to failure; by hiding this fact, they gained a few more days of active trading. Ultimately, these actions worsened the eventual crisis by spreading bad paper and false information. But is it fair to blame the Josephs for acting in what they assumed to be their own best interest? Their failure should have instigated panic throughout the nation, but because of the letter from New Orleans, they managed to escape that dubious distinction. Americans would cite conditions in New Orleans rather than New York as the reason pressure transformed into personal panics and local crises. New Yorkers might thank the Josephs for looking like victims rather than perpetrators, thus saving their city's reputation.

Early in the morning of March 17, the Josephs announced their failure and released news of the Hermann failure to all within earshot of New York City's financial district. The next morning, the postal system would begin to spread accounts of the Joseph failure outside the local area, but on the day it was made known, news traveled exclusively by word of mouth around Manhattan. The newspapers nonetheless preserved evidence of how panic spread. "Early in the forenoon the word was passed from street to street, and from counting-room to counting-room, that the firm of J. L. & S. Josephs & Co. had stopped in consequence of the failures in New Orleans," recounted one.[78] "As soon as it was known, the news flew like lightning – people rubbed their eyes, and would scarcely believe the reality of the fact. Crowds collected in Wall Street – and that busy avenue was filled with anxious faces through the live long day," reported another, which also noted, "The street is full of rumors, every one more frightful than another."[79] The Joseph failure sent a pulse of shock, fear, and gossip through the city.

The sources from this earliest period of panic convey the uncertainty of financiers. On receiving conflicting letters from his New York correspondents, one Bostonian wrote, "the accounts are so various & exaggerated it is difficult to ascertain the *Real* from the imaginary."[80] "Real" information was unavailable, but real effects of rumors were visible in the stock market where prices fell an estimated 10 percent. Financial uncertainty spread beyond the mercantile elite; as one newspaper reported, even "the hardy laborer looks with distrust upon *all promises to pay*."[81] "It has never fallen to our lot to witness such a general panic as existed in the city during the whole of the day," commented another correspondent who believed panic to be an overreaction. He continued,

Although there was certainly some cause for apprehension in consequence of the extended operations of the House of the Messrs Joseph and the influence which their failure and the failures in New Orleans might have on those connected with them; yet we must be permitted to say, that the alarm was far greater than was warranted by the facts of the case.[82]

This writer certainly had no means of assessing whether or not the panic was justified because on March 17, 1837, no one, not even the Josephs, knew all the "facts of the case."

The Josephs, nevertheless, shaped New Yorkers' understanding of their failure. Hone's diary reflected the success of their spin. As long-term causes, Hone indicted Democratic policies and the New York commercial community for trusting the Jewish partners of J. L. & S. Joseph, who were "almost strangers among us, and of that class or nation in whom we have no great reason to place too much confidence." But most directly, Hone blamed the Hermann failure:

> The great crisis is near at hand, if it has not already arrived, the banking house of J. L. & S. Joseph, the people whose new Edifice in Wall Street fell on Monday (a sort of forerunner of misfortune), stopped payment today and occasioned a great consternation in Wall Street, for their business has been enormous, and as it consisted principally of operations in Internal Exchanges, the merchants, jobbers, grocers, and other regular dealers are all implicated. The immediate cause of this disaster was the intelligence received from New Orleans by this day's mail of the stoppage of the House of Hermann & Co. and others connected with them, for whom the Josephs are under acceptances to the amount of two millions of dollars.[83]

Hone's diary entry testified to the certainty with which New Yorkers viewed the Joseph failure and the failures that would inevitably follow as deriving from the news from New Orleans.

The Josephs cultivated this notion and argued that good news from New Orleans could restore their business to health. They wrote to the Rothschilds, "Tomorrow's mail, we have strong hopes, will bring the cheering intelligence that . . . [the Hermanns] have resumed their payments, in which case we shall complete the arrangements immediately to resume our own."[84] Hone recorded in his diary, "It is rumored today that favorable accounts have been received from New Orleans which may enable the Josephs to resume their payments."[85] Indeed, with the afternoon arrival of the express mail, the Josephs received a second letter from New Orleans that mentioned a potential bailout for the Hermann firms. They immediately "permitted" its publication.[86]

This publication of private news by the press spread hope and faith in the Josephs' solvency through New York City. According to the *New York Daily Express*, the Josephs "immediately declared that they would resume payments," but a group of "the most distinguished of our bankers and merchants were of opinion that the step would be premature and strenuously advocated a more cautious line of conduct." Yielding to this advice, the Josephs announced that they would wait for "further intelligence from New Orleans." Praising the bill brokers as "princely-hearted men" with "the courage to meet the crisis," the *New York Daily Express* concluded, "Messrs. Josephs, in thus acting have sacrificed their feelings to the cooler judgment of the gentlemen in whose keeping they have placed their honor, and on whose friendship they have the most perfect reliance."[87] Less sacrifice and more scheme, the Josephs manipulated this negotiation with "the gentlemen" so that they appeared both eager and able to resume payments (even though they could not do so) and not at all at fault for the spark that set off the city's crisis (even though they were).

Just as the Josephs purposefully directed anxiety toward Hermann, Briggs, local newspaper editors brokered confidence in New York by printing the rumor that the source of the financial crisis was New Orleans. As Americans from Maine to Louisiana read reprints of these columns and learned of the Joseph failure, they would continue to trust New York's financiers. Canal Street, not Wall Street, would be considered the source of the panic.[88]

* * *

Whereas the New York papers piqued their readers' interest in news from New Orleans, the majority of the New Orleans papers offered no reprieve from anxiety. Out of what we can only assume to be an effort to protect the fragile local economy and the city's national reputation, most New Orleans newspapers did not report the local failures until late March, and even then they refused to provide names of failed firms or estimates of dollar amounts.[89] But John Gibson, editor of the *True American*, decided not to wait for the bankers to release an official account of the Hermann failure before publishing this news in his paper. On March 8, before the mid-morning departure of the New Orleans express mail bound for New York, Gibson cut a short paragraph from the previous day's newspaper to send to editors in New York; Washington, D.C.; and elsewhere. The excerpt headed north in a mail carrier's satchel alongside the letter addressed to the Josephs. Gibson's column would become the premier source of public information about the failure in New Orleans.[90]

Gibson's timing was perfect. The column offered newspaper editors around the country the latest news from New Orleans – just what their readers wanted in the days immediately following the Joseph failure. Any news about the failure in New Orleans that reached New York would have heightened the tense atmosphere created by the Joseph failure, but Gibson's column was particularly anxiety inducing. It provided very few specifics, and the details it did contain were wrong:

We are fallen on singular and anomalous times. In the midst of unexampled prosperity, when all the avenues of trade are open, when money is abundant for the ordinary operations of commerce, we are called upon to record several extensive failures involving an amount alarming to the general credit. On Saturday, one of our largest and most influential houses failed for SEVEN MILLIONS, carrying with it full *five millions more*. When and where this is to stop we know not. The rage for speculation has been so great, that there is no estimating the amount of responsibilities incurred. It does not appear to have been confined to real estate.[91]

Although Gibson omitted the name of the firm, it was true that a large house had failed. The dollar amount he included, however, exceeded the amount reported at the banker's meeting by at least $1 million. His estimate of additional failures doubled the sum under consideration by the bankers and represented more than a quarter of the state's total banking capital. This was an enormous overestimate of a sum already so high that it frightened the bank presidents enough to make them hold meetings on Sunday.

Where did the *True American* get this estimate? The answer must have been a leak from the bankers' meetings that had spent some time in the rumor mill. In a city of less than 100,000 people where the newspapermen worked only a few blocks from the exchange, which in turn was only a few blocks from the banks, information traveled fast. Gibson could stay in the building that housed the office of the *True American* to learn the daily commercial gossip. Situated on the corner of Magazine and Natchez Streets in the heart of the American section of the city, Bank's Arcade contained Gibson's newspaper office alongside offices of notaries, brokers, and attorneys. If information did not pass through walls, rumors certainly circulated in the building's shops, billiard hall, restaurant, and coffee room. Clerks, editors, and lesser merchants formed a local information network as they drank mint juleps and gin slings.[92]

Like their elite neighbors, who discussed the failure inside the city's banks, the men at Bank's Arcade wanted to employ the information to suit their own interests. But they knew very little. As Gibson would later complain, "it argues a strange state of things in the commercial world, when the operations of trade are made a matter of profound secrecy." Writing specifically of the public's curiosity about the failures, he grumbled, "everything is so involved in mist and secrecy in New Orleans, that it is almost impossible to get correct information." In fact, official information about the Hermann failure seemed never to surface. Another paper in the city would complain almost a month after the Hermann failure that "the first *definite* information we have been able to

FIGURE 9. In 2012, only one segment of Bank's Arcade survives at the corner of
Magazine and Natchez Streets in New Orleans. (Photograph by author.)

receive in relation to the extensive failures which have occurred in New
Orleans we obtain from the Louisville [Kentucky] Journal." While they
waited for "definite" and "correct" information about their own city to
arrive from elsewhere, New Orleanians speculated about their fate.[93]

Although they recognized how disastrous the failure would be for
business in New Orleans, the circle of men who gathered at Bank's
Arcade probably harbored some joy at seeing the city's biggest cotton
factors fail. For men who occupied the lower rungs of New Orleans's
commercial ladder, the failure promised new opportunities. In the first
weeks of the panic, Gibson hoped that the crisis would not "inflict severe
evils upon the middle class of dealers." He identified much more deserving failures: "For the last ten or twelve years, a monopoly of the cotton
business has been steadily growing up in Canal Street, till it has engrossed
more than half the capital provided for the community." The end of the
monopoly, he argued, would provide opportunity for the "industrious
and enterprising." While cultivating hope, Gibson's paper also fed
the uncertainties that led to panic through sentences such as "When
and where this is to stop we know not." As Gibson literally cut

these words out of the paper and sent them northward, he certainly did not try to stop the spreading of frightening rumors.[94]

On March 17, the same day that the Josephs failed, the *True American*'s column appeared in the *New York Herald* and the Washington *National Intelligencer*; both papers were sources for newspaper articles reprinted throughout the country. Arriving in these northeastern cities, the Bank's Arcade rumors entered the Jacksonian media cycle of newspaper exchanges that followed the routes of the post office emanating out from the nation's political and financial centers. The Richmond *Enquirer* in Virginia and the Tallahassee *Floridian* reprinted the *True American*'s column on Friday, March 18, the day after the Joseph failure. Over the next month, more and more Americans read Gibson's account of the crisis. Between March 18 and April 10, newspapers as far as Montpellier, Vermont, and St. Louis, Missouri, reproduced either the *True American* column or accounts of the New York panic that cited the Hermann failure as the cause. On April 15, readers of the *North Western Gazette & Galena Advertiser*, the newspaper of a lead mining town on the western edge of the westernmost state in the North, opened their newspaper to discover that they had been living through a financial crisis for nearly a month; even the last people in America to get the news learned to blame New Orleans. Regardless of party sponsorship, religious affiliation, or geographic location, the nation's newspapers carried Gibson's account of the failures in New Orleans. Accounts of the Joseph failure that also blamed New Orleans often followed the printing of Gibson's column; together these accounts solidified the idea that New Orleans was the starting point of the nation's panic.[95]

Rumors, however, spread for particular reasons. Just like Ormes and the Josephs, Gibson had his own motivations for setting his column into motion. Some New Orleans newspaper at some point would have printed an article on the failure, but Gibson did it quickly and with intention. Why did Gibson send these rumors to the *New York Herald* and the *National Intelligencer*? This choice reflected his ideas about the rapidly changing American economy. His reason for publishing such a sensational column could scarcely have been immediate profit because the paper was sold through semiannual subscriptions.[96] There are three more likely reasons.

First, in an odd combination that spanned the national political spectrum, the *True American* was a Whig paper with Loco-Foco sympathies. Gibson's politics, as he described them, were "on the side of the country, and of the South."[97] The *True American* constantly exchanged columns with the nation's other anti-Jackson papers, including the

National Intelligencer (which supported elitist, pro-national bank Whigs) and the *New York Herald* (which generally supported radically democratic, anti-bank Loco-Focos). Thus, Gibson's political imperative of anti-state banking may have outweighed his loyalty to the city's commercial best interest, a force that presumably explains the silence of the other papers. As the partners in Hermann, Briggs and the other large cotton brokerage houses filled the directorships of the state banks, Gibson had a political incentive to spread news of the disintegration of what he called "the credit aristocracy," who cultivated "overweening confidence."[98] Had the panic been less universal, his customers would have profited from the deterioration of confidence in the leaders of New Orleans's commercial community. In addition, Gibson's political allegiance corresponded with his profit motives. He recognized his readers as "independent and industrious" New Orleanians who struggled to compete in the market without the extensive networks of the more established merchants. As their informant, he sought to provide "observations" that he believed "salutary to the public weal." Thus, his definition of the "public weal" differed from that of other newspaper editors, and this might have prompted him to publish rumors about the Hermann failure.[99]

In addition to party politics and class agendas, the *True American* had a second more local political reason for printing its column on the failure. As its title indicates, the paper advocated "true" American-ness – a Protestant, Anglo-American-ness – in a city undergoing a contest for domination between a fading Francophone elite and upstart Anglophone Americans. The men behind the Hermann failure did not have English roots, neither were they Christian; they were immigrant German Jews. Although later *True American* articles would occasionally insinuate that Jews caused the panic, at this early stage, merely reporting on the failure was enough to unsettle this important non-"true" American firm. Politics both national and local, cultural prejudices, and the profits associated with advocating these views may have motivated the *True American* to break the silence observed by most New Orleans papers.[100]

Although the publication of the rumor did not increase Gibson's short-term profits, his third and final motivation could have been a strategy for long-term profits. By publishing the rumor and then sending the slip northward, his paper might rise in the esteem of other more nationally significant newspapers, thus encouraging them to send clippings from their papers directly to the *True American*. As Gibson explained, "it is a matter of course to furnish all our exchange correspondents every morning with slips, containing all editorial matter, ship news, market, etc. by express mail."[101]

Gibson bragged that at the office of the *True American*, "slips from seventy-six [newspaper] offices are regularly received."[102] By touting the most current political news, the *True American* could battle its local rivals for subscriptions. Eighteen newspapers were published in New Orleans in 1837, eight of which had been founded during the previous year.[103] Competition for annual subscriptions was fierce. Advertisers consistently filled three of the *True American*'s four large pages, offering a glimmer of truth to Gibson's claim that the paper was "more extensively read than any other journal in the city." Nevertheless, the *True American* included numerous appeals to readers to buy their own subscriptions rather than reading their neighbors' papers. One way to increase the number of paying readers was to tout the time-sensitive nature of the content in the paper and the advantage its first perusal could provide. As newspapers could send columns in the express mail for free, Gibson must have hoped to gain an edge over his competition and win over subscribers for the cost of paper and ink.[104]

Calculating and confident, Gibson's text conveyed terrifying news to most Americans, but Gibson did not print the only account of the failure circulating among New Orleanians.[105] One other newspaper saw profit in printing the city's rumors. In print for only two months at the time of the Hermann failure, the *Picayune* was the South's first penny press, and its editors worked hard to win readers, attract advertisers, and sign up subscribers. Without the patronage of a political party or long-term advertisers, the editors crafted a small paper that could be easily hawked on the street. To entice daily buyers, the *Picayune* devoted much of its column space to humorous anecdotes from life in New Orleans, reports on horse racing, and theater reviews.[106] Buried within columns covering a duel, a mysterious smell of ham and eggs, and a satirical encounter with the devil's servant, the March 8, 1837, *Picayune* featured a paragraph on the "reports" circulating around town about extensive failures.

Although the *Picayune* listed the same exaggerated sum as the *True American* for the "heaviest failure which ever occurred in the United States," it also reported the rumor of an additional failure. "Reports are in town," it asserted, "of the failure of one of the most extensive banking-houses in New York, that of the Josephs." As the Josephs did not fail until March 17, the rumor was false. Perhaps the appearance of this rumor indicates that the Hermanns attempted to redeem their reputations by blaming their New York correspondents, the same strategy employed by the Josephs. Although this posturing may have worked in New York City, the *Picayune*'s editors were not convinced. Despite printing the reports of the Joseph failure, the editors believed that "these rumors are groundless." Why print groundless rumors? Over the course of the next two months, as they reported record sales, the editors of the *Picayune* confirmed that rumors of catastrophe – fear of an uncertain future – sold newspapers.

Although printing a groundless rumor for profit insinuates market savvy, the reason the editors offered for the rumor's groundlessness implies their unfamiliarity with the operation of finance. The *Picayune*'s editors denied not that the Josephs *had* failed, but that they *could* fail. They argued that the Josephs should be safe from failure given the "extensive connections of these gentlemen, both in Europe and America."[107] The editors did not realize that the Josephs failed precisely because of the extensiveness of their connections. During the boom, the webs of connection that tied together mercantile houses, banks, cotton factors, and manufacturing enterprises inspired confidence and assured profits for all involved. But as soon as trade partners began to doubt the American market, these connections transformed into a web of failure trapping almost everyone involved in trade. Despite their integration of market principles into the newspaper business, the men at the *Picayune* misunderstood the structure of commercial relationships.

Newspapermen spread information about the financial world but were not necessarily its most skilled interpreters. Nevertheless, the crisis in the spring of 1837 spread not only through financial networks but also through networks of print. Without a printing press of its own, the two-month-old *Picayune* was published on the presses of the *True American*. One of the editors of the *Picayune* had been a former employee of the *True American*, thus gaining permission to use the press and access to the *True American*'s sources, however erroneous. The editors of both papers tapped into the rumor mill at Bank's Arcade, a site of physical connections where men ate, drank, and gossiped together. Meanwhile, the two editors of the *Picayune* were former colleagues at the *National Intelligencer*, the Washington, D.C., press, which through reprinting the column from the *True American* helped spread rumors and panic throughout the nation. John Gibson may have traded his physical facilities for an introduction to the editors of the *National Intelligencer*. Much like the commercial network of the Hermanns, the Josephs, and the Rothschilds, this network of New Orleans newspapermen relied on personal connections to do business and, in this case, to spread financial ideas to the broader public.[108] In March 1837, panic-inducing news traveled along these paths of people and print.

* * *

On learning the news of the Hermann and Joseph failures, the American public, like their fellow citizens in New York, panicked. In Baltimore, the

Rothschilds' correspondents reported, "the effect of the late extensive failures at the South and North has produced a want of confidence."[109] From the East Coast to the western hinterlands, the news generated anxiety and uncertainty. In Philadelphia, a correspondent of the secretary of the treasury explained, "No language can paint the dismay of the community." Despite its inaccurate portraiture, language not only transmitted the crisis from one place to another but also constituted panic as individuals struggled to find the right word to describe their dismay.[110]

Even one of the financial system's most ardent critics could not help but spread panic. After less than a month in retirement from the presidency, Andrew Jackson learned of the failure in New Orleans. In a long letter, he expressed his concern to his successor. Based on rumors circulating in Tennessee, the former president described his uncertainty about the extent of the failure: "it is said by some [Hermann, Briggs failed] for five millions, by others ten." Jackson feared that the uncertainties surrounding this failure would lead to an overwhelming demand on the nation's banks for specie, which could affect the solvency of the federal government. The possibilities were terrifying for everyone, even for the president who had dismantled the nation's centralized financial system.[111] For the next two months, the terror of financial uncertainty triggered by the news of actual or potential failures created personal panics and local crises with national and international ramifications.

For readers of Francis Wayland's textbook, the reason imprecise information about the failures in London, New Orleans, and New York provoked crisis wherever it traveled was obvious. Wayland cautioned:

> Now, it must at once be perceived, that the opinion of the value of stocks is made up very much from expectations of profit or loss, or anticipations of increase or diminution of risk. Hence, a rumor of war; of the failure of a company, or of a bank; of the probable insolvency of a government; or the news of a gain or loss of a battle, may make a very considerable difference in the price of those stocks which would be affected by such information. Hence, the great liability to fraud, in all the operations of the stock market.[112]

Wayland's recognition of the role of rumors in altering the value of stocks could also be applied to bills of exchange, bonds, or commodities. The process of interpretation, of forming "the opinion of the value" based on "expectations" and "anticipations," was made even more challenging because of rumors. "When such rumors actually arise without collusion," Wayland wrote, imagining precisely the layers of rumor, gossip, and print involved in the stories of failure surrounding March 4, 1837, "it requires great sagacity to judge of the probability of their truth, and thus to buy or sell, according to the true judgment to be formed from the facts actually in possession of the community."[113] The lack of facts and the inability of even insiders to form "true judgment" left all whose fortunes were connected with transnational trade with an acute sense of financial uncertainty. For individuals who held themselves responsible for their success or failure, the resulting anxiety proved overwhelming.

Phrenologists had their own means of explaining the spread of a financial crisis. They suggested that "Cautiousness," the mental organ that controlled one's assessment of risk, could be enlarged, producing "doubts, irresolution, and wavering ... A great and involuntary activity of it produces a *panic*, – a state in which the mind is hurried away by an irresistible emotion of fear, for which no adequate external cause exists."[114] Individually panicked people could not control their state, but the situation only worsened when they came into contact with people with enlarged "Sympathy" organs. Phrenology explained:

The very sight of a panic-stricken person, when we do not know the cause which has given rise to the alarm, excites a general uneasiness about our own safety; and if a great number of persons together, and at the same instant, perceive the terrified expression, it instantly rouses the faculty of Cautiousness to its highest pitch of activity in all of them, and produces the most intense feelings of dread and alarm.[115]

Panics, according to phrenology, were the product of the dire combination of two enlarged mental organs and not the product of any form of controllable human behavior.

But what separated many panicked people from a singular panic? As the failures that began in March escalated in size and scope during the two months that followed, individuals tried to protect themselves through actions that could be viewed as panicked responses to the changing times. As financial uncertainty set the panicked into motion, rising economic uncertainty prompted them to ask new questions about the causes of failure and to invent a single national event that would become known as the Panic of 1837.

CHAPTER 5

The Many Panics in 1837

"RIGHTEOUSNESS EXALTETH A NATION," exclaimed the motto of the *Colored American* below the date of its first issue, March 4, 1837. Of all the abolitionists who supported this mouthpiece of New York City's free black community, Arthur Tappan contributed the most money.[1] He was, after all, the president of the American Anti-Slavery Society, and he knew a great deal about experimenting with newspapers after his own efforts to turn the New York *Journal of Commerce* into an organ of Christian business journalism. More importantly, he had the money to devote to such causes. The profitable silk importing business he ran with his brother Lewis provided him with plenty of funds for his evangelical philanthropy. The Tappan brothers supported the American Tract Society, the American Bible Society, and the American Temperance Union. All of these organizations used print to convince individual Americans to take responsibility for their own lives and for the nation's soul. Northerners who believed in the mission of reforming the morals of their neighbors could hardly imagine more righteous businessmen.

Yet less than two months after the launch of the *Colored American*, the Tappan brothers failed. Their assets had become so illiquid, so tied to the collapsing credit system, that they could not pay their debts. Like the Joseph and Hermann failures, the Tappan failure signaled a change in the course of the panic in 1837.

Before the Tappans suspended their business, other individuals were doing everything they could to avoid failure. From dunning to dying, people in New Orleans, New York, and London chose continually more drastic measures over the course of their two-month wait for unusually slow transatlantic news. Their actions testify to their belief in the system of individual economic responsibility. They each calculated their own responsibility for the hard times: whether or not they had sinned, speculated, lived beyond their means, or acted dishonestly. Although some investors already argued that they were victims with no agency over their financial fates, the Tappan failure forced many to reevaluate the relationship between failure and individual behavior. Americans overwhelmed with financial uncertainty added to their burdens a new economic uncertainty. They searched for a larger system, something beyond individual behavior that could explain and take the blame for the crisis. Not even a decade old, the two-party system of mass politics offered an easy answer to questions of economic causation.

For people actively attempting to prevent their failure, panic was plural. Panic might look irrational in the aggregate, but each man and woman made conscious choices to try to save honor or money and sometimes both. The moral ambiguity of the Tappan failure nevertheless fed a desire for exculpation. It suggested a cause for the crisis larger than any one person's choices – a single cause for a single panic.

* * *

March 4, 1837, was, according to Philip Hone, "a dark and melancholy day in the annals of my family." Not yet aware of the simultaneous meetings of bankers in New Orleans and London, Hone learned that his son's firm had failed. He wrote in his diary:

Brown & Hone stopped payment to-day, and called a meeting of their creditors. My eldest son has lost the capital I gave him, and I am implicated as Endorser for them to a fearful amount. The pressure of the times, the immense amount they have paid of extra interest, and the almost total failure of remittances have been the causes of their ruin. This is a heavy blow for me, and added to the difficulty I experience in raising money on my property to meet my own engagements, almost breaks me down, but I have the consolation to know, and the public cannot fail to know it also, that the good name which it has been the object of my life to establish, cannot be compromised in this manner.[2]

Hone convinced himself on the pages of his diary that neither his son's errors nor his own were to blame for the "heavy blow" he sustained. He counted on "the support of the almighty" and concluded, "above all I hope to continue to say, as I now do in the privacy of my own chamber and in the presence of my God alone, that I am not conscious of ever having committed a mean or dishonorable action. This reflection must and will sustain me."[3] As he filled the pages of his diary with internal debates over the blame for his personal panic, "unfounded" rumors about him spread as his "embarrassments increase[d] daily."[4] He confessed that dealing with the possibility of failing "has almost made me crazy."[5] "Why should I be in such a scrape?" he asked himself.[6] If Hone had always acted morally in his business practices, his tenuous financial state seemed to prove that he was a victim rather than an accomplice of the commercial crisis. Fearing insanity, Hone struggled with the possibility that his own behavior was to blame for his financial woes or, worse yet, that his moral behavior did not matter.

His son, however, clearly thought that his own behavior could make a difference. Like most merchants during the months of pressure in transatlantic money markets, Hone's son and his partners had been "shinning" to meet their debts. They had sought high-interest, short-term loans to pay immediate debts while they waited for their own debtors to pay up. Although shinning could save a business in good times, the pressure of the previous months ensured that interest rates were so high, trustworthy paper so rare, and the repayment of debts so unlikely that the costs of the loans were more than most businesses could bear.[7]

To alleviate the need for shinning, creditors dunned their debtors. Although Joshua Bates had been "desirous that our correspondents should pay up" since the autumn of 1836, less insightful creditors demanded payment in the aftermath of the Hermann and Joseph failures.[8] But these large commercial collapses cast doubt on the value of bills of exchange and other paper instruments. One debtor informed his creditor that he could not find reputable paper in New York; he traveled more than two hundred miles to Washington, D.C., to pursue "an arrangement to pay you your debt."[9]

Forced to wait for others to pay up, debtors begged their creditors for leniency.[10] A Boston bill broker dismissed pleas for leniency by insisting in religious terms that "it is too late for repentance. The day of reckoning must come."[11] Even the Josephs, eager "to preserve our fair fame and honor," argued that if their creditors "grant us proper and merited indulgence and give us time to turn a large amount of our unavailable assets into money, we trust that our estate will make a good exhibit." Their creditors found no "merit" in this plea and almost immediately engaged in litigation to seek fractional repayment of debts.[12]

Though creditors had a legal right to sue their debtors for payment, the only people who definitely profited by suits were lawyers. "The houses which have suspended payment are uniformly composed of men of unblemished reputation and good business talents. There is no reason to believe that they will not treat their creditors honestly," remarked one New York newspaper that cautioned against pursuing payment through the courts. "Let the unfortunate houses settle their own affairs," argued the editorial, "and the business will be done better and sooner, and cheaper, than by any other process."[13] Lawyers' fees and court costs would diminish the amount of money received by creditors.[14]

One English merchant traveling in America experienced such difficulties in recovering his firm's money that he railed against the "extreme laxity in the laws throughout America, with respect to enforcing payment of debts." He found the laws useless: "In every State the laws are different, and there are so many facilities for evading payment, that legal proceedings are rarely had recourse to." Without federal bankruptcy legislation, creditors in every state confronted different laws often designed to protect debtors. The Englishman found that "it is common for a debtor to pay some of his creditors and leave others unpaid; and debts of preference are constantly spoken of and recognized, although they presuppose what in England the law stigmatizes as fraud and dishonesty."[15]

With different bankruptcy laws in each state, debtors found themselves characterized as honorable in one place and scoundrels in another. Solomon Andrews, a cotton factor, bill broker, and slave dealer, was, however, a scoundrel everywhere. A perfect example of a man attempting to negotiate between the bankruptcy laws of two states, Andrews acted according to Alabama law in paying off his brother and his clerk before paying the close to a million dollars owed to his other creditors in New York, New Orleans, and elsewhere. This preference, seen as "bad faith" by his distant creditors, was legal in Alabama, where, as a witness testified, "a debtor has a right to prefer a creditor & he is considered by the community under a strong moral obligation to protect endorsers & other honorary creditors."[16] Andrews's family members and friends might have benefited from the laws in Alabama, but a different culture of debt prevailed in Louisiana.

When Andrews sold his office furniture and horse to his clerk, quit Mobile in the middle of the night, "employed the name of his clerk to disguise" his withdrawal of $58,000 from the New Orleans Planters Bank, and booked passage on a northern-bound steamboat, his creditors had him arrested for his debts in Louisiana.[17] He petitioned for bankruptcy under an 1808 law "for the relief of honest and unfortunate debtors." According to Louisiana law, insolvent debtors could be released from jail and their debts only after proving that they had not committed fraud. The point of the Louisiana law was that, as one lawyer explained, "the shackles are struck from the limbs of the debtor; a spunge [sic] put upon his debts;

and with fresh hopes and tutored weariness, his bark is once more set adrift upon the currents of trade."[18]

To return Andrews to the seas of commerce, a jury had to decide that he had not committed fraud by absconding from his debts in Alabama. This would not be easy. The *True American* announced that the New York firm of Andrews's brother had failed two days before Andrews left his home in Alabama.[19] To blunt the effect of this evidence that Andrews was fleeing his debts, Samuel Hermann testified that Andrews had not "concealed himself" as an absconder would normally do. Hermann believed that when Andrews was arrested, he was not absconding because "Andrews told him that he was going to New York on business."[20]

Although Hermann's testimony raised doubts about the claim that Andrews was trying to abscond from New Orleans, he still faced charges of absconding from Mobile. Andrews brought witnesses to provide alternative justifications for his midnight flight. His clerk testified that one of his creditors threatened that if Andrews did not sign over his property "he would kill him."[21] Records of a witness's testimony revealed a different threat of physical violence:

What in witness's opinion induced Andrew to leave Mobile, was the difficulty which occurred in relation to the servant girl of Mr. Whiterman – at the time it was believed that she was an innocent & in some degree an unprotected female & that Andrews had violated or attempted to violate her. The Irish portion of the community were highly incensed & felt themselves called upon to redress the wrongs – She being an Irish girl – Rumors were constantly circulating that Andrews was to be mobbed, it was some times stated that he was to be rode on a rail & at others that he was to be emasculated.

According to this testimony, rumors of violence for sexual immorality, not financial immorality, caused Andrews's panic. His panic was visible, as the witness explained: "During the existence of these rumors of threatened violence, Andrews was very much alarmed & his fears were indicated in a manner which could not be mistaken by his appearance & his conduct." His lack of a poker face suggested to the witness that all was not right inside Andrews's head: "Andrews is a very timid man & his fear very easily alarmed."[22] Could a man with such easily enlarged organelles be an honorable debtor? The court was left to decide which fear – fear of failure or fear of violence at the hand of creditors or mobs – motivated his actions. Lawyers, judges, and juries struggled for years to sort out the cause of his panic and the results of his failure.[23]

Although Andrews's insolvency, like that of thousands of others', was sparked by the Joseph failure, Andrews seemed to know instinctively how to exploit the difference between state bankruptcy laws. Most people found themselves less certain about the law in the aftermath of unprecedented commercial catastrophes. Legal uncertainty thus mingled with financial uncertainty in the minds of panicked people. As the *New York Herald* commented, "The want of a general bankrupt law, is now awfully felt. The recent failures will lock up one hundred millions of property, and tie up the heads of a thousand persons."[24] Even though the law might "avenge irritation of feeling," court proceedings could not guarantee a quick, uniform, or fair end to people's panic.[25] Heads might be in knots for a long time.

Fearing the uncertainty of legal judgments against their property, some debtors prevented the law from being administered. "When men are driven to desperation," one newspaper opined, "law is but a weak barrier."[26] In early April, newspapers reported that in a single Mississippi county, more than a thousand suits had already been brought. When the governor refused a petition "to convene the Legislature for the purpose of passing a relief or replevin law," the citizens "called upon the Sheriff to resign just before the April term commences, threatening vengeance against anyone who will accept the office *pro tempore*."[27] Without a sheriff, judgments could not be executed, property could not be seized, and debtors could not be imprisoned. At least in this county in Mississippi, personal panics could be assuaged through threats of physical violence directed at the law's enforcers.

Whether out of fear of vigilante justice from "desperate" debtors or for some other reason, many creditors offered their debtors a compromise. Some allowed an extended payment period; others granted more time only if the debtor found an endorser who would guarantee the payment of the debt. Debtors thus asked their friends and family members to hold their property as collateral in exchange for a signature on a paper promise.[28] Like Hone, endorsers found themselves tied to the debts of their friends and family members.

In the spring of 1837, endorsers realized that worse than having misplaced trust in an individual, they had misplaced trust in the market. All types of collateral offered as security lost value as prices plunged. As one such endorser who held a mortgage on his friend's property wrote to a creditor, "We have fallen upon evil times, and those who have large amounts due to them must show some levity or great and inward distress must be the consequence." Without such "levity," the options were bleak: "if there can be no indulgence given in this matter [we] must sell the property put into our hands for the most that can be obtained, which at

this time, would not sell for half its real value."[29] Debtors seeking endorsements often offered collateral that was worth more than their debts to
shield endorsers from creditors, but in a rapidly deflating market, the "real
value" was difficult to determine. Those who depended on family and
friends suffered "inward distress" when collateral could neither protect
endorsers nor pay back loans.

As this endorser's allusion to "evil times" rather than evil actions suggests, begging debtors narrated their moral rectitude in the hopes of seeking
time from creditors. R. & J. Phillips, the Rothschilds' correspondents
in Philadelphia, blamed the Joseph and Hermann failures as well as the
diminished value of their collateral property for their "lamentable situation," which required "the dreadful necessity of suspending our payments."
The Phillips argued that they failed "at our most prosperous moment,
not by any act we can accuse ourselves of such as sacrifice or, injudicious
operations, or follies, but by placing too much confidence in others who
now cannot repay us & leave us to manage for ourselves as best we can."
For this reason, they believed they deserved the Rothschilds' "indulgence to
allow us the time necessary for such a trying occasion."[30] Good behavior in
bad times, according to this line of thinking, justified time.

Despite the networks they had built, individuals might see themselves
as forced "to manage for ourselves as best we can," but they still depended
on cooperation. Merchants relied on distant correspondents to inform
them of shinning firms so that they could avoid investing in paper tied to
these businesses. Moses Taylor warned his correspondent in Philadelphia
that he feared the Josephs would "carry others with them as many of our
Dry Goods Houses & grocers have sold them their southern paper for
notes." In exchange for this information, Taylor asked, "How do the
Phila. Houses stand it, who do these failures affect, & have you now the
same opinion of J.L. Hodge you had two weeks ago?" Taylor sought to
protect himself by asking about both the overall market and specific
individuals so that he could make informed choices.[31]

When direct information was not available, rumors often filled the void.
Eager for "any information it may be in your power to give us respecting
the New Orleans affairs," a bill broker in New York asked his correspondent in Philadelphia, "Do you hear anything certain from New Orleans
respective the difficulties there?"[32] Philadelphians could be no more certain
in their information about New Orleans than New Yorkers. Whatever the
answer to this question, it would rely on speculation. Taylor complained,
"All are occupied conjecturing what is next to happen. Who escape or
suffer & when we may hope for a better & more settled state of things.

Meanwhile all prospective operations seem to be quite neglected."[33] He was not alone in condemning rumor and conjecture as adding to panic and a stalled market. One of his correspondents in Boston wrote, "we have now serious failures reported and contradicted so that we don't know when to believe them."[34] Merchants could not invest in the paper that represented future transactions if they could not trust the words of their informers. Legal suits attested to the power of rumors. "A suit was about to be commenced against a person for reporting that a house had failed which was known to be solvent," reported one newspaper in mid-April. It cautioned, "suits will hereafter be commenced against every one who reports the failure of a solvent house."[35] Although "certain" information could end individual panic, uncertain or blatantly false reports produced more panics.

Rumors and facts traveled together from one merchant to another as information about distant places circulated. With the arrival of the latest Liverpool packet, Taylor warned a Cuban correspondent that "everything on the other side [of the Atlantic Ocean] looks gloomy" and that he should "look out."[36] "As a particular favor," Taylor had "been shown in confidence a letter from a London House & a house in Paris" that offered warnings about particular firms that had lost the trust of brokers in these foreign cities. Spreading the news about London's chain of troubled firms, he cautioned a correspondent that "such paper as G. Wildes & Co., T. Wiggin & Co., and T. Wilson & Co. cannot be discounted." The three Ws had not yet failed, but their bills of exchange, in large circulation in the United States, were losing value in London. To avoid losses, Taylor wrote, "I should therefore advise your being very cautious as to those with whom you have transactions & especially in regard to drawing or taking paper in the London Houses as it can hardly be foreseen who may be affected by the crisis."[37] When Taylor wrote this letter, the BOE had already bailed out the three Ws, but news of this decision had not reached the United States. Without this information, all London paper seemed risky.

After the Joseph and Hermann failures, creditors doubted whether any mercantile paper should be acceptable as payment for debts, but the right names on paper could still garner some trust. One Mississippi cotton factor attempted to convince his client that he had acted with caution by arguing that "the paper is very strong and I have not relied upon names of persons engaged in speculation, or upon merchants."[38] At around the same time, Taylor lost confidence in mercantile paper altogether, even his own. He informed a correspondent "I am buying up my own paper here, as in times like these, I am anxious to have as few engagements outstanding as possible."[39] With fewer bills on the market, he would be required to honor fewer promises for payment in specie. He paid bill brokers' fees to buy relief through certainty.

To Taylor, the only safe business was no business. He reiterated in letter after letter his "*firm determination to obstain* [sic] *from all exchange business whatever until confidence shall be somewhat restored* & affairs be placed upon a more stable footing. At the present moment, I would not exchange my paper against any that [could] be named!"[40] Like nearly every other panicked merchant, he abandoned his trust in his correspondents. As unfounded rumors of his own failure circulated, he ignored the dictates of "friendly feeling" and refused to "step forward" to help failing firms. Instead, he explained, "I intend to take care of myself."[41] In a moment of absolute uncertainty, Taylor only trusted himself.

Taylor was not alone in refusing to produce paper promises based on distant trade. Responding to the request of a Cuban correspondent who wanted to buy a bill of exchange on London, he wrote, "I applied to all the leading houses such as I consider safe and all have declined drawing at the present." Brown Brothers refused to sell Taylor a bill of exchange even if he convinced the BUS and John Jacob Astor, the multimillionaire, to back it.[42] Bills of exchange had lost their function as a circulating medium between the United States and London. Debtors could not pay back their creditors in anything except hard currency. Seeking to protect themselves, people hoarded their gold and silver coins. Reporting on Vicksburg, Mississippi, one cotton factor noted, "no one pretends to pay at all."[43]

By mid-April, the situation was the same in New York. Taylor summarized, "People are falling by the dozen & no one can tell where it is going to end. Confidence is entirely gone & paper will not sell at all."[44] As the month dragged on, uncertainty escalated. More than a month after the Joseph failure, he wrote, "Not a day passes without failures & we have yet to learn the effect produced in England by the crash here. When that blow is struck we may form some estimate of further prospects. Until then, it must be a matter of uncertainty as to who will remain solvent & who succumb under the general pressure."[45] Business in New York City stood still as Americans waited to receive English news.

Describing the "general pause," the Josephs wrote to the Rothschilds that they experienced "great anxiety" waiting for "the results from your side of the water as we do not know to what extent we may be liable for protested bills, should many failures take place in England." They, like all other panicked Americans, were waiting for "certain information."[46] By May 8, 1837, one lawyer estimated that upward of 280 failures had taken place in New York City in the previous seven weeks.[47] The accounts of these firms could not be reckoned without calculations of transatlantic debts and credits; in the absence of "certain information," Americans' personal panics intensified.

* * *

Just as New York merchants waited for British news to resolve their uncertainty, Londoners waited for the boats from America to bring correspondence as well as gold coins. Bad weather in the North Atlantic stopped the flow of information from the United States to Great Britain in early April 1837. Adverse winds prevented five packet ships containing approximately three weeks' worth of news from reaching the City. As a new round of bills of exchange would become due in early April, London confidence brokers faced the difficult prospect of betting that the delayed packets from New York would bring enough specie to restore the operations of the American houses to a more sure footing. On April 3, 1837, the London *Times* reported, "There exists a good deal of anxiety for further intelligence from New York, especially as such large amounts of American and other bills and engagements become payable tomorrow; there are now five packets due."[48]

April 4 proved a less disastrous day than March 4, but the absence of mail created "a most perplexing and embarrassing circumstance, and a great aggravation of the evils to which the higher class of merchants are exposed."[49] With optimistic hopes for shipments of gold, merchant banking houses temporarily renewed the paper promises of American correspondents – at least until the boats arrived. As the *Times* explained, "any failure of payment of a bill on the day on which it is due is fatal to credit; but the circumstances are in the present instance so peculiar, that the postponement of payment is proposed on the one side and assented to by the other, without any reproach being incurred by it." The chances that five consecutive packet ships would have failed to cross the ocean was "so unusual, that the merchant who has not taken that contingency into his calculation is exempt from all censure, and it would even be thought unfair to press him for payment." Whatever the cause of the local crisis, Londoners did not blame themselves for the lack of wind.[50]

In this uncertain atmosphere, few houses initiated legal proceedings to protest bills that exceeded the credit limits of correspondents. In response to the extended payment period, the *Times* joked, "the only parties who are likely to suffer are the notaries, and they probably will not be disposed to complain having reaped an abundant harvest for some time past."[51] Notaries on both sides of the Atlantic received payment for officiating over every protested bill. The financial pressure and commercial failures of the previous months had already proved lucrative for these panic profiteers. For the time being, the pens of notaries, lawyers, and mercantile clerks, along with those of more elite financiers, waited for accounts from New York.

Not everyone waited calmly for the wind to turn. Bates dealt with his uncertainties through frenzied movement. Traveling on icy roads that caused his carriage to break down five times, he curtailed a continental holiday to hurry back toward London. Once he reached the coast in Belgium, he "found the wind so violent that no packet would sail." Just as it prevented transatlantic communication, "remarkable weather" blocked his short journey back to London.[52]

While the packet ships that remained at sea contained accounts of the Hermann and Joseph failures and little specie, Londoners remained ignorant of affairs on the western side of the Atlantic. Despite the leniency in bill payment described by the *Times*, the market could not accommodate the overextended credits of the three Ws. When George Wildes & Co. sought assistance from the BOE in early April, London insiders realized just how significant the arrival of news and specie from America was to their market. The *Times* explained,

Whether the connexions of that house will ultimately escape injury from the situation into which it has fallen will depend on the successful collection of the sums due to it in America, for if they should not be realized to an extent sufficient to satisfy the Bank, all the collateral securities recently obtained in London must be put in requisition.[53]

The principals of George Wildes & Co. could only thank the directors of the BOE for their assistance and hope that their dunning letters proved effective. Thomas Wilson & Co. followed on the heels of Wildes & Co. on the dishonorable walk through the corridors of the BOE to plead its case before the directors. Timothy Wiggin & Co. was not far behind.[54]

Merchants, bankers, brokers, and newspaper editors on both sides speculated about the terrible consequences for correspondents when the news of such financial troubles arrived. In London, Bates wrote in his diary, "it is clear that when [Americans] get advices of the disasters here a panic will ensue so that the reaction here will be great."[55] Londoners thought New Yorkers would panic when they learned of the bailout of the three Ws, and New Yorkers thought Londoners would panic when they learned of the Hermann and Joseph failures. Fears of distant panic triggered by local news occupied the minds of many involved in trade and motivated frantic actions.

While the news from the United States remained trapped at sea, English financiers began to doubt the honor of their correspondents in America and sought new sources of information. The Rothschilds had already decided to send August Belmont, a twenty-four-year-old clerk who had risen quickly within the family's houses, to Cuba, where they believed there was "more to be earned than in America."[56] James de Rothschild, the head of the family's Paris house, wrote to his London nephews in late March, "I think that there will be some bankruptcies in America so it would be a good idea if Belmont goes there and he can then at least let us know what is going on."[57] Like many English bankers, the Rothschilds wanted a new set of eyes to survey the crisis in America.

Midway through Belmont's voyage, the Rothschilds learned "to our great astonishment" of the Joseph failure. The Londoners sent new instructions by the next packet. Atypical of Rothschild business strategy, they vested this non-family member with "full authority" and requested him "to take all steps necessary – so far as you can for us – to protect our property in order to work with the utmost care for our interests, so that we can come out of this unfortunate business with as little loss as we can."[58] The Rothschilds hoped to avoid financial trouble by capitalizing on the timely arrival of their agent. Belmont's New York stop began as an afterthought, but the Rothschilds found themselves relying on him to "recover" their assets.[59]

They quickly grew dissatisfied with their new agent. Whereas the Rothschilds wanted their property recovered, Belmont sought new profits. Belmont proposed buying depreciated paper and recently devalued sugar, cotton, and other produce for resale at higher prices in Europe.[60] A disgusted James wrote to the Londoners, "we received a letter from Belmont but I didn't have the patience to read it. He is a stupid man ... and we are not so desperate for new business and would rather sort the old business matters out so that there is no need for anyone to go to America."[61] Belmont obviously misunderstood the Rothschilds' desire to withdraw from American business, but they could not control him. After all, in their panicked reaction to the news of the Joseph failure, they had given him "full authority" to act for the house.[62] By authorizing Belmont in an attempt to avoid uncertain losses, the Rothschilds grew more anxious about their American investments.

Instead of dunning the Rothschilds' debtors and moving on to Cuba, Belmont decided to stay in New York. He found it impolitic to follow the Rothschilds' directives to appeal to the bankruptcy laws because, as he explained to them, "The laws of this country with regard to bankruptcy are so vague, enabling bankrupts to turn to various faculties that presently it seems not advisable to appeal to the law, as every foreigner who has got a claim, is considered to be an enemy of the country."[63] Nativism combined with a lack of a national bankruptcy law left Belmont unable to follow orders; his "stupid" behavior was not entirely his fault.

As the rates for reliable paper that could be used for payment in London soared, Americans hoarded their specie. One New York newspaper joked that the specie shortage derived from the democratization in the demand for gold jewelry. The editorial blamed America's obsession with symbols of wealth as the cause of the commercial crisis by listing whole classes of men and women who ought not to be sporting such finery:

There is no clerk, attendant on a store, headwater at any hotel, or respectable gentleman of color who does not wear a gold guard chain, whether he has a watch or not. There is no merchant or pawnbroker's clerk, young lawyer or physician, who does not sport a gold watch, seals, &c. There is no chambermaid, black, yellow, or white who does not wear gold ear-rings. Gilded rings and bracelets are for mechanics and farmers' daughters and ladies who act as market women.[64]

Although this statement was intended to be satirically humorous, the critique of America's buying habits relayed a serious concern for the availability of gold to balance payments between England and the United States.

Some described the credit crisis as a specie war. "Specie is the artillery of commerce, and we are now in the midst of the severest commercial conflict which has taken place for many years," remarked one newspaper.[65] In an era of "balance of power" political theory, British demands for specie could be reinterpreted as a legitimate concern for diplomacy. One newspaper editor used diplomatic terminology to describe how "The specie-balance-power of the world, as necessary as the political balance, is disturbed. The ship is sinking, for the ballast is all one side."[66] This argument favored sending gold back to Britain; other newspaper editors pointed out the folly of Americans believing that they could trap specie on the Western side of the Atlantic. One New Orleanian newspaper editor referenced the American Revolution as he argued that Americans had not actually "got old England under our thumb at last," as some were prone to argue during the boom years. As the demand for specie increased, the United States had lost its war against its "quandom [sic] mother."[67] The ferocity of debate surrounding both specie shipment and protested foreign bills contributed to the nativism observed by Belmont.

As a man with a German accent, Belmont found the practicality of collecting the Rothschilds' debts in New York daunting. This experience ensured that he could not meet his employers' demands, but it also taught him about American beliefs in individual economic responsibility. Belmont took pity on the "great many American merchants [who] have lately not been wanting of good will, remitting specie and bills at the present exorbitant rates."[68] In response, James called Belmont a "scoundrel" and instructed his nephews that "such an ass needs to be kept on a short leash." Offering debtors leniency and buying up deflated bills and commodities, Belmont found possibilities for profit in daily fluctuations. Given the slow transatlantic communication, the Rothschilds could not hold back their agent from becoming a panic profiteer.[69]

While the Rothschilds panicked by conveying authority to a doubtful agent already mid-journey, the heads of other American houses responded by sending agents immediately after hearing the news of American failures. "The commercial difficulties of the year 1836–7 and the failure of one of our correspondents in the United States" prompted Joseph Biggs, partner in a Liverpool and London mercantile concern, to book passage on a packet ship bound for New York at the beginning of May. "There are upwards of 50 cabin passengers," described Biggs. He had to sleep in a hammock because westbound passenger accommodations were in such high demand. "Several are European partners of American Houses," he recorded, "many are Americans returning to wind up their bankrupt concerns in New York." With his own spirits lagging, Biggs saw his fellow commercial travelers as "morose and disagreeable." Packet-line owners, captains, and crew profited from the increased fees paid by panicked passengers desperate to discover the condition of transatlantic credit for themselves.[70]

The long journey could not dissuade one of London's leading merchant bankers from relieving his panic by appraising the situation with his own eyes. When Melvil Wilson, a Thomas Wilson & Co. partner, heard the news of failures in America, he immediately booked passage. Although his father had founded the firm, Melvil Wilson bore responsibility for saving the house from failing in 1837. Refusing to wait any longer for letters from his correspondents, Wilson traveled for more than a month on choppy seas so that he could personally "look after their concerns." The night of his arrival, Wilson ate dinner with Hone, who joked in his diary, "I fear he will require many good dinners to reconcile him to the state of things he finds here."[71] Choosing to repair rather than repast, the next evening, Wilson sent his brother-in-law to excuse him from a dinner party hosted by Hone because he had, after only one day in New York, "sailed for England."[72] Spending approximately nine weeks sailing across the ocean and exactly one day on Wall Street, Wilson arrived back in London resigned to make the best out of his failure.

Not all panicked English merchants who traveled to the United States returned to face their failure as readily as Wilson did. An English merchant traveling in New York noted in his diary, "Two persons I have seen slinking about Wall Street absconded dishonourably from Leicester [England] some time since."[73] Some traveled further west in their attempts to flee their debts. The *New York Herald* announced in April, "About ten thousand mechanics are preparing to go west as soon as the rivers and canals are ready." Traveling on internal improvements, many of which would soon default on their payments to stockholders and bondholders, these economic migrants sought escape to "southern sections of Ohio, Illinois, and Indiana," where "paper cities" began to vanish from maps as quickly as they had been conjured through ink and paper.[74]

The newly independent Republic of Texas gained a reputation as a popular destination for dishonorable failures. Historians estimate that the population of Texas doubled in the four years after 1837. Once in Texas, no extradition laws would force absconders to return to the United States for trial.[75] Failed speculators fled to "that common sewer of the west & south," complained one Louisianan, "if a man is taken up here for any infamous crime and escapes, we always hear of him in Texas."[76] "Gone to Texas," abbreviated in "three ominous letters G.T.T." became a shorthand symbol found on abandoned businesses.[77] Like Frank Fulton in Lee's *Three Experiments of Living*, failed speculators hoped for rebirth inside and beyond America's borders.

Absconding to squat on western lands and perambulate from one property to another had become so common a practice that writers invented a new verb to describe this process: to absquatulate.[78] Like shinning and dunning, absquatulation was a form of personal panic. And because all of these actions seemed like attempts to avoid responsibility for failure, they all provoked questions of morality.

In New Orleans, business failure had become so universal during the spring of 1837 that legal authorities could not discern which actions were selfish and which were selfless. Who could they trust? In the case of E. W. Pennington, the answer was no one. Pennington was supposed to appear in court on April 15, 1837, to answer charges that he owed $2,002. His first attempt at absconding resulted in his pursuit and arrest by two sheriff's deputies. His next attempt required accomplices.

Once the deputies found and arrested Pennington, he asked them to escort him to a grocery shop where he could ask the proprietors to provide his bail. The owners of the store met with Pennington and the deputies; after a few preliminary questions, the deputies realized that the sheriff would need the creditors' permission to accept the grocers' note as bail. While one deputy trekked across the city with the unsigned note, the other waited above the shop with Pennington and the grocers. When Pennington "asked to go downstairs to get a drink," the deputy refused. He acquiesced, however, when one of the grocers "told him not to be afraid, that they would be responsible." Naïvely, the deputy trusted not only his charge but also his charge's friends.

The sound of glass shattering as Pennington descended the stairs made the deputy "uneasy," but he continued to allow the debtor his drink. After one to three minutes, the deputy grew suspicious that "he was gone rather long & went down after him & was told Pennington was somewhere in the store but after looking for him he could not find him." The clerks in the store misdirected the deputy, providing Pennington with time to get away. As Pennington performed his final escape act under the nose of one deputy, the creditors informed the other that they would graciously accept the bond of the grocers. The creditors, however, may have been as gullible as the sheriff's deputy. After Pennington's disappearance, the grocers refused to sign the note guaranteeing Pennington's court appearance.[79] His escape enabled theirs.

But the grocers did not need Pennington to abscond in order to escape paying his bail. Had the note been signed, it would have been an almost worthless guarantee because the grocers were "in insolvent circumstances at the time."[80] What had appeared to be generosity was actually fraud. When the grocers announced their failure, like so many other merchants, they crafted the necessary story of unjust failure. They blamed "the great pressure existing in mercantile business" and their "inability to collect their debts." They appealed to "justice" and "equity" as they begged their creditors for a "respite." Of course, they never acknowledged that by helping Pennington escape, they had already demonstrated their disrespect for the justice system. They constructed the story that served their interests.[81]

Perhaps the dishonorable actions of the failed grocers served the interests of the justice system. When Pennington could not be located, his creditors sued the sheriff's deputy for negligence, hoping to recover the $2,002. The court found in the creditors' favor, and the deputy appealed. The appellate judge observed in the insolvency of the grocers an escape for the deputy because his act of "negligence" did not change the fact that the guarantee would have been nearly worthless. The judge saw no need to punish the deputy for "a mere act of imprudence" without "bad motives or intentions." Justice, however, came with a cost. For the negligent deputy, the price of Pennington's escape was three rounds of court fees.[82] The legal system's profit was the original creditors' loss; they never collected their $2,002. Misplaced trust could prove costly in an atmosphere of unprecedented uncertainty where escape, if morally dubious, was possible and perhaps even rational.

For the absconding, New Orleans was not only a point of departure but also an international destination. In early February 1837, a court in Annonay, France, declared a merchant named Ennembord Richard Lioud "to be in a state of open failure or insolvency." Before the seizure of his property, Lioud "escaped to America, taking with him a very large sum of money belonging to his creditors."[83] While crossing the Atlantic, Lioud reinvented himself as Étienne Richard of Rouen. Richard arrived in New York and eagerly investigated purchasing property in several states so that he could spend his new life engaged in the "simple habits of agricultural work."[84]

Before Richard could buy his "forty acres" or "construct a little rugged dwelling," he fell ill while traveling in New Orleans. As his illness worsened, Richard became convinced that although his plan for his new life sounded wholesome, his conscience remained troubled. He explained that the dishonor he felt had come "to torture my soul, to aggravate the malady in my stomach, and to put me in my deathbed." In order to facilitate "the restitution of the family's honor" and to prevent his wife from doubting that he was "an honest man," Richard dictated a letter to be sent to his brother in France that would expose his identity to his creditors.[85]

Whether or not his commercial failure had been the result of his own actions, Richard believed that he was being punished. Before he died, he affirmed that by acknowledging his identity and returning his assets to his creditors, he was "repatriated with God." "My repentance is so sincere," he swore to his brother, "that I hope that I may recover the virtue that I abandoned."[86] According to the judge who awarded Richard's estate to the creditors who knew him as Lioud, the merchant had "sunk under the load of disappointment and remorse which his conduct brought upon him."[87] The judge's summary of the deathbed letter demonstrates that Americans understood the bankrupt's actions through a vocabulary of morality.

The "load of disappointment and remorse" conveyed by financial conduct weighed down the lives of some panicked people to such an extent that they no longer wanted to live. Interpreted in the nineteenth century as both sinful and a symptom of mental illness, suicide offered a final end to financial and moral uncertainty.[88] By the first week of May, shinning, dunning, suing, and absconding seemed like mild reactions to the hard times.

Panic's most desperate actions plagued New Orleans during the first week of May 1837. According to the *New Orleans Bee*, "never, in the same space of time, were committed so many murders and suicides."[89] Along with the suicides of several convicted criminals and two cases of self-immolation, Théodore Nicolet, the bill broker whom we first encountered in the introduction, ended his life.

For two decades, Nicolet sold bills of exchange drawn on banks in Liverpool, London, and Paris to New Orleanian merchants. His business thrived through caution. In 1830, he settled his accounts with Nathan Mayer Rothschild rather than risk becoming exposed to "unsafe" paper.[90] Six desks, two long tables, a comptoire, and two mahogany bureaus allowed the clerks in Nicolet's counting house to fill reams of letter paper with the details of the busy broker's sales. With a flying press and two copy presses, the clerks efficiently reproduced their work on sheets of tissue-thin cotton paper. Their boss, however, avoided ink stains. A man with nearly seventy shirts and sixty handkerchiefs of imported silks, he was an elegant bachelor who lived in a mahogany world. His bed, washstand, armoire, armchairs, shelves, safe, sofa, chairs, dining table, sideboards, desk, and even his commode were composed of the expensive wood.[91] He served as the consul for his native Switzerland and helped found New Orleans's first Francophone Evangelical Church.[92]

From his prominent place in the community, Nicolet descended quickly into a mire of debt and fear. In late December 1836, he found himself short on money and asked a friend to extend him more time to pay back his notes. Nicolet was far from alone in struggling with liquidity. As his friend commented, "the troublesome times had commenced and it was difficult to make collection on the 26th of December 1836."[93]

In February, March, and April 1837, Nicolet begged creditors to renew his notes. A friend remembered him regretting that "it was very hard for him ... but at this moment he could not pay the notes."[94] When Nicolet was unable to make his payments on four of his slaves, the seller repossessed them. Ben, Auguste, Henriette, and her ten-year-old daughter Heloïse served as the collateral for their own sale, which had been made on credit.[95] By early May, Nicolet's household included only two slaves: his cook Nancy and his servant Billy.[96] With so few servants, the mahogany would not be polished, but this was far from the worst of Nicolet's troubles. A friend recalled Nicolet confiding in him in late April that "he thought he would have to stop payment and that he would not survive it." At the time, the friend considered this last statement as "unimportant" compared to the more prescient news that this bastion of the community would fail.[97]

The rumors of Nicolet's insolvency spread. As a judge recounted, "the embarrassed state of Nicolet's affairs for some time previous to his death was a matter of notoriety."[98] Nevertheless, Nicolet's "bookkeeper and confidential clerk manager," his closest business associate, never believed these rumors. This man testified, "At the date of Nicolet's death, he had not been protested. He had at that date nearly four thousand dollars in the different banks."[99]

Whether or not he was still technically solvent, Nicolet planned his death. On the evening of May 2, 1837, he enclosed in a letter two bills of exchange repaying a last debt borrowed from a merchant in town. He begged the recipient "to excuse your faithful dying friend" for the form of his payment. He offered his "last farewell to you and your amiable family and at the same time my warmest thanks for all the kindness you have always shown me."[100] After working all night in his counting room, he scratched a final message in pencil to an "old friend" in Havre: "when you will have received this letter, your friend will have ceased to exist. Embrace your wife for me and tell my nephews the sad news of the occasion of our eternal separation."[101] The uncertainties of failure trumped Nicolet's concerns for his afterlife. Willing to spend an eternity paying for his immorality, Nicolet decided to escape the calumny of financial dishonor. The next morning, the forty-six-year-old man walked to a friend's house beyond the city's boundaries and "blew his brains out."[102]

People immediately blamed Nicolet's death on the commercial crisis. As one sugar plantation's overseer wrote to his employer in France, "his suicide is attributed to the losses that tried this honorable merchant in the derangement of commercial affairs."[103] Believing that the crisis had forced many men into terrible "despair," the editor of the *New Orleans Bee* blamed Nicolet's suicide on the insanity of the times. "When will this fatal madness end? Is there no honorable method of regulating a man's affairs but by abandoning them?" he asked. Nevertheless, the newspaper editor interpreted Nicolet's behavior as cowardly. "A man of education, sentiment, and character like Mr. Nicolet," argued the editor, "should have remembered that his misfortunes were no crimes." The editor assured that suicide itself was "An act so much to be condemned from a moral point of view." The real crime, he argued, was that "suicide finds some kind of excuse in society as it implies a fear of disgrace." The editor argued that Nicolet lived "in a community where bankruptcy, when unaccompanied by moral turpitude, is not dishonorable." Suicide was, then, "the effect of rash despair, and an inconsiderate disregard of the most obvious dictates of reason and duty."[104] In other words, Nicolet committed suicide because he had become irrational. He panicked.

Two days after Nicolet's death, his funeral allowed the public to express the grief, terror, anger, and uncertainty that had been accumulating for months. "An immense gathering of the most respectable citizens conveyed his body to its final sanctuary," reported the overseer, "and the many tears bear witness to the general dismay."[105] New Orleanians grieved for their own fates as they cried at Nicolet's burial. For years after the funeral, Nicolet's survivors – his friends and business partners – struggled to sort out the mess of financial fallout that he had "abandoned." Death might end a person's panic, but it spread financial uncertainty.[106]

* * *

As Nicolet wrote his suicide note, "great talk" circulated around Wall Street about another honorable failure. On Saturday, April 30, Arthur Tappan found himself, according to the *New York Herald*, "under the necessity of asking for an extension from his creditors." He had a half-million dollars in assets beyond the firm's liabilities, but his money was too tied up in illiquid inventory, real estate, and other investments to pay the $300,000 due on the first of May. Tappan found loans for half this amount, a testament to his good credit, as most of the banks would not lend money to anyone at any rate. But half a loan to the silk merchant was the equivalent of no loan at all. He could not justify paying only half his debtors. So as the papers all reported, "after a long consultation, he came to the conclusion to suspend entirely."[107]

Few expected Tappan to fail. "It was believed this House was firm enough to ride out any gale that could possibly occur in the money market," reported a newspaper from Massachusetts upon learning the news.[108] The surprise of Tappan's failure prompted Bennett at the *New York Herald* to assess the silk importer's business practices. "His manner of doing business has been singularly precise, scientific and accurate," the editor praised. The paper reported that through "legitimate" business practices, Tappan earned 10 percent of $1,500,000 in sales in 1836, which he spent supporting "his wild visionary notions about the negroes." "If he would quit this nonsense, and be rational on the black topic," Bennett argued, "we might take Arthur into our good graces."[109] To some critics, Tappan's "scientific" business practices mattered much less than his seemingly irrational investment in antislavery causes.

This was exemplified in newspapers' assessments of Tappan's refusal to do business with the slaveholding South. A month earlier, unfounded rumors had circulated in the nation's newspapers that Arthur Tappan had failed, but the *National Intelligencer* suggested that this would be impossible "because he is such a notorious abolitionist, he is thus saved from much of the embarrassment which is now felt by the holders of protested Southwestern paper."[110] Much to the delight of Southerners, abolitionism failed as a prophylactic for failure. As the proslavery editors of the New Orleans *Picayune* reported when news of his suspension arrived, "Arthur Tappan has failed in New York. His business has always been purely *illegitimate*."[111] Legitimate or illegitimate, the Tappan failure was too big to ignore.

Whereas slavery's advocates might see Tappan's failure as deserving, the merchant's correspondents rued his financial demise. Indeed news of Tappan's failure was explicitly addressed in nearly every mercantile letter written in New York during the first week of May. Taylor informed his correspondents that "A. Tappan & Co. have failed" and "the concern of Arthur Tappan & Co. has gone."[112] Hone confessed to his diary that "the number of failures is so great daily that I do not keep a record of them, even in my mind," but he recorded the Tappan failure because it was not supposed to happen. In Hone's anti-Semitic view, Jews and sinners could fail, but good Christian "Gentlemen" such as Tappan "were supposed to be out of the reach of danger."[113] A New York merchant informed the Evangelical minister Charles Grandison Finney of the failure: "Today a concern has stopped that I hoped and tried to pray might be spared – Arthur Tappan & Co." He sought an explanation why such a moral man should fail, but could only console himself that God had "wise & good reasons for it or it would not have been so." "Truly the Lord seems to shake terribly the earth," he confessed.[114] This writer's biblical allusion to a divinely ordained earthquake reflected his conclusion that the crisis was beyond human control. The *National Intelligencer* employed a different metaphor of natural disaster to explain the crisis: "Mr Tappan has made a good fight, but he is at last tumbled down by the whirlwind of the times."[115]

Whether a tornado or an earthquake, "the times" no longer seemed to follow the rules of individual responsibility for economic success and failure. Even those who had experienced "collisions of opinion" with the merchant were dismayed. One wrote, "he has been a munificent giver to the great objects of Christian philanthropy engaging the attention of the world for twenty years past; and when such men are wrecked in their business, the fall is a common calamity."[116] As a "calamity," a "wreck," a "whirlwind," and an earthquake, the crisis called for new economic causation.

"The distress and ruin caused by these failures will be tremendous; general bankruptcy seems inevitable," Hone predicted.[117] The distress caused by Tappan's failure would stretch the crisis beyond the financial bankruptcy of his commercial connections. "Among all the suspensions in Pearl street, we presume none has created livelier regret than that of the firm of A. Tappan & Company," concluded a New York newspaper.[118] America's white, male reformers and religious revivalists as well as the disenfranchised women and free people of color who raised funds, wrote petitions, and distributed the literature that Tappan's donations produced regretted the failure of a man who literally financed the crusade for American "righteousness."[119]

The *Emancipator*, the weekly newspaper of the American Anti-Slavery Society, commented, "We believe our readers will feel deep regret at the announcement, that the house of Arthur Tappan & Co. have been obliged to suspend payment." Indeed, after Tappan's fall, the *Emancipator* started to cover the financial crisis as a topic of interest to its antislavery readership. The *Emancipator* blamed his failure on "the present unprecedented pressure"; Tappan was a victim.[120] Abolitionists understood slaves to be economic victims, but the application of this idea to free men was unsettling.[121] Abolitionists, like everyone suddenly feeling economically powerless, started constructing an explanation out of familiar systems that were larger than any individual. For some, explanations naturalized the crisis by comparing it to uncontrollable forces of nature. For others, God or the devil was behind the crisis. For the editor of the *Emancipator*, slavery was the obvious villain.[122]

The *Emancipator* worked hard to demonstrate "the principal cause of the present pressure in the monetary world, viz. *speculating in slaves and the souls of men*."[123] To make his case, the editor culled articles from Southern newspapers that had been reprinted in the New York City press. He looked for accounts of the precarious finances of cotton factors, planters, and banks in Mississippi, Alabama, and New Orleans. He used these "extracts" as evidence of the causal relationship between the system of human bondage and the financial crisis, even though few of these original reports actually mentioned slavery. For example, an article clipped from the *New Orleans Bee* suggested that "it is dreaded that all the notes on mortgages of property lately sold in Louisiana and Mississippi, will be little better than waste paper."[124] This article was intended to report on a horrific prospect for investors, but on the pages of the *Emancipator*, the devaluation of southern financial instruments pointed to the evil of the idea of owning humans as property. The *Natchez Courier* sympathized with the indebtedness of Mississippi planters by explaining that they had bought ten thousand slaves in 1836 "*on a credit.*" Through the clever use of parenthetical interjections, the *Emancipator* converted this article into an explanation of the link between speculation and sin: "It was a very easy matter to buy – (the way to hell is easy) – but when *pay* day came – (and so they'll find it at the judgment) – it was not so easy to pay."[125] In its columns, the *Emancipator* gathered evidence of violent reactions to the legal suits that had led to the "sacrifice of property, unheard of in the annals of calamity."[126] An article from the New Orleans *Commercial Bulletin* rued the "incalculable" distress in Mississippi where "Negroes and estates are being sacrificed by the sheriffs for a mere song."[127] To the readers of the *Emancipator*, the "property" sold at sacrificial prices to liquidate planters' assets had faces, names, and souls. Readers of the original articles were meant to pity the sacrifices of southern property owners; readers of the *Emancipator*'s version pitied the slaves.

Other southern sources of the words reprinted in the *Emancipator* empathized with the individual settlers who had purchased land at the height of the bubble. As one *New Orleans Bee* article decried, "these are the innocent victims upon whom will fall the calamity of blasted homes and broken fortunes."[128] To the *Emancipator*, however, the "calamity" demonstrated that all Americans, white as well as black, were victims of the sin of slavery. Moreover, the power behind slavery's ability to create financial crisis and victimize the enslaved and free alike was rooted in an even larger power: divine retribution. The *New Orleans Bee* described the situation in Mississippi as "the winding up* of those extravagant and enormous speculations in the lands which have been proceeding undisturbed during the last three years." Through the power of his asterisk, the editor of the *Emancipator* interjected, "The 'winding up' is to come at that day when God, as the God of the oppressed, shall 'make inquisition for blood.'"[129] God's wrath for slavery's injustice was one of many new explanations of the financial crisis to focus on forces larger than individual choice.

The editor of the *Emancipator* was not alone in connecting financial instability to a larger cause of both slavery and punishment for sin. Samuel E. Cornish, the volunteer editor of the *Colored American*, would soon find himself forced to beg his readers for payment because of "the expense attending his feeble health, the pressure of the times, and the calls of his growing family."[130] This paper, founded the day the panic began by the free African American community and funded by Tappan, argued that "*our commercial distress and financial miseries come from the South*. The protested drafts, the foreclosed mortgages, and the dishonored obligations of that '*cursed region*,' are making destructive inroads upon northern enterprize [sic] and northern prosperity."[131] Cornish's identification of the crisis with a divine curse reflected the reports of the previous months that dated the origin of the crisis to the Hermann failure in New Orleans rather than the failure of the Josephs in New York or the changes in discount policy made by the BOE. Where the *Emancipator*'s rereading of southern newspaper articles isolated blame to southern slavery, the *Colored American* expanded the reach of the system of slavery to northern "prostration and ruin" by blaming "the deep and damning concessions, made by merchants and men in authority to the hydra system of Slavery, which carries God's blasting curse with it, wherever it goes."[132] Although the two newspapers made the same abolitionist argument, the *Colored American* assumed that its readers would accept that slavery undergirded northern as well as southern trade. The *Emancipator*, on the other hand, laboriously illustrated the link between slavery and northern business. This work of reading slavery into the articles of southern presses evidenced the lack of American acknowledgment of the centrality of slavery to the economy. For that matter, they did not recognize an economy at all.

* * *

In several pamphlets published during and after the crisis, Charles Francis Adams, the son of John Quincy Adams and grandson of John Adams, tried to use the theories of political economy to explain recent events. He found himself and political economists more generally facing "the difficulty of attaining a position elevated enough to look over the whole surface of action. Hence a danger of mistaking the relative importance of events, of giving to an exception the character of a rule, and of making a partial view weigh as much as if it were a general one." He could not see a bird's-eye-view economic perspective, but he, like many other writers, was starting to want one.[133]

The quest for a systemic explanation of the crisis resulted in nearly endless newspaper editorials and pamphlets as well as novels and sermons. Americans throughout the nation hungered for answers to their questions about the causes and effects of the financial crisis. As a newspaper in New

Orleans reported, "even the preachers are haranguing their congregations upon the subject from the pulpit."[134]

In Boston, the wealthy Unitarian parishioners of Nathaniel L. Frothingham invested a great deal of their time in trying to explain the crisis, so much so that Frothingham felt the need to stop them. One of America's most bookish religious figures in this period of enthusiastic revival, Frothingham preached and published a sermon on "The Duties of Hard Times" designed to dissuade his listeners and readers from seeing the crisis as anything other than the product of individual sin. Frothingham argued that Christians ought to ignore the "mysteries" of the "commercial world." Beginning his sermon with a four-page history of "anarchy and war" in ancient Israel, he dismissed the trials of "transient depressions and anxieties, and simple changes of fortune, which we are so accustomed to call public distress." Real "distress" involved blood, not banks.[135]

Comparing his listeners and readers to King David's military advisors, Frothingham exhorted them to "deliver ourselves from the evils of our condition" through "thoughtfulness."[136] "How can we apply the remedy till we have come to understand the source and the character of the disease?" Frothingham asked. Despite the fact that this question might seem to beg his audience to apply empiricist science and rational inquiry to economic conditions, the minister ironically demanded the opposite. Divine "scourges" of the past that brought about disease, drought, insects, war, as well as "the desolations of the earthquake, the tempest, the flood," he argued, could be understood through science and observation.[137] The "commercial world" of the "present day" with its "fluctuations of trade" and "vexed questions concerning credit and capital," however, was too complex to be explained in the midst of the crisis. He argued that studying economic troubles was a waste of time because "the science of it is itself as yet new."[138]

Frothingham wanted his audience to return to the arguments that had been made before the crisis began by locating the causes of their personal crises in their "greedy passions and ambitious indulgences, and the haste to be rich, and headlong schemes, and strange delusions."[139] Ending with a message of hope, he implored his audience to "Increase not a general panic by unreal terrors. Extend not wider that want of confidence, which is one of the worst features of the day." Ironically, by condemning inquiry into the economy, Frothingham enabled the continuation of "unreal terrors."[140] His parishioners suffered not only from the financial uncertainty of ignorance about whether they would fail but also from the economic uncertainty of changing epistemology.

Frothingham's sermon contributed to a growing commitment by writers to the word "panic" to describe the crisis. He was far from alone. In an early May sermon entitled "Views of Duty Adapted to the Times," Portsmouth, New Hampshire's Andrew Preston Peabody labeled the "unprecedented convulsion" in the "commercial world" a "panic." He began by locating the cause of "alarm and dismay" in financial causes. "It is not that your estates are wasted, or your specie sunk, or your merchandise consumed," argued Peabody, "But, credit, a mere creature of public faith and general good will, is undermined and crushed."[141]

Peabody's sermon explicitly put the work of the church at the service of the commercial community. He explained that "Causes, that operate on the public mind," alone were sufficient "to account for a period of commercial distress." Implicating without explicating the ultimate uncertainty at the root of the crisis, he argued that the causes of distrust could be "great or small, real or imaginary, whether flowing from the errors of men in power or of men in trade." Whatever the cause of distrust, Peabody ensured that "a panic, though brief and groundless, is never harmless; but may aim a more deadly blow at national commerce or wealth, than a war or a famine could." Peabody labeled the crisis a "panic." Like many other writers, he implied that it was a short, irrational event that had a singular and most often political cause.[142]

Ministers, even Peabody, regarded "the pressure of the times as a dispensation of Providence for our admonition and discipline."[143] Few newspapers, however, called directly on God or the devil for an explanation. The New Orleans *Picayune* was an exception. In a humorous serial column entitled "The Gentleman in Black," the *Picayune*'s editors discussed the crisis with Mephistopheles Jr., the son of the devil's servant. Dressed in "the deepest black," this fictional character was inspired by Goethe's story of Faust, which had recently been translated into English. Mephistopheles Jr. provided the editor with his analysis of the sins of New Orleans: the theater, the horse racing, and of course the crisis.[144]

In late March, the young devil argued that "failures, stoppages, suspension of business and payments have now become so common – I might say fashionable – that I fear you will tire your readers with a repetition of them."[145] The readers of the *Picayune* did not tire of the newspaper's satirical local reporting; in fact, circulation increased 150 percent during the spring of 1837.[146] On March 12, 1837, the editors punned on the success of the newspaper when Mephistopheles Jr. asked, "How *is your paper* taken? It has never been *protested* in any instance has it?" The editor's response applied the terms of the failing credit system to the newspaper's success. When "Hundreds of gentlemen" could not get a copy of the "paper," these potential subscribers "protested." The "confident" editor "increased the circulation" but could not "meet the demand." These kinds of puns attracted readers because they not only explained financial uncertainty in understandable terms but also elicited laughter.[147]

As the numbers of failures increased, the *Picayune* reported that mere "squalls among the banks" transformed into "something worse than an equinoxical storm."[148] This language naturalized the crisis as a normal, if extreme, feature of business. By mid-April, the *Picayune* described the crisis as a "vortex" from which "thousands of innocent persons will doubtless suffer, but they will be martyrs in a good cause." Whether the editors actually believed anyone in New Orleans was "innocent" or were merely pandering to their guilt-stricken readers, their columns argued for a cleansing of the local business community, a baptism by fire. They argued against relief efforts: "Better – far better, let the old rotten fabric burn out of its own accord, without attempting to extinguish it, when we shall be able to build up a much more enduring system."[149] Whether as a hurricane, a tornado, or a conflagration, the local crisis could not be controlled by individuals.

The *Picayune*, however, spun the crisis as a source of relief for individuals. In late April, the devil assured, "The times were never worse nor never better than now." He continued:

Never *worse*, because money was never known to be so scarce as at the present time – never brought such exorbitant interest rates. Never *better*, from the circumstance that the people can now see their errors, now know what fluctuations and what depressions must unavoidably rise from the high credit system, which has been constantly increasing since 1825. Had this state of things been allowed to exist longer, the suffering it must eventually have occasioned would have been much greater.[150]

Financial certainty, he suggested, was a good thing whether or not it was good news. Although the editors occasionally implied that the devil might have a causative role in the city's failures, Mephistopheles Jr. alternated in his arguments between a new species of economic victimhood and the old arguments about individual responsibility.[151]

This simultaneous argument for victimhood and agency reflected an explanation for the economic disaster that was circulating through the nation's press. The editors asked the Gentleman in Black, "What has been the prime cause of all this pecuniary distress? Some lay it to the Specie Circular, some to this thing and some to that." He responded, "All nonsense. Many of the acts of Gen. Jackson's administration may have had a tendency to create a pressure, but if we look to the real first cause, we shall find it in the base purposes to which many of the banks have lent their issues." He blamed "aristocratic speculators" and "monopolizers" for illegitimately employing the financial resources of New Orleans's banks and argued they should "go to work, go to Texas, or into obscurity." Over the course of the crisis, he expressed pity for only two groups: "their unfortunate families" and "the poor devil who does business on his own account, independent of, yet at the same time dependent upon, others."[152] Despite his willingness to see some merchants as victims of the crisis, the *Picayune*'s devil argued that individuals had caused the crisis. He refused, however, to name names. This was not, as the paper claimed, because the editors refused to ally themselves with a political party. On the contrary, the devil's servant's son blamed unidentifiable "bankers," "speculators," and "monopolists" in order to support the argument expressed by the newspapers of the Democratic Party. This explanation rooted in groups of anonymous and immoral financiers stood in contrast to the explanation spread by Whig newspapers that blamed nameable people and policies for the crisis. Partisan explanations either blamed bankers, speculators, and monopolists or Andrew Jackson, the Specie Circular, and before long Martin Van Buren.

By taking the political turn, the *Picayune* provided its readers with a blamable system more dislikable to them than slavery, more empirical than the devil, and more acceptable than asking readers to blame themselves. Like the ministers who called the many panics and local crises a singular panic, the editors of the *Picayune* sought a scapegoat. Like nearly every other newspaper in the nation, these partisans claiming impartiality blamed the crisis on the new and fractious system of mass political parties.

* * *

Along with the news of financial catastrophe, America's newspapers spread the idea that panic was the result of politics. In serial pseudonymous articles, Whigs and Democrats blamed different culprits with the same purpose: to turn economic uncertainty into political power. These arguments were expanded and graphically depicted in other printed sources such as pamphlets and political cartoons. As the anonymous author and self-publisher of "The Times; or The Pressure and Its Causes Examined" explained:

When we attempt to discuss the reason of [our present difficulties], and trace the relation between cause and effect, we separate into political parties, and differ in our opinions not according to our means of information, or our natural endowments and our intelligence – but according to our political biases, our prejudices and the warmth of our feelings. One party of us charge it upon the measures of the administration; and by the other it is attributed to overtrading, overbanking and speculation.[153]

This author, like every other advocate of political causation, claimed "a sincere desire to ascertain the truth" and then provided a partisan explanation.[154] In this case, the author argued, "*it is in ourselves*, that the fault of the times have their origins."[155] Although this sounds like an affirmation of individual economic responsibility, the author employed the term "ourselves" to reference the Democratic triumvirate: merchants, bankers, and speculators.

Each of these faceless culprits appealed to different factions within the Democratic Party. Merchants' international connections appealed to nativist sentiments. Jackson had cultivated the vague symbol of monstrous banks and bankers or "the minions of the banks" as his opponents in his nearly decade-long conflict with Nicholas Biddle to court both hard-money and state-banking factions of his party. The term "speculators," on the other hand, provided a means of blaming what sounded like individual morality without insulting voters.[156] Who, after all, would refer to one's own self as a "speculator"? In fact, "overtrading, overbanking, and speculation" were all accusations that could only be retrospectively assessed by those who claimed no complicity.[157] So this particular pamphlet's deceivingly individualistic argument and search for "truth" was actually one of thousands of restatements of a common argument that deployed an indictment of familiar yet anonymous villains as a shield for the administration.

Whigs made similar claims to "truth" to advocate their own explanation of the crisis. For example, one Whig paper reported its partisan explanation of "Cause and Effect" as emerging from the lips of "a man of extensive business, and without political bias, being really a business man, and not a politician."[158] The Whigs claimed mercantile knowledge and banking experience in their explanation of the crisis, but this came treacherously close to admitting that they were the party of financial malevolence. To avoid this charge, Whigs consistently pointed out that some of the nation's businessmen were Democrats. As one letter in the Whig *National Intelligencer* complained of a Democratic newspaper, "In pronouncing those who buy and those who sell stocks 'gamblers,' 'false reporters,' 'Faro bank men,' 'lottery dealers,' &c. the *Globe* wounds where it should heal." The paper assured that "such speculations are confined to

FIGURE 10. In the lithograph "Uncle Sam Sick with La Grippe," Edward
Williams Clay visually depicted the nation's financial disease and political cures.
Andrew Jackson ("Dr. Hickory"), Thomas Hart Benton ("Apothecary Benton"),
and Martin Van Buren ("Aunt Matty") administer "mint drops" and "juice of
Humbug" to an ailing Uncle Sam, who threatens "if you don't leave off ruining my
Constitution, with your quack nostrums, I'll soon give you your walking ticket
Aunt Matty, and call in Doctor Biddle to prescribe for me." Through the window,
"Doctor Biddle" arrives bringing with him "Bonds lotion" and "Post Note pills"
for temporary relief and an assurance of "assistance" from the English "Dr. John
Bull." Alluding to the failing state of the treasury, the bald eagle humorously
suggests copying the escapist tactics of many panicked people: "I must fly to
Texas, for I shall be starved out here." (New York, 1837. Courtesy of the
American Antiquarian Society.)

no party; that if the roll should be called, and the names answered in
person, the friends of the Administration will be found among the chief
of sinners."[159] Despite this claim to bipartisan speculation, Whigs assured
that the crisis was not a financial problem but a political one. Visualized in
striking political cartoons, such as E. W. Clay's "Uncle Sam Sick With La
Grippe," Whigs continuously diagnosed the crisis as a political disease that
required a political cure (Figure 10).

To make this case, they turned to the word "panic." Its original meaning described individual irrational responses to fear, but by 1837, this term
also connoted a political cause to a collective crisis. "Panic after panic is

created," accused the *New York Daily Express*, cleverly using the passive voice to blame "the Government" for the "tremendous shocks" and the "storm" felt by merchants. The article continued by comparing the American merchants to those in London and Liverpool. The column exclaimed, "A little panic seizes upon the merchants there, and what an affright there is! How the post chaises fly! How the merchants groan! Even the Bank of England is in commotion! But what a feather of pressure have the English merchants suffered in comparison with ours!" The article asserted that "The Government of England is the friend of the mercantile and manufacturing classes." In contrast, it argued, "The Government of the United States is their most bitter enemy. When difficulties crowd upon English merchants, the Government rushes to the rescue; but when difficulties fall upon our merchants, the Government comes with specie humbugs, Treasury Circulars, and the like nonsense of blockhead politicians."[160] Arguing that the change of policies by the Jackson administration caused the crisis, the Whigs reasoned that only different government intervention could end it. In order to convince the voting public that new policy making was required, Whigs first had to convince Americans who were not involved in finance that a crisis was really happening that had ramifications for those who were not just dishonest speculators.

Like the *Picayune*, most Democratic papers suggested that the mercantile failures cleared the land of dishonest businessmen and created new opportunities. In other words, the crisis was a good thing, if it existed. Democratic newspapers suggested that the crisis was an illusion fabricated by "the bankites of Philadelphia and New York" who were working "to create a panic."[161] They blamed Whig newspapers for "adding the terrors of an excessive panic, to destroy all confidence" by ringing "a daily alarm bell" in the form of a daily commercial column that reads like "a panic letter." Referencing the highly politicized panic of 1834, Democrats blamed the failures of "well-doing merchants" on "panic-makers" with partisan motives.[162] Democrats claimed that there was no scarcity of currency. Instead, they argued, the crisis was the result of a collapse in confidence stimulated by the daily "panic letters" in newspapers, which were designed to destroy the solvency of the state banking system in order to clear the path for a new national bank. In other words, politics fueled panic-inducing newspaper accounts. Panic, then, was merely the product of print.

Whigs retorted, "The cry of panic is no party whoop. Distress is no phantom invoked for the promotion of special political ends and objects. Panic-makers, so called, are without employment; the product of their industry is found ready-made in every section of the Union."[163] Unemployment, hunger, and desperation became featured stories in Whig newspapers to show the severity of local crises and the spread of effects beyond the mercantile elite. Whig newspapers pressed Democrats to "go to New York, and ask your own partisans, who are falling amid the general crash brought on by Gen. Jackson and his myrmidons, . . . whether *they* are becoming bankrupts for the sake of creating a panic?" Likening the crisis to the common metaphor of biblical distress, the Whig papers lambasted Democrats for denying that innocent Americans had become victims of a power larger than themselves. "Go accuse the victim of the plague, who is already writhing in the grasp of death, with endeavoring to create a false alarm! Proclaim that 'all is well' while Pestilence and Famine are desolating the country and cities are wrapt in flames!" blasted a Whig newspaper.[164]

Both Whigs and Democrats employed romanticized language in order to explain crises that were, in their actual operation, rather technical. But newspapers did not help educate Americans about the actual process of failure described by merchants with words such as "shinning"; "dunning"; "distress"; "embarrassment"; and, perhaps most evocatively, "gloom." Political explanations and financial explanations of the crisis employed different vocabularies. Whereas merchants most commonly called the period between March and May 1837 a "crisis," American politicians preferred the word "panic." Labeling the crisis a panic worked for both Democrats and Whigs because it implied that it was manufactured, the product of politically assailable policies.

The word "panic," like plagues, famines, and earthquakes, turned Americans into victims. Both parties' arguments cast responsibility onto representative figures, either partisan officeholders or legions of anonymous financiers who transferred individual guilt to the political system. After the Tappan failure, more Americans than before accepted the idea that they were victims, that their potential failure was not a punishment for their individual immorality, and that the federal political system provided the explanation and the means for ending the crisis. The Democratic author of "The Times" wrote, "However much the present distress may have been magnified by imagination and fear – whatever portion of it may be ascribed to an undue panic and want of confidence – still, enough is real to make the present year stand out as a time of distress and difficulty which has no parallel in our history." By the words "our history," the author referenced a single national story; as he clarified, "the present period has never been paralleled since the organization of our government." To this

Democrat, who was willing to concede "the *existence* of these difficulties," the distress of individuals or of local communities had become a singular national event of historical significance.[165] The word "panic" enabled the process of transformation that turned individual suffering and local crises into something much more useful: a national event. The politicization and nationalization of the many panics in 1837 resulted in the invention of the Panic of 1837.

* * *

By the first week in May, the *New York Commercial Advertiser* estimated that "the number of the heavy suspensions that have taken place since the day on which the Josephs failed, is now 260, to say nothing of countless smaller ones, which, in the crash of millions, are not taken into the account."[166] Two months after the Joseph failure, most of the major New York commercial houses had failed. The *Picayune* similarly reported that it had no new failures to report because "there is nobody left to fail!"[167] Americans were still waiting for news of "the effect in England of the bad news in America." Meanwhile, they moaned that "the state of suspense is horrible."[168] Times were so bad that a correspondent for the *National Intelligencer* wrote, "I am weary of writing you. I am disgusted with the reiterated bad news every day's events compel me to tell."[169] Whether this was a heartfelt statement or the words of a "panic-maker," the stories of individual failures became useful tools for people with political aspirations.

By May, even those without a political voice had adopted the language of partisan arguments about panic, sometimes with overwhelming personal consequences. For nineteen-year-old Caroline White of Boylston, Massachusetts, the crisis had not yet directly affected her life, but the discussion of the panic threatened to create a rift within her parents' home. Despite the fact that neither the sender nor the recipient could vote, Caroline's letter to her seventeen-year-old brother Charles confessed her interpretation of the crisis:

All that I hear of is "the times"; all that I say must be the "times," and all my senses has [sic] to partake of the "times." They do not worry me much; but they make me sick. It appears to me that for a number of years past, the whole nation has been madly bent on speculating and living on credit; but credit without cash will not stand many years, and now credit has expired, those who have lived on it must fall. Southern planters, a year or two since, bought a vast number of slaves on credit, expecting their cotton crops would pay principal & interest for slaves, and leave a handsome fortune besides; but instead, they raised so much that cotton fell in price, and they were left greatly in debt; so that they could not pay the northern merchants and manufacturers their dues, and they failed. Thus there was one source of the troublous times, and it has caused a most disastrous train of evil. I suppose that all might be accounted for, in a somewhat similar fashion, though Gen. Jackson and his constituents have a great share attributed to them. For my part, I have picked up the idea, (extremely heretical at home however) that the banks are a little more than half to blame, though some ought to be attached to both sides; indeed, if I happen to say a word against the "banking citadel" it produces so much excitement, that I think they know it is rather feeble or they would not be alarmed at my weak weapons.[170]

Those who took the Democrats' side in the debate over the cause of the crisis, such as Caroline White, argued that the Whigs' argument was rhetorically weak. Nevertheless, the question of the role the government and banks played in fomenting the crisis was not just about rhetorical strength. During the same months that individuals reconceived their crisis as political, the crisis challenged nations, states, and local communities to test their systems of political economy. The practical results of these experiments would come to define the significance of 1837 for policy makers and theorists.

CHAPTER 6

Parallel Crises

It was a matter of minutes. The meeting on April 6, 1837, was the first one recorded in the sixtieth volume of the minute books of the Court of Directors of the Bank of England. A few pages in, a clerk's clear penmanship noted a significant historical event not in terms of centuries, years, or even months, but as fractions of an hour. In perfectly formed oblique and horizontal lines, the clerk spelled out the situation:

Resolved,

That the Governor & Deputy Governor be requested to wait upon his Majesty's Ministers to represent to them the further aid required by Messrs. Wildes & Co., and that they are unable to offer to the Bank any further security than their own personal engagement – and to draw the attention of His Majesty's Ministers to the consequences which may be likely to ensue upon the suspension of the House in question.

At 4 o'clock the Court adjourned to enable the Governors to carry into effect the foregoing Resolution.

At ½ past 5 o'clock the Court was held again, – when the Governor stated that accompanied by the Deputy Governor, he had had an interview with the Chancellor of the Exchequer, and from whom he had received the following letter dated this day.[1]

In exactly ninety minutes, two of the world's most powerful capitalists not only traveled to and from the British Empire's political capital but also obtained a letter resolving any doubts about the role the government would play in the crisis. Although the two men had "waited" on the minister and although the long wait for transatlantic news had motivated George Wildes & Co. to seek the BOE's assistance, no delay could be discerned in the decision of the BOE directors to save this failing firm.

Years later, another clerk transcribed these same minutes into a book labeled "American Accounts, 1836–1842" to justify the actions taken by the BOE in this climactic and controversial period.[2] Twice written in the primary sources, the story of how the most powerful financiers in the world decided to bail out one of the world's largest merchant banking firms with no collateral is worth retelling, even if we must return to the beginning of the panic in 1837.

Between March and May 1837, weeks' worth of news stalled at sea, heightening the financial and economic uncertainty of panicked people in London, New York, and New Orleans. When the packets finally arrived in London, the London *Times* reported that "the arrear of intelligence [was] almost equally great on both sides of the Atlantic."[3] Parallel delays had fomented parallel local crises. When the *Times* printed its account of the Hermann failure, it characterized events in New Orleans as "an exact parallel to proceedings here." The failure in New Orleans, explained the paper, "threatened to disorganize the commercial affairs of the whole city. In fact, it serves to complete the parallel between the New Orleans merchants and those of London."[4] In April, the many panics in 1837 were not only personal but also parallel citywide events. Signed by individuals and traded within networks of correspondents, bills of exchange linked the destabilization of the commercial communities in all three cities. But without communication, events in each city developed independently.

The threat of community-wide failure forced individuals in each of these cities to come together and advocate for the practical application of theories of political economy. National political structures and geography mattered as local communities sought solutions to their crises. Americans could not expect the efficiency or the clarity experienced in London. American finance had been decentralized. Its political system was more layered. And its geography was more expansive. New Orleans was physically more distant from the center of American political power than New York. With hopes of communicating as quickly as leading financiers and politicians in England, Americans in 1837 had just begun inventing devices that would "annihilate" distance through electric current.[5] But even if messages arrived in Washington, D.C., from New Orleans and New York instantaneously, no single authority determined the policies of political economy. States and even municipalities influenced the financial system. And at all three levels of governance – nation, state, and local community – the agendas of elected politicians and self-appointed community leaders influenced policy.

During the same two months of financial uncertainty and cascading failure that forced many individual panicked people to reconsider their fundamental ideas about economic responsibility, the crisis provided a testing ground for different systems of political economy. More than minutes and less than a year, the two months of panic in 1837 set the stage for more than a century of theoretical disputes about the intersection between governments and financial systems. And as more and more Americans turned to the political system as an explanation of the crisis, their accounts bore the prejudices and polemics of partisanship. Many of the meanings ascribed to the panic took shape as institutions and groups of individuals tried to end it.

* * *

Less than one week after the Joseph failure, seven of New York's most respected businessmen traveled to Philadelphia as members of a Committee of Circulation and Conference.[6] Although they labeled themselves a committee, these men were not elected by voters or nominated by a government officer. Instead, they were a group of self-appointed leaders determined to speak for the mercantile community of New York City and, by extension, for merchants throughout the nation. They reached their destination in a back room of a marbled edifice on Chestnut Street during the morning of March 24, 1837.

By the time the New Yorkers arrived, Nicholas Biddle had presided for fifteen years over the BUS, but this once nationally chartered bank had become a pale imitation of itself. Despite the fact that the building still echoed the architecture of Greek temples, the BUS had an entirely new business structure.[7] Under its Pennsylvania charter, the BUS no longer wielded the resources of federal deposits or acted as a national clearinghouse for bank notes and bills of exchange. Nevertheless, it remained highly regarded by those looking for trustworthy credit instruments on both sides of the Atlantic.[8] Hoping to translate the BUS's symbolic power into a more tangible form, the committee wanted Biddle to do what New York's banks could not: issue paper credit instruments to replace the increasingly dubious bills of exchange. Despite its limitations, the BUS's new charter proved less restrictive than the charters of banks established during the 1830s in New York State.

Between resigning his U.S. Senate seat in January 1829 and becoming secretary of state to Andrew Jackson in March 1829, Martin Van Buren served as New York State's governor. In his two-month term, he signed into law "An Act to Create a Fund for the Benefit of Creditors of Certain

Monied Corporations." This state banking law required newly chartered banks to participate in an experiment in regulation that became known as the Safety Fund System. In addition to a board of commissioners with the power to investigate the books of any bank within the system, the Safety Fund was primarily a pool of money designed to protect creditors from bank failures. All the banks in the system were required not only to pay a fee into the fund based on a percentage of their capital but also to pay specie for all of their paper money on demand. If a bank refused to exchange its notes for coins, depositors and bank note holders would be paid from the fund. The other member banks, however, would have to reimburse the fund for the lost capital. Thus, the Safety Fund System was designed to create "safe" banking not only through governmental surveillance but also by incentivizing self-policing by the bankers themselves.[9]

The system represented a middle ground between the theories of political economy of the hard-money Loco-Focos and the commercial Democrats, who advocated for state-chartered banks. It created state control over banking and protected citizens from bank paper while allowing new banks to be chartered. Whigs who favored a more national, centralized policy pointed out the system's flaws: it took into account neither the possibility of the failure of all the banks at the same time nor the influence of financial networks that reached beyond New York State's boundaries.

The committee that met with Biddle found the Safety Fund System too restrictive and sought a means to circumvent its limitations. Its members implored Biddle to buy $5 million of "domestic exchange and notes" that had "heretofore caused no losses of any magnitude" with bank notes that had a future payment date, otherwise known as "post notes." Safety Fund Banks could not issue post notes because they were not payable on demand, but the BUS could. To replace foreign bills of exchange, the committee suggested that Biddle sell bonds backed by the "high credit of the Bank of the United States" in European money markets. John A. Stevens, author of the merchants' proposal, "confidently believed" that these measures would "have a salutary influence in the existing crisis in restoring confidence – in invigorating the efforts of solvent houses to sustain themselves and in letting loose masses of money now hoarding, which it is thought would soon seek investment in such undoubted securities."[10]

Although the plan might ease the shortage of currency, it might also weaken rather than revive confidence. After all, it circumvented a system designed to protect people from banks, and it involved an allegiance with the figurehead of Whig opposition to Democratic financial policies. The Safety Fund had been designed to prevent this sort of circulation because, as Stevens admitted in his letter, the plan could lead "to an imprudent and injurious expansion of business."[11] Stevens, of course, hoped this would not happen, but the possibility was dangerous in both financial and political terms. With the Democratic press suggesting that merchants and their "overtrading" and "overbanking" had caused the crisis by exactly this type of paper credit, the plan was not likely to convince Democratic voters that more paper would restore banking safety. Besides, by appealing to Biddle, the loser of Jackson's bank war, the plan implied partisanship.

When the press learned of the proposal, William Leggett found it so partisan and so contrary to the Democratic explanation for the cause of the crisis that he likened the committee to quack doctors. He excoriated, "There is a new theory in medicine which administers as a remedy that which caused the disease. The merchants and Mr. Biddle are now for applying this theory to business. An excessive inflation of bank credit caused the evil; and they now propose a still further inflation as the cure." Leggett employed an arsenal of metaphors, from children's fables to the biblical flood, to ridicule the idea that more credit would yield confidence. He concluded, "We doubt if the community can be rescued from the dreadful consequences of a deluge of bank credit, by a further effusion from the fountain of evil."[12] But where was the fountain of evil's source? A few weeks later, Leggett reported that he was "disclosing the foreign origin of Mr. Biddle's notable scheme of 'relief' – a scheme which bore on its face that it was adopted at the suggestion of the merchants of this city, although it had already been made the basis, in London, of extensive financial arrangements between the Barings and the Bank of England."[13] The hint of an accusation of treason that lurked behind this passage complemented the Democratic argument that "evil" bankers, merchants, and speculators had caused the crisis not only by "overbanking" but also by allowing foreigners to invest in America.

The plan looked political on a smaller scale as well. Within New York State, the Safety Fund System protected "country" bank note holders by taxing the large capital of New York City's banks, most of which did not rely heavily on bank notes to conduct their business. This rift between country and city bankers allowed the state's newspaper editors to fill their columns with partisan attacks on the paper circulations of upstate banks and the intrigues of city banks to undermine the Safety Fund System. The committee's trip to Philadelphia confirmed the latter.[14] The plan also posed political troubles between New York City and its rival Philadelphia.[15] In his letter, Stevens implored Biddle that "no local feelings or mistaken views of State interests can interfere." Stevens and the other bankers hoped that even though the BUS was now chartered by Pennsylvania, Biddle would supply new paper money to restore confidence in New York. But after years of plotting and counterplotting between financiers in New York and Philadelphia, this plan invited local animosity as well as partisan invective.[16]

Without sleeping on the proposal, Biddle promised to present the suggested measures "to the Board of Directors by whom they cannot fail to be considered with the respectful attention due to all that concerns the distinguished community you represent." He assured the committee that "the Bank of the United States, tho' no longer national in form, has lost none of the desire to be useful to any portion of our common country."[17] In a letter sent the next day, Biddle promised the committee that he would "permit no unnecessary delay" in determining a course of action, but that the board of directors was "not prepared today to make any specific recommendation."[18] Clearly, this was not fast enough for the New Yorkers. To convince Biddle and his board of the urgency of their decision, Stevens and the "self appointed committee of the merchants of New York" extended an invitation to the Philadelphian to see the crisis in New York City for himself.[19]

More than mere altruism motivated Biddle to accept Stevens's invitation. Biddle recognized the possibilities of a display of the BUS's authority in New York. As a shrewd politico, he could not have missed the opportunity to win supporters for his crusade for federal rechartering of the BUS. With news arriving from London that the BOE had extended credit to its commercial community, newspapers called for Biddle to demonstrate his institution's analogous role in the United States.[20] Biddle needed the support of the public to convert his cultural power over the nation's economy back into its institutional form. In addition, the board of directors required convincing. As a private, state-chartered bank, the BUS was not required to save its competitors. Responsible to their stockholders, the directors hesitated about risking further debt on New York's behalf at this precarious moment.

Three days after the New Yorkers left Philadelphia, Biddle journeyed to New York to, in Hone's words, "ascertain the true state of things."[21] On his arrival, Biddle wrote to his board, "The condition of things I found more alarming than I had anticipated and required to my judgment some strong measure to put down a feeling of despondency & despair which threatened the worst consequences." Not sure that the amount of paper currency the BUS could offer would be enough of a "strong measure" to end the crisis, Biddle noted that he was "too busy to do more than to add the appearance of respect and regard."[22] All Biddle could do was instill in the commercial community the belief that he would help; he hoped that this idea alone might restore confidence. He was supporting a current economic belief among businessmen, if not yet among theorists, that a destruction of confidence rather than any more tangible economic factor produced financial crises. If panic was nothing more than a failure of confidence, an "appearance of respect and regard" might be a solution. Practically, even if Biddle believed in a more material cure for the crisis, he could offer nothing more while in New York.[23]

On March 28, 1837, Biddle scheduled an appointment with what one newspaper described as "the principal merchants and bankers" at the appropriately named Merchants' Bank on Wall Street.[24] A few hours before Biddle's arrival, Hone and a number of other businessmen met "for the purpose of agreeing upon a letter to be presented to Mr. Biddle, requesting the Bank of the United States at Philadelphia to step forward in this most appalling crisis and save the commercial community of New York."[25] Unlike Stevens's earlier private correspondence with the bank, this meeting was purposefully acknowledged to the public. In New York's financial district, all eyes turned toward Biddle. According to Bennett in the *New York Herald*, when Biddle arrived on Wall Street, "[he] drew more attention towards him than Mr. Webster or Mr. Clay or Mr. Van Buren could do any day." As the hour of Biddle's arrival at the Merchant's Bank approached, "an immense crowd gathered around the door."[26] As Hone described it in his diary, "an assemblage of woebegone countenances" attended the meeting. With a hint of envy, Hone said the "assemblage" revered Biddle as "the sun to which alone they can look to illumine the darkness." Even Hone looked to the Philadelphian as a savior of confidence. As he confided to his journal, "He can do much, and most assuredly will."[27]

During the panic in 1837, Biddle's "sun" certainly shone brighter in New York than it ever had before. During the Jackson administration, the Safety Fund System had made many New York bankers inured to concerns over the destruction of the BUS and empowered others to actively support the dismantling of Biddle's power.[28] Hone asked himself rhetorically, "Did ever man enjoy so great a moral triumph?"[29] And from the words of newspaper writers throughout the states, Biddle's visit was indeed interpreted as "not a little mortifying" and "humiliating" for the New Yorkers and the height of altruism for the Philadelphian.[30]

In front of the crowd gathered at the bank, the commercial leaders publicly read their letter asking Biddle for exactly the same financial remedies that Stevens had already requested in private. Other than the signatures of representatives of 103 firms, the publicly presented letter differed from Stevens's private one only in that it explicitly argued that Biddle's assistance would "not only be of service to this city, but to the United States at large."[31] By asking Biddle to help New York for the benefit of the nation, the city's "self appointed" mercantile leaders explicitly fed him the national power he craved.

Although he doubted the efficacy of the BUS's financial commitment, Biddle fulfilled his role as provider of confidence. In his written reply presented to the committee in an interview the next day, Biddle flattered the "spirit and intelligence" of the New York commercial community. He assured the New Yorkers that he would not "permit myself to doubt that this city will preserve its high character before the world." Just as individuals panicked when they lost faith in one another, he explained, the city's greatest threat was the doubt of its citizens. In an exhortation of trust, Biddle assured New York's mercantile leaders that "the surest ground of confidence for others, is confidence in ourselves."[32] Biddle's confidence-boosting words encouraged the revival of commerce and encouraged the members of the New York commercial community to rediscover their confidence as local leaders.

Despite Biddle's advice, learning to trust again required more than a revival of faith. In his letter to the New Yorkers, Biddle acknowledged that it was not only the lack of confidence among New York's commercial community that had caused the crisis but also "that recent weeks in the South & in Europe have ... produced a paralysis of private credit which deranges the whole system of our foreign and domestic exchanges."[33] In other words, as he explained in a letter to his European correspondents, "The disasters in New Orleans and in London had nearly destroyed all confidence in private bills and left no means of remittance except specie." He continued, "Of this the supply in the banks was very small, for altho' much has undoubtedly come into the country, yet owing to the perverseness of the Government it had ceased to be available for the purposes of commerce." The immediate cause of the collapse in confidence in New York City was, according to Biddle, the failure of the Hermanns and the trouble in the London money market, but ultimately he blamed the Jackson administration's financial policies for the credit crisis that required his "prompt and vigorous interposition."[34]

With a failure in trust stretching as far as New Orleans and London, Biddle thought "the appropriate remedy seems to be to substitute for the private credit of individuals the more known & established credit of the Bank, until public confidence in private stability has time to recover."[35] He feared "a general suspension of specie payments" by the "commercial community." And although he would have preferred to discriminate against those who "ought to fail ... as victims of their own rashness," he felt that "in moments of financial panic such a discrimination was impossible, and all that remained was by some vigorous effort to rally back the spirits of those who were about to throw up every thing in a moment of despair." By calling the crisis a panic, Biddle argued that it was the "temporary" product of his political opposition. He suggested that foreign credit and his own institution's reputation could "dissipate an alarm calculated to do infinite mischief" by ending the "momentary despair" of New York's "mercantile community."[36]

Over the course of the next month, Biddle would convince the board of the BUS to draw on credit it had been offered at the BOE and issue the post notes and bonds. Explaining this decision to his British creditors after the fact, Biddle declared that the BUS's long-term paper credits had already "inspired confidence here."[37] If Biddle's plan actually did so, the effects of that confidence were not immediately apparent in New York City. Hone opined, "these measures have had the effect to inspire some degree of Confidence, but the actual state of things continue as bad as ever." He summarized, "Money is exorbitantly dear."[38] Any increase in confidence vanished as failures continued. A little more than a week after Biddle left town, the *Morning Courier and New-York Enquirer* editorialized, "If our merchants, bank directors, monied and business men generally, would but feel the same confidence in the result of the late measures by the Bank of the United States which Mr. Biddle himself does, all would be well."[39]

Privately, even Biddle had doubts. In letters to his board, he expressed his concern that no amount of credit provided by the BUS could fill the gap created by the increasing quantity of protested paper. Even after the New York State Canal Fund proposed issuing another $3 million in stock, the crisis continued.[40] Biddle's opposition could not have agreed more with the banker's private appraisal of the insatiability of the demand for reputable paper. In the pages of the *New York Herald*, Bennett pointed out the obvious: "In the face of all these propositions of relief, the stock market fell, and the failures continued without any special intermission." The editor continued, "The evil is too enormous and too complicated for any relief from a beggarly five millions or even ten millions."[41] He was right. The crisis stretched too far geographically, involved too much money, and was too multifarious in nature for any existing financial institution, even the BUS, to end.

* * *

Although the BUS might have been a symbol of confidence to desperate merchants and hopeful Whigs, it was not exempt from the pressures on international credit. Biddle's bank would struggle through similar threats to its specie as the New York banks. In fact, within half a decade, the only remnants of the BUS would be its marble edifice on Chestnut Street, the lawsuits of angry creditors, and thousands of upended lives.

When visiting Philadelphia in 1841, Charles Dickens stayed on Chestnut Street and described the building across from his window as "a handsome building of white marble, which had a mournful ghost-like aspect dreary to behold." The next morning, he discovered its identity: "It was the tomb of many fortunes; the great catacomb of investment; the memorable United States Bank."[42]

The BUS's failure in 1841 would color the memories of many. Biddle's biographers referred to him either as a thwarted villain or a tragic hero of mythical proportions, a fitting fate for America's evangelist of Greek-style architecture.[43] For the BUS's clerks, debtors, and creditors, the failure enabled tales of self-made manhood and of victimization.[44] The clearest victims of the failure, however, were the thousands of people who found themselves reinventing their own lives in the pens of the domestic slave trade because, unbeknownst to them, their lives had been mortgaged to finance their own enslavement.[45] In the 1840s, the trust managing the bankruptcy of the BUS became one of the largest slaveholders in Mississippi. This meant that holders of BUS bonds and stocks suddenly became owners of portions of securitized people. To pay creditors, the executors sold many slaves, but conditions may have been worse for slaves not sold. One agent sent to assess a foreclosed plantation described the conditions as "a wretched state of things." He reported, "several of the Negroes now there are sickly & inefficient from overwork & exposure – some frost bitten, some ruptured, some branded on their hips as runaways – all without shoes & most of them without winter clothing or blankets."[46] For these people, the BUS's failure caused physical pain and suffering.

For all of those who cheered or booed the many rises and falls of the BUS, 1837 would be remembered as featuring intense political battles even though, in the midst of the crisis in April 1837, little actual politics occurred. Congress was not in session. Jackson had retired. Van Buren had barely begun to govern. No elected official had appealed to the BUS. And Biddle's role in the crisis was brief and mostly symbolic.

Both Biddle and his New York hosts actively shaped the legacy of their participation in the crisis. They did everything in their power to appear significant. Every aspect of financial maneuvering was coupled with an almost theatrical posturing. The group of New Yorkers who claimed the right to speak for merchants throughout the nation in their appeal to Biddle constructed an identity of national leadership. The genius of the New Yorkers' response to the financial crisis was that despite their potential personal ruin and likely loss of social position, they collectively harnessed the power of panic not only to preserve the existing hierarchies but also to claim national financial authority. Nevertheless, as the crisis proved larger than the New Yorkers imagined, they realized that if they could not be the national leaders they imagined, they could at least blame the national leaders they had elected.

* * *

While the New Yorkers turned toward the government in Washington to find a national resolution to their crisis, reports of Biddle's appearance traveled across the Atlantic. Londoners recognized the international significance of the meeting between Biddle and the New Yorkers, even if they missed the local and state politics associated with the event. Even though London newspapers based their coverage on the same New York City newspapers and correspondence that implied the superficiality of the Biddle meeting, the efforts of the BUS looked much more successful from across the Atlantic.

In late April, Londoners had been waiting for transatlantic news for weeks with "much alarm and apprehension" as they struggled through their own crisis. The initial reports from New York, however, "happily disappointed all." The London *Morning Chronicle* described the "prompt and energetic measures adopted to check the mischief ... The Bank of the United States came forward at this critical moment and rendered every assistance in its power." Implying that the BUS could have done more if it still had the powers held under its former federal charter, the newspaper article hinted at the recent actions of Britain's own central bank.

The positive London interpretation of the BUS was a reflection of the BOE's own struggle to balance public duty and private interests. The unfolding local London panic peeked through the editor's hope that his report would "revive the drooping spirits of those who anticipated numerous failures in the United States, and be the means of placing the American houses in firm position." Although glowing reports might invigorate the spirit of London investors, the American houses needed more than words to save them.[47] They needed the credit of the BOE. "We have no alternative left but [to] suspend payment unless we can be assured of an advance," wrote George Wildes & Co., asking the BOE to help it meet the payments that would come due in April.[48] Unfortunately, the firm could offer the BOE no additional collateral.

This was bad news for the BOE directors; they had hoped that the loans provided to Wildes in March would have been sufficient. Now, should the stockholders demand it, they would have to find a way to justify not only the first round of loans but also either a bailout with no additional security, a glaring deviation from standard practice, or the failure of a firm that could rattle the British Empire's financial stability. The urgency of this request and its unorthodox terms prompted the Court of Directors to send the governor and deputy governor on their ninety-minute journey to Westminster and back. The directors resolved to present the details of the Wildes case to the political official in charge of fiscal policy, the chancellor of the exchequer, to give a difficult decision the scent of public approval. By inviting the chancellor to participate in the Wildes decision, the BOE hoped to spread the blame for the fallout.

Much more than two and a half miles separated the BOE from the chancellor's office on Downing Street; the distinct communities that surrounded these buildings mirrored the difference between these two institutions and their response to the crisis. The BOE was located in the City, a place where social networks were constructed through the prospects of financial profit. Westminster, home of the chancellor's office, was the capital of the British Empire, where parties gained control of Parliament by calculated coalitions and offices resulted from patronage. A financial crisis that threatened the empire's trade could be disastrous for the leaders of both the City and Westminster, but responsibility thus far had fallen exclusively to the BOE and the merchant bankers who had pledged support for the American houses. By bringing the news of the Wildes failure to Westminster, the directors of the BOE opened the question of whether national commercial disasters were the responsibility of the government.[49]

When the BOE officers arrived, the sitting chancellor faced a difficult choice. In 1837, the party in power in the British Empire, the Whigs, was not entirely committed to free trade. It had other more pressing concerns. Whig power rested on a precarious balance between advocating political reform and aristocratic central rule. Economic policy threatened the Whig coalition.[50] The sitting chancellor, Thomas Spring Rice, would risk his political career by issuing any opinion regarding banking. As both a member of the Irish landed gentry and a moderate advocate of free trade associated with the Political Economy Club, Spring Rice's credentials had helped him win the highest Treasury office in 1835. After a career of navigating political fault lines, he did not want to misstep by offering his opinion on a sensitive matter when it was not absolutely required. He spoke for the government as a whole when he pronounced, "that when the responsibility of a decision rested solely on the Bank of England, we did not feel ourselves at liberty or justified in recommending to you any particular course." As an able politician, he offered the directors a consolation for his inaction. "Be assured that whatever decision you came to on full deliberation of your Court should receive from His Majesty's Government the most favorable interpretation," he informed the directors. In lieu of entire or even joint responsibility for the pending disaster, Spring Rice offered his best spin.[51]

For Spring Rice, the request of the BOE for government intervention was the precursor of many that would follow. That same April morning, before the BOE governors' trip across London, a delegation of "merchants, brokers & other inhabitants connected with the trade of Liverpool" began their journey toward the capital. In 1837, Liverpool-based merchants imported 90 percent of Britain's cotton. Since January, the price of cotton had declined by more than 30 percent. Unable to sell their cotton without ruinous losses, the Liverpudlians looked to London for help.[52] When the delegation arrived in London, it sought assistance from the City and Westminster. During the next few days, the delegates met with both Spring Rice and the directors of the BOE and presented a memorial signed by nearly two hundred individuals and firms. The memorial attested, "That the distress of the Mercantile Interest is intense beyond example and that it is rapidly extending to all ranks and conditions of the community so as to threaten irretrievable ruin, in all directions; involving the prudent with the imprudent, the Manufacturer with the Merchant, and the Weavers, Spinners, and Labourers generally with the Manufacturers themselves." Claiming the threat of widespread economic strife, the memorialists begged Spring Rice to intercede on their behalf with the BOE. As a precedent, they cited events in 1826 when the BOE accepted merchandise as collateral for loans. They argued that the current distress "beyond example" required such exceptional measures.[53]

By appealing to the political leadership, the northerners hoped to use their Whig connections to influence the financial leaders. Economic unrest among laborers might empower radical politicians who would threaten the Whigs' recent political conquest of the manufacturing districts. With a politician's polished sympathy, the prime minister, Lord Melbourne, expressed his "most serious regret that any circumstances should have occasioned serious commercial embarrassments ... & the hope that the native industry of the Country may be soon restored to that state of prosperity which it has enjoyed during several successful years." The memorialists lacked adequate influence to win more than sympathy from politicians, let alone convince the BOE directors to loan them scarce specie.

The BOE directors had difficulty in deciding to assist their friends in the City; they had no interest in aiding provincial strangers. In addition, the chancellor refused to lobby the BOE directors for their cause. Spring Rice explained that he had "uniformly & steadily declined any interference in the management of the Bank." He justified his decision to ignore the commercial crisis based on his "Feeling confident that the Bank possesses the means of pronouncing a proper decision & that the directors would be governed by their sense of duty to the public." Despite the confidence expressed by Spring Rice, the BOE directors decided that "duty to the public" did not mean sending its depleted specie northward, especially without the typically required collateral. The memorialists failed to convince the BOE to help them. By rejecting their appeal, the directors of the BOE defined the institution's duty to merchants during a crisis: none.[54]

Elected solely by fellow shareholders, the BOE directors catered to a different public than the British government. Although BOE policy makers were mostly concerned with the money market and bankers within the City, not everyone agreed with this nearsighted focus. The *Morning Chronicle* asked, "How can the commercial interests of the country ever be in a wholesome state while the controllers of the monetary system administer such partial laws, and act so diametrically opposite to every principle of honour, consistency, and justice?" Of course, as a private institution with public duties, "the controllers of the monetary system" issued no "laws" and made no claim to impartiality; they also claimed no power over the nation's commodity trade. The "great secrecy" about the BOE's deliberations fed the newspaper's speculation "that the recent measures of the Bank have been dictated by interested motives."[55] But no clear line existed between the directors' private interests and public duties. As one member of Parliament later argued, "Scarcely two persons are agreed upon the question of what the Bank ought to do for the purpose of regulating the currency: so that, while every one is calling upon the Bank to do its duty, no one can say with certainty, what that duty is."[56] Perhaps the intercession of Spring Rice on the Liverpudlians' behalf might have convinced the BOE directors that their duty was to save the merchants of the cotton trade. Without this governmental pressure, the directors struggled to follow what the Palmer Rule dictated as the duty of the BOE: balance the ratio between gold and paper.

The struggle of the BOE directors to follow this rule involved not only their fears of the collapse of the international financial system but also personal obligations. In contrast to the Liverpudlian outsiders, Wildes did not need the intercession of politicians to argue its case at the BOE because, as the *Morning Chronicle* had guessed, the directors were financially and theoretically "interested" in the question of Wildes's survival. Several of the twenty-three men who had been elected to the Court of Directors on April 5, 1837, had pledged their assets in connection to the March loan to Wildes.[57] When the court deliberated over the bailout the next day, they had every incentive to prevent the firm's bankruptcy.

In addition to these financial interests, the BOE's loan to Wildes represented a developing concept in banking theory, the idea of a lender of last resort, an institution that supplies sudden demands for liquidity when the market cannot meet the demand. By extending a loan of specie to Wildes, the BOE hoped to sustain confidence in paper financial instruments and squelch the doubts that would lead to a run on the nation's gold supplies. Thus, the BOE directors could make the case that providing Wildes with an unsecured loan implied dutifully protecting the currency.[58]

Shortly after Spring Rice declined to give an opinion about the financial crisis, the directors made a radical choice in order to preserve the existing financial system. Like all conservative revolutionaries, they hoped that it would not set a precedent for change. Again, the clerk's perfect penmanship recorded the decision:

A Motion was made and seconded,

That in the opinion of this Court the Bank ought not to make Advances to Commercial Houses without sufficient and approved security.

Upon which an Amendment was moved and seconded,

That it is expedient under the great difficulties in which the Country may be placed by the suspension of any of the principal Houses carrying on the American Trade, for this Court to depart from its accustomed mode of acting – and to afford such aid as may be necessary for closing the concerns of Messrs. Wildes & Co.

And the Question being put thereon,

The said Amendment was carried in the affirmative.[59]

The formality of these sentences masks their deviancy. The "Motion" affirmed existing policy but the "Amendment" declared a revolution in central banking. Despite their hedging, the directors established a precedent for protecting the "Country" from "great difficulties." With duty redefined, the BOE bailed out Wildes without any collateral.

* * *

In 1837, on both sides of the Atlantic Ocean, experiments in applying the theory of a lender of last resort occurred simultaneously within different systems of political economy. The BUS, unlike the BOE, had been relieved of any duties demanded by a national government. In addition, the regulated national currency of the centrally controlled British Empire contrasted with the decentralized monetary system and divided national and state governments in the United States. The British could respond to their financial problems more quickly than Americans because official leaders of the national financial system existed, and these men could travel to the political capital, discuss a problem, and return with a definitive answer in minutes. To the Liverpudlians' disadvantage, geographical proximity to the center of financial and political power mattered in England.

Distance mattered even more in the geographically expansive United States. Any attempt at centralizing financial power in America would fail to provide equal access for northeastern New Yorkers and southwestern New Orleanians, who were, unlike British subjects, equal citizens separated by difficult overland and sea routes. These differences in political economy and geography resulted in different responses to local crises in 1837. Americans increasingly cast events in the terms of national politics; British bankers and merchants demanded intervention from the government and its favored bank from the onset.

* * *

The story of bank bailouts did not end with the BOE directors' choice to save Wildes; in fact, most of the story was written and its significance determined outside the banks. The bailout came with conditions: it was to be used only for "closing the concerns of Messrs. Wildes & Co."[60] The next week, Wildes sent out a circular announcing that "the operations of our House will henceforth consist only of liquidation." It blamed "the severe pressure experienced in the Money Market." Under the guidance of a board of inspectors, the BOE would continue to loan Wildes money for another two months, allowing the firm more time to accommodate its bills circulating in the Anglo-American economy.[61]

The BOE's bailout of Wildes did not end the crisis in the City. "There are of course rumors about everybody," Bates recorded in his diary in response to an erroneous rumor that Baring Brothers was in trouble.[62] Not every house, however, was as secure as Baring Brothers. By May 11, both Thomas Wilson & Co. and Timothy Wiggin & Co. requested and received assistance without the usual collateral from the BOE.[63] The three Ws found themselves in the same situation – they had overextended credit to American correspondents, had not received the anticipated specie from the United States that would cover their debts, and needed the BOE's help to liquidate their concerns.

The BOE's decision to sustain the three Ws received mixed reviews. Surveying "the evils of the times that threaten us" in his diary, Bates praised the BOE for saving "the commercial world" from "a state of perfect stagnation and discredit."[64] Few expressed such decisive approval. Although the *Times* reported, "the interference has proven to be an instant and sensible relief in a very large circle," the *Courier* asserted that it was by "no means clear that the course that has been adopted with respect to the American houses generally is the best." The *Courier* enumerated "two very pernicious consequences" from the bank's actions that highlighted the difficulty of brokering confidence in a crisis. First, the BOE's support "inevitably prolongs a state of insecurity, and paralyzes commercial operations by hindering individuals from knowing whom to trust or how to act." Second, "it allows the principal culprits, that is the money dealers, to get out of the pit they had dug for themselves." The BOE's policy granted creditors neither certainty nor revenge. Despite these perceived shortcomings, the *Courier* refused to blame the BOE directors for their choice to support the three Ws because of the "novel and extraordinary circumstances of the case." The editor hoped that the BOE directors would "use every practicable effort to bring the present anomalous state of things to a close." Public opinion confirmed the BOE's decision.[65]

The classification of the times as "novel and extraordinary" and "anomalous" reflected the state of economic thought in 1837. Political economy theorists agreed that crises were abhorrent to the ideal relationship between supply and demand that formed the basis of their analysis. Businessmen were uncertain not only about the trustworthiness of paper but also about the economic processes taking place. Even in London, a center for political economy clubs and publications, the crisis eluded theoretical explanation. Indeed, even the directors of the BOE could not explain the "anomalous" times.[66]

The *Morning Chronicle* described the BOE as having "whirled about in so many directions" that it appeared to act "contrary to all rule."[67] In such times, the rules were unclear to the directors as well as the public. Some of the statements issued by the BOE seemed to diminish the directors' choice to save Wildes by regarding it as a necessity, whereas others highlighted the decision-making process by claiming the bailout as a "merit for the Bank." "There is understood," reported the *Times*, "to be a very large party in the Bank parlour who are wholly opposed to the Principle of the assistance given to this and other houses." The *Times* informed its readers that this dissent has "very much puzzled and mystified the city." Ruling out government interference, the *Times* complained, "there is much difficulty in conjecturing what other power there can be able to compel the Bank to do that which was thought inconvenient or impolitic." But conjecture they did: "In the novel as well as difficult situation into which commercial affairs have been brought, nothing can exceed the eager curiosity and interest with which every new incident is watched."[68] Rather than believing that they could look to the past for explanations of the present, the BOE directors agreed with the *Times*'s opinion that "it is no exaggeration to say that the calamity of 1825 has been very far exceeded."[69] The confusion within the BOE about policy mirrored the general confusion in people's minds about the relationship of the current crisis to any larger explanation of political economy. By arguing that the times were anomalous, advocates of *laissez-faire* found a loophole in their doctrinaire position of rejecting government or any other regulatory involvement in markets.[70] In a crisis without precedent and therefore without a theoretical model, one could be a free trader who supported this bailout without feeling like an oxymoron.

The London *Times* found proof that the present case was "out of the ordinary range of commercial difficulties" by the troubled task of assessing blame for the crisis. The paper reported that "all houses below the first class" had been injured by "a calamity as much beyond their control as any great political crisis, or even a war itself." Although less elite financiers had confided in the credit system that led to the crisis, the newspaper expressed fears that the "possible consequences to the whole of the manufacturing districts" would "tend to throw the great multitudes out of employ." If the bankers did not understand the crisis they had partially caused, the "great multitudes" certainly shouldered no blame and bore the material brunt of economic depression.[71]

As the BOE directors "continu[ed] their manifestoes on the original cause of these difficulties," the *Times* pejoratively noted that they were "exculpating themselves, as usual."[72] "Manifestoes" about the bank's policies and the protection of the nation's currency were not the sole province of the directors. The British banking system inspired print, as a member of Parliament early in 1840 exclaimed to a roaring response, "Mr. Richardson, the bookseller, of Cornhill, has printed and sold no less than 2,000 [different] pamphlets on the currency question, within the last two years and a half ... Why, there is scarcely a morning of the year that we do not see or receive a new paper or publication on the subject."[73] The decision to bail out Wildes would be remembered as a pivotal choice in debates over regulation of financial markets; the two handwritten copies of the minutes in the BOE's archives presaged thousands of rewritings of the story in print.

* * *

The directors had a reason to write. Spring Rice's refusal to involve the government in the crisis meant that the BOE directors were left entirely responsible for the ramifications of their decisions. The directors argued that they were merely responding to factors beyond their control and therefore should not shoulder the blame. Spotlighting international causes of the crisis, the BOE cited events on the other side of the Atlantic and the "unfavourable winds" that held precious specie and information in suspension between the United States and Britain.[74]

In mid-April, after more than a month without news from America, Londoners discovered that New Orleans and New York had been experiencing similar crises. The London *Times* reported on April 18, 1837, that the Hermann businesses had submitted "a pressing application for assistance" to the "principal banks of New Orleans." According to the first set of letters that arrived in London, New Orleanian banks had not yet made a decision about whether or not to bail out the Hermanns. The *Times* reported, "much private influence was exerted (an exact parallel to proceedings here) to induce the banks to afford the assistance required, and many individuals had offered in that case to become the securities for the house in question, whose fall, under such a weight of engagements, threatened to disorganize the commercial affairs of the whole city."[75] Although the crises in New Orleans and London might have been operating in parallel, they were not identical.

Londoners imagined that the commercial community in New Orleans would act with as much speed and decisiveness as the BOE. In their optimism, they failed to realize that the economic organization of New Orleans was vastly less developed than the centuries-old structure of the City. Located more than a thousand miles from America's northeastern centers of politics and finance, New Orleans's merchants and bankers could not call on a central government or its agents for immediate relief. Instead, New Orleanians operated under an entirely decentralized system of political economy. No Safety Fund System united Louisiana's banks. New Orleans was more fragmented than New York. It was divided into three municipalities, each without the will to regulate. Its banks were numerous and uncooperative, and its failed merchants could inspire little confidence.

The response of the London commercial community to the crisis had been so organized that it formed the basis for new banking theories that continue to inform policy. By contrast, the New Orleans commercial community was so disorganized that reports from the city varied daily. Outsiders looked for news that New Orleanians would save their cotton factors in the same way the BOE had saved the three Ws. Locals knew that New Orleanians lacked both the institutional organization and the cultural power to cultivate an image of strength in a time of ultimate weakness.

By the time the London *Times* reprinted the New Orleans *True American*'s first report of the Hermann failure in late April, the banks in New Orleans had failed to organize a collective response to the panic for almost two months. With sixteen banks, each with approximately ten board members, more than one hundred men with their own pressing concerns had to agree to risky actions. The boards of individual institutions such as the Citizens' Bank of Louisiana could not decide on an appropriate response to what one correspondent described as "the merchants' dreadful times."[76] Although several banks agreed to lenient terms for the businesses of the Hermann family, "an early and a satisfactory adjustment" involving all of the banks in New Orleans never materialized.[77] After opting out of the collective plan to support the Hermanns, the directors of the Citizens' Bank reluctantly granted the failed firms extended time to pay back several loans. Two of the eleven directors voted against this policy and preserved in the minutes their right to "record their reason for so doing."[78]

The dissent among Citizens' Bank directors was smaller and less publicized than the disagreements among the pamphlet-writing directors of the BOE. Whereas the BOE directors battled behind a single pair of parlor doors and then published their arguments to invite public debate, the disagreements among New Orleanians about how a bank should function in a period of commercial crisis took place in sixteen separate buildings without the printing institutions or the theoretical interest to call for public reflection by the bankers. Only post-panic investigations called by state and federal legislatures would expose the rifts within New Orleans bank boards.[79] In London, these debates formed the foundation for banking theory and fodder for the institutionalization of *laissez-faire* economic theory in journals such as the *Economist*.[80] In New Orleans, the dissent of directors vanished into the least accessed recesses of the archives.[81] London might have been in the vanguard of *laissez-faire* theory, but New Orleans put that theory into de facto practice. The state of Louisiana had chartered all of the banks in New Orleans, granted them the right to print paper money, and for the most part left them alone. In the extremely diffuse political economy of New Orleans, no one regulated finance: not the federal government (except for the loose oversight of the deposit banks), not the state government, and not the municipal governments.[82]

Even the local press was divided about how to shape the public image of New Orleans. For more than two weeks, the *True American* and *Picayune* printed the only accounts of the Hermann failure. On March 21, 1837, the *New Orleans Bee*, the official newspaper of Louisiana's state government and an organ of the Democratic Party, finally reported on the "temporary alarm created by the suspension of two of our most respectable commercial houses." Unlike the *True American*'s report, the *Bee* coupled this sentence with a discussion of the continued high value of New Orleans real estate to ensure its readers that "our credit and responsibility [are] not to be easily disturbed." The editor of the *Bee* justified breaking the silence about the failures "in order to prevent misapprehension abroad, as well as to disabuse the timarous [sic] at home, who are too ready to lend a willing ear to stories circulated by persons who have nothing to lose themselves, [and] sport with the dearest interests of the industrious portion of our community." Thus, the *Bee* accused the *True American* of circulating "stories" designed to shatter confidence in New Orleans commerce. By disputing the source of the reports circulating in the national and international press on the Hermann failure, the editor of the *Bee* tried to convince people to have confidence in New Orleans.[83]

Although partisanship might seem to color this feud, attempts to boost confidence in New Orleans were not purely political maneuvers, as the *Bee* was not the only paper to publish a retort to the *True American*. Also reporting on the crisis for the first time, the official Whig paper, the *Commercial Bulletin*, ensured its readers that "Nature has destined New Orleans for a city of immense magnitude and despite of all partial difficulties she will advance constantly and rapidly to the consummation of her destiny." But by waiting so long to cover the Hermann failure, the confidence-inspiring *Bee* and *Commercial Bulletin* had allowed the doubt-inducing *True American* to control the image of New Orleans in the wider world for two weeks.[84]

Once the *Bee* and the *Commercial Bulletin* began to recognize the escalating crisis in print, they grew concerned about the effects of their own reporting. "Should the journalist raise his voice in this moment of peril, and public calamity ... the alarm becomes more general," commented the editor of the *Bee*. He assured his readers that his reports were designed to draw "the attention of our Legislature ... and induce them to adopt a code of laws ... similar to those which control most of our other civil and political institutions."[85] Like the directors of the BOE and the self-appointed leaders of New York City, the editor of the *Bee* saw intervention as the only escape from the crisis. As a Democrat, the *Bee*'s editor did not turn to national institutions of finance and politics for relief. Instead, he was determined to use the crisis as a means to buttress support for a decentralized although not unregulated financial system.

Specifically, the editor of the *Bee* wanted to see the passage by the Louisiana Senate of the banking act proposed by Forstall. By advocating that a law could counteract the crisis, the editor implied that the crisis was understandable. Initially, he claimed that the crisis was "an ordinary one" and assured his readers that "after the present derangement, the equilibrium will be restored without serious injury to anyone."[86] When news arrived from Liverpool that cotton prices had plummeted to 50 percent of what factors had extended to planters, the *Bee* changed the buzz. The new circumstances, according to the *Bee*, "extend the calamity to a wider extent than ever was witnessed in a similar crisis, and further than has been dreamed of in the worst fears of those who are not versed in the mysteries of economics."[87]

The "mysteries of economics" stumped its opposition as well. The editor of the *True American* argued that the causes and effects of the crisis were "beyond the control of any one man, set of men, or even the government."[88] He grew frustrated with the inability of the city's press and its "very clever economists" to explain the situation. He lamented, "We too have written and written till we are tired. We have tried to tell the public what we thought upon the matter, – we have endeavored to trace things to their true sources, but the failures would continue, and nobody is the wiser for what we have written." Despite his frustration, Gibson assured his readers that "the evil is reaching to such a height that silence is criminal."[89] By mid-April, silence was not an option for any editor. Like financiers who would lose their credit when they lost their reputations, newspaper editors who did not publish news would lose their subscribers.

Editors provided so many descriptions of the crisis in part because their vision was so local. Although New Orleans's newspapers were partisan, they did not adopt the singular explanations of the national political presses. Whereas most papers called the crisis a "panic" to imply that their opponents had unnecessarily caused it, the *Bee* could not decide on a word to describe the event because it could not decide on an interpretation. "The excitement, the terror, the panic – or whatever you please to term the state of public feeling," wrote the editor of the *Bee*, "pervades all ranks: merchants have no confidence in each other; and banks distrust their rivals." Merchants and bankers, however, were not distinct categories. As the *Bee* exposed, merchants dominated the bank boards: "almost one fifth of the bank directors are now insolvent, or have suspended payment; and hence it is difficult if not impossible to acquire the combined action of our banks on any specific mode of relief to merchants."[90] As the leadership of both the failing commercial community and the troubled banking community overlapped, insider lending came under attack in the press. "Were Banks created for making money without regard to the interests of the community?" asked the *True American*, provoking weeks of debate about "whether banks are really salutary to the public good or not." The *True American* asserted, "perhaps no question since the reformation, has engrossed so much of public attention, as that of banks."[91] In the first month of the crisis, neither Catholic nor Protestant bankers tried to provide the newspapers with an alternative story whereby the bankers looked like the community's saviors. Unlike in New York, New Orleans's leading businessmen did not engage in theatrical performances of public duty.

In early April, the arrival of the news of the first time the BOE bailed out the three Ws brought the idea of collective action by the banks back into the public spotlight. The London correspondent of the *Bee* reported that "the conduct of the [BOE] directors will ... be carped at and inculpated for not letting matters take their own course, though it might have involved hundreds of innocent parties in the gulf [of] bankruptcy." The directors of the New Orleanian banks, despite a few extended loans to the Hermann firms, had generally followed the advice of the critics of the BOE by "letting matters take their own course." Whereas Londoners praised concepts of *laissez-faire* while promoting intervention, New Orleanians followed free trade policies because they had not developed any alternative.[92]

Some of the newspapers prodded the bankers to take action. "Relief, – relief, – relief, – this is the watchword with all sorts of people, poor, rich, broken, and solvent," intoned the *True American*.[93] "On the least symptoms of a panic in the commercial world," Gibson opined, "the first course of monied institutions should be to relieve those who are perfectly solvent."[94] Others saw immediate relief as a waste of time and advocated long-term change. The *Picayune* argued, "To attempt any relief in the present crisis of affairs, may smother for a while the fire which is now burning at the root of our mercantile interests, but it will break out again and blaze with redoubled vigour."[95] A few days later, the *Picayune* argued that any attempt at relief was "too late" and "ridiculous in the extreme" because "We have now in this city over *one hundred millions of dollars* in protested paper."[96] Despite such an enormous sum, some believed that relief could still be found. As a cotton factor wrote to a correspondent, "they cannot hold out in [New Orleans] a month longer unless relief comes from some quarter, and where we are to look for it while all the world is in distress, I do not know."[97]

New Orleanians, however, did not look as far as "all the world" or even New York or Washington for relief. Instead, on the evening of April 11, the sixteen presidents of the city's banks looked to one another. The Union Bank of Louisiana appropriately set the stage for discussions of collective actions. Founded in 1832, the Union Bank of Louisiana built a neoclassical headquarters to administer its capital, which had been raised by state bonds sold in Europe and backed by private mortgages on land and slaves. Even though the columned face of the building conveyed a message of financial and physical strength, the building's small size parlayed the bank's limited power.[98] Unlike its models, the BOE and the BUS, the Union Bank of Louisiana was one small bank among many in a provincial city.[99]

At the meeting, the presidents of the city's banks decided that the best way to "secure the continuance of confidence" was to agree to formalize the relationship between the city's financial institutions by designing a series of resolutions to regulate the exchange of bank notes. A bank would "in no instance whatever" redeem another bank's notes for specie at its counter. Instead, it would provide customers with its paper and collect other banks' notes. On a daily basis, the banks would settle their accounts with one another through commercial paper, and they would make no demands of payment in specie until December. They would all increase their discounting of paper by 10 percent to provide liquidity for struggling merchants. And perhaps most importantly, each bank would submit a "statement of its condition and of its operation" that would be reviewed at a meeting of the presidents to be held weekly on Sundays at nine in the morning. Uniting local finance, the presidents would collectively "devise proper modes of action for the Banks." But to act together, the banks' directors first had to decide that the plan complied with the public duties of their state charters and the private interests of their shareholders.[100]

Although all of the presidents left the Union Bank with copies of the resolutions proposed at the meeting, each president formulated independent strategies for convincing his particular board. For Forstall, the meeting represented a realization of his prior attempts to regulate the city's paper financial instruments. In March, he had proposed a different plan to two of the city's largest banks, which he had capitalized through bond sales with Baring Brothers. They responded with letters "declining to concede to the arrangements proposed."[101] Simultaneously, his act stalled in the state's upper house. When he walked into the Citizens' Bank boardroom with the proposal formulated at the Union Bank, Forstall was closer than ever before to witnessing bank regulation in New Orleans.

Shortly before midnight on April 13, the Citizens' Bank board members agreed to the plan with several additional amendments designed to protect their bank's assets. News had recently arrived from Europe that the Citizens' Bank bond sales in Amsterdam had provided the bank with a large amount of credit in London and Paris. Because the plan allowed the banks to wait until December before balancing their accounts with one another, the directors were concerned that they would become a "Creditor Bank." They proposed amendments to the plan that demanded both an importation of specie and greater influence over the daily operations of "Debtor Banks."[102] Like the directors of the BOE and the BUS, the directors of the Citizens' Bank aimed to stabilize the city's precarious currency while protecting their own interests.

Both the solution presented by the New Orleans banks and public opinion about the plan reflected uncertainty. Devoting a full column of his paper to the meeting, the editor of the *Bee* first speculated that the banks planned to act "in imitation of what was done in New York by the banks for the merchants there – that of substituting public credit for private, or bank notes for individual." But as the editor mentioned on the same page, "the measures of relief that have been adopted [in New York] are limited in their operations, and necessarily public confidence will be restored only gradually." Rather than endorse the New York plan, the *Bee* proposed that the banks immediately "extend their discounts and circulation" to demonstrate their confidence and end "the panic which now chiefly or solely prostrates private credit and public confidence." Shortly before the paper went to press, someone supplied the editor with a copy of the resolutions actually adopted. He was pleased with the results.[103] Some, however, thought the New Orleans banks had gone too far. The *True American* opined that the banks had become "panic-struck themselves."[104] Even the pro-bank *Bee* doubted that the banks could act cooperatively: "we can place little faith on a unanimity of action as well as feeling on their part."[105]

As if to fulfill public doubts about unanimity, the arrangement between the banks lasted less than a day. On April 14, the Gas Light & Banking Company, a state-chartered internal improvement company with the right to issue paper money, violated the terms of the agreement by paying out specie in exchange for another bank's paper. When W. F. C. Duplessis, one of the Citizens' Bank directors, learned of the news, he arranged a "special meeting" to submit the resolution that "this Bank declines continuing the arrangement."[106] The board had spent hours deciding to join the union of banks; it agreed to withdraw from the arrangement within minutes. Viewing less cautious banks as enemies attempting to erode the Citizens' Bank gold supply, the board agreed to protect its institution at the risk of destroying overall confidence in the city's paper money. As the *Bee* commented, "[the] banks feel it to be their duty to secure themselves first, and afterwards think of benefiting the community."[107]

For another month, despite daily demands in the newspapers for "the influential and monied institutions of New Orleans to act promptly, unanimously, definitely, and efficiently," the city's business leaders did not form a collective plan to end the local crisis.[108] "The commercial horizon is so obscured," described the editor of the *Bee*, "that scarcely a ray of hope glimmers in the vista – All is darkness, doubt, and despair."[109] Unlike the New Yorkers who managed to cultivate confidence in their leadership despite their worsening finances, New Orleanians failed to craft a public image of confident leadership. As one cotton factor wrote,

All confidence and credit [are] destroyed. The best and strongest houses, and the richest planters cannot sell bills on any point. No one has the smallest confidence in our Banks or in any Bank except that of the U. States [BUS], the credit of which is so firmly established, that even in the midst of the ruin which surrounds us every man calls for its notes at a premium, instead of specie! Those and specie are the only money used. You cannot buy a barrel of corn without one or the other, and both are likely to be exhausted.[110]

Without a national paper currency, Americans trusted the closest thing – the paper of the former national bank. Despite the fact that, in 1837, the BUS held a diminished specie supply and banking powers only in the state of Pennsylvania, the cultural value ascribed to Biddle's bank sustained the financial value of its paper in New Orleans and elsewhere. But the BUS could not safely produce enough bills to replace the specious private paper throughout the nation. As the New Yorkers had already discovered, the BUS was not capable of ending the linked local crises.

In stark contrast to the failure of leadership in New Orleans, the express mail brought news of another collective initiative in New York City. Whereas the meeting with Biddle represented a unified effort of just over one hundred banks and mercantile firms, more than three times that number formulated a new agenda for relief by appealing directly to President Van Buren. After months of bemoaning the lack of local organization in New Orleans, the editor of the *Bee* criticized the New Yorkers for being "hirelings and dependents of the United States Bank." Furious that New Yorkers claimed to represent the commercial community in New Orleans, he hoped that Van Buren would inform the "committee of bank nabobs sent from New York . . . that they do not represent the whole people of the United States."[111]

Without a rival group forming in New Orleans or anywhere else, the self-appointed leaders of the New York commercial community claimed authority to speak to the president on behalf of the nation's merchants. The story they would narrate converted the parallel crises in New Orleans and New York into one national panic and simultaneously cropped the crisis in London out of the picture. Their portrait of panic was singular and it demanded singularly political solutions.

* * *

Two days after Biddle's meeting with the New York merchants, the *New York Herald*'s second-page headline ran, "Dangerous State of the Country – The only Remedy – in immediate meeting of Congress." Although parallel panics took place in New York, New Orleans, and London, the *Herald* explained these crises as a single national event: "We are in the midst of a commercial panic which threatens to break up all the business of society – to ruin whole States – to lay waste to large districts – to sweep half our banking institutions from the land – to excite the most inflamable [sic] passions, and to create a revulsion that will retard the country for years." Bennett argued that "the only remedy is a general revision of our tariff, distribution, and commercial laws," which only Congress could do. He dismissed the plans for relief proposed by "the principal bankers of New York and Philadelphia" as "limited." Bennett called out to his readers, businessmen and laborers alike, "Why do not the people meet and call upon the Executive to interfere, and to assemble Congress at once?" Although he may not have agreed with the New York commercial community about much, Bennett shared its interpretation of the crisis as national and New York as the center of both trade and public opinion. New Yorkers recast their local crisis as "the panic" and demanded a change in the nation's political economy.[112]

After the failure of another month of public meetings, private counsels with the mayor, and appeals to the state legislature, the merchants of New York answered Bennett's call. By May, with the likelihood of runs on the banks increasing daily and threats of revolution ringing in the streets, New York's Whig businessmen had grown so desperate that they prepared to ask their arch-political enemy for help. Only President Van Buren could call an extra session of Congress and only Congress could create a central regulatory institution.

The New Yorkers faced a difficult mission in convincing the president to act decisively, let alone do so against his political interests. The New Yorkers hoped that the clever magic practiced by the man known as the "little magician" or the "red fox" on his ascendancy from New York to national politics could be applied to the country's finances.[113] Van Buren had won the 1836 election by a "razor-thin majority of 50.2 percent" of the popular vote through a diverse coalition of interests.[114] His greatest opposition came from the "business community," so failing merchants provided him with little political capital.[115] Nevertheless, the shifting and divided group of business leaders in New York included some commercial Democrats. One friendly banker warned Van Buren that Jackson's policies had "brought this flourishing country to the eve of a fiscal revolution."[116] This may have been Jackson's intention, but the destruction of confidence in paper money threatened the prosperity of Van Buren's home state as well as the success of his Safety Fund banking law.

Two weeks after the inauguration, Silas Wright Jr., the chairman of the Senate Finance Committee and one of Van Buren's most loyal supporters, traveled home to Canton, New York. When he reached New York City, he sent the president a long report. He had heard rumors of the Joseph failure in Philadelphia but what he found in New York exceeded his fears. He learned through rumors that "the mass, numerically counted, consider the [Treasury] order as more or less the cause of all the pecuniary embarrassments under which the country is now suffering." He argued that "the majority have hitherto been made to believe" that only the repeal of the Specie Circular would save them. Wright disagreed with this opinion and set out "perambulating the city" to talk with "regular merchants" as well as "the most deliberate and thinking men." Conveniently for a follower of Jackson, he reported that many people of "sound opinion" blamed the crisis not on the "Treasury order" but on the failures that followed the Josephs' suspension.[117]

He witnessed squabbling within the commercial community as many blamed the "Jew Brokers" and "the mad character of the speculations" pursued by the houses that had failed. Blaming the morality, if not the religion, of the failed, the men Wright met on his walk also told him exactly what he wanted to hear: "nothing but further similar failures could afford the relief which the fair business men required." He reported:

I have heard many men of all political parties declare that it was nonsense [to] talk any longer of Treasury orders and Currency Bills, or of any [ac]tion of the national or state governments as either having [oc]casioned the mischief, or as being able to furnish the remedy; [that] the evil exists in the spirit of mad speculation which has had rule for the last two years and that the remedy is to bring these speculations to the test of truth and fact.[118]

Doing nothing, it seemed, would be the most helpful policy. Van Buren agreed.

Petitions and memorials poured into Washington asking the president to reconsider Jackson's policies. Merchants, bankers, and brokers despaired that the Specie Circular would remain law until Congress reconvened the following December.[119] In mid-April, the Democratic mayor of New York City called a meeting at City Hall. There, the son of the founder of the First Bank of the United States, Alexander Hamilton Jr., surmised that if the Specie Circular was not repealed, the banks would have to suspend specie payments. He advised the banks to seek legislative sanction. Although Hamilton's suggestion met with unanimous disapproval from the mayor and the others at the meeting, the publication of this fearful prediction in the nation's press suggested that the federal government's funds deposited in state banks might be in danger.[120] The potential suspension of specie payments by deposit banks should have concerned Van Buren, but no one outside his inner circle of correspondents had any idea whether the president was paying attention. No words of encouragement or plans of government assistance echoed from the White House. Instead, Van Buren wrote to Jackson about "the dreadful state of the money market in New York" and his desire to "weather the present tempest." Similar to Chancellor Spring Rice, President Van Buren decided that the commercial crisis was not his problem.[121]

In late April, long after the momentary spike in confidence after Biddle's visit had waned, Hone led New York's commercial community to cross party lines and call on the president for help. Much like the directors of the BOE, Hone and his mostly Whig colleagues saw a chance to exculpate themselves for the crisis by appealing to the government. By seeking help from Van Buren, the merchants focused attention on federal inaction, thereby shifting blame for individual panics and local crises from their own questionable business practices to the policies and rhetoric of the government.

The desperate New York commercial community genuinely sought economic relief from the president but did not actually expect Van Buren to find an immediate solution to the crisis. Rather, by implying that the federal government could provide an economic panacea, the New Yorkers laid a publicity trap for the president. If Van Buren offered assistance after the New Yorkers' appeal, Whigs could claim political victory over Democrats. If Van Buren failed to help, Whigs could blame the turmoil of the panic in 1837 on the paralysis of Democratic leadership. Regardless of the president's reaction to their appeal, Hone and his fellow businessmen engineered an escape from blame. At the same time, they transformed parallel crises occurring across national boundaries into a singular, national panic.

On the evening of April 25, 1837, Manhattan's Masonic Hall, the headquarters of the city's Whig party, overflowed with thousands of New Yorkers determined to confront the president.[122] Philip Hone presided over what some newspapers called a "great meeting of merchants" and others described as "a mere partisan assemblage, a convocation of whigs to pass resolutions for party effect."[123] The contest for control over public opinion about the culpability of either the commercial community or the federal government began immediately.

Despite the fact that many of these men had failed to meet their debts, Hone described the meeting in his diary as "the largest and most respectable assemblage I ever witnessed."[124] Although Hone may have respected the failed and failing merchants, others disagreed. Reflecting his readers' significantly more skeptical perspective on the city's business leadership, Bennett averred, "[the] leaders and instigators are the same clique of speculators by whose ambition and avarice, opposing the ambition and avarice of Mr. Van Buren and his friends, the country has been hurried into the present crisis." Blaming both parties, Bennett's unusual account of the meeting praised the crowd of lesser merchants, clerks, and laborers gathered outdoors.[125] Hone feared "violent and inflammatory measures" from this same crowd.[126] Both Hone and Bennett, however, saw a benefit in channeling violence and vengeance into civic duty.

Many of New York's merchants affixed their names to a petition to be delivered to the president. The men at the meeting formally drafted resolutions and appointed a committee to "repair to Washington and remonstrate with the Executive ... in the name of the merchants of New York, and the people of the United States."[127] Although the petition claimed the power to represent "the people of the United States," an article from the *New York Evening Post* reprinted in the *Washington Globe* suggested that this was blatantly false. "In short," the article argued, "the resolutions are whig in language, whig in spirit, whig in what they state and what they omit to state, offered by a whig, at a meeting of whigs, with a whig president and whig vice presidents, and adopted by whigs who have appointed a committee of whigs to carry them into effect."[128] As much as Hone and the other leaders implied partisan neutrality through words such as "merchants" and "the people," their opponents suggested that the meeting, and even their "language," was merely an attempt to strengthen a platform designed to reverse the decentralization of the Jackson administration by nationalizing financial policy.

By recasting the meeting as purely partisan and by refuting the blame of the federal government for the "storm which has lately burst over the mercantile community," Democratic papers unconsciously concurred with their opponents on two points that would shape the legacy of the panic.[129] First, by labeling the meeting as the product of "the whigs," Democrats agreed that the crisis could be understood in terms of national politics rather than in terms of transnational financial networks, international diplomacy, state regulation, local conditions, or personal morality. Second, by agreeing that the crisis was a single "storm," both parties claimed that a single event beyond the control of individuals was at work. In the rhetorical battle to describe this meeting, both parties constructed a single, national, political event – a panic.

At Delmonico's restaurant the next evening, the committee prepared for the meeting with Van Buren by composing "pretty well spiced" resolutions as they ate a multi-course meal.[130] How they paid for this feast is not certain, but with paper money quickly depreciating, the dinner offered evidence that financial ruin did not necessarily lead elites to the same material deprivation experienced by the rising numbers of unemployed workers.

Fifteen of the committee members volunteered to go to Washington and present a speech to the president.[131] Isaac Hone, Philip's nephew, prepared the speech, which Van Buren would later request "in writing" in order "to avoid any misapprehensions to which oral communications are liable."[132] The speech asked for three measures: the immediate repeal of the Specie Circular, a postponement of lawsuits against the federal government's debtors, and "an extra session of congress at as early a day as possible." All of the proposals sought to instill confidence in New York's commercial community as "the promoter and the index of our National Prosperity, and whose fall will include the ruin of thousands in every region of our territory." Thus, following the example of the petition prepared for Biddle, Isaac Hone expressed national ramifications of the local crisis.[133]

Shrewdly, the younger Hone sketched details of New York City's suffering as a synecdoche for the nation's. First, he outlined the commercial distress: the depreciation in real estate by more than $40 million, the more than 250 failures of commercial firms in two months, the decline of $20 million in stock value, and the loss of 30 percent of the value of merchandise in the city's warehouses. Then, Hone played his ace against a president who claimed to represent farmers and laborers: "within a few weeks not less than twenty thousand individuals depending upon their daily labor for their daily bread, have been discharged by their employers because the means of retaining them were exhausted." The commercial concerns may have weighed more heavily on the merchants, but twenty thousand unemployed and hungry laborers meant trouble for Van Buren. With indebtedness threatening their status as independent men, the elites used the language of family and democracy to beg Van Buren "to interpose the paternal authority of the Government, and abandon the policy which is beggaring the People."[134]

On May 4, 1837, Van Buren formulated his response. As expected, the president refused to act. Employing strikingly similar language as that of the chancellor of the exchequer, the president drafted his opinion that it would be "inconsistent with the public good and with my official duty to take either of the steps proposed."[135] In the letter he sent to the merchants, he explained his opinion on the Specie Circular: "I have not been able to satisfy myself that I ought, under existing circumstances, to interfere." In terms of calling Congress, he could not "see at present, sufficient reasons to justify me in requiring an earlier meeting than that appointed by the Constitution." Much like the British prime minister, he expressed his "deep sympathy with those who are now suffering from the pressure of the times," but he did nothing.[136] Van Buren allowed the New Yorkers to represent the nation. Although he might have sympathized with their despair, he clearly implied that the embarrassments ultimately were theirs. Van Buren refused to accept the commercial crisis as his responsibility.

On May 6, 1837, the committee of merchants returned to New York "under strong excitement" and immediately organized a meeting. Philip Hone wrote, "It is a dangerous time for such a meeting – combustibles enough are collected to cause an awful conflagration. Men's minds are bent upon mischief; ruin and rashness. Distress and despair generally go together, and a spark may blow us up." According to his diary, he decided to honor his obligation to preside over the meeting to use his "influence" to "prevent violence."[137] Certainly, like Biddle, he also relished the chance to shine as a confident leader. Over the past three months, the city's working class had rioted and organized political rallies. Anticipating an angry mob, Hone asked himself, "Where will it all end? – In Ruin, Revolution, perhaps, Civil War."[138] Hone admitted to his diary that just as he and his peers presented themselves as national mercantile leaders, they were losing control over New York City. Ultimately, no one knew how the panic would end.

Hone was not the only New Yorker fearing a revolution instigated by laborers paid for their work with valueless bank paper and merchants who could trade neither paper nor goods. Bennett blamed both parties for the crisis by arguing that "every fresh public meeting ... only increases the panic." Distrust and calls for violence spanned the political and social spectrum. Both Van Buren's Democrats and the mercantile Whigs, he argued, "[were] busy in urging a revolution, insurrection, bankruptcy, the destruction of all credit, and the general disruption of confidence."[139] Bennett confirmed the crisis in leadership that Hone had admitted in his diary. No one knew how to relieve New York or the nation of its panic.

As "great anxiety pervaded throughout the city," Hone told himself that the best way to deal with the anger of his peers was to channel it into "an example ... to the lower orders of the people." Despite the distrust, debt, and panic of his peers, Hone still believed that he and the other failed business leaders were above the "lower orders." With the purpose of stabilizing the financial system and confirming the social hierarchy, he "determined to exert all my power and influence to give a proper direction to the action of the committee." By channeling the energy of the angry men into creating "a party opposed to the men who have brought us into our present unhappy situation," Hone hoped the existing political system – not a revolution of the social order – could end the panic or at least redirect blame away from New York's commercial community.[140]

After the meeting on May 8, 1837, at the Masonic Hall, Hone recounted in his diary that "the Report was accepted, the Resolutions adopted, the meeting adjourned, and the immense multitude retired without the slightest act of indecorum." Hone bombastically praised the assembly as "the finest fellows in the State of New York." He beamed, "[the proceedings] do us credit, and will have a favorable influence over the minds of men in other parts of the Country." Affirming his belief that New York's business leaders held sway over the nation, Hone hoped the peaceful meeting would attract adherents throughout the nation to "wrest the state from Mr. Van Buren at the next Election."[141] Virulent political attacks, he hoped, could erase the idea of violent personal attacks from the minds of the panicked people of New York.

* * *

Hone's plan to turn the crisis into a national, political panic worked better than he could have imagined. The New Yorkers may have lost their attempt to control the crisis through national intervention, but they won the contest to control the history of the crisis. Proof of this victory appeared in 1924 when Reginald McGrane published the first monograph-length history of the Panic of 1837. He described the panic as a singular, national crisis featuring "the clashing ambitions of Andrew Jackson, Nicholas Biddle, and Martin Van Buren." The parallel panics in New York, New Orleans, and London – let alone the personal panic of individuals in any of those places – had entirely disappeared from the history of 1837.[142]

For economists, however, the legacy of 1837 was its innovation in banking policy. Theorists considered the BOE's decision to bail out the three Ws either a groundbreaking policy for managing liquidity crises or a colossal mistake. Few economists studied the vacuum of authority in New Orleans or the politicized attempts to restore centralized regulation in New York. These American stories lacked the clarity of interpretation and the separation of political and economic systems that appealed to proponents of *laissez-faire* and their later critics. The national story of Jackson's war with the BUS propelled the American economic history narrative to focus on the period before and after the actual crisis in the spring of 1837.

For both political and economic historians, however, the crisis had not yet reached its climax during the months of acute financial uncertainty in the spring of 1837. For historians, the political story would climax as Jackson's deposit bank system experienced bank runs and was put to the test of nationwide specie suspensions. For economists, the same runs and suspensions invited criticism or praise of policy. But neither of these stories describes the experience of panicked people. For those who had already lived through two months of terror, the specie suspensions were anticlimactic and ended rather than began the panic in 1837.

CHAPTER 7

States of Suspense

Nothing builds suspense like a scandal involving a corpse. When Sophia Bricker opened the door to her brother's bedroom on the morning of May 4, 1837, she thought the body in his bed looked a little too still. She called a doctor, but it was too late. John Flemming was already "quite dead." The physician "attributed his death to apoplexy or nightmare." Mrs. Bricker recalled that her brother had returned home at about half past ten on the night before his death and appeared "not more depressed than usual."[1] This was odd. By all accounts, Flemming should have been unusually depressed. That very afternoon, a growing scandal involving New York City's Mechanics Bank prompted Flemming to resign his post as president. As Philip Hone recorded in his diary, "it was very naturally reported that he had committed suicide."[2]

The circumstances surrounding Flemming's sudden demise demanded investigation. When the coroner presented his findings to a jury, it "returned a verdict of 'death from mental excitement.'"[3] Hone confessed to his diary that it was "the awful state of things which caused it."[4] Had Flemming killed himself because of his panic or had his panic killed him? The determination of whether Flemming had been the cause of his own destruction or the victim of a force beyond his control mirrored the question at the heart of the financial crisis: had the past two months of trouble been a result of human agency or an uncontrollable nightmare?

Regardless of who or what was to blame, panic resulted in tragedy. John Flemming's death ushered in the final stage of the panic in 1837. The scandal undermined any vestige of confidence in banks and bank paper. Within two weeks, the crisis would be over in New York and New Orleans. Within a month, the crisis would end in London. But the end of the panic in 1837 was not the end of the economic, cultural, or political fallout, which endured into the 1840s and beyond. People around the globe felt the ramifications of the destabilization of the financial system for many years to come.

How did the panic in 1837 end? The suspense about unanswered financial and economic questions found resolution, ironically, in two new genres of suspension: the suspension of specie payments and the suspension of individual agency.

The suspension of specie payments by banks throughout the United States and the three Ws in London brought an end, at least for a little while, to financial uncertainty because failure, for many, became a certainty. From a historical distance, the suspension of specie payments by nearly every American bank looks like a national event, but at the time, the suspensions were plural, local, and dependent on choices made by identifiable bankers. The men in charge of banks who decided to suspend specie payments prevented the types of widespread bank runs that so many later writers would associate with panics. The agency of these men ended the period of panic in 1837, but instead of touting their accomplishment, the bankers claimed to have had no choice. They denied their agency in part because their decision had political implications. Suspension defied bank charters and trapped federal funds, so bankers had to put aside their partisanship to choose to suspend. This bipartisan effort nevertheless yielded an intense political fight that would be remembered as the beginning, rather than the end, of the Panic of 1837.

Like the bipartisan suspension of specie payments by the nation's banks, the American writers who theorized economic victimization and suspended individual agency came from opposing camps. Democrats and Whigs, northerners and southerners, and novelists and political economists agreed with uncoordinated unanimity that something larger than individuals was to blame for the failure that surrounded them. Many jettisoned the concept of self-made failure and, with this, wrote their own experiences out of the panic.

The stories historians and economists have subsequently told about the Panic of 1837 are derived directly from these choices made in May 1837. The states of suspense that ended the actual period of panic in 1837 obscured the role that individuals and communities played in one of the most influential national and international events of the nineteenth century.

* * *

During the evening of May 9, 1837, Aaron Clark, lottery dealer turned banker and Whig politician, had no time to relish his inaugural day as New

York City's mayor. As a newspaper reported the next afternoon, "at a late hour," Clark met with a group of his fellow bank presidents, who wanted him "to be prepared against scenes of popular violence" that they expected the next morning. Fearing a riot on his first full day in office, he called into active duty "an adequate number of troops" and stockpiled "a good supply of ball cartridges in readiness at his office."[5] "Fortune's Favorite," a nickname devised by Clark's political opponents to reference his gambling past, was not counting on luck.[6]

What prompted such martial mayoral actions? The banks of New York City were under siege; at least the city's bank directors believed this to be true. But were they? Despite the fact that mobbed banks now serve as the symbol of financial panic, only two bank runs received extensive coverage in the nation's newspapers in 1837. Both took place in New York City during the week between John Flemming's death and Aaron Clark's inauguration, and both were linked by one scandal that, like panic itself, started months earlier.

Shortly before the flour riot in February, New York State officials grew concerned that banks were lending their capital to "speculators, and especially Eli Hart, and others, to enable them to monopolize and speculate in flour." The New York State Assembly authorized a committee to investigate the lending practices of the banks holding state charters. During the financial crisis, this investigation probed the books and interrogated the officers of most of New York State's banks, including twenty-four banks in New York City.[7]

On the morning of May 2, the *New York Herald* printed rumors that the investigation had discovered a scandal. According to this article, "before the present revulsion took place," Mechanics Bank president John Flemming had agreed to a proposition offered by Bullock, Lyman & Co., a Wall Street brokerage house: "you permit us to draw checks against you for $245,000, alternatively to be placed in the Dry Dock [Bank] and Mechanics Bank, we paying the interest daily."[8] The broker's cashier would confirm in later testimony that this arrangement was called "kiting, or kite flying."[9] Like the kited bills of exchange drawn between firms in the Hermann network, this deal between bankers and brokers also involved artificial supplies of credit. Although kiting provided banks with revenue and merchants with funds in the right place at the right time, the process was dangerous because if the firm should fail to make its payments, the banks would find their accounts "overdrawn" by a considerable amount.[10]

This is precisely what happened at the end of April, when Flemming decided to no longer extend credit to Bullock, Lyman & Co. because its collateral (Dry Dock Bank stock) had lost half of its value.[11] When the firm failed, the directors of the Dry Dock Bank found themselves holding the hot potato; according to the investigation, Bullock, Lyman & Co. owed the Dry Dock Bank upward of $141,000.[12] Had New Yorkers known these figures, they may have run on the Dry Dock Bank first. Instead, people wrongly associated Flemming's resignation and mysterious death with financial insolvency at the Mechanics Bank. Despite the fact that Flemming had acted to protect the Mechanics Bank by grounding Bullock, Lyman & Co.'s kite, the implication of his suspicious death was that the Mechanics Bank was unstable.

As a correspondent to the *National Intelligencer* reported, "It being rumored that [Flemming] had killed himself, holders of the bills were frightened, and ran on the bank."[13] Despite the attempts of Democratic newspapers to convince readers of Flemming's "perfect integrity" and that "the absurd tales about *suicide*, so rife yesterday, were entirely unfounded," note holders and depositors demanded specie from the Mechanics Bank on May 4.[14] The *New York Times*, a paper affiliated with commercial Democrats, suggested that the run had been inspired by a conspiracy of "panic makers" who wanted to "destroy our Banks" to speed the federal rechartering of the BUS.[15] An eyewitness reported to the *National Intelligencer* that "the tellers are counting out specie as fast as they can; not in large amounts, however, but in *fives* and *tens*."[16] Counting out specie in small denominations was a stalling technique used by banks to prevent tellers from redeeming too many bills during operating hours; thus, the *New York Times* could have correctly read the situation.[17] But the small denominations could also indicate that the run was perpetrated by working people who were worried about protecting their small but hard-earned assets. The latter is more likely. According to a report the next day in the *New York American*, "the run commenced at 10 A.M. and had full scope until 5 P.M. – and great as the reports of an existing *Run* may have been, the entire amount of specie drawn from the bank yesterday was *Fourteen Thousand Dollars!*"[18] The bank stayed open later than usual to ensure that all who demanded cash were paid. As Hone condescended, "the Bank was kept open two hours beyond the usual time of closing and the hungry harpeys [sic] were gorged with specie to the contentment of their savage appetites."[19]

In a rare show of support for a competitor, the city's other banks brought bags of coins to the tellers. Because the Mechanics Bank was a member of the Safety Fund system, the other banks had every motivation to reinforce the specie supply to ensure that no resources from the Safety

Fund would be drained. An eyewitness reported that one of the officials conducting the investigation into the scandal, "read a statement on the steps of the bank, that all was safe, and has pledged his word in the evening papers, but that does not quiet the alarm."[20]

Of course, not everyone who had gathered outside the Mechanics Bank was alarmed. One newspaper asked that

Persons who are friendly to the banks and the merchants would not congregate as speculators about the doors of the bank to-day, nor make a current in and out to gratify an unimportant curiosity about what is going on in the interior. Nine-tenths of the men in attendance yesterday were merely lookers-on. Their presence served to increase excitement, and give consequence to the occasion, and, besides, prevented the alarmed bill holders from having that free and ready ingress which belongs to them.[21]

Crowds gathered "curious to see what a 'run on a bank' really was."[22] What they saw, however, could hardly be described as a panic. The Mechanics Bank survived easily.

But two banks were involved in the kiting scandal. The *Herald* described Bullock, Lyman & Co. as "a pair of brokers in Wall Street, who 'hunted in couples,' and appeared to be always flush of money, handling $50,000 or $60,000 as if it were so many love letters and billets of invitation."[23] The *Herald* shifted the focus from the Mechanics Bank to its more vulnerable other half. The Dry Dock Bank was a state-chartered, joint-stock company founded in 1825 to fund an internal improvement project: a dry dock.[24] Unlike the Mechanics Bank, the Dry Dock Bank was not a member of the Safety Fund. It was, however, a pet bank, a depository of federal funds. This put the Dry Dock Bank in a politically precarious position, especially because reports of the scandal coincided with the meeting between the delegation of New York merchants and President Van Buren. If the Whigs wanted to prove the instability of the Democratic Party's decentralized banking system, they could target the Dry Dock Bank without upsetting their own interests in the Safety Fund.[25]

After the Thursday run at the Mechanics Bank had ended, the New York City banks refused to accept Dry Dock Bank paper. This may have been a conspiracy, as some newspapers suggested, but it also may have been a justified response to the financial troubles of the institution.[26] Over the next few days, newspapers reported a wide range of estimates on the liabilities and assets of the bank that suggested that it was insolvent; months later, the state's investigation found the bank to be solvent but illiquid.[27] Regardless of the actual financial condition of the Dry Dock

Bank, the refusal of the city's other banks to receive its paper destroyed creditors' confidence. According to the *New York Express*, "this course alarmed the bill holders, who immediately went to the bank and demanded specie; and the crowding continued until 3 o'clock, when the bank closed, with a notice that all demands would be promptly met by the bank at 10 o'clock on Monday."[28] But could the bank keep its promise? The answer relied in part on the liquidity of the bank's investments and in part on the unlikely generosity of the city's bankers.

After the Dry Dock Bank closed its doors that Saturday afternoon, the city's bank presidents and cashiers met at the mayor's office. They examined the Dry Dock Bank's books and unanimously decided "*not* to afford the required aid." Unable to secure a bailout, "the officers cleared the bank of all books, specie, and other valuables, and locked the same up."[29] "As early as 7 o'clock this morning," reported the *New York Express* on the next business day, Monday, May 8, "crowds began to collect at the Dry Dock Bank for admittance, and by 10, the usual time of opening the bank, the street was filled with people." The newspaper explained, "It was soon given out that the bank had suspended payment, and that its doors would not be again opened. The sensation in Wall Street was very great. Thousands upon thousands, rich and poor, male and female, were collected, some with large sums and some with small sums."[30]

Panic was palpable, and it changed the bank presidents' minds: "At 11 o'clock, the mayor announced from the steps of the bank, that all the banks in Wall street had resolved to receive and pay the bills of the Dry Dock Bank."[31] According to the *New York Commercial Advertiser*, "This information caused an abatement of the panic, and the crowd gradually melted away."[32] This was good news for holders of Dry Dock Bank paper, but depositors, including the federal government, which had approximately a quarter of a million dollars of public money in the institution, could not expect to see their funds returned. The *National Intelligencer*, eager to rally Whig animosity toward the Democratic system of deposit banks, provided extended coverage of the event and the precarious financial condition of the bank's books to its national correspondents, arguing that "the failure of that Bank cannot be by itself as great an evil as the Bank itself was."[33]

In the morning, the Dry Dock Bank suspended specie payments; that evening, the committee of merchants returned from their interview with Martin Van Buren. Reflecting on the combination of events, Bennett argued, "political agitation adds to financial panic."[34] For individuals still searching for an explanation for their financial anxieties, the next two days would connect the dots between panic and politics.

* * *

Bank runs played a very small part in the Panic of 1837. No particular bank was targeted after the Dry Dock Bank shut its heavy doors on May 8. Newspapers and correspondents reported, rather summarily, on how "a general run was made on every bank."[35] Few vivid scenes made it into newspapers and the only graphic illustration of a mob swarming a bank, E. W. Clay's lithograph "The Times," relegated this scene to the background.[36] Hone, however, recorded in the words of his diary a picture of panic at the New York Savings Bank. Although this institution had been established as a philanthropy by wealthy men who argued that working people ought to invest their small savings safely and abstemiously, Hone's description sounded anything but safe:

[The tellers] paid three hundred and seventy-five depositors $81,000. The press was awful; the hour for closing the Bank is six o'clock, but they did not get through the paying of those who were in at that time until nine o'clock. I was there with the other trustees, and witnessed the madness of the people, – women were nearly pressed to death, and the stoutest men could hardly sustain themselves; but they held on, as with a death's grasp upon the evidences of their claims, and, exhausted as they were with the pressure, they had strength to cry, "Pay! Pay!"[37]

Hone labeled the run madness, but, like all the personal panics of 1837, these individuals' demands for specie made perfect sense. The desire to replace the dubious rustle of paper in pockets with the clink of coins, especially by the financial neophytes who were the clientele of the savings bank, proved easy to portray as madness by those who wanted to see the crisis as beyond the control of rational and responsible individuals. The rich trustees and the poor depositors alike were exhausted by financial uncertainty and seeking to end the crisis by obtaining or retaining specie. As a New Yorker wrote to President Van Buren, "the public has become alarmed, panic has seized all classes."[38]

One newspaper tried to dissuade panicked laborers from redeeming notes by arguing that a worker who ran on a bank for small bills should "be looked upon as an enemy to his fellow operatives, whom he is doing his best to keep out of employ."[39] This rhetoric, however, could not convince the holders of bank notes that paper promises were worth much more than the depreciating cotton pulp on which they were printed. Requesting coin was not only rational for individuals but also perfectly legal. In fact, the banks' state charters required the convertibility of paper into gold. To retain their charters and suspend specie payments, as Alexander Hamilton Jr. had suggested in early April, the banks would have to win legislative sanction.

Political economy theory, however, suggested that suspension should not be necessary. In his textbook, Wayland argued, "it is morally certain, that all the bills of the bank can never be presented for payment at the *same instant*."[40] By the close of business on Tuesday, May 9, the bank presidents had empirical proof that it did not take the return of all of a bank's notes to shake moral certainty. A fraction of a bank's circulation could jeopardize the institution's liquidity and solvency as it rattled confidence in the underpinnings of the credit system. Real life did not necessarily conform to theory. And theory could not entirely explain the events unfolding in the spring of 1837, let alone describe them.

Despite the lack of visual or textual descriptions, the general run had significant consequences. On May 8 and 9, the New York banks distributed at least half their reserves, more than $1,300,000 in specie. The bank presidents estimated that in two more days, their vaults would be empty.[41] One newspaper reported that on the mayor's inauguration day alone, $700,000 in specie had been drawn out.[42] None of these figures, however, was confirmed by an outside source. The bankers had every reason to exaggerate the sums because they would soon face a difficult choice.

The city's bankers, including Mayor Clark, shared Hone's haunting fear that the financial distress would lead to "Ruin, Revolution, perhaps, Civil War."[43] They met after the inauguration to prevent any further runs. All but three banks resolved to suspend specie payments the next morning, and Clark agreed to muster soldiers. A group prepared resolutions imploring the state legislature to legalize the suspension by either issuing an injunction against distributing specie or amending the Safety Fund law as well as individual bank charters. Another group circulated copies of the resolution to the city's newspaper editors for publication in the morning papers. To prevent a riot or a revocation of their banking privileges, the bankers sought public approval through force, law, and print.[44]

Before the banks opened for business on May 10, the final three boards of directors resolved to join the general suspension. The directors of the National Bank, one of the three institutions that had not agreed to the decision made at the mayor's office, blamed "circumstances or combinations not under their control" for putting the board in a situation where "it finds itself compelled to direct that specie payments be for the present suspended."[45] The bankers may have felt like victims of an uncontrollable situation, but they made the choice to suspend specie payments. By doing so, they prevented the nationwide bank runs that would come to define later panics, allowing only two publicized runs and one bank failure into the historical record.

* * *

But did the bankers choose to violate their charters to save the financial system or were they conspiring to bring about political change? Before the suspension, Bennett made a case for the latter.

When the *New York Herald* appeared on the morning of May 9, the first column of news suggested a massive conspiracy theory. He argued first that the city's bank presidents' true purpose for meeting after the Saturday run on the Dry Dock Bank had been "to pave the way, and prepare the public mind for a general suspension of specie payments by all the banks in this city and state." Next, he argued that the presidents selected the *Morning Courier and New-York Enquirer*, a Whig paper, "on that sacred night, to promulgate the feelers for that suspension." In a paragraph describing "the state of the American houses in England," the *Courier and Enquirer* printed on May 8 the following lines:

> The suggestions we have thrown out would be still more incomplete than they are, if we did not call on the banks to act in concert among themselves, and with the people. None of them are so strong, that in the present state of things they may wrap themselves up in fancied security, and think they can avoid the common danger.

"These ominous hints," Bennett read between the lines, "are, no doubt, easily understood by the 'specie-suspending' confederates, who, with the mayor of this city at their head, and the devil at their tail, have brought the country to its present horrible condition." In other words, Bennett, who like many Democrats blamed the banks for the nation's financial troubles, believed that these lines were meant as an encoded signal that the time for suspension had arrived. He worried, however, that "the people do not – and will not understand these sly hints, and obscure inuendoes." He demanded that the bankers "talk in common, every day language, that we can understand," asking "what is the use of mystification now?" His article attempted to decode this message so that the public could claim its specie from the banks before the suspension took place. His title, "Suspension of Specie Payments by the Banks," was not a headline reporting on the news; it was a prediction of news that would break the next day.[46]

Bennett's article also may have been a cause of the suspension. Whether or not Bennett was right about the bank presidents' plan, his writing fed the demands for specie that would legitimize the suspension. Had Bennett taken his conspiracy theory one step further, he might have considered the possibility that the bank presidents had leaked the "sly hints, and obscure inuendoes" in the *Courier and Enquirer* so that Bennett would publish a demystified version that would encourage people to run on the banks.[47] Who ultimately was to blame for the specie suspension? We will never know. All of these layers of rumor and print, however, suggest an overwhelming desire by all involved to see order in chaos.

As much as Hone and the other bankers feared potential "civil war" with the suspension of specie payments, Bennett offered a much calmer prediction.[48] He argued that the banks should "become bold faced villains, and to suspend at once, without any more ado about the matter. There is no danger of excitement – no fear of public commotion – no alarm to be entertained from the people. The hard times have cowed down and trampled down all classes alike."[49] Bennett's prediction served as a foil to a letter from the Josephs to the Rothschilds written on the same day. They reported, "The excitement is without parallel and apprehensions of serious riots are entertained."[50] On May 9, no one knew exactly what would happen the next morning, but everyone from the mayor to Bennett's readers knew that change was coming.

*   *   *

Too pressing to wait for the next packet's departure, the ink on the newspapers and commercial letters written on the afternoon of May 8 was barely dry when it caught up with a ship that had been cleared by customs a day earlier.[51] The news aboard the *Roscoe* would prove troubling for London's bankers, who would be left to wonder about the survival of America's people, banks, and (most importantly to them) specie.

For months, the "regular" sailing packet ships had been delayed by bad weather in the mid-Atlantic. The *Roscoe*, captained by a man who held the record for the fastest westbound voyage, reached the eastern coast of the Atlantic only three weeks after leaving New York City's harbor.[52] The *Roscoe* arrived in Liverpool on Monday, May 29, 1837, and its paper cargo journeyed an additional two hundred miles to reach the City of London the next afternoon.[53] It traveled down the many corridors of the BOE to reach the Court of Directors' parlor where it destroyed the near unanimity of twenty-six of the world's most powerful bankers.[54]

The directors of the BOE had gathered to discuss whether their institution should continue to support the liquidity of the three Ws. As had become typical during the financial crisis, the directors received a letter from the houses begging the BOE for its support. "In consequence of the temporary and almost universal suspension of credit throughout the principal commercial cities of the United States we are deprived of almost every kind of remittance for the debts due to us, and are consequently unable to meet our outstanding engagements," the houses confessed to the BOE. They implored the directors to consider the national significance of their choice because of "the magnitude and importance of the trade between the two countries." Again they argued that their appeal was of "such an especial character as to warrant a departure from the ordinary rules of the Bank when affording assistance to individual Houses placed under temporary difficulties." Believing that the houses' "difficulties" were indeed "temporary," the directors granted the firms' request for extended time in exchange for the security of assets, "which may be reasonably calculated as good upon the restoration of credit in America." With the commitment of the private bankers who had guaranteed the houses' credit, the directors passed a resolution to extend their assistance to the three Ws until the end of the year.

Before the governor adjourned the court, however, the *Roscoe*'s news reached the BOE. Quickly, one director moved to amend the motion, calling for further consideration. The news of the bank runs in New York challenged the "reasonably calculated" value of the firms' assets based on the increasingly unlikely "restoration of credit in America." The directors resolved, "The annihilation of commercial credit in the United States, the numerous failures of Commercial Houses in that Country, and the suspension of remittances, must ... so seriously affect the Houses in question, as to cause great doubt of their ultimate solvency." A director proposed an amendment requiring "adequate security" for additional assistance.[55] Aware that the houses would not be able to find such collateral, those who proposed this amendment did so to curtail support of the three Ws. Facing the personal, local, national, and international ramifications of their choice, the directors needed time. The amendment was seconded and the meeting adjourned until the next morning when, according to rumors, the discussion continued for the entire day in the "most agitated and contradictory character."[56]

People in the City "anxiously watched" the directors for any sign that they would "desert those houses that have hitherto depended on them."[57] After the second day of debate, the *Times* reported that "the Bank

Directors met again this morning, but it soon became evident by signs of uneasiness among parties interested in the result that some demur had arisen to the application of the American houses for further assistance." A "depression" on the stock market was in part attributed to "the continued suspension of the Bank's decision."[58] As news of the bank's deliberations reached Paris, correspondents confirmed the international significance of the BOE's "deliberations" and the "anxiety" produced by "the deplorable accounts from New York by the Liverpool packet."[59] Rumors circulated that the private bankers who had endorsed the loans to the three Ws "expressed a wish to withdraw altogether."[60] Without this collateral, the BOE directors would force their shareholders to shoulder all of the risk in supporting the American houses and, by extension, the transatlantic trade. On the streets of the City, the directors' indecision, according to the *Times*, "produced the awful state of suspense."[61]

Once more struggling with whether sustaining international trade was part of their duty as protectors of the national currency, the directors decided again to share the burden of their decision with the government. On the third day of their deliberations, June 1, 1837, the governor and deputy governor traveled across London to meet with Prime Minister Melbourne and Chancellor of the Exchequer Spring Rice.[62] The Liverpool packet bound for New York was detained to include the outcome of this meeting. Commenting on this extraordinary deviation from protocol, the *Times* averred, "There has probably never existed in the annals of commerce a more anxious and eventful period than the present."[63]

When the BOE Court of Directors reconvened after the midday meeting, they listened to a letter that must have sounded all too familiar. Lord Melbourne and Spring Rice expressed that they were "deeply impressed with the public inconvenience which would result to the manufacturing and commercial interests from a suspension of the houses engaged in the American trade." They wrote to the BOE directors that they were "most anxious ... that these calamities should be mitigated if not averted." Nevertheless, the ministers continued to argue that "it is not within their province or consistent with the line of duty which they have proscribed to themselves to direct or influence the decision of the Bank of England." Refusing to commit their support to any particular action, the ministers hoped that the BOE directors would decide to continue to support the houses but offered "to put the most favorable interpretation on whatever Resolution the Court of Directors may adopt."[64] Again, Westminster offered nothing but spin. This time, however, the government's refusal to intervene meant the directors were free to extricate themselves from the support of the American houses. With the government's promise of "favorable interpretation," the directors of the BOE could cut the institution's losses without fear of political backlash.

At nine o'clock in the evening after three full days of debate, the directors approved the amendment and ended their support of the failing American houses by a margin of a single vote. As merchants and private bankers, the directors were so personally interested in the decision that some threatened to resign based on the vote's outcome.[65] Even in the globe's most powerful financial institution, panic was personal.

The next morning, the three Ws suspended specie payments. As the *Times* reported, "Such an extent of failure has probably never occurred in the city in the same day." Without the BOE's months of support, it would have been much worse. "Had it occurred six months ago, and taken the city by surprise, it would have been difficult to say who was entirely beyond the sphere of its influence," reported the *Times*. Despite the fact that "all bills connected to American business have been in so much discredit for a long time" and traders had "ample time to prepare for the worst," many in the City were furious.[66] Countering the "loud" complaints of individuals who blamed the BOE for bringing on their difficulties, the *Globe and Traveller* argued that the directors "would not have been justified in wasting the property entrusted to them by the Shareholders, in any attempt to bolster up a cause which was desperate."[67] The directors had decided that their public duties were best served by protecting the BOE's private interests.

Many in London disagreed, believing that the actions of the bank were ultimately detrimental to the public. Their arguments were strengthened the next week when several additional American houses failed.[68] Without financial details from any of the failed houses or the BOE, outsiders could only guess the extent of the liabilities that would now go unpaid. One thing was certain: the securities held by the BOE would "be peremptory claimed for the protection of the Bank."[69] The failure of several of the firms that had guaranteed the three Ws raised questions about the solvency of the BOE, the sagacity of the directors' decision, and the preferential status of the BOE's debts. Some claimed that the BOE committed "downright robbery" if, as rumored, the directors created "a secret arrangement to absorb the whole of the property [of the three Ws] in the event of any serious disaster." The *Times* suggested that the BOE's "bolstering [of certain houses] enables a few artful men to secure all that is owed them, and leave little or nothing to the rest."[70]

Only a few weeks earlier, the concept of the lender of last resort seemed like a saving grace; after the three Ws suspended payments, investors began to question whether the involvement in the market of the BOE or any governmentally sanctioned institution was fair. Free trade might be harsh, they argued, but at least it would not be preferential. Others questioned whether "bolstering" large financial institutions set a precedent for risk taking or whether it enabled credit markets to survive. Debate ensued in pamphlets and Parliament. None of the writers used the phrases "too big to fail" or "the moral hazard problem," but the end of the BOE's support for the three Ws raised questions that remain current nearly two centuries later. The reign of "terror over the city" ended during the first week of June, but the questions of political economy as applied to the financial market had only begun to dominate discussion in the City.[71] London's local crisis produced a renewed interest in banking practices and economic theory – an important intellectual product of the panic in 1837.

* * *

Some creditors certainly fared better than others. In an act of indubitable preferential treatment by the BOE, the firm of William and James Brown & Co. requested and received assistance.[72] Joseph Shipley, the American-born partner who appeared at the BOE, reported back to the firm's headquarters in Liverpool, "The Bank views our position as altogether different from most of the others, as it really is." Receiving a week's loan, he concluded, "We have gained some little triumph already to stand even for a week amid the general wreck."[73] In a 1901 letter, a Liverpool financier recounted Shipley's triumphant arrival in Liverpool with the news that the firm received more support from the BOE:

I was standing at my Father's shop door, when I saw coming down street at full galop [sic] a Post Chaise ("Po Chay") and four horses ridden by Post Boys all covered with mud. It stopped next door (Brown, Shipley) and out jumped Mr. Shipley all covered with glory, up went the windows in front and out popped the heads of the Clerks who gave three rousing cheers. It was the year of the panic, and Mr. Shipley had been to London to negotiate a loan with the Bank of England. He had been successful and thus saved the credit of the house. It made quite an impression upon your future Uncle, who really didn't think he would be writing to his pretty niece in the next century a description of it. You must remember it was before railroads and telegraphs and things, which accounts for the "Po Chay."[74]

Aside from a vivid picture of Shipley's arrival, this writer's language illustrates important shifts in the financial lexicon. Although the correspondent marked the passage of time through the change in the speed of communication (the "railroad and telegraphs and things"), the content of communication had changed as well. Shipley had written about the spring of 1837 as "the general wreck," but in the memory of this author, 1837 was "the year of the panic." The difference between "the general wreck" and "the panic" reflected half a century's worth of economic theorization about the causes of financial crises. Moreover, this letter was written on the precipice of even more dramatic changes. The "pretty niece" would soon see trains and telegraphs giving way to cars and telephones. Similarly, this elderly man employed financial language that was quickly becoming outdated. In the early twentieth century, "panics" lost out to "depressions" as markers of historically significant economic events. In the middle of the nineteenth century, however, when Shipley described the crisis as "the general wreck," the idea of a panic was in the process of being invented.

Wrecks were unpredictable disasters beyond human control. Shipley's use of this phrase suggested that he believed the local crisis to have been caused by something larger than the individual economic choices of the wrecked. This way of thinking was becoming common. As Joshua Bates prematurely gloated in his diary before the Brown loan, "thus, only my House is left and although it is sad to see so many fallen around me, I should be thankful that my firm is preserved amid the wreck."[75] Despite the fact that he prided himself on his skill, Bates's choice of passive voice phrasing suggests that luck rather than skill allowed Barings to survive and eventually realize significant profit from others' despair.[76] But Barings was neither alone nor merely lucky, as banker James Morrison wrote on June 9, 1837:

The last ten days has been a horrid dream! All the Ws are gone and with them many others, indeed, as far as respects the American Houses, one looks about to see who is left standing, not who has fallen, the list is a brief one now! We are almost alone. All who had not resources like myself or Baring are gone.[77]

The few houses with "resources" that remained solvent could demand exorbitant fees for their paper and could use their good credit to buy up cotton, land, and dishonored bills at the newly diminished prices. Capitalists, after all, would need new investments.

The nightmare ended quickly for many investors in London. After the three Ws published the statements of their affairs, newspapers reported, "the feeling of alarm, which prevailed in the city on Saturday, has subsided." The papers rejoiced, "we are all in good spirits again."[78] Because the failures affected, "more or less, every person engaged in the foreign trade of the country," the *Times* praised the "candour and frankness which have allowed such important documents to be submitted to the public eye." As the *Times* noted, "they have produced on the whole a much more tranquil feeling than before existed." From "despondency" to tranquility, the "altered feeling" produced a "very marked" increase in activity and prices at the stock exchange.[79]

Although discussions of malfeasance by the BOE eventually prompted parliamentary investigation and a new bank charter, business quickly improved.[80] As Bates recorded, "Money matters in the city seem to improve and no new failures are looked for and it seems generally expected that prices will rather improve and business soon become active."[81] The reason for the end of London's crisis was simply stated by the *Globe and Traveller*: "We now know the extent of the evil, and are better able to grapple with it than before."[82]

The *Times*, however, warned, "it will be a very mistaken notion for the public to fall into, if they infer from any appearance of tranquility on the surface of things, that this is an evil likely to be of short duration, or limited in its effect and consequences." Indeed, the global results of the crisis would take a long time to become visible, but by the second week in June, any trace of panic disappeared from London as the local crisis ended.[83]

* * *

In New York City, people's panics ended the day after the *Roscoe* sailed beyond the reach of coastal vessels when the city's banks suspended specie payments. During the early morning of May 10, 1837, Mayor Clark marshaled his troops. Hone joined the throngs of people waiting for something to happen on Wall Street. As one newspaper reported, "those from whom turbulence was naturally to be expected have, for the most part, drawn their specie during the last four days." Instead of the expected violent mob, the newspaper described, "the people in the street, today, are of the better classes – and, under the circumstances of the case, all are rejoicing at the resolution at which the banks have arrived."[84] Although Hone was far from rejoicing because he knew that "men of Capital will suffer by the deterioration of the value of the circulating medium," he certainly was not planning to riot. Hone looked around him and saw that "men's countenances wore a more cheerful aspect than for several days past." He hoped that "the suspension of specie payments will restore confidence." Like so many of his contemporaries, Hone believed that a restoration of confidence would end thousands of personal panics, placate New York's local crisis, and rejuvenate trade.

Hone predicted that "honest men who are in debt and wish to pay, and mechanics who are willing to work will have cause to rejoice."[85] Despite the benefits of escaping debt, the suspension posed a special problem for working people because of a shortage of small change, the currency of daily life. Banks were not allowed to print bills for denominations less than $5.00, and bill brokers charged steep fees for silver change. Hard-times tokens, cheap coins minted by local storekeepers as advertisements, and shin plasters, small-denomination bills printed by private companies, provided a means for exchange after the suspension. Although people may have appreciated the satirical engravings and minted witticisms on them, this illegal currency faced the constant problem of depreciation.[86] Claiming to have been inspired by "a good angel," Bennett sought to remedy the "great and unmerited injury having been done to many of the gentler sex, by the suspension of specie payments and the difficulty of procuring small change." He offered "every female, widowed, married, or single, pretty little girls and all," the chance to redeem $5.00 in small notes at the *Herald*'s office one day during the following week.[87] With nothing but depreciating paper money to buy food, people who could not count themselves among the "men of Capital" might not have as much reason to "rejoice" as Hone imagined.[88]

The resolution printed in the morning papers justified the specie suspension by claiming that it was "expedient and necessary," absolving the bankers from the burden of choice.[89] Hone thought the suspension was a choice. He interpreted the relocation of a meeting of the trustees of the Savings Bank to the mayor's office as an attempt by some of the bank's

FIGURE 11. These three "hard-times tokens" from 1837 are each impressed with a different humorous message ridiculing (from left to right) the value of the penny, President Martin Van Buren, and the suspension of specie payments. (Private collection.)

officers to avoid explaining their choices to the public. After the meeting, he confided in his diary, "I . . . expressed myself freely in reprobation of the pusillanimity which led them to give up the ship of which they had the command."[90] Hone may have recognized individual choices, but some merchants, such as Moses Taylor, understood the banks' actions as collective decision making. Taylor wrote to a correspondent, "I would much rather we all fail than to have the banks suspend."[91] For merchants who relied on their distant correspondents' trust, New York's bank suspensions threatened their international reputations, credit, and income. If, as Taylor predicted, "[the] measure will probably be adopted by Banks generally throughout the U. States," Americans would have no access to specie and no choice but to deny international creditors payment.[92] Coupled with the falling price of cotton in Liverpool, the American specie suspension would ensure that many transatlantic mercantile firms failed.[93] In terms of foreign policy and future credit, the suspension of specie payments was quite a controversial decision.

Private reprobation, however, was countered with public "universal approbation," according to one newspaper.[94] Indeed, the decision received little criticism from newspaper editors – reflecting bipartisan support. One Whig paper expressed the consensus that "The thing is much to be regretted in itself, but cannot and ought not to be any longer deterred. It is better that the Banks should suspend while yet they have a considerable amount of specie in their vaults, than wait till it is all drawn out."[95] A commercial Democratic newspaper confirmed that "we blame them [the banks] not for what they could not help."[96] By declaring that "This course was forced on the banks," editors absolved the bankers from responsibility for their decision.[97] Like individuals, the banks could claim to be economic victims.

Even hard-money Democrats viewed the suspension as something other than merely the product of human agency. As Leggett wrote in the *Plaindealer*, "It is as palpable to the mind, as the universal light of day to the senses, that the present anarchical and chaotick [sic] condition of financial affairs is the result, the direct and inevitable result, of the unholy alliance between politicks [sic] and banking."[98] The editor of the *New York Commercial Advertiser*, a Whig paper highly sympathetic to the banks, "call[ed] upon our citizens, one and all, to avoid excitement, and to conduct themselves with all possible forbearance, toward the banks, and toward each other."[99] Even Bennett, no friend of the city's banks, agreed with the suspension, urging his readers to be "cool and quiet." He suggested, "Let us breathe – look around us – and reconstruct society on a new basis."[100]

As news of the New York bankers' choice to suspend specie payments spread on the first day after the suspension, stocks rose 15 percent.[101] Taylor wrote to a correspondent, "Since the suspension of specie payment by our City Banks there seems to be a reviving feeling of confidence among mercantile men."[102] "The merchants are the most excitable class of men in the world," Hone admitted to himself, "[they are] in the garret or in the cellar." If as Hone asserted, the stock market was "the mercury in the thermometer of public opinion," the temperature stopped fluctuating shortly after the initial excitement.[103]

As investors waited to learn the results of the specie suspension, the feverish pace of stock sales leveled off. In the days after the suspension, Hone echoed reports in the newspapers that confirmed "a dead calm has succeeded the stormy weather of Wall Street and the other places of active business, all is still as death, no business is transacted, no bargains made, no negotiations entered into." He concluded, "men's spirits are better because the danger of universal ruin is thought to be less imminent. A slight ray of hope is to be seen in countenances where despair only dwelt for the last fortnight, but all is wrapped up in uncertainty. Nobody can foretell the course matters will take." Hone expressed his uncertainty through the language of unpredictable bodily illness: "the fever is broken but the patient lies in a sort of Syncope, exhausted by the violence of the disease and the severity of the remedies."[104] In mid-May, a comatose calm replaced frenzied financial anxiety.

By mid-June, Taylor was predicting "a material improvement in prices ere long."[105] Almost a month later, he wrote, "Money is getting easy here & the prospect for business appears to brighten every day. It is quite time we had a change for the better."[106] The New York bankers had ended their local financial crisis and started a chain reaction that brought an end to financial uncertainty to the rest of the nation.

* * *

As the post office carried the story of the New York suspension beyond the city, banks throughout the country joined in a unified suspension of specie payments. Citing a fear that the New York suspension would result in a drain of their stores of specie, bankers in New Jersey, Connecticut, Providence, Philadelphia, and Baltimore decided within a day of the New York suspension to do the same "in self defense."[107] Even the BUS suspended with general approval. Over the next four days, the news from New York triggered suspensions along the Erie Canal, in Boston, and throughout New England. By the end of the week, gold and silver coin could not be obtained at most banks from Portland, Maine, through Norfolk, Virginia. As a rural New Hampshire newspaper reported on May 19, "We learn from every quarter, in which the news of the suspension of the New York banks has been received, that the example is followed without exception." The paper provided a list: "Philadelphia . . . Baltimore, Trenton, Albany, New Haven, Hartford, Portland, Portsmouth, Newburyport, Haverhill, Worcester." By the next week, entire state banking systems, like those of Indiana and North Carolina, suspended specie payments.[108]

New York, however, was not the only starting point for the nation's suspensions. By May 10, banks located far from the main routes of financial information in Tallahassee, Florida, and Natchez, Mississippi, had already suspended payment. The news of these distant suspensions had not reached New York in time to influence the bankers there. Only three days after the New York suspension, most New Orleans banks suspended specie payments.[109] With an average nine-day journey in the express mail, the news from New York could not have reached New Orleans in time to trigger this parallel suspension. Andrew Jackson saw this as a "simultaneous movement" inspired by "all the Whig papers from New York to Louisiana recommending the suspension at the same time and then, sudden as a water spout, suspension of specie payment from one end of this continent to the other."[110] Although full of partisan venom, Jackson's attribution of the simultaneous nationwide suspension to local newspapers not only echoed Bennett's conspiracy theory but also implied the significance of local context to economic action. The local context in New Orleans, much like that in New York, prompted that city's bankers to protect the gold in their vaults. In the South, as well as in the North, the nation's banks ended the panic in 1837 to protect local concerns.

* * *

Out of fear that their vaults would be raided if other local banks suspended, depositories of the federal governments' funds participated in the national suspension. The inability of the federal government to access its money spotlighted a flaw in the decentralized financial system. As the *National Intelligencer* commented, "for all purposes of the Government, [its gold and silver] might as well be at the bottom of the Ocean . . . as in the vaults in which it has now become inaccessible." The newspaper elaborated, "the Government, with more than twenty millions of dollars in the Deposit Banks, is as much bankrupt as the Dry Dock Bank . . . for the ability to meet *all* engagements is essential to the character of solvency."[111]

Who was to blame for the illiquidity and potential ruin of the federal government? Attempts to answer this question flew off printing presses.

Some writers had difficulty waiting to assign blame until after the suspension actually happened. On May 10, a Philadelphian Whig writing under the pen name "The Examiner" argued that "the greatest evil that could befal [sic] this country, not only as regards her prosperity at home, but her honor and character abroad, would be a general suspension of specie payments by the banks." Nevertheless, he predicted this would be the case if the "governments of the Union and the States, as well as the whole people" did not pursue "the prevention of such a catastrophe." When the column was published as part of a pamphlet, the author added a "P. S." indicating that "less than two hours after the foregoing was first published, news reached Philadelphia of the intention of the New York Banks to suspend specie payment."[112] Blaming the suspension on government inaction was one tactic of Whig writers.

"Neckar," a pseudonym for a "Citizen of New-York," offered the opposite Whig perspective on the crisis in a serial column in the *Morning Courier and New-York Enquirer*. This author blamed the actions of the federal government, especially the destruction of the BUS and the Specie Circular. He argued that with more specie at his command, Biddle could have eased America's credit by arranging a larger loan from the BOE: "but the specie was stowed away in western banks, or was uselessly occupying secret corners in the hiding places of a deluded people." "The consequence was," he continued, "that specie began to rise in value; a panic ensued, and a general suspension of specie payments was, as we all know, the final result." He concluded, "the suspension of specie payments was brought about by the ill-advised measures of the general government, who promised the people plenty of gold when they needed their votes to sustain them in power."[113] In other words, Jacksonian policy caused the crisis; different policy could fix it. Many other pamphlets and newspaper columns argued for the same "remedy" as Neckar: reinstatement of the BUS.

Charles Francis Adams wrote a follow-up pamphlet to his earlier account of the pressure. Although he was a Whig and used the suspension as a justification for chartering a national bank, his narrative of the crisis was unusual because it did not focus on the bank war:

On the fourth of March last, the late President in his valedictory address congratulated the public upon the astonishing prosperity of the country; and so far as the present writer had an opportunity to observe, none, even of his most bitter opponents pretended to contradict him. Yet ... on that very day the bubble, which he took for prosperity, broke. On that day happened at New-Orleans the first great commercial bankruptcy, the precursor of the general suspension of specie payments which took place in May. The operations of our banking system had reached their condition of the utmost tension, and the cords then began to snap. The inducing cause was the re-call of capital borrowed from Europe.[114]

Despite his dismissal of Jackson's judgment, Adams's argument allowed the crisis to be of international origins even if its effects were national. "There are numbers of persons who will cavil at this explanation," he imagined, "for they have been in the habit of ascribing exclusively to the agency of President Jackson what may after all be quite as fairly charged to their own imprudence and short sight." Blaming political leaders vindicated individuals but bestowed power to parties. He continued, "The atmosphere of party scorches everything within its reach, and most naturally those who imagine they suffer by its influence."[115] Nevertheless, even his pamphlet argued for a solution to the crisis through a partisan plan of national policy making.

Some pamphlets took absurd forms to cement the political causation of the specie suspension. *The Autobiography of Sam Simple*, for example, used a farm allegory to make the typical argument that bad policy caused national dishonor. In this case, the tyrant "Aunt Deborah Crabstick" attempts to kill the reliable old cow, a stand-in for the BUS, and hoard eggs, symbolizing specie. Ultimately, the family nearly starves from her policies, but the story ends happily when Uncle Sam and the old cow return and remove Crabstick from power. "We have had weeping and wailing enough," argued the author, "and if we can extract a little mirth from our sufferings, it may serve for a time to lessen the weight of our sorrows."[116] This attempt to simplify the politics and policies of the 1830s counted on laughs to spread the Whig message: recharter the BUS.

Another allegorical Whig pamphlet, "The Vision of Judgment: Or, A Present for the Whigs of '76 & '37," relied on humor and personification of animals to explain the crisis and suspension of specie payments. In this story, an "ass" wearing a "lion's skin" and his mentor, a "clever fox," plot against a "noble mastiff" who guards a "large bag, marked U.S." The "Vision of Judgment" stands out from both serious treatises and humorous satires because it quite literally illustrated the Jackson years. These rare images of the crisis, however, do not depict bank runs or meetings of bankers and politicians. Instead, the lithograph conveying the specie suspension depicts how "the golden ball," a symbol of the policies pursued by hard-money Democrats, "was found to have been *hollow* within and only *gilt* without." "From it, as from the fabled box of Pandora," the text explained, "issued every evil thing which could be imagined. Poverty,

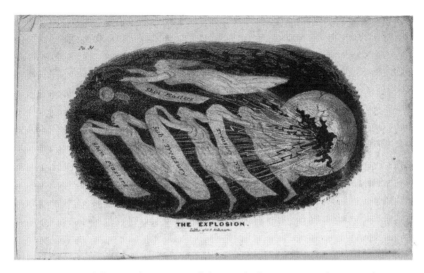

FIGURE 12. "The Explosion," a lithograph by H.R. Robinson, depicts a politicized interpretation of the suspension of specie payments. It appears between pages 30 and 31 of "Vision of Judgment, Or a Present for the Whigs of '76 and '37" by Junius Jr. (New York, 1838. Courtesy of the American Antiquarian Society.)

Distress, and Famine came forth, followed by a ghostly train, bearing in their arms whole bundles of paper."[117] This symbolic representation of the specie suspension clearly assigned blame to political causes.

"The Vision of Judgment" explicitly claimed Whig partisanship in its title. Some responses to the suspension, although arguing for a political causation, did not reveal their partisan affiliation. For example, "The Pressure and Its Causes: Being the Old Fashioned Notions of an Old Fashioned Man" read the phrenology of Uncle Sam in its first chapter measuring the nation's Acquisitiveness against its "other leading organs." "At the present moment ... he is in 'pretty considerable of a darned bad fix,'" explained the author in the fake vernacular used by Whigs to ridicule Jackson's western appointees. "And, while he is trying to wriggle himself out," the author continued, "it may not be a bad speculation, in these hard times, to try to study out how he got in." This phrenological reading, although certain to evoke a chuckle, was designed to blame the crisis on one of the causes cited by Democrats: speculation. Situating the cause in America's national character, the "Old Fashioned Man" blames northern speculators in Maine timberlands as well as southern speculators in plantations and slaves. He blames banks. He slyly claims not to "go to the ridiculous length of accusing the British government of employing emissaries to ruin the country, in the factors and merchants who sell goods to those who wish to purchase," although he seems not to be too uncomfortable blaming merchants, the third of the Democratic triumvirate of causes. With Whig tropes and Democratic causation, the pamphlet is designed to confuse the reader into believing that it is nonpartisan and that its real concern is for the morality of the country. "Since the suspension of specie payments by the Banks, the writer has heard a little club of lads estimating the value of a quarter dollar," wrote the author about what he believed to be the worst effect of the crisis: it taught America's youth dishonorable behavior. "Any governmental policy, or individual feeling which throws obstacles in the way of a just liquidation of our debts," the writer concluded, "is *not* honesty, and is *not* policy."[118] In other words, specie suspension taught Americans, young and old, the wrong lesson.

Democrats turned vague moral lessons learned from the crisis into partisan rhetoric. "The moral effect of these revulsions is seldom considered by those who produce them. They wickedly and falsely charge them upon the government; and thus prevent that useful lesson of warning which might be drawn from them," argued the Democratic "Citizen of Massachusetts" who wrote "The Times: or, the Pressure and its Causes Examined" to blame the Whigs for the crisis. The "lesson" of this implicitly Democratic pamphlet is not to speculate and, if possible, to stay on the farm in New England rather than moving to coastal "commercial cities" or western "uncultivated wilds." In terms of more systematic proposals, the author had no easy solution like the Whigs. He could only argue in the negative:

> Let us restrict business within safe bounds. Let us make no more paper money, but annihilate that which already exists. Let no more of our public lands be sold to speculators, or to any but actual settlers. Above all let us have no United States bank, which is the grand object of the fancy-stock men to accomplish during the sitting of the next Congress.[119]

If the Whigs were more concrete in their blame, they were also more concrete in their suggestion for how to solve the nation's fiscal problem. More than the Whigs, however, the Democrats, as the party in power, needed a positive proposal for dealing with the suspension of specie payments.

Since the beginning of the financial crisis in March, Van Buren had received many letters begging for his help. As one New Yorker wrote, "friends and enemies are looking to you for some measure which shall . . . promise relief to this suffering city."[120] On May 15, the president publicly answered these requests. With "great and weighty matters claiming the consideration of Congress of the United States," President Van Buren called the legislative branch to an extra session that would convene in September.[121] When the New York merchants made the same request less than two weeks earlier, Van Buren had argued not only that he believed there were not "sufficient reasons to justify me requiring an earlier meeting than that appointed by the Constitution" but also that incomplete state elections posed "obstacles to the immediate convocation of Congress."[122] After the nationwide suspension of specie payments, however, Van Buren found reason enough to call even an incomplete Congress into session.

Because the U.S. Treasury had lost all access to its funds, he could no longer leave financial policy to the states. In addition, as a result of the deposit banks' suspension of specie payments, the Treasury could no longer legally deposit funds in the pet banks. Worse yet, merchants claimed that they could not pay import duties in specie, as Van Buren required. Thus, little specie was flowing into the Treasury. Meanwhile, the Distribution Act called for additional payments to be made to state governments in the summer and the fall. The federal government's financial mess was so complex that even Jackson begrudgingly confirmed his successor's opinion that "the call of congress was a necessary measure."[123]

By calling Congress, Van Buren committed to some form of action. The shape and substance of this federal policy, however, were far from determined. Van Buren saw his election as a referendum against the BUS, but the commercial Democrats' state banking system had failed, and advocating a specie currency as hard-money Democrats demanded had become impossible. His need for a new plan grew stronger every day. So during the summer of 1837, pamphlets with titles such as "What Will Congress Do?," "A Practical Plan for a National and State Currency," "The Outline for a Plan for Regulating Domestic Exchange," and simply "The Remedy" competed for the eyes of the president, legislators, and voters. Without a plan to save the liquidity of the government, the nation, as a political entity with unpayable debts, might become another victim of the panic.[124]

* * *

The very idea of a panic victim was created by individuals during and after the crisis. Hannah Farnham Sawyer Lee, the author of *Three Experiments of Living*, wrote a sequel that reflected this new idea. Written as the financial crisis worsened, *Rich Enough: A Tale of the Times* shifted its climax from individual failure to what the main character, a speculating proto-industrialist, described as the "perplexing" times. He lists the financial causes of the panic: "bills come back protested – bad news from

England – sudden and unlooked-for failures – no one can tell where it will
end." Turning from predictions to causes, the narrator explains, "some
attributed the thick-coming evils to the removal of the deposits, others to
interrupted currency; some to overtrading, and some to extravagance."[125]
The novel favors none of these partisan explanations.

In place of these familiar causes, the novel constructs a model of a
system. "All men ... are subject to the reverses of life, but particularly
men of extensive business connections," a pro-agrarian character explains
as she launches into an explanation of international finance through
domestic metaphor: "They are like the spider in his cobweb dwelling;
touch but one of the thousand filaments that compose it, and it vibrates
to the centre, and often the fabric is destroyed that has been so skillfully
woven."[126] Men and women were not only trapped in spider webs, but
the entire "community" suffered the "desolation" of a natural disaster – an
epidemic of "yellow fever, or cholera" or "a whirlwind" – that "made no
distinction of persons." Lee could not explain the crisis in terms of biblical
disasters: "No pestilence visited our land; it was not the plague." Instead,
she described a new economic form of punishment that blighted the
moral and immoral alike. She consoled her readers that financial failure
could no longer be seen as the marker of spiritual failure because "the high-
minded and honorable fell indiscriminately with the rest." Making sense of
both "sudden and un-looked for failures" and how "the banks concluded
to issue no specie," Lee's explanations of the economy adapted to the
changing times.[127] The experience of crisis changed the moral of her
stories; individual choices were no longer the only force that powered
economic change. Instead, both frugal and greedy individuals found themselves at the mercy of forces beyond their control.

Although the moral of Francis Wayland's political economy textbook
would not suspend agency as radically as Lee's novel did, Wayland
rethought the complete control of individuals over their economic fates.
While the nation's financiers panicked, the Brown University president
revised his *Elements of Political Economy*. As he sent the manuscript of an
abridged version to the printer in October 1837, he had already begun
rewriting some passages in the longer textbook to explain the "sudden
paralysis of mercantile confidence" as the cause of the crisis.[128] The text of
the shorter version, designed for "the advanced students of both sexes in
our High Schools and Academies," reiterated his argument for individual
responsibility. The lesson seems so clear: "If men were content to grow
rich somewhat more slowly, they would grow rich more surely." But the
exercises at the end of the chapter on "The Disadvantages to which a Paper

Currency is exposed" prompted students to think about systemic solutions. One question asked them to consider the role of the government in regulating banking: "What means can a legislature take to prevent banks from issuing bills, when they have nothing with which to redeem them?" Another suggested to students that even the failed choices of individuals might be remedied by larger forces: "If men are universally anxious to accumulate more rapidly than their capital will admit, is there any remedy to these fluctuations? What can prevent them?" Although the student is expected to answer that only moral, nonspeculative behavior can prevent "fluctuations," the open-ended question suggested the possibility of other answers, answers that, like Lee's spider web metaphor, might suggest an economic system beyond the reaches either of individual morality or partisan policy making.[129]

Wayland took the opportunity on the Sunday following the general suspension to combine his academic interest in political economy with his religious duty to his congregation. He asked to "be pardoned for introducing, on this occasion, discussions so foreign to the ordinary topics of pulpit discourse. The subject and the crisis are both peculiar; and this peculiarity is my only excuse for doing, for once, what I hope I may not soon have occasion to do again."[130] Wayland, like advocates of the BOE's lender of last resort policies, argued that the "peculiarity" of the times allowed him to express sentiments contrary to his theoretical beliefs. For example, from his pulpit, Wayland admitted that failure was no longer the product of individual morality: "When a wide-spreading calamity overtakes a nation; when the same stroke of adversity falls not upon one but upon all; when the cup is pressed to the lips of men of every rank and of every occupation, we naturally look for some common cause to account for so universal an effect." The common cause he suggested was neither the new concept of economic victimization suggested by Lee nor the increasingly accepted concept of victimization from partisan policy making. Instead, as a scholar concerned with identifying laws of political economy and as a Baptist minister with a strong belief in God's active role in human life, Wayland asserted, "Conscience naturally inquires, what is the moral law for the violation of which a most merciful God inflicts so grievous a punishment upon the creatures whom he hath made." In other words, Wayland blamed God as the "ultimate cause" of the "wide-spreading calamity."[131]

In looking for the "moral law" that provoked divine retribution, Wayland brought Democratic arguments about the origins of the crisis into the church. Mixing moral aspersions and critiques of the financial system, he blamed greed, gluttony, covetousness, "practical atheism," "reckless expenditure," and "an enormous extension of paper currency." Although he claimed to be "an American citizen belonging to no party," he defended Van Buren's administration by arguing, "I can foresee no good, but much evil, as result of universally calumniating the motives of those in authority." And even more strongly supporting the idea that the immoral behavior of bankers, merchants, and speculators rather than the government contributed to the "immediate causes" of the crisis, he asserted, "that our calamities do not arise mainly from the government is, I think, evident from the fact that Great Britain where no such cause exists is suffering an equal if not a greater calamity, and a calamity of precisely the same nature." In line with his academic arguments in favor of free trade, he argued, "were the government to feel authorized to do any thing, it seems to me that it would be very difficult for any man to tell us what would relieve the present distress." Advocating universal confidence between Americans, Wayland offered no practical solution to the problem.[132]

As an ambivalent supporter of a national bank, he cautioned those eagerly proposing this solution to remember "that men are much more easily convinced of mistakes by kindness, and confidence, and reason, than by sarcasm, and calumny, and invective." Certainly struggling with his own theoretical debates over the "laws" of political economy and their relationship to "moral law," Wayland exhorted his parishioners and the readers of his published sermons that "Those who administer the government of this country, at such a time as this, hold surely no enviable office. They need our help and we need theirs in order that we all may be safely carried through the present alarming crisis."[133] The "help" proposed by Wayland, either as theoretical political economist or as moralizing minister, could hardly provide a policy solution for what had become a single, national "crisis."

* * *

William Gouge, however, had a vision. In 1833, Gouge had written *A Short History of Paper Money and Banking in the United States*, which was so popular among hard-money Democrats that it sold out of its cloth edition, was reprinted in a dense twenty-five-cent paper edition, and was serialized and excerpted by several newspapers.[134] The book proposed not only diminishing the banks' power by gradually eliminating paper currency but also divorcing the federal government's funds from the banking system.

On May 29, 1837, Gouge wrote a new pamphlet adding structure, quite literally, to what he considered to be "the true policy of the United States government," which was "to separate its fiscal concerns from the private concerns of individuals and corporations." He imagined replacing the fifty-seven state-chartered banks and branches located in thirty-six cities that held the federal government's deposits with thirty-six "Sub-Treasury Offices." Rather than the banks' "costly buildings" erected to "impress passers by with an idea of their great wealth," most of the Sub-Treasury Offices could be located in existing structures that housed "the Custom Houses, Land Offices, and Post Offices." New buildings would only be required in the seven cities that collected the most federal funds – New York, Boston, Philadelphia, Washington, New Orleans, Louisville, and Detroit. Unlike the many transactions that occupied bankers and their clerks, "The receiving of the money due to government, the safe-keeping of the same, the payment of it when legally demanded, and the transmitting of certain amounts from one place to another," were the only tasks that would be required of the officers of the Sub-Treasury.[135]

Gouge's idea for how to protect the nation's money involved not only physically removing it from the books and the vaults of the nation's suspended banks but also building new structures that would allow the nation to look solvent. Gouge envisioned new physical approaches to bookkeeping through interior design: "the safety room in each of the principal Sub-Treasuries should be fitted up with sliding shelves of such a size as to contain a definite number of pieces of coin, say 1,000 or 5,000 dollars in half-dollars, eagles, or half-eagles." His organization of an exclusively specie currency had practical benefits: "By simply drawing out the shelves it could be seen whether they were full or not, and, in this way, the amount of money in the largest Sub-Treasuries could be ascertained in a few moments." To prevent against counterfeit coin, Gouge's system added another feature to his design: "the weight of each shelf should be marked on it as tare, and suitable scales provided. Then by putting the money shelves into the scales the accuracy of the ocular examination could [be] tested." Gouge added that weighing rather than counting would save money because what took bank clerks hours "would occupy only minutes." The convenience of bank paper, its portability, was a liability to Gouge. He argued that with the Sub-Treasury's specie-laden vaults, thieves "could not conveniently carry off any very great amount." Even fire, Gouge asserted, posed less danger in the Sub-Treasury because although a bank's valuable paper might burn, "The most it would do in the safety-room of a Sub-Treasury, would be to melt the gold and silver." Perhaps most importantly after the scandals and the uncertainty of the spring of 1837, Gouge argued, "In the Sub-Treasury books there would be no fictitious accounts to confuse and confound plain people – no room for mystification." In fact, under this gouging-free system, who needed books, let alone accounts? The ability to perform an "ocular examination" and to weigh the nation's funds provided ultimate confidence that nothing could endanger the nation's finances.[136] Opposed to credit in nearly any form, Gouge's supporters were not disturbed that physical accounting amounted to hoarding the resources of economic development; slower growth suited the Loco-Foco aim of increasing both the theoretical and monetary value of labor.

As Gouge saw it, the suspension of specie payments provided the perfect opportunity for implementing his plan to change the structure of the nation's finances. With its concrete and efficient structure, Gouge hoped his system of Sub-Treasury Offices, also known as the Independent Treasury system, would be adopted by the extra session of Congress. As an analyst in the Treasury Department, he was perfectly positioned to feed his ideas to Levi Woodbury, the secretary of the treasury, and through him to the president.

Gouge correctly surmised that his plan would appeal to the president, who was trapped financially by the suspended deposit banks and politically by the Whig support of a new federally chartered bank. On September 4, 1837, Van Buren outlined a plan not only to withhold the October distri-bution to the states and to issue "Treasury Notes" while the government waited for specie payments to resume but also to "separate the fiscal oper-ations of the Government from those of individuals or corporations."[137] Van Buren's version of the Independent Treasury lacked Gouge's architec-tural vision but gained a distinctly partisan tone.

One of the principal products of the "excited state of public feeling," Van Buren explained, had been that the crisis "became connected with the passions and conflicts of party; opinions were more or less affected by political considerations, and differences were prolonged which might otherwise have been determined by an appeal to facts, the exercise of reason, or by mutual concession." Unable to escape the system of eco-nomic understanding that he identified, the president spun a narrative of the spring's crisis that blamed bankers, speculators, merchants, and for-eign investors. The "facts" he recited conveniently left out the policies cited by Whigs as the cause of the crisis: the Specie Circular and the bank war.[138]

Unwilling to accept the national boundaries of the crisis defined by the Whigs' accusations toward Jacksonian fiscal policy, Van Buren looked abroad. He tried to focus attention on how, as Wayland had argued, Great Britain was experiencing "the same overwhelming catastrophe," but he could not stop himself from turning this fact into supporting evidence for his "remedies" through national policy making. "The most material difference between the results in the two countries," Van Buren added, "has only been that with us there has also occurred an extensive derangement in the fiscal affairs of the Federal and State Governments, occasioned by the suspension of specie payments by the banks." By drawing attention to the differences between the crises in America and Britain, Van Buren ultimately confirmed political causation and demanded national solutions.[139]

By September, the transnational reach of the spring's crisis had become mere justification for national politics. National politicians, following Van Buren's lead, would tell and retell the story of the crisis in their dueling partisan perspectives for years.[140] Although the decision to cancel the distribution of federal funds to the states was resolved in the extra session, the debate over Gouge's plan continued for nearly a decade. The Independent Treasury became law in 1840, was repealed in 1841, and was reestablished in 1846.[141] As legislative justification for or against what would become known as the "Divorce Act" (implying an end to the marriage of banks and federal funds), Democrats and Whigs reiterated accounts of a "panic" fomented by their opponents. By transforming the many panics and local crises into *the* panic, these masters of rhetoric eclipsed any aspect of the events of the spring that did not directly support the policies they advocated. These political narrations fed America's textbook accounts of the crisis, teaching future generations that politics was the ultimate problem with America's economy.[142]

* * *

In early May, before local crises crystallized into a national panic and before the arrival of the news from London of the failure of the three Ws, the international implications of the situation were less clear. In fact, the day the banks suspended, a correspondent wrote to Van Buren that in light of the bad news from recent transatlantic packets, he foresaw "Bankruptcy of the English Banks, Commission Houses, & great merchants, and in my opinion, a stopping of specie payments by the Bank of England."[143] This correspondent was only partially correct in his predictions. Others, such as Hone, more accurately predicted that the nationwide American bank suspension would only prompt the English to "scold furiously, and stigmatize the Yankees as a nation of swindlers."[144]

When news of the nationwide specie suspensions in the United States arrived on June 12, 1837, Londoners nearly channeled Hone's words. Newspapers reported it was "a robbery committed upon their foreign creditors" and "an attempt to cancel private obligations under the cloak of a general banking failure."[145] Despite these criticisms, newspapers reported no new "mischief" brewing in London or Liverpool.[146] One reason for the calm acceptance of this news was that British newspapers reported that some Americans interpreted the suspension as a national crisis that might result in "a revolution, which will overturn the Van Buren administration" rather than an international specie war with Great Britain.[147] But the main reason why this news barely disturbed the City was that the local crisis had already ended. As the *Times* had determined a week earlier, "we may ... already have sustained all the evil that the crisis in New York can do to us."[148] By the third week of June, the Rothschilds reported that "Business appears to be in general improving & a steady demand continues for cotton."[149]

On June 20, 1837, the causes and consequences of the crisis disappeared from newspapers as England mourned the death of King William IV. As the *Times* reported, "The money business in the city has seldom occupied so little attention as it has done to-day, and even the American Houses have ceased to be a subject of remark; everyone is now occupied more or less in watching the first incidents of the new reign."[150] The ascension of Queen Victoria inaugurated a new era of British history and a new period of speculation.[151] As Bates recorded in his diary shortly after the king's death, "Money matters seem to grow gradually better. Gold is flowing into the bank ... This abundance of money will lead to speculation of some sort either in stocks or in goods and confidence will gradually be restored and business increased."[152] On the same day that the *Times* scathingly reviewed the BOE's policies, the business news was eclipsed by optimistic reports that Queen Victoria might make her first visit to Parliament.[153] In the newspaper business, a reinvigoration of national politics trumped the old story of rumor and ruin in international trade.

Although London's panic ended quickly, the BOE's decision produced long-term global consequences. In London, holders of the three Ws' bills of exchange immediately "[gave] notice of legal proceedings to compel payment" by the BOE.[154] Decades of legal suits passed before the BOE could claim to have settled the accounts. In the 1880s, the BOE was still pursuing legal claims on the property pledged by the late Melvil Wilson and the other deceased partners of Thomas Wilson & Co. The consequences of the panic in 1837 outlived many of the people who had panicked.[155]

As news of the failure spread outside of London, thousands of legal suits followed. The *Times* predicted that "every part of the globe must in succession be visited by its influence."[156] Indeed, the creditors and debtors of the fallen firms spanned the globe. T. Wilson & Co. was "largely connected" with banks in Canada and did "much business in the East Indies and China." It had also brokered loans for banks, governments, and corporations in Brazil and Denmark in addition to the United States.[157] The geography of George Wildes & Co.'s debts and credits spanned the globe. Merchants, banks, and corporations in Liverpool, Glasgow, New York, Boston, Philadelphia, New Orleans, Montreal, Hamburg, Antwerp, Paris, Bordeaux, Buenos Aires, Mexico City, Calcutta, and Canton – among many others – either were owed money by or owed money to George Wildes & Co.[158] The BOE's lawyers would spend decades trying to balance these accounts by forcing payments through the courts of many nations.

By July, Baring Brothers had hired an attorney in New York to begin filing legal claims on its local debts.[159] Lawyers throughout the United States would profit from the protracted settlement of paper debts and personal bankruptcies.[160] In an unusual association of lawyers with honesty, the *New York Herald* defended attorneys who "bring suits for clients and try to make debtors pay their debts," in contrast to the suspended banks that enabled debtors to get away.[161] The differing state bankruptcy laws and the interstate nature of commercial transactions – the state jurisdiction over the national economy – complicated the process of receiving payment for debts through the American legal system.[162] After Martin Van Buren lost his bid for reelection in 1840 to the Whigs' rhetorically charged "Log Cabin Campaign," the federal government passed the Bankruptcy Act of 1841. This law alleviated a judicial system encumbered with complicated bankruptcy cases but infuriated those who held onto a belief in self-made failure. The act was repealed after only thirteen months, but 41,000 individuals filed petitions.[163]

Joseph L. and Solomon Joseph were among the filers. In legal documents, they attested to all the paper instruments of their failure – their liabilities as well as their assets; the judgments against them by London and New York bankers; and the suits they pursued against others in New Orleans, Charlestown, Philadelphia, Havana, and elsewhere. These records explain the Josephs' pre-panic business. The schedule of their belongings paints a compelling picture of how they had lived during the boom of the 1830s. One schedule includes the nearly two hundred items of "wearing apparel," from chemises to shoes, that had attired Joseph L. Joseph, his wife Frances, and their six children. In their three-story house on Houston Street, a guest could sit on one of the six sofas or forty-six chairs and enjoy two pianos, two pier glasses, three portraits, nine pictures, three bronze heads, two marble heads, "one Hercules in small marble, one

Paris and Helen on Wooden Pedestal," a musical clock, and a marble cupid.[164] They had lived well for a while. As a neighbor, Hone witnessed the sale of the belongings of one of the brothers, presumably Solomon, in mid-April 1837. He surmised in his diary, "the articles sold ... were exceedingly costly and sold at a great sacrifice, but a difference of a few hundred dollars in the sale of the furniture of people who have failed for millions will make but a trifling difference to their creditors."[165] He was wrong; the amount may have been trifling but the principle mattered to the Josephs' creditors.

Just as the Josephs had manipulated the news of the Hermann failure to preserve the reputation of their brokerage house, Joseph L. Joseph tried to save his home. He sheltered his possessions by assigning title of his home and property to his brother-in-law. His creditors employed this fact as evidence of fraud. Arguing in support of the dismissal of Joseph's bankruptcy case, the lawyer for the Atchafalaya Rail Road & Banking Co. noted that

[Joseph L. Joseph] collusively and fraudulently procured his furniture of the value of $3000 or there about to be placed in the name of Myer Levy his Brother-in-law and nominally divested himself of the title and ownership thereof with the intent fraudulently to place the same beyond the reach of his creditors and to retain and enjoy the same for his own use and benefit ... and that every attempt on the part of creditors to subject the same to execution has been and still is litigated and resisted by him ... and that he now fraudulently retains said furniture under the cover and cloak of such fraudulent transfers and operations and pretenses.[166]

"Cover and cloak" might shield elite décor, but these actions destroyed Joseph's reputation. He may have lived well, but his besmirched past pushed his family's future to the historical sidelines. The last source on the Josephs may well have been their bankruptcy files.

Lewis Tappan, another failure of 1837, wanted to prevent just such historical vanishing acts. In 1841, one month before the Bankruptcy Act came into effect, Tappan invented a system that would not allow failures or frauds to disappear: credit reporting. His Mercantile Agency institutionalized the previously informal system of intelligence that had inspired merchants and financiers to cultivate correspondents. Within a decade, he employed two thousand informants whose reports occupied thirty clerks to fill more than one hundred volumes of six hundred to seven hundred pages each with reports on tens of thousands of Americans involved in trade.[167] Constantly enlarged, amended, and indexed, Tappan's books centralized accounts of success and failure and evaluated morals as well as assets. Even though Tappan's informants somehow missed the Josephs, his system of espionage, recording, and reciting transformed the practice of long-distance trade.[168] Words continued to convey confidence or the lack thereof, but after 1841, intelligence could be purchased. Confidence became commoditized.

Without confidence, creditors created an untold volume of litigation regarding commercial failure. Lawsuits over bills of exchange, bad debts, and other commercial complications of insolvency produced such a backlog in the courts of the three municipalities of New Orleans that the state legislature formed a new commercial court to make room in judges' dockets for other types of cases.[169] The BOE sent agents there to negotiate protested bills. Meanwhile, other creditors commissioned agents in New Orleans to negotiate an end to their debts through the literal substance of paper promises: cotton.[170] Even the BUS saw opportunity in New Orleans. Biddle contacted his correspondents in the Gulf South and authorized them to extend credit to cotton planters in exchange for cotton. The BUS became a cotton factor.

* * *

As agents of American and European creditors competed in the New Orleans cotton market, Edmond Jean Forstall was too embroiled in his own banking scandal to take advantage of the opportunity for buying cheap cotton. Although Forstall's scandal would not result in the same tragic end as the one involving John Flemming, both started with choices made during prosperous times.

Back in 1835, when Bates declined Forstall's Citizens' Bank bonds, the New Orleanian turned to Hope & Co. in Amsterdam. F. de Lizardi & Co., a firm associated with Forstall's firm managed in part by Alexander Gordon, his longtime partner in Liverpool, would channel the specie from the sale in the Netherlands back to New Orleans.[171] To sell the bonds, the Dutch financiers required that the state guarantee the Citizens' Bank bonds (see Figure 4 and Figure 5). To gain this legislative support, Citizens' Bank agreed to a new charter that imposed racist, sexist, and nativist limitations on shareholders to make certain that only propertied, white, male Louisianans controlled the bank.[172] Louisianans wanted foreign capital but not foreign control.

The first installment of specie arrived in the spring of 1837, just in time to reassure the public of the reputation of the Citizens' Bank following the Hermann and Joseph failures.[173] When most banks in New Orleans suspended specie payments in May, Forstall protected his bank's coins by suggesting limits on the circulation of each bank in the city.[174] As a member of the General Committee on Banks formed by both houses of the Louisiana State Legislature, Forstall compiled evidence for more than half a year. Justifying his plan for circulation limits, he drew up a detailed table entitled the "Statement of the Situation of the Banks in New Orleans, on the 23 December 1837."[175] In the meanwhile, he attempted to prove his institution's trustworthiness by directing the tellers to continue to redeem notes issued before the national suspension.[176] He cultivated such a trusted reputation that the First Municipality in New Orleans contracted an issue of small denomination notes exclusively with the Citizens' Bank.[177]

When the Citizens' Bank suspended specie payments on June 6, nearly a month after the rest of the New Orleans banks, the directors recognized that they had a choice between two evils: "the suspension of specie payments throughout all the United States leaves no alternative to the Bank [but] to liquidate itself or to assimilate its currency to that now becoming the only medium of exchange." All but one bank director agreed that "a liquidation in the present unprecedented commercial crisis would jeopardize the assets of the bank, which it is its imperative duly to protect."[178] A few days later, the sole dissenter recorded his objections in the minutes, arguing that the suspension of specie payments "truly degrades the credit and the character of this institution by putting it purposely on a level with that which this very institution denounces as depreciated and hazardous."[179] Despite the fact that they came to opposite conclusions, both the dissenting director and Forstall's majority believed they were fulfilling their obligations to the bank's investors. This division within the directorate of the Citizens' Bank not only confirms the real choice bankers made in suspending specie payments but also suggests a hint of brewing dissatisfaction with Forstall's leadership.[180]

In fact, even before the Citizens' Bank suspended specie payments, Forstall found a disturbing letter undermining his authority in the *True American*. At a special meeting of the board of the Citizens' Bank, Forstall read the letter's accusation "that the Lizardis (of London) had received a loan from the Citizens' Bank of Louisiana." The letter's author, under the moniker "A Stockholder," was infuriated that the bond issue sold in Amsterdam was funding Forstall's foreign and private business partners. Forstall and the board instructed the cashier to "submit the affairs of this bank to any Stockholder that may apply to investigate the same." Resolving that "the assertions contained in the letter alluded to in the above article are fake and malicious," the bankers insisted in the minutes that "no loans hav[e] ever been made by this Bank to Messrs. Lizardi of London or Paris either directly or indirectly."[181] Because of the slow transportation of information across the Atlantic, the board members had no idea that they were wrong.

Forstall's international associates had, without his knowledge, loaned themselves money rightfully belonging to the Citizens' Bank. Crippled by the pressure in the money markets in the beginning of 1837, Gordon offered some of the proceeds of the Citizens' Bank bond sale to the BOE as collateral for a loan. When the three Ws failed, some of this money remained in the BOE's vaults. Forstall was trapped by the circumstances surrounding the crisis in London and the anxiety over specie and foreigners in his own local crisis.[182]

As agents of foreign creditors flocked to New Orleans to buy cotton at depreciated prices, nativist sentiments prompted demands to know, as another bank's board expressed, "the extent of the engagements of said Citizens' Bank with Foreign Houses and Institutions." The board of the Citizens' Bank initially characterized this request as "absurd and ridiculous," but Forstall knew that accusations alone could injure the reputation of the bank and thus the value of its paper.[183] "In consequence of the calumnies daily circulating against this institution," Forstall requested a public investigation by state officials and officers of several other banks.[184] But no investigation proved necessary because by the end of June, uncontestable news of the use of Citizens' Bank funds by the Lizardis reached New Orleans. Forstall recorded his "disapprobation of the extraordinary and unaccountable conduct of the agents of this Bank Messrs Lizardi Hermanos of Paris and of Messrs Lizardi & Co. of London." Forstall "declared ... that he was not a partner of the firms above named," but he was a partner in a local affiliated firm and had acted as their agent.[185] Forstall tendered his resignation, but the directors feared this act would further damage the reputation of the bank.[186] When other issues split the board of directors, in the fall of 1838, Forstall's opponents launched new accusations of inappropriate allocations of funds at the president. Rightly or wrongly, Forstall resigned, citing "sudden and much-to-be-lamented division in the directory of the Citizens' Bank."[187]

In his resignation letter, Forstall congratulated the directors for "having passed through a revulsion unparalleled in the annals of commerce" and preached ideas of responsible banking to ensure the survival of the institution. He argued that banks "hold, as it were the morals of the people in their hands" and "according to their good or bad management, they become the benefactors or the curse of their country." He suggested that banks should protect the reputation of their debtors. "To destroy the credit of the debtor of the bank," Forstall warned, "is to destroy the property of the bank; it is demolishing one's own house."[188] In the case of the property banks, this was especially true. The securitized property was the "whole estates" – the homes, lands, and slaves – of "thousands of families."[189] Forstall proposed a safeguard. He argued that only "accountability" could destroy what he described as "fictitious paper," by which he meant the kites flown by insolvent merchants such as Samuel Hermann.[190]

Hermann and his sons cost the Citizens' Bank and creditors throughout the transatlantic commercial community a fortune. In June 1839, Louis Florian and his partners in Hermann, Briggs & Co. expressed in a letter to the editors of the *New Orleans Bee* their determination "by industry and exertion to become masters of our affairs by paying *every* person whom we owed to the [last] cent if possible." They still owed $2 million of the $6 million involved in their original failure. Despite their best intentions and their open acknowledgment that "we had in our credulity, in common with others, gone too far," they feared that they might "sink in our present struggle."[191] Indeed, they would never be able to pay these debts, and they dragged down many others with them.

Samuel Hermann, once the richest cotton factor in New Orleans, ended his life destitute and probably dependent on his daughter and son-in-law for food and shelter.[192] Hermann originally tried to save his showcase home from his creditors through several legal maneuvers that involved transferring ownership to his wife. But in 1844, she sold it to Felix Grima, a notary who had been involved in the original 1831 construction contract.[193] Grima's purchase of the house reflected the opportunity that the panic offered to notaries: he had collected significant fees for officiating over many of the transfers of property required to pay the debts of Hermann, his family, and the rest of the city's failures.[194] Grima undoubtedly profited from panic, and this taught Hermann's youngest son Lucien a lesson. Whereas his two older brothers, Louis Florian Hermann and Samuel Hermann Jr., struggled to restart their lives in the cotton business, Lucien Hermann displayed the economic acumen his father had lacked during the pressure of 1836. He abandoned the stress of factoring for the steady income of a notary.[195]

Eventually, Forstall also found a post-panic career path that both mitigated his risks and increased his wealth. The 1840s posed great challenges to Forstall, but he turned them into opportunities. Although he enjoyed the success of finally seeing his Banking Act become law in 1842, he personally owed a great deal of money to the Lizardi family. After they closed their New Orleans branch in 1838, the Lizardis tried to collect from Forstall.

In 1843, he settled his debts with his entire life's savings. Meanwhile, Louisiana's legislature and the property banks planned to repudiate the bonds that he had been so instrumental in selling to Europeans. Forstall interpreted this as besmirching his own honor. With few business prospects, he devoted his time to a campaign in the state legislature, Washington, and Europe to negotiate terms with foreign bondholders to try to preserve Louisiana's credit. This work earned him renewed respect from European bankers and brokers.[196]

In a letter to Baring Brothers in 1848, Forstall proposed opening a "permanent agency" for the Londoners. He described his conception of this new business: "In my opinion, it would require a head manager, an efficient and responsible accountant able in case of accident to replace the manager, and an active produce clerk." He summarized, "The agency so organized and working under the absolute control and instructions of its Principals would combine all the safety and efficiency that could be desired of a commercial establishment of the first order." As a condition of this potential employment, he promised never again to become embroiled in his own mercantile and financial commitments. He was already preparing: "I have been freeing myself of all responsibility whatsoever so that my name may in future be used only for the agency, to which I would bind myself to devote the whole of my time."[197] With less grand plans, Baring Brothers proposed to employ Forstall as its agent, but it would only staff the office with "a lad."[198] Forstall traveled to London to negotiate and once again win these bankers' confidence. In 1849, Forstall agreed in writing to their terms: "I hereby pledge myself not to incur any other liabilities and strictly and faithfully and in all cases to follow your direction or those of your agent T. W. Ward, Esq. of Boston."[199] Serving in this capacity until his death in 1873, Forstall ultimately won a type of confidence that would prove both permanent and profitable.[200]

Forstall's future would lead to stability, but in 1838, as he submitted his resignation to the Citizens' Bank, he foresaw very unstable times. He warned the directors that new problems with credit, confidence, and cotton might destabilize America's banks, which had recently resumed specie payments. He warned the board members not to accept the renewed confidence in the financial world too confidently. His caution about "fictitious paper and kites" included a warning: "the amount of which in our Banks is becoming alarmingly large."[201] Indeed, the same credit system that had trapped individuals, communities, and nations was beginning to weave a new web. In the enthusiasm after the panic in 1837, few bankers shared Forstall's skepticism of the revived system of confidence and the national recovery it promised to produce.

* * *

In the spring of 1838, after angry debates between bankers throughout the nation, some banks resumed specie payments, inspiring hope that the nation's economy had recovered from the events of 1837.[202] Americans imported fewer British goods than earlier, thus improving the balance of trade between the two nations and increasing optimism of Americans' ability to meet their obligations. Many banks appealed to state legislatures to gain the faith of the state as security for new loans. Internal improvement projects gained new resources from bond sales. British and Dutch investors bought state-backed bonds and stocks. In the South, banks became cotton factors; they sold the staple in Britain to balance their debts. The BUS took the lead.[203]

Samuel Jaudon, the BUS's representative in London, served as a commission agent in Liverpool who both negotiated credit from English investors to finance the advances to planters and sold cotton at artificially high prices. Several British merchant banking houses, including the Lizardis, competed with the BUS for America's cotton. As a New Orleans agent for a Boston textile manufacturer reported at the end of December 1837, "There is nothing doing in Cotton – nearly all of that going forward to Europe is on [account] of the Bank."[204] The BUS was winning control over the entire American cotton crop. Because of adverse environmental conditions that resulted in a small crop, this was easier in the winter of 1837 than it would have been in almost any other year. American cotton recovered 50 percent of its value. Prices for other goods returned to near pre-panic levels. Positive interpretations of the economy led to an inflow of British capital, increased cotton prices, and state expenditures.[205]

By December 1838, one year after his earlier letter, the New Orleans agent of the Boston textile manufacturer recognized a problem. He complained to his correspondent of artificially high prices: "so much of the present crop will be under the control of the Banks & agents of European Houses that it is doubtful the article will decline, while speculation may enhance prices."[206] The BUS's corner of the cotton market nearly succeeded, but environmental conditions in Britain affected the supply of credit.

In an exaggerated repeat of the events leading to the panic in 1837, millions of pounds sterling of specie exited the vaults of the BOE in 1839. This time, instead of blaming the American houses, the BOE directors recognized that a poor harvest necessitated wheat imports expending the national specie supply. To protect the currency of the country, the BOE directors again raised discount rates. A new wave of commercial failures traveled through the networks of commercial correspondents from London to New York to Canton and everywhere in between. Textile demand declined and cotton prices fell when British manufacturers stopped buying American cotton. The flow of capital into America began to dry up. The pressure on American money markets transformed into a commercial crisis. Pessimism replaced optimism.[207]

In March 1839, the BUS suspended specie payments again; this time there would be no amendment to its charter. Instead, the assets and liabilities of the failed BUS would be settled over the next two years. The failure of the BUS triggered bank failures throughout much of the United States. In addition, payments on state loans floated before the panic in 1837 became due in Europe. States counted on profitability of internal improvement projects to fund the interest on these debts, but with less consumption of imports and lower prices, canals and railroads could not generate this income.[208] Never receiving the final installment of the Distribution Act, many states experienced a shortfall in their capital supplies, which were pledged many times over to support the loans to state-chartered banks. Nine states defaulted on their loans. Foreign investors feared a general repudiation of state debts and drastically reduced the flow of capital and credit to the United States.[209] Even the BOE needed Barings to negotiate a loan from the Bank of France to protect British currency from what had become a global crisis. Although the actual crisis in 1837 was more acute, the panic in 1839 brought on the worst deflation Americans had yet experienced.[210] The English called the years that followed "the hungry forties."[211]

Measuring the depression is nearly impossible. Aside from the census every ten years, tariff accounts by customs houses, and commodity price listings in newspapers, no governmental or private sector statisticians collected precise data. We can determine drastic deflation in prices, but we can never know the extent of unemployment in part because the data were not yet collected. Some economic historians have compared the period between 1839–43 and 1929–33 and argued that the former was a deflation and not a depression because, unlike in the twentieth century, production levels did not decrease.[212] But the formulas for defining a "depression" or a "deflation" were invented by later economists imagining an economy driven by industrial production and mass consumption. Quantitative research that uses stature to measure the standard of living has found that children born during the early 1840s were five centimeters shorter than children born only ten or fifteen years earlier. Similarly, a decline in the average height of Ohio National Guardsmen began with the cohort born in the late 1830s. This suggests that the hard times of the late 1830s and early 1840s produced "nutritional hardship" that could be physically measured in the bodies of Americans.[213] The extent of the shattered economy of these years could also be judged by the private accounts of people's starvation, unemployment, inadequate relief from private societies, and dreams of going ahead suspended with many, in reality, left behind.[214]

***

In the late summer of 1837, Ralph Waldo Emerson advised the recent graduates of Harvard college and inductees into Phi Beta Kappa to employ "Drudgery, calamity, exasperation, [and] want" as their instructors because "The books of an older period will not fit this."[215] Few invited Emerson's harsh instructors; most merely reacted to the hard times.

The future leaders of the Civil War, North and South, would be shaped by the economic catastrophes of the 1830s. The experience of business failure during the Panic of 1839 set John Brown on a path to abolitionist martyrdom. Meanwhile, a struggling young lawyer named Judah P. Benjamin, who would later hold several Confederate cabinet positions, built his New Orleans practice out of the post-panic legal boom. The aftermath of 1837 also shaped lives in the West. Bank failure in upstate New York in 1837 propelled Joseph Smith Jr. to move his fledgling Mormon flock westward. When her new husband's employer could no longer afford to build better accommodations for their young family, Harriet Beecher Stowe began housekeeping in a tiny Ohio home in 1837. She drew on this experience of domestic economy in the title of her 1852 bestseller, *Uncle Tom's Cabin*. The literature of the American Renaissance also bore the panic's mark. While the dark worlds of Nathaniel Hawthorne and Edgar Allan Poe waited for the recovery of the publishing industry, Herman Melville and Anna Warner stockpiled experiences of economic calamity that would fuel their later fiction.[216]

Writing a future based on the experiences of the past was not just a task for individuals, as Emerson had suggested; it was a work of national politics. In October 1837, John L. O'Sullivan issued a call for revision in the first issue of his pro-manifest destiny *Democratic Review*: "All history has to be re-written; political science and the whole scope of all moral truth have to be considered and illustrated in the light of the democratic principle."[217] On the opposite end of the political spectrum, Abraham Lincoln delivered one of his first public addresses in January 1838. He mourned the loss of the memory of the Revolution to "the silent artillery of time." The young Whig lawyer and future credit reporter argued that the current generation needed to restore "the temple of liberty" by becoming the new pillars "hewn from the solid quarry of sober reason."[218] Both Whigs and Democrats envisioned themselves in a moment of revision with practical implications for America's future.

Perhaps no event in history would be more actively "rewritten" than the panic in 1837. Although the period of panic would dramatically influence the political, cultural, and social history of the nineteenth century, it would be forgotten. After the banks suspended specie payment in May 1837, the many panics experienced by individuals and the local crises in New York, New Orleans, and London were edited out of the new politicized narratives.

As the economy revived, the year 1843 offered American schoolchildren their first chance to learn from history textbooks about the economic chaos that dominated their young lives. Despite admitting that recent events were "not yet ripe for the regular historian," Charles Goodrich decided to include the Jackson, Van Buren, and Harrison administrations in the 1843 edition of his schoolbook *A History of the United States*. Although he assured readers that he "confined himself chiefly to a narration of facts and events" and was reserving judgment to "the future historian," the "facts" he recounted were as Whig as the "facts" recited by President Van Buren in September 1837 were Democratic.[219]

Goodrich's 384-page text described approximately 350 years of history. So if the textbook divided the chronology equally, each page should cover about a year. The account of the three-month period between March and May 1837 spanned four pages; what should have been covered in a quarter of a page took sixteen times the space. The panic in 1837 equated to more than 1 percent of the story of the nation and its colonial antecedents.

Goodrich conveyed the financial uncertainty during those disproportionately significant three months: "Men who had been living in affluence, and who supposed themselves worth an independent fortune, were distressed, and not a few of them, who retired in comparative ease and comfort at night, awoke bankrupt, and without a home, in the morning." All explanation of this personal distress, however, turned not to individual choices but to national politics. "The work of mercantile ruin progressed" in the passive voice, and "suitable remedies" could only be devised by the "representatives of the nation." Just as individual failures had no agency,

Goodrich explained the suspension of specie payments as "the unavoidable result of the diversion of specie to the west, and the drain upon the banks in the Atlantic cities for exportation to Europe."[220] Through skillful linguistic slight of hand, this account masked both the choice to suspend economic agency and the choice to suspend specie payments.

Goodrich never referred to the spring of 1837 as a "panic." This term would not appear as a description of the financial crisis in textbooks until 1851, and it would not appear in any history book as a proper noun – "The Panic of 1837" – until after the Panic of 1857.[221] By 1871, accounts of this event had become so standardized that textbooks could abbreviate, as William Swinton's text summarized: "Soon after President Van Buren came into office, the country suffered great distress from a terrible crash in business and money matters. This is known as the 'Panic of '37.' Nearly all the banks of the country had to suspend specie payment. This caused an immense number of failures and wide-spread suffering."[222] Familiar, yes; factual, no.

By the time Swinton wrote his textbook, the agency of individuals had been lost, and the chronology of the crisis had been revised. By 1871, specie suspension led to failure, rather than the reverse. Few actually remembered the correct order of events. One memoirist writing in the late 1880s explained that when he started to work on Wall Street in 1857, "the facts" of the 1837 crisis "were still fresh in the recollection of several speculators, bankers, and business men, with whom I had the honor of being acquainted." By 1888, however, "Of those who gave me lively descriptions of their vivid recollections of that panic, but few now survive." He therefore felt obliged to tell their story because "there will soon be none of those, who took an active part in the exciting events of that period, left to tell the tale."[223] Ironically, the tale that these "active" participants remembered fifty years later did not involve their participation. Even the last gasps of memory breathed a narrative of a single, national event.

The death of memory was coupled with other reasons why writers in the late nineteenth century elided the story of the months of financial crisis that had been so disproportionately important in the history textbook of 1843. The end of the second party system made the Whig and Democratic arguments about policy making obsolete. Even more importantly, the politicized narrative of a single national panic did not matter to the new economic theory that explained the nineteenth century's booms and busts. In the business cycle, panic was not even a phase. Barely remembered and no longer needed for political or economic purposes, the history of the panic in 1837 vanished.

EPILOGUE

Panic-less Panics of 1837

Define the Panic of 1837. The most recent editions of textbooks vary in their answers.[1]

Chronology is far from consistent. Dates for the beginning of panic range from "late 1836" through the May 1837 bank suspensions.[2] In some textbooks, there is no panic at all because when Van Buren took office, he "was immediately faced with a catastrophic depression."[3] Or, as another puts it, "no sooner was Van Buren in office than a severe depression, called the Panic of 1837, struck."[4] The dates for the end of the Panic of 1837 are equally varied. One text argues, "The panic of 1837 subsided by 1838."[5] Another asserts, "credit continued to collapse through 1838 and 1839."[6] A third extends the panic further, echoing generations of political history by claiming, "The Panic of 1837 lasted six long years."[7]

Finding a uniform answer to the question of the panic's cause proves equally problematic. Some textbooks clearly blame domestic policies.[8] Others cite foreign, especially British, causes.[9] Some textbooks perform intricate narrative maneuvers so that they can blame both foreign and domestic causes.[10] Others end up blaming both without seemingly meaning to do so. For example, one textbook first argues, "the Democrats bore no direct responsibility for the economic downturn"; on the next page, however, this same text claims, "the Specie Circular contributed to the Panic of 1837."[11] Other textbooks try to avoid this issue by relocating blame to impersonal and ahistorical economic forces. One text employs the adjective "inevitable" to describe the "cycle" in 1837; another describes Jackson's effect on "the swings of the economic pendulum."[12]

When I first started working on the Panic of 1837, I thought there were two competing accounts of this event, one composed by historians and the other by economists. After a decade of work on the subject, I see many more variants in the definition of the Panic of 1837. As these textbooks illustrate, the subject is elusive in its chronology and causation. I have come to realize and the previous chapters illustrate that the people of 1837 contributed to this confusion by redefining a plurality of experiences into a single event. One could argue that the generations of writers between these primary sources and this book have also contributed to the many Panics of 1837 by defining and redefining this event to make it useful as evidence for a theory, a turning point in a narrative, or a touchstone for comparison with the present.

To truly see the panic as plural, we need to trace the evolution of these historical and political accounts. We will find that the most common element among these versions is a lack of attention paid to the actual experience of panic. This book has painted the panic back into our picture of the Panic of 1837. The pages that follow explain the dangers of losing sight of panic and the rewards of re-centering definitions around the panic in 1837. Ironically, the story of the panic-less Panics of 1837 begins before anyone started to panic in 1837.

* * *

Early in 1837, John Horsley Palmer, former governor of the BOE and author of the Palmer Rule, circulated a pamphlet justifying the BOE's deviation from its policies during the pressure of 1836.[13] Palmer argued that his rule "was never intended to apply under any extraordinary events that might arise."[14] Palmer's statement disturbed Samuel Jones Loyd, the future Lord Overstone, so much that he fired back with his own pamphlet.[15] He admonished that the BOE's rule breaking was unjustified because nothing "extraordinary" had happened. Indeed, Loyd insisted that pressure in the money market was an ordinary part of "an established cycle." He wrote, "First we find [the state of trade] in a state of quiescence, – next improvement, – growing confidence, – prosperity, – excitement, – overtrading, – convulsion, – pressure, – stagnation, – distress, – ending again in quiescence."[16] His account represented an innovation: he saw a cycle within crises.

He was not entirely alone in recognizing that crises followed a pattern. Around the same time, Americans Condy Raguet and Charles Francis Adams published similar explanations of patterns within crises.[17] Indeed, since the eighteenth century, writers casually referenced the recurrence of crises. But only Loyd's pamphlet would be remembered by later economists, who saw in his language not the description of a single cycle from start to finish but what they wanted to see: a chain of cycles from one crisis to the next.[18]

Loyd's description of a cycle might be remembered, but his point was relatively unimportant to the mainstream of economic thought of his time. Theorists of political economy generally ignored crises because they were, as Palmer suggested, anomalies that temporarily suspended the normal state of equilibrium.[19] Critics of classical political economy, however, wrote about the forces that created gluts and scarcities during the devastating economic conditions that followed the Napoleonic Wars of the early nineteenth century.[20] These theories did not suggest a cycle intrinsic to business. Instead, they suggested that crises were singular events caused by forces, such as wars, beyond the calculations of political economy. As the list of failures grew in 1837, some commentators discussed previous crises as precedents. Nevertheless, they doubted that similar moments were "produced by causes so exciting and extensive," because, in their view, every crisis was the result of particular historical causes.[21] Several decades passed before the application of the concept of the cycle to crises – so clear to the practical Loyd – piqued the curiosity of more quantitatively minded students of the economy.

Meanwhile, other writers with practical experience noted the frequency of crises. Inspired by the devastating conditions of the English industrial workers that he observed while employed in his family's mercantile firm, Friedrich Engels also saw crises as repetitive. They "reappear as regularly as the comets," he wrote in 1843, as he criticized what he saw as willful ignorance on the part of political economists not to recognize that financial crises were an integral part of the system of trade. To Engels, crises existed because prices did not adequately communicate the required balance between supply and demand. Their periodic recurrence and increasing intensity, he hoped, would encourage an economic revolution to dismantle the system of private property.[22] In the late 1850s and early 1860s, Karl Marx, Engels's fellow critic of classical political economy, pushed his critique further. Marx wrote, "Instead of investigating the nature of the conflicting elements which erupt in catastrophe, the apologists content themselves with denying the catastrophe itself and insisting, in the face of their regular and periodic recurrence, that if production were carried on according to the textbooks, crises would never occur."[23] In the two decades between the observations of Engels and those of Marx, however, the textbooks had begun to change.

By the 1860s, theorists within the tradition of classical political economy began not only to recognize a cycle of crises but also to search for its causes by analyzing numerical evidence. In 1862, Clément Juglar, a French physician and economist, published the first book-length argument about the regular recurrence of crises. His list of financial crises in England, France, and the United States suggested a seven- to ten-year period between crises.[24] In 1867, John Mills explained commercial crises as part of a "credit cycle" that was caused by the psychology of businessmen. Mills's approach was groundbreaking. He used the increasingly important technology of the curve to plot financial factors (such as "bank circulation" and "pauperism") against the four stages of the cycle (which he identified as "excitement," "collapse," "depression," and "activity").[25]

Whereas Mills found causes of the cycle in the minds of men, William Stanley Jevons compared Juglar's dates to data on natural phenomena beyond human control. In 1875, he noted that the cycle of sunspots closely correlated with the cycle of crises. He speculated that these flares of extra energy produced bumper crops that glutted the market, causing crises. To address the discrepancy between the eleven-year solar cycle and Juglar's ten-year commercial cycle, Jevons discarded several events as "unfounded panics."[26] For Jevons, a new definition solved his data problem. By the mid-nineteenth century, 1837 had become evidence for an economic theory.

* * *

While Juglar, Mills, and Jevons hunted for patterns, other historically inclined writers hunted for historically particular causes. Jevons was not alone in trying to clarify the terms of financial catastrophe. The process of distinguishing between descriptors occurred as much in newspapers and in school history textbooks as in the literature of economic theory.

In 1857, Members of the New-York Press published a pamphlet with a long but significant title: *'37 and '57: A Brief Popular Account of all the Financial Panics and Commercial Revulsions in the United States, from 1690 to 1857; with More Particular History of the Two Great Revulsions of 1837 and 1857*. Writing in the midst of what would eventually become known as the Panic of 1857, these journalists explained their vocabulary: "The distinction between a Panic and a Revulsion in the commercial world, is obvious. A Panic is a pressure in the money market *without* adequate cause. A Revulsion, on the contrary, is pressure *with* adequate cause." For the authors of this pamphlet, neither '37 nor '57 should be called a panic because their causes (political or otherwise) mattered; they were "Great Revulsions."[27]

As the preface of this pamphlet made clear, uncovering "the causes of financial revulsions" promised "a renovation of our business system as shall prevent the recurrence of similar periods of panic and disaster."[28] The causes of mere panics could be dismissed; revulsions demanded further study by anyone who dared. This document's culled newspaper columns, timelines, and quotations offered readers the chance to be their own historians. Journalists and economic theorists, writers in not yet entirely distinct genres, shared the belief that the study of the causes of financial distress promised the only cure.[29]

Interest in determining the cause of the crisis in 1857 led many writers to look backward to the events of 1837. Despite the determination of the authors of *'37 and '57* to emphasize the equal severity of the two Great Revulsions, few authors expressed this perspective. Most turned the language of panic from 1837 on itself. One writer ridiculed the inexperience of the previous generation by arguing that "the great Panic of 1837 ... could easily have been foreseen, or at least accounted for by the merest tyro in political economy."[30] Another dismissed the previous panicked generation by arguing that "nobody seemed to know what ought to be done."[31] Even Samuel Hurd Walley, who had been a banker and a lawyer in 1837, looked back with disdain on his fellow panicked Americans who had passed off "the terrible crash" as inconsequential. He remembered the language as particularly troubling: "'It was only a panic.' A great failure for millions was only a 'suspension,' and that but 'temporary.' Men of that day, the masses, even, were deluded."[32] To Walley, the use of the term panic in 1837 reflected an overly optimistic, delusional dismissal of events that would ultimately lead to economic devastation in the later 1830s and early 1840s.

In 1865, the phrases "Panic of 1837" and "Panic of 1857" entered the index of Samuel Goodrich's frequently revised and reprinted *A Pictorial History of the United States*.[33] In this and many other history textbooks, the Panic of 1837 neatly filled the period between Van Buren's inauguration and James K. Polk's election to the presidency. This association of the Panic of 1837 with presidents symbolized the politicization of this event in historical accounts. These political narratives reflected the politicized sources printed during and immediately following the panic in 1837. For writers supportive of the Democratic Party, the panic began with the suspension of specie payments on May 10, prompting President Van Buren to call on Congress to save the nation from the banks. For pro-Whig writers, the panic began at the same time, but as they wrote the story, the banks suspended specie payments as a *result* of Van Buren's stubborn refusal to reverse any of Jackson's economic policies. Accounts of the Panic of 1837 frequently lasted through the Harrison and Tyler administrations to the election of 1844. Less than twenty years after 1837, the panic had evolved from a ten-week experience into a seven-year event.[34]

The textbooks of the late 1860s barely, if at all, mention the experience of panic in the spring of 1837.[35] By 1879, Samuel Goodrich's *The American Child's Pictorial History of the United States* explained, "Congress met, and the people expected them to provide a remedy for the existing state of things; but they could do nothing, though they remained in session for six months. The panic continued for several years, and the country did not recover from its effects till 1842."[36] Goodrich's 1879 explanation of the crisis not only reflected the longer definition of the Panic of 1837 but also suggested a new meaning for the event. The reader is meant to deduce that the people were wrong to have "expected" Congress to "provide a remedy." The pronouncement that Congress "could do nothing" implied a new interpretation of the crisis, one in support of *laissez-faire* economic policy. Goodrich, whose book bears subtle Whig overtones lingering from earlier overtly Whig editions, was loath to suggest that Van Buren's steadfast commitment to Democratic policies was the correct course of action. Instead, his book instructs that government was and (more importantly for young Americans learning their civics lessons) will always be powerless to stop financial crises.

Less diplomatic than Goodrich, John William Burgess heaped praise on Van Buren. Published in 1897, Burgess's *The Middle Period* explicitly used the Panic of 1837 as an example of appropriate *laissez-faire* policy: "Mr. Van Buren and his advisers decided very properly not to involve the Government, but to let the people work themselves through the disaster by the natural course of business. This, as is usual in such cases, turned hosts of supporters into opponents."[37] To Burgess, governments and economics operated in separate systems, and panics were no longer the legitimate province of politics. For Burgess, the Panic of 1837 was mostly relevant because the "supporters" that were turned into "opponents" by Van Buren's inaction led to his reelection defeat and the first Whig presidential triumph in American history. Had the Whigs lost and Van Buren won, the Panic of 1837 might have disappeared from historical memory entirely.

So by the late nineteenth century, the historical version of the Panic of 1837 had developed into a seven-year political event. The panic in 1837 had disappeared from history. By the early twentieth century, economists produced the same result, a panic-less Panic of 1837, but by very different means.

* * *

Economic theorists' attention fluctuated in sync with the crises they studied. In his 1858 address, Walley expressed this sentiment: "any discussion of [financial revulsions], ... must be comparatively uninteresting, unless listened to while the revulsion is in process."[38] In other words, during panics, people grow interested in them. Or, as historian Ann Fabian has succinctly stated, "Panics produce texts."[39] Each new crisis has brought a new generation of theories reflecting the latest words and numbers.[40]

Sometimes, a new crisis provoked a theorist to revisit an earlier argument. For Jevons, new evidence published in the late 1870s led him to return to the problem of sunspots and crises.[41] He looked to history for evidence of "decennial crises" and formulated a list complete with question marks that literally conveyed his uncertainty about how to distinguish the "principal" crises of the past: "(1701?), 1711, 1721, 1731–32, (1742? 1752?), 1763, 1772–73, 1783, 1793, (1804–5?), 1815, 1825, 1836–9 (1837 in the United States), 1847, 1857, 1866, 1878."[42] The 1830s stand out as the only crisis in this list that spanned four years. Through the power of the parenthesis, Jevons clearly tried to mask the fact that the crisis in 1837 had been lumped together with the crisis in 1839. He could only make the math work by referencing the whole period from 1836 to 1839 as "1837 in the United States"; one year symbolized four.[43]

Despite this remarkable inaccuracy, he concluded, "I can entertain no doubt whatever that the principal commercial crises do fall into a series having the average period of about 10.466 years. Moreover, the almost perfect coincidence of this period with Broun's estimate of the sun-spot period (10.45) is by itself strong evidence that the phenomena are causally connected."[44] If the sun caused crises, humans did not. Crises had become a normal aspect of business or, in Burgess's term, "natural."[45] With this conclusion, Jevons not only naturalized crises as unstoppable physical phenomena but also defined the economic and natural worlds in the same terms: numbers.

In Jevons's work, as well as in that of Mills and Juglar, economic arguments about cycles of crises no longer depended on words but on tables and graphs.[46] All this quantification revealed something unanticipated: the numbers between crises never returned to some state of equilibrium. Instead, throughout the entire time series, normal appeared to be in flux. Some credit Juglar with this discovery. In 1927, Wesley Mitchell recognized in studying Juglar's work that "the developments in the non-crisis periods offered quite as much a problem as did the crises themselves."[47] In 1939, Joseph Schumpeter wrote of Juglar's work, "His great merit is that he pushed the crisis into the background and that he discovered below it another, much more fundamental, phenomenon, the mechanism of alternating prosperities and liquidations." He continued, "Henceforth, although it took decades for this new view to prevail, the *wave* ousted the *crisis* from the role of protagonist of the play."[48] It was curtains for panics.

The business cycle upstaged cycles of crises and won a prominent place within economic study. "The more intensively we work, the more we realize that this term is a synthetic product of the imagination," Mitchell wrote of business cycles in his review of the subject's derivation, which would cite Loyd as the subject's theoretical founder. He continued, "Overtaken by a series of strange experiences our predecessors leaped to a broad conception, gave it a name, and began to invent explanations, as if they knew what their words meant." By the twentieth century, "strange experiences" as well as "names" and "words" no longer mattered. The focus of study had shifted and narrowed. Mitchell summarized, "Recent writers upon business cycles differ from one another less in principle than in emphasis. Everyone who studies the problem with care must realize that many processes are involved in the alternations of prosperity and depression." Crisis, expressed in terms of revulsion or panic, no longer held a central position between "prosperity and depression." Instead the four "phases" described by Mitchell included "depression, revival, prosperity and recession." He explained, "The word 'crisis' is not dropped, but is used like the words 'panic' or 'boom' to indicate degrees of intensity."[49] As an intensifier rather than a phase, a word rather than a data point, crisis was all too easy to ignore.

By the early twentieth century, words had ceded their place in economic theory to equations, graphs, and statistics. Economists found long as well as short business cycles, but the biggest challenge they faced was that they had, in Mitchell's terms, "no statistical evidence of business cycles as wholes."[50] Business cycles, like the experience of panic for those in 1837, only looked like singular entities in hindsight. Moreover, "statistical evidence" became tantamount to existence. As a founder of the National Bureau of Economic Research (NBER) in the United States, Mitchell built the institutional structure that would allow students of business cycles to gather, create, and access numerical data. Based upon these data, his team

defined the beginning of the "American business cycle" as the period from
1834 to 1838. Nevertheless, out of 277 tables and charts in the NBER's
classic study *Measuring Business Cycles*, Mitchell and his coauthor
included only one reference to the 1830s.[51] More recent crises supplied
better data for study. As Mitchell boasted in 1927, "the leading commercial nations are learning to keep more adequate records of their economic
activities. Of the extraordinary business fluctuations through which the
world has been passing of late, we have fuller knowledge than of any
earlier cycles."[52] Although Mitchell did not indicate precisely what the
"records" tracked, numbers had clearly replaced words as descriptors of
economic change. More recent "fluctuations" proved to be better subjects
of study for this methodology; "earlier cycles" literally disappeared from
books filled with numbers, graphs, and eventually equations.

Quantitative data begged for manipulation. With an increasing focus on
the underlying numbers rather than the actual experience of the economy,
mathematics visualized business cycles as Schumpeter's "waves" – curves
on a graph. The plotting of smooth lines to connect points of data dulled
sharp moments of crisis. As economists started collecting, processing, and
charting data from the time before official quantification, their perspective
widened, and the detail disappeared. The brief but acute periods of crisis
blended into the longer periods of depression. Economic theory about the
business cycle no longer coincided with the lived experience of sudden
economic change.[53] By smoothing out periods of crisis, the models lost
track of the cause of the economic uncertainty that had originally provoked curiosity about panics. The business cycle destroyed the evidence of
its own creation. The cycle never looked so natural.

By the twentieth century, natural no longer meant unalterable. As
Mitchell had suggested, economists increasingly used data to model the
economy with the hope that this "fuller knowledge" would enable them to
reengineer it.[54] As an American translator of Juglar commented in 1915,
"just as modern medicine is overcoming the dangers threatening the physical man, so is modern finance overcoming panic."[55] Although theorists
hoped to eradicate panic from human experience and had been hoping to
do so since the mid-nineteenth century, they only succeeded in removing it
from the study of economics.

* * *

By the 1920s, panic may have lost its place in economics, but for historians,
the concept of the business cycle suggested new approaches to the old story
of politicized panic. In the first paragraph of *The Panic of 1837: Some*

Financial Problems of the Jacksonian Era, Reginald Charles McGrane expressed the hope that his study would "show the several stages in one particular business cycle and its concomitant political aspects." To accomplish this goal, he would "describe the economic forces and the leaders involved in the great crisis of 1837." True to his word, McGrane's only identifiable human subjects were politically significant figures: President Andrew Jackson, President Martin Van Buren, and BUS President Nicholas Biddle.[56]

Moreover, McGrane's chronology reflected his politicized sources. On the first page of chapter 1, he wrote, "The panic of 1837 was one of the most disastrous crises this nation has ever experienced . . . and for seven long years the people of this land struggled to free themselves from its oppression." Later in the book, he makes clear his view that the panic began in May, when "the banks of the United States suspended specie payment, and the country found itself in the throes of the disastrous panic of that year." These sentences demonstrate that he did not recognize the spring of 1837 as especially significant to his account because the suspension led to the "throes" of panic, rather than vice versa. With inanimate banks choosing to suspend specie payment and a "country" passively finding itself in a panic, McGrane ensured that individual experience and individual economic choices (unless they were made by political leaders) played no part in his story of the "dictatorial" Biddle and his Democratic "protagonist[s]."[57] McGrane's scholarship combined both the politicization and the theorization that had erased the actual experience of panic from the historical record.

In 1927, Leland Hamilton Jenks, another historian eager to locate historical antecedents of then-current economic ideas, took a transatlantic approach to the American economic events of the 1830s. In contrast to McGrane, Jenks focused his study, *The Migration of British Capital to 1875*, on "the principal ways in which the migration of capital has influenced the rise of an invisible empire of which London is the metropolis – the empire of British enterprise." With the rise of American economic power, Jenks looked to Britain's past for policies to guide his nation's future. Jenks entitled his third chapter, which covered the same period as McGrane's book, "A Cycle of Anglo-American Finance." This title suggested a similar agency-less economic event. Jenks's focus on British primary sources, however, prevented him from ignoring the spring of 1837. In a subsection entitled "Crisis in Anglo-American Economy," Jenks briefly covered the international period of financial uncertainty in the spring of 1837. Although it shared with McGrane's work a common disinterest in the agency of ordinary people, Jenks's study innovated a new chronology for the same event. This account represented the first version of the Panic of 1837 that started in 1836 in England.[58]

Jenks's focus on financial sources made his chronology attractive to economists. In 1952, R. C. O. Matthews, a British economist, produced an entire monograph on the period covered in Jenks's third chapter. Matthews claimed, "our aim will not be to test any particular theoretical model of the trade cycle, but rather to see what explanation or explanations are suggested by the facts themselves." Based on nearly exclusively quantitative data, Matthews's account largely missed the experience of crisis. Indeed, his chapter entitled "The Pattern of the Cycle," which summarized the "several phases," jumped directly from "The boom, 1835–1836" to "The recession, 1837." In his chapter on "The American Market and Its Fluctuations," he did devote five pages to "The turning-point and the panic of 1837." Thus, he safely confined panic to America. The British crisis, barely visible in the numbers, disappeared from Matthews's economic analysis.[59]

As Matthews's study suggests, economists remained relatively uninterested in the experience of panic after 1929. Instead, the Great Depression provided the most statistically accessible case study of the function of business cycles. The 1930s would serve as the foundation for models of macroeconomic engineering. Later in the twentieth century, its most prominent students would gain positions of power within American financial and policy-making institutions.[60] But crises gained few students.[61]

*** * * ***

After 1929, the study of panic initially lost out to the study of depression in history departments.[62] In a series of journal articles published between 1932 and 1956, Samuel Rezneck documented the experience of economic depression in America during the nineteenth century. Soon, however, even this essential stage of the business cycle lost economic theorists' attention. In the epilogue to the 1968 volume collecting his essays, Rezneck offered an explanation: "[it is] illustrative of the historically close relation between economic facts and economic theory, that, since World War II, the efforts of economists . . . have shifted from the study of the business cycle, including depressions, to the analysis of the secular forces of economic growth, with or without fluctuations." This disinterest in both depression and panic reflected a growing belief in the mid-twentieth century that, as Rezneck argued, "the present period represents the close of an age of sharp, recurring economic and social fluctuations extending back into the nineteenth century." He hoped that the Great Depression would teach future policy makers to believe in "prevention and avoidance of the extreme swings of the business cycle by the application of a new social and political philosophy of constant vigilance."[63] Rezneck cast the lack of economic study of depressions in the postwar period as evidence of the success of government's "constant vigilance."[64]

Historians may not have been flocking to the study of depression in the postwar period, but historical narratives found new use for versions of the panic-less Panic of 1837. Two books by historians that featured the Panic of 1837 won the Pulitzer Prize for History in the 1940s and 1950s; each marshaled a different version of the Panic of 1837 in support of twentieth-century beliefs.

Arthur M. Schlesinger Jr. wrote *The Age of Jackson* during World War II as an ode to democracy in the midst of its fascist challenge. In a chapter entitled "Panic," he merely summarized the spring of 1837: "Credit tight-ened, specie fled the country, and in its wake the shades of depression fell fast across the land." Panic may have been the chapter title, but depression and more specifically "the political exploitation of the crisis" were its subjects. For the pro-Jackson Schlesinger, the signal lesson of the Panic of 1837 was not, as it had been for Burgess, a favorable verdict on *laissez-faire*, but a forerunner of the democratic triumph of Franklin D. Roosevelt. Schlesinger saw Andrew Jackson as part of a tradition of American leaders ("Washington, Lincoln, Wilson, Franklin Roosevelt") who, when faced with a crisis, acted in the best interest of "the people" rather than as a puppet of business interests or as a totalitarian.[65]

Twelve years after *The Age of Jackson*, Bray Hammond's Pulitzer Prize–winning *Banks and Politics in America: From the Revolution to the Civil War* reflected the change from World War II to the Cold War. As the economic systems of capitalism and communism battled for global dominance, Hammond's book tried to show an American precedent for moderation; he wrote, "Nothing is more firmly established in 20th century thought than that government has over-riding economic responsibilities, especially in respect to money." Hammond's account turned the Panic of 1837 into a case study of the foibles of *laissez-faire*. To do so, he recast Biddle as the "resourceful and energetic protagonist" who successfully managed the nation's first central bank and brought unprecedented pros-perity to the nation until the agrarian Luddites, led by Andrew Jackson, destroyed the bank, Biddle, and American economic growth. In writing about the policy making that followed the suspension of specie payments in May, Hammond, unlike Schlesinger, cast Biddle in the role of Roosevelt.

Also unlike Schlesinger, who relied on politicized sources, Hammond consulted the papers of the largest banks on both sides of the Atlantic to reconstruct the flow of credit. Tellingly, his chapter "Panic, Suspension, Resumption: 1837–1838" drew attention back to Jenks's chronology and the transatlantic crisis in the spring of 1837. His focus on the BUS and the BOE, however, was intended to be more of a lesson for central bankers than an account of Americans' panic.[66] Hammond and Schlesinger disagreed about chronology and about which party to blame for the hard times of the 1840s, but both their narratives ignored the experience of panic.

* * *

The experience of panic would remain on the sidelines as new battles broke out in response to Hammond's book. Attacks came from within the traditional historical discipline as well as from the new field of econometrics, a branch of economics that reconstructed quantitative data from historical sources and plugged these figures into economists' latest models.[67] In his 1969 book *The Jacksonian Economy*, Peter Temin set out "to refute the commonly accepted view that Andrew Jackson's policies toward the Second Bank of the United States produced the dramatic boom and crises of the 1830s." In fact, Temin sought to relocate the cause of the crisis entirely outside of the United States and thus beyond the reach of both Democrats and Whigs.[68]

As an econometrician, Temin applied monetary theory to nearly global historical data of the 1830s to avoid the "errors" derived from "the nature of the sources used to compile the traditional account." To avoid "the opinion of informed contemporaries" and to try to see "how the system as a whole behaved," he turned to a different source base. He explained, "The primary source materials are the data presented in the tables and the Appendix; they are numbers rather than words." He used this evidence to show that "The economy was not the victim of Jacksonian politics; Jackson's policies were the victims of economic fluctuations."[69] In Temin's view, these "fluctuations" had everything to do with policies made beyond American borders, including the Chinese opium trade, the Mexican silver trade, and (echoing Loyd and Jenks) the policies of the BOE in London. To Temin, his quantitative evidence not only suggested new, or long forgotten, causes for the Panic of 1837 but also pointed toward its culmination in "deflation" rather than "depression."[70] As Temin purposefully excluded any source that could have suggested the lived experience of his numerically expressed factors, his account of the Panic of 1837 is perhaps the most panic-less story of this period.

Although Temin found clarity in numbers as sources, his explanation of his findings could not avoid the ambiguities of words. Temin supplied two definitions of panic, one rooted in quantifiable finance and the other based on qualitative appraisals of human thought. Together, these two definitions imply a panic that began and ended within the first two weeks of May 1837. In the first paragraph of his chapter entitled "The Panic of 1837," Temin writes that in the beginning of May, "the crisis had become a panic." This sentence suggested that "panic" was a synonym for the collapse of the credit market represented by specie suspension. This definition was useful for Temin's argument about policy making because it enabled him to draw and then challenge parallels to similar events during the Great Depression.[71] A few pages after his correlation between panic and credit markets, Temin provided a second definition. Here, he explained the effects of the suspension of specie payments in these words: "panic – the anticipation of worse things to come – ended."[72] In this definition, panic was a mental state: "anticipation of worse things to come." Anticipation is a hard concept to quantify and even harder to model.[73] Given his quantitatively minded audience, this definition received little attention. Temin's critics, his fellow economists, challenged his numbers with other numbers.[74] For much of the late twentieth century, neither of Temin's definitions of panic mattered, because panic was not a number.

Not all economists, however, neglected refining the concept of crisis during the Cold War. Charles P. Kindleberger's *Manias, Panics, and Crashes: A History of Financial Crises* appeared for the first time in 1978. As economist Robert M. Solow explained in a foreword to the posthumous final edition, Kindleberger "mistrusted iron-clad intellectual systems, whether their proponents were free marketers or social engineers."[75] He sought a model of crises that would provide practical advice for policy makers. In each edition, Kindleberger synthesized the history of financial crises over an increasingly global space and lengthy time. In the entries for the English and American crises of the 1830s in his ten-page table of crises from 1618 to 1998, Kindleberger listed the period of "Crisis (crash, panic)" in England as occurring in November 1836 and in America as taking place in September 1837. By any definition of crisis, crash, or panic, this chronology was wrong.[76]

Kindleberger's chapter "Anatomy of a Typical Crisis" provides hints as to why he may have erred in the details. To describe a crisis, he turned to old words, the terms of the nineteenth century. As he wrote, "'Overtrading,' 'Revulsion,' 'discredit' have a musty, old-fashioned flavor."[77] Although these words undoubtedly "flavored" a book full of twentieth-century jargon, Kindleberger had no alternative language. These terms were artifacts of a subject lost to his field for nearly a century. Their study had declined with the rise of the business cycle and no new terminology had been invented. For more than a century, economists' emphasis on theoretical models blurred the detail. Chronological precision was, ironically, lost to an obsession with numbers. Numbers, however, would soon provide economists with a means of reevaluating the role of the human mind in their models.

* * *

Just as the study of crises eventually led to their disappearance from economic theory, the modeling of rational behavior and perfect information has recently been challenged by scholars' awareness of imperfection. In 1996, and again in 2001, economists studying information asymmetry won the Nobel Prize in Economic Sciences. In 2002, the prize committee recognized behavioral economics.[78] These two subfields have presented economists with new approaches to old questions, including the origins of crises.

Although Kindleberger disliked the dismissal of crisis behavior as "irrational," his own work hinted at a new research avenue that might kill *homo economicus*, the ideal profit-seeking man whose panic was rational enough to be the foundation of business cycle models.[79] Kindleberger turned to behavioral metaphor in the final edition of his textbook: "Revulsion and discredit may lead to panic ... as investors crowd to get through the door before it slams shut."[80] The bank run, the most visually dramatic experience of panic, has provided a new model for understanding acute information asymmetry and irrational behavior. Bank runs played a relatively small role in the history of 1837. Nevertheless, over the course of the many crises of the nineteenth century, the image of a bank run became the visual symbol of panic, first as engravings in newspapers and later as photographs.[81] Lost amid the sinking fortunes of the study of crises, bank runs made a triumphant return in the economic literature of the late twentieth and early twenty-first centuries because they offered a quantifiable window into Temin's second definition of panic – anticipation of worse things to come.[82] Of course, in the jargon of modern economics, the definition of panics as "sudden crises of systemic illiquidity" is less vivid than the image of men losing their top hats as they push their way through slamming bank doors.[83] But this interest in people, thought, and communication suggests that economics, as a discipline, may be on the verge of taking the words, stories, and details of history as seriously as it has taken numbers, models, and policy implications.[84]

"The idea that economic crises, like the current financial and housing crisis, are mainly caused by changing thought patterns goes against standard economic thinking," explained George A. Akerlof and Robert J. Shiller in their 2009 book *Animal Spirits*. Akerlof and Shiller nevertheless argued that the crisis in 2007 "was caused precisely by our changing confidence, temptations, envy, resentment, and illusions – and especially by changing stories about the nature of the economy." As for panics, these economists argue, "their origins lie in human nature."[85] This suggests that recent economic events have once again renewed interest and provoked change in the theoretical study of crisis.

Similarly, historical scholarship has recently returned the Panic of 1837 to a significant place in America's past. Although the emphasis on social history in the 1960s through the 1980s deemphasized the Panic of 1837, the question of America's capitalist transformation or market revolution has brought the economic story of ambition, speculation, panic, and failure into the spotlight.[86] Transnational approaches to the colonial period and economic subjects such as slavery, cotton, and the dissemination of political economy have also reinvigorated questions of the Atlantic world and the "invisible empire" studied by Jenks nearly a century ago.[87] Nonetheless, like the textbooks, the great syntheses of our time struggle to balance the varied chronologies of the Panic of 1837 as well as the national political and international financial causes.[88]

Inspired by cultural historians' studies of early American experiences and understandings of failure, my doctoral dissertation documented the pathways of panic and the chronology of the crisis in 1837.[89] In the five years that have transpired between my dissertation defense in 2007 and the completion of this book in 2012, some articles, monographs, and syntheses have employed a periodization that recognized the centrality of the spring of 1837.[90] Even Wikipedia, a gauge of popular knowledge, changed its chronology of the crisis. The very first entry on the "Panic of 1837" wiki, posted two days before I defended the prospectus of my dissertation in 2003, described this event with two sentences: "The Panic of 1837 was a depression in the United States. The panic started on May 10, 1837 in New York City with the failure of banks and record unemployment levels."[91] Nearly a decade later, the expanded Wikipedia entry of August 9, 2012, defines the Panic of 1837 as "a financial crisis or market correction in the United States built on a speculative fever." It explains, "The Panic was followed by a five-year depression."[92] As this new definition suggests, common knowledge now separates panic from depression.

FIGURE 13. Edward Williams Clay's lithograph "The Times" is often mistaken for a picture of the Panic of 1837 when it is, in reality, an argument about panic's political causes. Chronology is the key to understanding Clay's interpretation of the crisis, which supports the longer and later periodization of politicized sources. The flag reads "July 4ᵗʰ 1837, 61ˢᵗ Anniversary of our Independence," thus the image takes place more than a month after the panic in 1837 ended. The bank run in the background is rare in the iconography of 1837. "The Times" includes many types of panicked action; in addition to a bank run, it depicts dunning, shinning, suing, pawning, begging, and failing. (New York, 1838. Courtesy of the American Antiquarian Society.)

This is an important first step to realizing the importance of the experience of panic to both history and economics. Beginning his work of synthesis with Loyd, Mitchell claimed in 1927 to have summarized "the foundations upon which our contemporaries have built their more elaborate theories." But his history of the evolution of business cycle theory failed to dig down to bedrock. He bragged that recent theories "conserve all of permanent value which the older economists achieved."[93] His quantifiers, however, missed an essential force: the cultural construction of the crisis, which takes place during the crisis itself.[94] This history is of "permanent value" because it teaches us to see even chronology as argument.[95]

***

For readers of many modern history textbooks, the picture of the Panic of 1837 is E. W. Clay's lithograph "The Times" (Figure 13). Clay staged

America's financial ills as if they were a theatrical production. In the foreground, the characters evoke sympathy or scorn. Shoeless tradesmen huddle beside overpriced commodities and broadsides advertising schemes, frauds, and high prices for coins and credit. A respectable widow and child, dressed in neat mourning black, beg for relief from a fat mortgage holder. A dark-skinned soldier, stogie in his mouth, watches a drunk pass a bottle of gin to a young mother lying barefoot and spread-eagle on the dirty straw of a lean-to. The troubles of a commercial community in crisis fill the background. Crowds throng the liquor store, pawnbroker's shop, sheriff's office, and almshouse. Attorneys wait on clients emerging from luxurious carriages. Clerks sit idly by the Customs House windows above a sign demanding specie for payment of duties as ships (and their cargoes) rot in the harbor. Well-dressed and laboring men run on the "Mechanics Bank," which has posted a sign reading "No Specie payments made here"; soldiers march toward the unarmed crowd. No billows of smoke emerge from the stacks of the railroad engine or steamboat. Signs on the city's offices, hotel, and factory respectively read "to let," "for sale," and "closed for the present." A woman draws the shutters closed above the pawnshop of "Shylock Graspall." A fort labeled "Bridewell," an infamous English poorhouse and debtors' prison, prepares to welcome a new inmate while a veteran tenant hangs from a gibbet. All the while, in an expression of visual gallows humor, the well-tended fields produce crops that have no hope of being transported to markets or of alleviating the hunger in the city.[96]

At first glance, the scene portrays familiar tropes of financial crisis: unemployed workers, bank runs, stagnant commerce, and a crashed real estate market. Remove the top hats and bonnets, and we can easily see our twenty-first-century selves begging for leniency from creditors and paying high prices for fuel. But this is not 2007 in 1837 costume, nor is it really what panic looked like in 1837. We need look no further than the flagpole for proof that the image is an argument, not an illustration. July 4, 1837, the nation's anniversary, occurred more than a month after people stopped panicking and started politicking. As this date suggests, Clay intended to make a political argument. The Whig interpretation can be seen at the top and bottom of the image. The suicides of several figures leaping out of a burning hot air balloon labeled "Safety Fund" allude to problems with Democratic financial policy. Jacksonian emblems on the sun, together with a fallen broadside of his famous quotations, or "popular sayings," suggest that the former president had something to do with the current hardships.[97] Like so many writers of novels and newspapers, Clay's art served to replace individual, local, and international panic with something more usable: a single, national, political event.

By restoring the history of how the local crises and the many panics in 1837 came to be called the Panic of 1837, we gain not only accuracy but also a new use for this event. The definition and redefinition of "The Subprime Mortgage Crisis," "The Panic of 2008," and "The Great Recession" suggest that the most recent hard times are in the midst of a similar process of cultural construction.[98] With headlines such as "To Some, the Widening Crisis Seems Driven by Fear, Not Facts," journalists writing during early 2008 noted that economic events were to an extent driven by words rather than numbers, by rumors rather than an unknowable reality.[99] Even the old question of individual responsibility for financial crisis has resurfaced in headlines that hark back to the novels and sermons that predated the panic in 1837: "Economy Fitful, Americans Start to Pay as They Go: Living Within Means; Easy Credit Era Over, Some See a Trend Back to Thrift."[100] The recent refashioning of 1930s iconography on magazine covers suggests a shortsighted search for models.[101] The choice to see the Great Recession as the Great Depression is as much a choice as to see one panic out of many. Those who determine the representation of the crisis shape its meaning and more importantly its theoretical and political uses.

1837 does not necessarily offer a better model than the Great Depression. Rather, it teaches a different lesson. Experience shapes economic understanding, and this shaping is the process of human agency. Even when economic events seem beyond the control of any individual, the shaping of their meaning remains within our grasp. In 2008, *The Economist*'s covers depicted hurricanes and tornadoes as images of the unfolding financial crisis; these images perhaps unknowingly referenced an earlier perspective on panic crafted in an earlier moment of economic uncertainty.[102] Just as the emphasis on the Great Depression serves as a historical blinder to a richer past, arguments for economic events as natural disasters serve to dismiss the undeniable role of individuals in constructing the economy in such a way that it could become uncontrollable. The same metaphors of natural disaster were important in the spring of 1837 when the process of obscuring the history of crisis began. To balance ideas of an engineered economy and ideas of an economy with its own agency, economic history must keep the panic in the picture.

In order to make sense of our own hard times and the crises that will surely come in the future, we need to reconsider nearly two centuries of historiography that have labeled panics as insignificant events easily overlooked theoretically and easily dismissed politically. By recovering the lost history of the many panics between March and May 1837, and between 1837 and today, we may be able to recover an idea that has been eclipsed by the seemingly more useful stories constructed afterward. The most useful story of the crisis in the spring of 1837 might well be the rediscovery of the history of panic itself.

* * *

In New Orleans, in the spring of 1827, a merchant in his mid-thirties hosted a meeting of "those who occasionally turn their thoughts upon a future existence." For an afternoon, they forgot the bustling cotton trade. They had already found a minister to preach "the principles of the Helvetian Church in all their purity"; now they needed a church. To build it, they would have to raise money. The merchant became their treasurer. His name was Théodore Nicolet.[103]

During the first year, half of the necessary funds rolled in from local subscribers. The New Orleanians sought deeper pockets in New York City. In a letter designed to win confidence from these distant donors, they promised that the "church will be built free of every description of debt, and that thenceforth our interests cannot be shaken by any earthly power."[104]

Debt, however, would destroy both the church and its treasurer. A decade later, the church had sold its organ, and the congregation had "gone to pieces."[105] As for Nicolet, he panicked. In Portland, Maine, about as far from New Orleans as one could travel within the United States, the *Eastern Argus* reported:

Theodore Nicolet, one of the oldest and most respected merchants at New Orleans, in a fit of despair caused by the return of foreign bills protested, committed suicide by shooting himself with a pistol May 3d. He committed the act in a field outside the town. His age was 43. He was a native of Switzerland.[106]

Notes

Introduction

1. For Nicolet and the French Evangelical Church, see Notarial records of square 97, 300–306 N. Rampart St. and 1033–1035 Bienville St., Vieux Carré Survey, HNOC; "Religious Intelligence," *The Christian Advocate* 6 (1828): 515, 566; and "French Church," *Louisiana Advertiser* (New Orleans, LA), Apr. 12, 1827. For Nicolet as consul, see Jean Boze to Henri de Ste-Gême, May 3, 1837, fol. 275, Ste-Gême Family Papers, MSS 100, HNOC.

2. Inventory of the Property of Théodore Nicolet, Grima, Felix. V. 16, Act 425, May 12, 1837, NONA. For Nicolet's age, see Will of Théodore Nicolet, filed May 5, 1837, mf vrd410, vol. 5, p. 456, NOCA.

3. Jean Boze to Henri de Ste-Gême, May 3, 1837, fol. 275, Ste-Gême Family Papers, MSS 100, HNOC; and *New Orleans Bee*, May 4, 1837.

4. Jean Boze to Henri de Ste-Gême, May 3, 1837, fol. 275, Ste-Gême Family Papers, MSS 100, HNOC.

5. For the origins of the term "capitalism," see Jürgen Kocka, "Writing the History of Capitalism," *Bulletin of the German Historical Institute* 47 (Fall 2010): 7–24; and Raymond Williams, *Keywords: A Vocabulary of Culture and Society*, rev. ed. (New York: Oxford University Press, 1983), 50–52. Precise dating of the emergence of the concept of the economy varies greatly in range from the mid-nineteenth century to the mid-twentieth century. Daniel Breslau, "Economics Invents the Economy: Mathematics, Statistics, and Models in the Work of Irving Fisher and Wesley Mitchell," *Theory and Society* 32, no. 3 (June 2003): 379–411; Timothy Mitchell, "Fixing the Economy," *Cultural Studies*, 12, 1 (1998): 82–101; and Margaret Schabas, *The Natural Origins of Economics* (Chicago: University of Chicago Press, 2005), 1–5.

6. "Correspondence of the *Courier and Enquirer*, New Orleans, April 16, 1837," *NI3*, Apr. 27, 1837.

7. For the process of naming an event, see Lloyd Pratt, "In the Event: An Introduction," *Differences: A Journal of Feminist Cultural Studies* 19, no. 2 (2008): 1–8. Hayden White has argued that events are constructed only in retrospect and to serve a function within a historical narrative. Hayden White,

"The Historical Event," *Differences: A Journal of Feminist Cultural Studies* 19, no. 2 (2008): 9–34. Al Young offers an example of this process in *The Shoemaker and the Tea Party: Memory and the American Revolution* (Boston: Beacon Press, 1991).

8. Noah Webster, *An American Dictionary of the English Language*, 2 vols. (1828; New York: Johnson Reprint Corporation, 1970), s.v. "panic."

9. The earliest reference to the "panic session" that I have found is *The Globe* (Washington, D.C.), Jan. 15, 1835.

10. Webster, *An American Dictionary*, s.v. "crisis."

11. In his study of English, French, German, Spanish, and Italian dictionary entries and titles of economic publications, Besomi finds that in 1837, the word crisis "became the most used catchword in titles," which implied that "the source of disruption can be exogenous or endogenous" (79, 80). Daniele Besomi, "Naming Crises: A Note on Semantics and Chronology," in *Crises and Cycles in Economic Dictionaries and Encyclopedias*, ed. Daniele Besomi (London: Routledge, 2011), 54–132.

12. "Correspondence of the *Courier and Enquirer*, New Orleans, April 16, 1837," *NI3*, Apr. 27, 1837.

13. Mary Beth Norton et al., *A People and A Nation: A History of the United States*, brief 5th ed., vol. 1, *To 1877* (Boston: Houghton Mifflin, 1999), 1:251–52.

14. David Goldfield et al., *The American Journey: A History of the United States* (Upper Saddle River, NJ: Prentice Hall, 1998), 1:302.

15. The epilogue provides a much more thorough account of the transformation of historical and economic writing related to the Panic of 1837.

16. John Larson and Edward Balleisen have provided notable recent exceptions to this longer and later periodization. John Lauritz Larson, *Internal Improvement: National Public Works and the Promise of Popular Government in the Early United States* (Chapel Hill: University of North Carolina Press, 2001), 211; John Lauritz Larson, *The Market Revolution in America: Liberty, Ambition, and the Eclipse of the Common Good* (Cambridge, UK: Cambridge University Press, 2010), 92; and Edward J. Balleisen, *Navigating Failure: Bankruptcy and Commercial Society in Antebellum America* (Chapel Hill: University of North Carolina Press, 2001), 34–37.

Chapter 1

1. Scott Sandage, *Born Losers: A History of Failure in America* (Cambridge, MA: Harvard University Press, 2005), 25–26.

2. Percentages calculated based on figures for real GDP (column Ca-9) in Richard Sutch, "Table Ca9-19 – Gross domestic product: 1790–2002 [Continuous annual series]," *Historical Statistics of the United States, Millennial Edition Online* (Cambridge, UK: Cambridge University Press), http://dx.doi.org/10.1017/ISBN-9780511132971.Ca1-26.

3. Patricia Cline Cohen, *A Calculating People: The Spread of Numeracy in Early America* (Chicago: University of Chicago Press, 1982), 224.

4. "The Dollars," *Burton's Comic Songster: Being Entirely a New Collection of Original and Popular Songs, as Sung by Mr. Burton, Mr. Tyrone Power,*

Mr. John Reeve, Mr. Hadaway, &c. &c. (Philadelphia: James Kay, Jun. & Brother, 1837), 9, 10.

5. Joshua D. Rothman, "The Hazards of the Flush Times: Gambling, Mob Violence, and the Anxieties of America's Market Revolution," *The Journal of American History* 95, no. 3 (Dec. 2008): 651–77; Walter Johnson, *Soul by Soul: Life Inside the Antebellum Slave Market* (Cambridge, MA: Harvard University Press, 2000), 138; Jane Kamensky, *The Exchange Artist: A Tale of High-Flying Speculation and America's First Banking Collapse* (New York: Viking, 2008), 280–89, 308–13; and Malcolm J. Rohrbough, *The Land Office Business: The Settlement and Administration of American Public Lands, 1789–1837* (Oxford, UK: Oxford University Press, 1968), 221–302.

6. Daniel Walker Howe, "Charles Sellers, the Market Revolution, and the Shaping of Identity in Whig-Jacksonian America," in *God and Mammon: Protestants, Money, and the Market, 1790–1860*, ed. Mark A. Noll (Oxford, UK: Oxford University Press, 2002), 62–65; Daniel Walker Howe, *What Hath God Wrought: The Transformation of America, 1815–1848* (New York: Oxford University Press, 2007), 285–327; and Harry L. Watson, *Liberty and Power: The Politics of Jacksonian America*, rev. ed. (New York: Hill and Wang, 2006), 54–57. On the relationship between religion, reform, and economic thinking, see Thomas Haskell, "Capitalism and the Origins of the Humanitarian Sensibility," *American Historical Review* 90 (1985): 339–61, 547–66.

7. In 1830, agriculture claimed nearly 70 percent of the American labor force. Robert A. Margo, "The Labor Force in the Nineteenth Century," in *The Cambridge Economic History of the United States: The Long Nineteenth Century*, ed. Stanley L. Engerman and Robert E. Gallman (New York: Cambridge University Press, 2000), table 5.3, 213.

8. Andrew Combe, *The Principles of Physiology Applied to the Preservation of Health, and to the Improvement of Physical and Mental Education* (New York: Harper & Brothers, 1834), 163.

9. J. M. Opal, *Beyond the Farm: National Ambitions in Rural New England* (Philadelphia: University of Pennsylvania Press, 2008), 155.

10. Combe, *Principles of Physiology*, 163. Combe was a British phrenologist whose works circulated widely in the United States. By "country" here, he probably means Scotland, but Americans could describe their nation similarly. *Oxford Dictionary of National Biography*, s.v. "Combe, Andrew," by L. S. Jacyna, http://www.oxforddnb.com/view/article/6017.

11. Larson, *The Market Revolution in America*, 169.

12. For the political reforms in the United States, see Howe, *What Hath God Wrought*; and Sean Wilentz, *The Rise of American Democracy: Jefferson to Lincoln* (New York: W. W. Norton, 2005). For the era of reform in Britain, see Lawrence H. White, *Free Banking in Britain: Theory, Experience, and Debate, 1800–1845*, 2nd ed. (London: Institute of Economic Affairs, 1995), 63; Peter Mandler, *Aristocratic Government in the Age of Reform: Whigs and Liberals, 1830–1852* (Oxford, UK: Clarendon Press, 1990); Ian Newbould, *Whiggery and Reform, 1830–41: The Politics of Government* (Stanford, CA: Stanford University Press, 1990); T. A. Jenkins, *The Liberal Ascendancy,*

1830–1886 (New York: St. Martin's Press, 1994); and Ian Machin, *The Rise of Democracy in Britain, 1830–1918* (London: Macmillan, 2001).

13. Debates continue over which is more important for the long-term development of the economy – banking freedom for economic growth or central banking for economic stability. The economic history of the 1830s has often been written to provide evidence in this debate.

14. Otto Gatell suggested the term "bank wars" to refer to the many state and federal banking disputes, but this was a period of both intra-national and international bank wars. Frank Otto Gatell, "Sober Second Thoughts on Van Buren, the Albany Regency, and the Wall Street Conspiracy," *Journal of American History* 53, no. 1 (1966): 40. The experience of the "flush times" is the subject of Joshua Rothman, *Flush Times and Fever Dreams: A Story of Capitalism and Slavery in the Age of Jackson* (Athens: University of Georgia Press, 2012).

15. The earliest known coins date back to 600 BCE. Niall Ferguson, *The Ascent of Money: A Financial History of the World* (New York: Penguin Press, 2008), 24.

16. C. C. Marsh, *The Science of Double-Entry Book-Keeping: Simplified by the Introduction of an Infallible Rule for Dr. and Cr. Calculated to Insure a Complete Knowledge of the Theory and Practice of Accounts* (Philadelphia: J. Towar & D. M. Hogan, 1830).

17. John Adems Paxton, *A Supplement to the New-Orleans Directory of the Last Year* (New Orleans, 1824).

18. On credit reporting, see Balleisen, *Navigating Failure*, 146–51; Sandage, *Born Losers*, 99–188; Rowena Olegario, *A Culture of Credit: Embedding Trust and Transparency in American Business* (Cambridge, MA: Harvard University Press, 2006); and Joshua Lauer, "The Good Consumer: Credit Reporting and the Invention of Financial Identity in the United States, 1840–1940" (PhD diss., University of Pennsylvania, 2008). On the telegraph, see Richard R. John, *Network Nation: Inventing American Telecommunications* (Cambridge, MA: Harvard University Press, 2010); Richard R. John, *Spreading the News: The American Postal System from Franklin to Morse* (Cambridge, MA: Harvard University Press, 1998), 87–89; and Howe, *What Hath God Wrought*, 690–98. On stock tickers, see David Hochfelder, "'Where the Common People Could Speculate': The Ticker, Bucket Shops, and the Origins of Popular Participation in Financial Markets, 1880–1920," *Journal of American History* 93, no. 2 (2006): 335–58.

19. Joshua Bates to Messrs. Thomson Bonar & Co., Feb. 8, 1828, Reel 56, BBLOC. As a banking term, "correspondents" became a part of the vocabulary of finance in 1819 replacing the previous term "connexion," but it gained real significance in the 1830s. Fritz Redlich, *The Molding of American Banking: Men and Ideas* (1947; New York: Johnson Reprint Company, 1968), 1:51.

20. Edmond J. Forstall to Baring Brothers & Co., Feb. 27, 1829, Reel 51, BBLOC.

21. Alexander Gordon to Edmond Forstall, July 28, 1830, HC5.7.6, BA.

22. Edmond Forstall to Thomas Baring, Apr. 30, 1835, Reel 51, BBLOC. For more on Forstall, see *The Encyclopedia of American Business History and Biography: Banking & Finance to 1913*, ed. Larry Schweikart (New York: Facts on File, 1990), s.v. "Edmond J. Forstall" by Irene D. Neu, 186–201.

23. Howard Bodenhorn, *State Banking in Early America: A New Economic History* (Oxford, UK: Oxford University Press, 2003), 250–60; Redlich, *Molding of American Banking*, xiv(a)–xv(a), 1:205–8, 2:32–44; Richard Holcombe Kilbourne Jr., *Debt, Investment, Slaves: Credit Relations in East Feliciana Parish, Louisiana, 1825–1885* (Tuscaloosa: University of Alabama Press, 1995); Harold D. Woodman, *King Cotton and His Retainers: Financing and Marketing the Cotton Crop of the South, 1800–1925* (Lexington: University of Kentucky Press, 1968), 98–125; George D. Green, *Finance and Economic Development in the Old South: Louisiana Banking, 1804–1861* (Stanford, CA: Stanford University Press, 1972); Larry Schweikart, *Banking in the American South from the Age of Jackson to Reconstruction* (Baton Rouge: Louisiana State University Press, 1987); and Irene Neu, "J. B. Moussier and the Property Banks of Louisiana," *The Business History Review* 35, no. 4 (1961): 550–57.

24. Douglass C. North, *The Economic Growth of the United States, 1790–1860* (Englewood Cliffs, NJ: Prentice Hall, 1961), 178–80, 233; Stuart Bruchey, *Cotton and the Growth of the American Economy, 1790–1860: Sources and Readings* (New York: Harcourt, Brace, 1967), 222; and James E. Winston, "Notes on the Economic History of New Orleans, 1803–1836," *Mississippi Valley Historical Review* 11, no. 2 (1924): 207.

25. Angela Lakwete, *Inventing the Cotton Gin: Machine and Myth in Antebellum America* (Baltimore: Johns Hopkins University Press, 2003); Adam Rothman, *Slave Country: American Expansion and the Origins of the Deep South* (Cambridge, MA: Harvard University Press, 2005); and Daniel S. Dupre, *Transforming the Cotton Frontier: Madison County, Alabama 1800–1840* (Baton Rouge: Louisiana State University Press, 1997). Agricultural improvement in the biology of cotton may have also increased productivity and profit. Alan L. Olmstead and Paul W. Rhode, "Biological Innovation and Productivity Growth in the Antebellum Cotton Economy," *Journal of Economic History* 68, no. 4 (Dec. 2008): 1123–71.

26. Nick Crafts, "The Industrial Revolution," in *The Economic History of Britain since 1700*, 2nd ed., ed. Roderick Floud and Deirdre N. McCloskey (New York: Cambridge University Press, 1994), 1:44–59; and Joel Mokyr, "Technological Change, 1700–1830," in *Economic History of Britain*, 1:12–43.

27. Leland Hamilton Jenks, *The Migration of British Capital to 1875* (New York: Alfred A. Knopf, 1927), 67; and North, *Economic Growth*, 77.

28. North, *Economic Growth*, 189–203; and Dupre, *Transforming the Cotton Frontier*, 9–38.

29. Jenks, *Migration of British Capital*, 73; and North, *Economic Growth*, 257.

30. North, *Economic Growth*, 256–57; and Rohrbough, *Land Office Business*, 177–98.

31. North, *Economic Growth*, 194, 233.

32. Scott Reynolds Nelson, *A Nation of Deadbeats: An Uncommon History of America's Financial Disasters* (New York: Alfred A. Knopf, 2012), 96–100; North, *Economic Growth*, 234, 288; and Margaret G. Myers, *A Financial History of the United States* (New York: Columbia University Press, 1970), 100.

33. Peter Evans Austin, "Baring Brothers and the Panic of 1837" (PhD diss., University of Texas at Austin, 1999), 55.

34. North, *Economic Growth*, 81–86, 219–20, 238; and Austin, "Baring Brothers," 57–58. Historians of English economic and social history debate the relative significance of home and foreign markets and whether the increased investment in manufacturing created the demand for products or whether the demand for products inspired increased investment. For a summary of this debate, see Stanley L. Engerman, "Mercantilism and Overseas Trade, 1700–1800," in *Economic History of Britain*, 1:182–204.

35. North, *Economic Growth*, 67, 195–97.

36. For the Erie Canal's financing, see Nathan Miller, *The Enterprise of a Free People: Aspects of Economic Development in New York State during the Canal Period, 1792–1838* (Ithaca, NY: Cornell University Press, 1962), 77–111. For a broader survey of state-based canal financing, see John Lauritz Larson, *Internal Improvement: National Public Works and the Promise of Popular Government in the Early United States* (Chapel Hill: University of North Carolina Press, 2001), 71–107, 195–224.

37. For a recent survey of the economic literature on the rise of commercial agriculture, see Jeremy Atack, Fred Bateman, and William N. Parker, "The Farm, the Farmer, and the Market," in *The Cambridge Economic History of the United States*, 245–84. Emily Pawley argues that agricultural improvement, often in subtle forms, led to a new system of valuing land and its products. Emily Pawley, "'The Balance Sheet of Nature': Calculating the New York Farm, 1820–1860" (PhD diss., University of Pennsylvania, 2009).

38. Edmond J. Forstall to Baring Brothers & Co., Feb. 27, 1829, Reel 51, BBLOC. Philip Ziegler, *The Sixth Great Power: A History of One of the Greatest of All Banking Families, the House of Barings, 1762–1929* (New York: Knopf, 1988), 150; and Neu, "Edmond J. Forstall," 189–90.

39. Winston, "Economic History," 201, 205.

40. Charles Daubeny, *Journal of a Tour through the United States and in Canada Made during the Years 1837–8* (Oxford, UK, 1843), 138–39.

41. Winston, "Economic History," 203; and Robert Greenhalgh Albion, *Rise of the New York Port, 1815–1860* (1939; New York: Charles Scribner's Sons, 1970), 105.

42. According to Winston, in 1836, some sixty thousand people lived in New Orleans all year and an additional forty thousand moved there for the winter season. Winston, "Economic History," 200–1; and Allan R. Pred, *Urban Growth and the Circulation of Information: The United States System of Cities, 1790–1840* (Cambridge, MA: Harvard University Press, 1973), 5.

43. Johnson, *Soul by Soul*, 5–6. For slaves as collateral, see Edward E. Baptist, "Toxic Debt, Liar Loans, and Securitized Human Beings: The Panic of 1837 and the Fate of Slavery," *Common-place* 10, no. 3 (Apr. 2010), http://www.common-place.org/vol-10/no-03/baptist/; and Richard Holcombe Kilbourne Jr., *Slave Agriculture and Financial Markets in Antebellum America: The Bank of the United States in Mississippi, 1831–1852* (London: Pickering & Chatto, 2006).

44. Joseph G. Tregle Jr., *Louisiana in the Age of Jackson: A Clash of Cultures and Personalities* (Baton Rouge: Louisiana State University Press, 1999); and John M. Sacher, *A Perfect War of Politics: Parties, Politicians, and Democracy in Louisiana, 1824–1861* (Baton Rouge: Louisiana State University Press, 2003).
45. Daubeny, *Journal*, 138.
46. The term "Creole" is heavily laden with meaning in Louisiana. For alternate definitions of the term used by historians, see Tregle, *Louisiana*, 337–43; and Sacher, *Perfect War of Politics*, 11–14. For a cultural history, see Virginia R. Dominguez, *White by Definition: Social Classification in Creole Louisiana* (New Brunswick, NJ: Rutgers University Press, 1986).
47. On networks of businessmen in other cities, see Robert F. Dalzell Jr., *Enterprising Elite: The Boston Associates and the World They Made* (Cambridge, MA: Harvard University Press, 1987); and Naomi Lamoreaux, *Insider Lending: Banks, Personal Connections, and Economic Development in Industrial New England* (New York: Cambridge University Press, 1994). For networks of clerks, see Patricia Cline Cohen, *The Murder of Helen Jewett: The Life and Death of a Prostitute in Nineteenth-Century New York* (New York: Vintage, 1999), 9–11; Thomas Augst, *The Clerk's Tale: Young Men and Moral Life in Nineteenth-Century America* (Chicago: University of Chicago Press, 2003); Brian Luskey, *On the Make: Clerks and the Quest for Capital in Nineteenth-Century America* (New York: New York University Press, 2010); and Anthony Rotundo, *American Manhood: Transformations in Masculinity from the Revolution to the Modern Era* (New York: Basic Books, 1993).
48. John, *Spreading the News*, 37–38.
49. Albert C. Lerder et al., *A Guide to New Orleans Architecture* (New Orleans: New Orleans Chapter of the American Institute of Architects, 1974), 7, 9.
50. For images of New Orleans's banks, see John Gibson, *Gibson's Guide and Directory of the State of Louisiana and the Cities of New Orleans & Lafayette* (New Orleans: John Gibson, 1838).
51. Alejandra Irigoin, "The End of a Silver Era: The Consequences of the Breakdown of the Spanish Peso Standard in China and the United States, 1780s–1850s," *Journal of World History* 20, no. 2 (June 2009): 207–44.
52. I am grateful to Scott Reynolds Nelson for discussing this conceptualization of bank notes with me. Nelson, *A Nation of Deadbeats*, 13–18.
53. Jenny B. Wahl, "He Broke the Bank, but Did Andrew Jackson also Father the Fed?" in *Congress and the Emergence of Sectionalism: From the Missouri Compromise to the Age of Jackson*, ed. Paul Finkelman and Donald R. Kennon (Athens: Ohio University Press, 2008), 190.
54. For these examples and more, see Bank Note Collection, AAS.
55. Stephen Mihm, *A Nation of Counterfeiters: Capitalists, Con Men, and the Making of the United States* (Cambridge, MA: Harvard University Press, 2007), 1–19; Howard Bodenhorn, *A History of Banking in Antebellum America: Financial Markets and Economic Development in an Era of Nation-Building* (New York: Cambridge University Press, 2000), 197; and Joshua Greenberg, "Lemons and Diddles: The Culture of Early Republic Paper Money" (American Antiquarian Society Seminar Paper, Worcester, MA, 2011).

56. Mihm, *Nation of Counterfeiters*, 248–49.
57. For overviews of the workings of the BUS and its many functions, see Howe, *What Hath God Wrought*, 374; Peter Temin, *The Jacksonian Economy* (New York: W. W. Norton, 1969), 44–58; Bray Hammond, *Banks and Politics in America: From the Revolution to the Civil War* (1957; Princeton, NJ: Princeton University Press, 1991), 300–25; and Richard Timberlake, *Origins of Central Banking in the United States* (Cambridge, MA: Harvard University Press, 1978), 27–41.
58. Mihm, *Nation of Counterfeiters*, 105; Hammond, *Banks and Politics*, 323–24; Stuart Weems Bruchey, *Enterprise: The Dynamic Economy of a Free People* (Cambridge, MA: Harvard University Press, 1990), 181–82; and Kilbourne, *Slave Agriculture*, 11–55.
59. Many have argued that land speculation was key to bringing about the Panic of 1837. For examples, see Robert P. Swierenga, "Land Speculation and Its Impact on Economic Growth and Welfare: A Historiographical Review," *Western Historical Quarterly* 8, no. 3 (July 1977): 283–302; and Ted R. Worley, "Arkansas and the Money Crisis of 1836–7," *Journal of Southern History* 15, no. 2 (May 1949): 178–91. For a case study of land speculation before the Panic of 1837, see Dennis East, "The New York and Mississippi Land Company and the Panic of 1837," *Journal of Mississippi History* 33, no. 4 (1971): 299–331.
60. Jane Knodell, "Rethinking the Jacksonian Economy: The Impact of the 1832 Bank Veto on Commercial Banking," *Journal of Economic History* 66, no. 3 (2006): 558. For the workings of bills of exchange, see Larry Neal, "The Finance of Business during the Industrial Revolution," in *Economic History of Britain*, 1:157–62; and Edwin J. Perkins, *Financing Anglo-American Trade: The House of Brown, 1800–1880* (Cambridge, MA: Harvard University Press, 1975), 4–15. The BUS also dominated the domestic exchange market; see Bodenhorn, *History of Banking*, 174–77.
61. Temin, *Jacksonian Economy*, 33.
62. For the BUS as a source of confidence, see Stanley L. Engerman, "A Note on the Economic Consequences of the Second Bank of the United States," *Journal of Political Economy* 78, no. 4 (July 1970): 726.
63. William Leggett, "Thoughts on the Causes of the Present Discontents," *Plaindealer* (New York), Dec. 10, 1837, in *Democratick Editorials: Essays in Jacksonian Political Economy by William Leggett*, ed. Lawrence H. White (Indianapolis, IN: Liberty Press, 1984), 98.
64. *Cyclopedia of Commercial and Business Anecdotes*, ed. Frazar Kirkland (New York: D. Appleton, 1868), s.v. "Commercial Croakers."
65. The literature on banking and politics in the 1830s is enormous and fraught with the partisanship of the past and the present. For recent syntheses of the secondary sources, see Howe, *What Hath God Wrought*; and Wilentz, *Rise of American Democracy*.
66. On Jackson's language choices, see Howe, *What Hath God Wrought*, 376, 380–81.
67. Scheiber argues that Jackson's 1833 executive order ending federal deposits at the BUS and the Deposit Act of 1836 illustrate the significance of shifting opinions on the security of banks in the Jacksonian era. The opinions, he

argues, established real economic pressures that contributed to the Panic of 1837. Harry N. Scheiber, "The Pet Banks in Jacksonian Politics and Finance, 1833–1841," *Journal of Economic History* 23 (June 1961): 196–214. For a reevaluation of the financial effects of these actions and an overview of the existing literature, see Knodell, "Rethinking the Jacksonian Economy."

68. For conflicting interpretations of these policies, see Howe, *What Hath God Wrought*, 373–95; Wilentz, *Rise of American Democracy*, 360–74, 392–401; and Bruchey, *Enterprise*, 184–92.

69. Temin argues that based on the changing valuation of the dollar, 1834 was the only year that the importation of gold would have been profitable for English merchants. Temin, *Jacksonian Economy*, 79.

70. Ibid., 80–82; and W. E. Cheong, "China Agencies and the Anglo-American Financial Crisis, 1834–1837," *Revue Internationale d'Histoire de la Banque* 9 (1974): 134–59.

71. Peter Temin, "The Economic Consequences of the Bank War," *Journal of Political Economy* 76, no. 2 (1968): 257–74; and Irigoin, "The End of a Silver Era," 225–39. For primary sources on the China trade, see *China Trade and Empire: Jardine, Matheson & Co. and the Origins of British Rule in Hong Kong, 1827–1843*, ed. Alain Le Pichon (Oxford, UK: Oxford University Press, 2006).

72. Peter Rousseau, "Jacksonian Monetary Policy, Specie Flows, and the Panic of 1837," *Journal of Economic History* 62, no. 2 (2002): 457–88.

73. Warren E. Weber, "Early State Banks in the United States: How Many Were There and When Did They Exist?" *The Journal of Economic History* 66, no. 2 (2006): 433–55.

74. For a thorough discussion of the architecture of the Hermann house, see Samuel Wilson Jr., "Architectural Analysis of the Hermann-Grima Historic House," in *Women Who Cared: 100 Years of the Christian Women's Exchange*, ed. Charles L. Dufour (New Orleans: Christian Woman's Exchange, 1980). For more information, see Christian Woman's Exchange records, Manuscripts Collection 257, LARC; and *A New Orleans Courtyard, 1830–1860: The Hermann-Grima House*, ed. Shingo Dameron Manard (New Orleans: Christian Women's Exchange, 1996).

75. Carl Kohn, quoted in *Women Who Cared*, 34–35.

76. Neu, "Edmond J. Forstall," 189–92. For the new structures in New Orleans, see Gibson, *Guide*, 302–72; and Winston, "Economic History," 222–23.

77. Bruchey, *Cotton and the Growth of the American Economy*, table 3.A; and Winston, "Economic History," 206–7.

78. T. B. Thorpe, "Making Cotton," *Harper's New Monthly Magazine* 8, no. 45 (1854): 452–59, reprinted in *Cotton and the Growth of the American Economy*, 171–76.

79. Bruchey, *Cotton and the Growth of the American Economy*, 222; and Norman Sydney Buck, *The Development of the Organisation of Anglo-American Trade, 1800–1850* (New Haven, CT: Yale University Press, 1925), 30–65.

80. For in-depth accounts of the business of cotton factors and specific New Orleans factors, see Robert Roeder, "New Orleans Merchants, 1790–1837" (PhD diss., Harvard University, 1959), 222–86; and Woodman, *King Cotton*, 3–71.

81. For sources on the workings of bills of exchange, see Chap. 1, n. 60. For domestic bills, see Bodenhorn, *History of Banking*, 152–54; and Howard Bodenhorn, "Capital Mobility and Financial Integration in Antebellum America," *Journal of Economic History* 52, no. 3 (1992): 587. For an overview of the credit system in the transatlantic trade, see Stanley Chapman, *The Rise of Merchant Banking* (London: George Allen, 1984), 109.

82. Bill of exchange, *The Bank of England vs. Samuel Hermann & Son*, docket no. 19999, original suit records, First Judicial District Court (Orleans Parish), NOCA (emphasis reflects handwriting in original).

83. For the transportation technology used to communicate in the 1830s, see George Rogers Taylor, *The Transportation Revolution, 1815–1860* (1951; New York: M. E. Sharpe, 1977); and Albert Fishlow, "Internal Transportation in the Nineteenth and Early Twentieth Centuries," in *The Cambridge Economic History of the United States*, 543–642.

84. This can easily be compared by examining the "latest dates" sections in all three cities' newspapers.

85. Gibson, *Guide*, 224–25.

86. Robert G. Albion, *Square-Riggers on Schedule: The New York Sailing Packets to England, France, and the Cotton Ports* (Princeton, NJ: Princeton University Press, 1938), 11–13, 317.

87. Gibson, *Guide*, 224 (emphasis in original). John, *Spreading the News*, 37–42, 83–87, 91, 157–59. Kielbowicz argues that the postal service offered to carry exchange news slips not exceeding two columns to minimize the bulky transportation of entire exchange papers. Richard B. Kielbowicz, *News in the Mail: The Press, Post Office, and Public Information, 1700–1860s* (New York: Greenwood Press, 1989), 169.

88. For population figures, see Pred, *Urban Growth*, 18.

89. Albion, *Rise of the New York Port*, 391.

90. Aaron H. Palmer to NMRS, May 8, 1837, XI/38/199, RAL.

91. Miller, *Enterprise of a Free People*, 99–111.

92. Diary of Philip Hone, Jan. 1, 1837, 12:313, BV Hone, Philip, MS 1549, MCNYHS.

93. Edwin G. Burrows and Mike Wallace, *Gotham: A History of New York City to 1898* (New York: Oxford University Press, 1999), 596–98.

94. Diary of Joshua Bates, Jan. 9, 1836, DEP 74, vol. 2, BA.

95. Joshua Bates commented on the arrangements made in the aftermath of the fire. Joshua Bates to Thomas Wren Ward, July 22, 1836, LB 5c, BA.

96. Burrows and Wallace, *Gotham*, 598.

97. Diary of Philip Hone, Jan. 1, 1837, 12:313, BV Hone, Philip, MS 1549, MCNYHS.

98. Elizabeth Blackmar, *Manhattan for Rent, 1785–1850* (Ithaca, NY: Cornell University Press, 1989); Richard Bushman, *The Refinement of America: Persons, Houses, Cities* (New York: Alfred A. Knopf, 1992), 353–65; Burrows and Wallace, *Gotham*, 598–601; and Christine Stansell, *City of Women: Sex and Class in New York, 1789–1860* (Chicago: University of Illinois Press, 1987), 41–42.

99. For an example, see map of Timothy Wiggin & Co.'s property in New York City. "Map of Property in the Second Ward of the City of New York Belonging to Timothy Wiggin Esq.," C5/239, BOEA. The AAS holds printed records of the Josephs' land speculation on Staten Island. *Articles, &c. of the New Brighton Association* (New York, 1836).

100. NMRS to JLSJ, Aug. 30, 1836, II/10/1, RAL.

101. For credit reporting, see Chap. 1, n. 18. On the development of networks of exchange dealers and merchant bankers in London, see Stanley Chapman, *Merchant Enterprise in Britain: From the Industrial Revolution to World War I* (New York: Cambridge University Press, 1992), 81–106. For Baring Brothers' system of credit rating and the importance of honest correspondents, see R. W. Hidy, "Credit Rating before Dun and Bradstreet," *Bulletin of the Business Historical Society* 13, no. 6 (1939): 81–88.

102. Pred, *Urban Growth*, 27–32; and Albion, *Square-Riggers*, 274, 302–3. For the classic study of New York in opposition to Philadelphia and other American Atlantic ports, see Roger G. Albion, "New York Port and Its Disappointed Rivals, 1815–1860," *Journal of Economic and Business History* 3 (1930–31): 603, 608, 612–13. The subject continues to provoke debate. Rohit Aggarwala, "Twin Cities of the New Republic? Comparing the Commerce of New York and Philadelphia, 1790–1812" (Conference paper presented at the Pennsylvania Historical Association Annual Meeting, Philadelphia, Oct. 2006).

103. Albion, *Square-Riggers*, 9, 274.

104. Asa Greene, *The Perils of Pearl Street, Including a Taste of the Dangers of Wall Street* (New York: Betts & Anstice, and Peter Hill, 1834), 162–63.

105. Bills of exchange would be labeled "First of Exchange second of same time and date unpaid" to signify the number of duplicates of a bill and the condition that the other bill be "unpaid" for its acceptance. For examples, see Bill of exchange, *Brown Brothers & Co. vs. Joseph Hoxie & Co.*, docket no. 17642, original suit records, First Judicial District Court (Orleans Parish), NOCA.

106. Moses Taylor to Philo J. Sheldon, May 1, 1837, Moses Taylor outgoing letterbook, vol. 2, series 1, MTP.

107. NMRS to JLSJ, Nov. 19, 1836, II/10/1, RAL.

108. For the history and meaning of the term "merchant banker," see Norio Tamaki, "The Merchant Bankers in the Early 1830's," *Keio Business Review* 13 (1974): 59–70; and Ralph W. Hidy, "The Organization and Functions of Anglo-American Merchant Bankers, 1815–1860," *Journal of Economic History* 1 (1941): 53–66. "American houses" was a term employed by writers in the 1830s. For example, see James W. Gilbart, *The History of Banking in America: With an Inquiry How Far the Banking Institutions of America Are Adapted to This Country; and a Review of the Cause of the Recent Pressure on the Money Market* (London: Longman, Rees, Orman, Brown, Green, & Longman, 1837), 165, 190.

109. David R. Green, *From Artisans to Paupers: Economic Change and Poverty in London, 1790–1870* (Aldershot, UK: Scolar, 1995), 1; and David Kynaston, *The City of London*. Vol. 1, *A World of Its Own, 1815–1890* (London: Chatto & Windus, 1994), 9–20.

110. Stanley Jevons, quoted in Lars Tvede, *Business Cycles: The Business Cycle Problem from John Law to Chaos Theory* (Amsterdam: Harwood Academic Publishers, 1997), 47.

111. *The Political Economy Club: Names of Members, 1821–1860: – Rules of the Club: – and List of Questions Discussed, 1833–1860* (London, 1860), 32. For more on London's Political Economy Club, see Agnar Sandmo, *Economics Evolving: A History of Economic Thought* (Princeton, NJ: Princeton University Press, 2011), 61.

112. The original rules of the club, reprinted in the 1860 rule book, indicate that it was the responsibility of the club's members "to watch carefully the proceedings of the Press, and to ascertain if any doctrines hostile to sound views of Political Economy have been propagated; to contribute whatever may be in their power to refute such erroneous doctrines, and counteract their influence; and to avail themselves of every favourable opportunity for the publication of seasonable truths within the province of this science." The rules do not define particular "sound views of Political Economy," but according to Lawrence H. White, the club was founded to promote free trade. *The Political Economy Club*, 24; and White, *Free Banking in Britain*, 72. For the origin of the idea of the economy, see Intro., n. 5.

113. For the structures of the City, see Daniel M. Abramson, *Building the Bank of England: Money, Architecture, Society, 1694–1942* (New Haven, CT: Yale University Press, 2005); and Iain S. Black, "Spaces of Capital: Bank Office Building in the City of London, 1830–1870," *Journal of Historical Geography* 26, no. 3 (2000): 351–75. For the layout and functions of an eighteenth-century London merchant banking house, see David Hancock, *Citizens of the World: London Merchants and the Integration of the British Atlantic Community, 1735–1785* (Cambridge, UK: Cambridge University Press, 1995), 85–114.

114. The firms with headquarters in London were Thomas Wilson & Co., George Wildes & Co., and Timothy Wiggin & Co. (the "three Ws"); F. de Lizardi & Co.; Morrison, Cryder & Co.; Baring Brothers & Co.; and NMRS. Meanwhile, W. & J. Brown & Co. headquartered its firm in Liverpool. Ralph W. Hidy, "Cushioning a Crisis in the London Money Market," *Bulletin of the Business Historical Society* 20, no. 5 (1946): 132.

115. Stuart Jones, "The Cotton Industry and Joint-Stock Banking in Manchester, 1825–1850," *Business History* 22, no. 2 (1978): 165–80; A. Andreades, *History of the Bank of England: 1640–1903*, trans. Christabel Meredith (London: P. S. King & Son, 1909), 248–77; and Sir John Clapham, *The Bank of England: A History*, vol. 2, *1797–1914* (Cambridge, UK: Cambridge University Press, 1945), 99–185. As R. C. O. Matthews explains, "the joint-stock principle greatly facilitated entry to the banking business, making it possible for newcomers to challenge the position of established banks to an extent that would otherwise have been impossible." R. C. O Matthews, *A Study in Trade-Cycle History: Economic Fluctuations in Great Britain, 1833–1842* (Cambridge, UK: Cambridge University Press, 1954), 193. Joint-stock companies remained morally dubious until the late nineteenth century. Paul Johnson, *Making the Market: Victorian Origins of Corporate Capitalism* (Cambridge, UK: Cambridge University Press, 2010), 2.

116. White, *Free Banking in Britain*, 35, 44.
117. According to Matthews, the rule required that "at what were called 'times of full currency,' when the reserve was at a maximum and the exchanges such as to cause neither import nor export of specie, the securities should be equal to two-thirds of the liabilities; and that *thereafter* the securities should be held constant, whatever happened to the bullion." Matthews, *Study in Trade-Cycle History*, 168 (emphasis in original). White identifies a third "free banking school" that advocated the elimination of the BOE's controls entirely. Although directors of the BOE included believers in both principles, the specie principle clearly won out in 1836. Andreades, *Bank of England*, 273–77; William F. Hixson, *Triumph of the Bankers: Money and Banking in the Eighteenth and Nineteenth Centuries* (Westport, CT: Praeger, 1993), 105–12; and White, *Free Banking in Britain*, 63–88.
118. The ratio was, as Matthews explains, "a general guide to the Bank of the sort of level to be aimed at. It was the constancy of the securities in face of gold movements that was the crucial part of the doctrine." Matthews reviews the BOE's varied deviations from its rule. Matthews, *Study in Trade-Cycle History*, 168, 170–75.
119. Joshua Bates explains the purpose of raising discount rates in his letter to the BOE; see Joshua Bates to Directors of the Bank of England, Oct. 26, 1836, Committee of the Treasury Minute Book, vol. 22, G8/29, BOEA.
120. For American politics of the streets, see David Waldstreicher, *In the Midst of Perpetual Fêtes: The Making of American Nationalism, 1776–1820* (Chapel Hill: University of North Carolina Press, 1997).
121. E. J. Forstall to Thomas Baring, Aug. 13, 1835, HC5.7.6, BA.
122. Neu, "Edmond J. Forstall," 187.
123. Hope & Co. agreed that the bonds were not suited for the London market. Hope & Co. to Baring Brothers & Co., Mar. 15, 1836, HC8.1 Part IV, BA.
124. Joshua Bates to Thomas Wren Ward, July 22, 1836, LB 5c, BA.
125. Diary of Joshua Bates, May 21, 1834, Aug. 30, 1834, Apr. 22, 1834, DEP 74, vol. 2, BA.
126. For Bates's foreboding about the conflict between American politics and the potential for financial profits, see Diary of Joshua Bates, Mar. 16, 1834, Sept. 26, 1834, Dec. 14, 1834, Oct. 26, 1835, DEP 74, vol. 2, BA.
127. Diary of Joshua Bates, Mar. 5, 1836, DEP 74, vol. 3, BA.
128. Diary of Joshua Bates, July 30, 1835, DEP 74, vol. 2, BA.

Chapter 2

1. Kynaston, *City of London*, 105. Rothschild employed carrier pigeons to great profit after the Battle of Waterloo. Howe, *What Hath God Wrought*, 695.
2. Lord Ashburton, quoted in Kynaston, *City of London*, 107.
3. Richard Hildreth, *The History of Banks: To Which Is Added, a Demonstration of the Advantages and Necessity of Free Competition in the Business of Banking* (Boston: Hilliard & Gray, 1837), 77.
4. JLSJ to NMRS, June 30, 1836, XI/38/15, RAL.

5. Behavioral economists challenge the foundational premise of *homo econom-icus*, the rational and self-interested individual, as a flawed model. Edward J. O'Boyle, "Requiem for *Homo Economicus*," *Journal of Markets and Morality* 10, no. 2 (Fall 2007): 321–37; and George A. Akerlof and Robert J. Shiller, *Animal Spirits: How Human Psychology Drives the Economy, and Why It Matters for Global Capitalism* (Princeton, NJ: Princeton University Press, 2009).

6. "Imperial Parliament – Joint Stock Banks," *Albion, or, British, Colonial, and Foreign Weekly Gazette* (New York), June 25, 1836.

7. "Joint Stock Companies," *Preston Chronicle* (Preston, England), May 14, 1836.

8. Some variations exist between the texts printed in newspapers and in the official record. "Imperial Parliament – Joint Stock Banks," *Albion, or, British, Colonial, and Foreign Weekly Gazette* (New York), June 25, 1836; and *Hansard Parliamentary Debate*, HC Debate, May 12, 1836, vol. 33, col. 878, http://hansard.millbanksystems.com/commons/1836/may/12/joint-stock-banks.

9. Vindex, *Letter to William Clay, Esq. M.P. Containing Strictures on His Late Pamphlet on the Subject of Joint Stock Banks: With Remarks on His Favourite Theories* (London: James Ridgway and Sons, 1836), 10; and *Derby Mercury* (Derby, England), May 11, 1836 (emphasis in original).

10. Vindex, *Letter to William Clay*, 9.

11. Gilbart, *History of Banking in America*, 95.

12. Vincent Stuckey, *Thoughts on the Improvement of the System of Country Banking: In a Letter to Lord Viscount Althorp*, 2nd ed. (London: J. Hatchard and Son, 1836), 18.

13. *Times* (London), Feb. 14, 1837.

14. *Times* (London), May 3, 1836.

15. *Caledonian Mercury* (Edinburgh), May 5, 1836; and *Jackson's Oxford Journal* (Oxford), May 7, 1836.

16. *Times* (London), May 25, 1836.

17. *Times* (London), May 19, 1836.

18. *Times* (London), May 23, 1836.

19. *Times* (London), May 19, 1836.

20. *Journal of Commerce* (New York), Apr. 23, 1836, reprinted in the *Times* (London), May 25, 1836.

21. *Newcastle Courant* (Newcastle-upon-Tyne, England), May 21, 1836.

22. *Brighton Patriot* (Brighton, England), May 31, 1836.

23. *Derby Mercury* (Derby, England), June 1, 1836; *Hull Packet* (Hull, England), June 3, 1836; and *Newcastle Courant* (Newcastle-upon-Tyne, England), June 4, 1836.

24. *Times* (London), June 17, 1836.

25. Whereas some writers confirm contemporary accounts of inflation, Clapham argues that the paper money supply in England was actually contracting in 1834–36. Clapham, *Bank of England*, 149. The scholarly debate over mone-tary factors is enormous. For reviews of the literature, see Daniel Feller, "Politics and Society: Toward a Jacksonian Synthesis," *Journal of the Early Republic* 10 (Summer 1990): 131–61; Knodell, "Rethinking the Jacksonian Economy," 541–74; and Richard Sylla, "Review of Peter Temin's *The*

Jacksonian Economy," EH-Net, Aug. 16, 2001, eh.net/book_reviews/jackso-nian-economy.

26. *Times* (London), June 17, 1836.

27. *Times* (London), June 13, 1836.

28. For a summary of the Distribution Act or Deposit Bill, see Wilentz, *Rise of American Democracy*, 436–46. Cambreleng had been at the center of the investigation of the BUS earlier in the Jackson administration. Thomas Payne Govan, *Nicholas Biddle: Nationalist and Public Banker, 1786–1844* (Chicago: University of Chicago Press, 1959), 184–85, 195–98; and Gatell, "Sober Second Thoughts," 19–40.

29. C. C. Cambreleng, "Armament of Fortifications," *Appendix to the Congressional Globe*, 24th Cong., 1st sess., 1836, 312–16.

30. For the rise of models, see Robert M. Solow, "How Did Economics Get That Way and What Way Did It Get?" *Daedalus* 126, no. 1 (1997): 39–59; and David M. Kreps, "Economics – The Current Position," *Daedalus* 126, no. 1 (1997): 59–87.

31. Patricia Cline Cohen has demonstrated the "very real limits to the quantitative abilities of even some of the most acute quantifiers in the 1840s." Cohen, *Calculating People*, 204.

32. "Army Appropriations Bill," *Journal of Commerce* (New York), Apr. 29, 1836; and "Army Appropriations Bill," *Journal of Commerce* (New York), Apr. 30, 1836.

33. Cohen, *Calculating People*, 175–226.

34. Stewart Davenport, "*Das Adam Smith Problem* and Faculty Psychology in the Antebellum North," *History of Political Economy* 40, no. 5 (2008): 243–64; Stewart Davenport, *Friends of the Unrighteous Mammon: Northern Christians and Market Capitalism, 1815–1860* (Chicago: University of Chicago Press, 2008); Joseph Dorfman, *The Economic Mind in American Civilization: 1606–1865*, vol. 2 (New York: Viking, 1946), 503, 707–8; Michael Joseph Lalor O'Connor, *Origins of Academic Economics in the United States* (New York: Columbia University Press, 1944), 1–3; and Michael O'Brien, *Conjectures of Order: Intellectual Life and the American South, 1810–1860* (Chapel Hill: University of North Carolina Press, 2004), 877–937.

35. For the use of numbers by governments, see Mary Poovey, *A History of the Modern Fact: Problems of Knowledge in the Sciences of Wealth and Society* (Chicago: University of Chicago Press, 1998), 305–6; and Cohen, *A Calculating People*, 150–204. For the ways in which newspapers conveyed partisanship, see Jeffrey L. Pasley, "The Cheese and the Words: Popular Political Culture and Participatory Democracy in the Early American Republic," in *Beyond the Founders: New Approaches to the Political History of the Early American Republic*, ed. Jeffrey L. Pasley, Andrew W. Robertson, and David Waldstreicher (Chapel Hill: University of North Carolina Press, 2004): 31–56; Jeffrey L. Pasley, "*The Tyranny of Printers*": *Newspaper Politics in the Early American Republic* (Charlottesville: University Press of Virginia, 2001), 6–8; John, *Spreading the News*, 154–55; and Stephen Campbell, "The Spoils of Victory: Amos Kendall, the Antebellum State, and the Growth of the American Presidency in the Bank War, 1828–1834," *Ohio Valley History* 11, no. 2 (2011): 3–25.

36. "By The Journal of Commerce Express," *Journal of Commerce* (New York), Apr. 29, 1836.
37. Wilentz, *Rise of American Democracy*, 443–46.
38. *Times* (London), June 17, 1836.
39. *Times* (London), June 13, 1836.
40. Matthews argued that "It was not until 1836 that widespread publicity was given to the extent of dealing in American securities in London, but large and growing capital export to the United States had by then already been taking place for several years." He does not delve deeper into why the increase in publicity happened at this moment. Matthews, *Study in Trade-Cycle History*, 88.
41. *Times* (London), June 13, 1836.
42. Diary of Joshua Bates, May 19, 1836, DEP 74, vol. 3, BA.
43. Hope & Co. to Baring Brothers & Co., May 3, 1836, HC8.1 Part IV, BA.
44. Diary of Joshua Bates, June 18, 1836, DEP 74, vol. 3, BA. For more on Joshua Bates's role in Baring Brothers, see Ziegler, *Sixth Great Power*, 112–44.
45. Joshua Bates to T. W. Ward, July 22, 1836, LB 5c, BA.
46. Hone makes no mention of Bates discussing his concerns about the American trade when they met in England in August 1836. The Bank of England had already increased discount rates for American houses, but Hone does not record any English doubts about America. Diary of Philip Hone, Aug. 29, 1836, 12:117, BV Hone, Philip, MS 1549, MCNYHS.
47. By the 1870s, one of the actual pillars in the 'Change was known as the "Rothschild pillar." Frederick Martin, *The History of Lloyd's and of Marine Insurance in Great Britain* (London: Macmillan, 1876), 292.
48. Quotation in Niall Ferguson, *The House of Rothschild*. vol. 1, *Money's Prophets, 1798–1848* (New York: Penguin 1998), 296.
49. Ferguson, *House of Rothschild*, 299–304.
50. *Times* (London), Aug. 9, 1836.
51. David Salomons, quoted in Ferguson, *House of Rothschild*, 300.
52. Hope & Co. to Baring Brothers & Co., Aug. 5, 1836, HC8.1 Part IV, BA.
53. On his deathbed, Nathan Mayer confirmed the transfer of all his business into his sons' names with the proviso that "My dear wife Hannah . . . is to co-operate with my sons on all important occasions and to have a vote upon all consultations." He expressed the desire that his sons "shall not embark on any transaction of importance without having previously demanded her motherly advice." Nathan Mayer's inclusion of Hannah Rothschild as a participant in the family business suggests that the Rothschild women, who have often been considered the forgers of family bonds through marriage and children rather than active participants in the family's business, may have been significant partners in commerce. Ferguson, *House of Rothschild*, 297–98.
54. Samuel Hermann & Son to NMRS, Apr. 5, 1834, XI/112/115, RAL.
55. *Das Fuellhorn* (1835), quoted in Bertram W. Korn, *The Early Jews of New Orleans* (Waltham, MA: American Jewish Historical Society, 1969), 116.
56. "Death of Rothschild," *Journal of Commerce* (New York), Sept. 10, 1836; and C. Z. Barnett, *The Rise of the Rotheschildes: Or, The Honest Jew of Frankfort: A Drama, in Two Acts. Founded Upon Facts* (London: J. Pattie, 1838).

57. For evidence of Hermann's 1835 trip, see JLSJ to NMRS, June 30, 1836, XI/38/15, RAL.
58. JLSJ to NMRS, June 30, 1836, XI/38/15, RAL.
59. NMRS to JLSJ, Aug. 19, 1836, II/10/1, RAL. This was only the beginning of Nathan Mayer Rothschild's sons' more conservative business dealings. Ferguson, *House of Rothschild*, 309–15.
60. Clapham, *Bank of England*, 152. For a timeline that depicts the flow of information westbound across the Atlantic between June and October 1836, see Rousseau, "Jacksonian Monetary Policy," 484, fig. 4. For an explanation of the Palmer Rule, see Matthews, *Study in Trade-Cycle History*, 168.
61. Andreades, *History of the Bank of England*, 265.
62. Joshua Bates to T. W. Ward, July 9, 1836, LB 5c, BA. Matthews, *Study in Trade-Cycle History*, 58.
63. *Times* (London), Oct. 28, 1836.
64. Minutes, Aug. 24, 1836, Committee of the Treasury Minute Book, vol. 22, G8/29, BOEA.
65. Ibid.
66. Clapham, *Bank of England*, 149; Frederic S. Mishkin, "Asymmetric Information and Financial Crises: A Historical Perspective," in *Financial Markets and Financial Crises*, ed. R. Glenn Hubbard (Chicago: University of Chicago, 1991), 69–108; and Charles W. Calomiris and Gary Gorton, "The Origins of Banking Panics: Models, Facts, and Bank Regulation," in *Financial Markets and Financial Crises*, ed. R. Glenn Hubbard (Chicago: University of Chicago Press, 1991), 109–73.
67. Clapham, *Bank of England*, 147–49. Matthews adds a third source of capital from savings bank funds. Matthews, *Study in Trade-Cycle History*, 172.
68. Temin, *Jacksonian Economy*, 79–82, 137.
69. Jackson nearly provoked a war with France to receive these payments in gold. According to contemporary accounts, these coins were sent to the mint to be transformed into American coin and not directly to the federal government's many banks. *Journal of Commerce* (New York), May 17, 1836. It is possible that private bankers shipped English gold to France to make these payments, but I have not discovered any evidence of this.
70. Temin and Matthews have no definitive answer for the destination of the BOE's gold in 1836. Matthews generally agrees with Pattison's appraisal but suggests that important capital movements to the United States actually occurred earlier in the decade. Temin is less convinced by 1830s arguments and existing data. *Jacksonian Economy*, 137, 173; and Matthews, *Study in Trade-Cycle History*, 85, 92–93.
71. *Times* (London), Oct. 28, 1836.
72. Bates to T. W. Ward, Sept. 6, 1836, LB 5c, BA.
73. Minutes, Sept. 7, 1836, Committee of the Treasury Minute Book, vol. 22, G8/29, BOEA.
74. Ibid.
75. Ibid.
76. *NYH*, Sept. 27, 1836.
77. *NYH*, Sept. 28, 1836.

78. Rousseau dates the arrival of this news to October 10, 1836. Rousseau, "Jacksonian Monetary Policy," 486, 484, fig. 4. It may have arrived on October 8, 1836, via the packet ship *England*, the arrival of which was reported in the *NYH* on October 10, 1836. The *NYH* does not directly report on the reversal of the BOE's policy, but it does report on the BOE's increase in the interest rate from 4.5 percent to 5 percent on October 11, 1836.

79. *NYH*, Oct. 1, 1836. Rousseau argues that money markets were already tight because of domestic financial policies. Rousseau, "Jacksonian Monetary Policy."

80. Although the financial markets in New York and London were generally integrated in this period, London traders responded more strongly to news from New York than vice versa. Richard Sylla, Jack W. Wilson, and Robert E. Wright, "Integration of Trans-Atlantic Capital Markets, 1790–1845," *Review of Finance* 10 (Jan. 2006): 634.

81. NMRS to JLSJ, Aug. 30, 1836, II/10/1, RAL.

82. *NOTA*, Oct. 15, 1836.

83. Hermann returned to New Orleans on Dec. 1, 1836. *Commercial Bulletin* (New Orleans), Dec. 2, 1836.

84. *Boisdore vs. Citizens' Bank*, 9 La. 506, docket no. 2956 (May 1836) Orleans Parish, UNO.

85. Citizens' Bank Minute Book, vol. 2, June 29, 1837, July 3, 1837, CBLARC; George G. Green, "The Citizens Bank of Louisiana: Property Banking in Troubled Times, 1833–1842," *Papers of the 15th Annual Meeting of the Business History Conference* (Bloomington: Indiana University Press, 1968), 58–71; and Neu, "Edmond J. Forstall," 192–94.

86. Hope & Co. to Baring Brothers & Co., May 3, 1836, HC8.1 Part IV, BA.

87. *NYH*, Nov. 3, 1836.

88. *NYH*, Nov. 4, 1836.

89. *NYH*, Oct. 11, 1836. For the rumors of a conspiracy, see *NYH*, Nov. 11, 1836.

90. Bates, diary, Sept. 17, 1836, DEP 74, vol. 3, BA.

91. Joshua Bates to T. W. Ward, Sept. 6, 1836, LB 5c, BA.

92. Bates, diary, Sept. 17, 1836, DEP 74, vol. 3, BA.

93. Bates to T. W. Ward, Sept. 9, 1836, LB 5c, BA.

94. Bates to T. W. Ward, Sept. 6, 1836, LB 5c, BA. For Baring Brothers' system of credit rating and the importance of honest correspondents, see Hidy, "Credit Rating," 81–88.

95. Under the wind-powered packet system, European news came in fits and starts that often left New Yorkers at least a month behind events in London. Albion, *Square-Riggers on Schedule*, 318–22.

96. Andreades, *Bank of England*, 265.

97. Minutes, Oct. 26, 1836, Committee of the Treasury Minute Book, vol. 22, G8/29, BOEA; and Oct. 26, 1836, American Accounts, C5/282, BOEA.

98. Ibid.

99. Ibid.

100. Ibid.

101. *London Circular to Bankers*, Dec. 2, 1836, 161.
102. Diary of Joshua Bates, Oct. 9, 1836, DEP 74, vol. 3, BA.
103. *Times* (London), Oct. 10, 1836.
104. *Commercial Bulletin* (New Orleans), Dec. 2, 1836.
105. "Extract of a Letter Dated Liverpool October 25, 1836," *Commercial Bulletin* (New Orleans), Dec. 3, 1836.
106. *Hermann, Briggs & Co. vs. Western Marine & Fire Insurance Co.*, 13 La. 516, docket no. 3446 (May 1839) Orleans Parish, UNO.
107. The water levels were so low in many southern rivers that planters struggled to send their cotton to market. Alexander Trotter, *Observations on the Financial Position and Credit of Such of the States of the North American Union as have Contracted Public Debts* (London: Longman, Orme, Brown, Green, and Longmans, 1839), 103–4.
108. *Hermann, Briggs & Co. vs. Western Marine & Fire Insurance Co.*, 13 La. 516, docket no. 3446 (May 1839) Orleans Parish, UNO.
109. Ibid.
110. Ibid.
111. *NYH*, Dec. 26, 1836.
112. "Ocean Steam Navigation Company," *Commercial Bulletin* (New Orleans), Dec. 1, 1836.
113. *NYH*, Sept. 6, 1836.
114. "Ocean Steam Navigation," *Daily National Intelligencer* (Washington, D.C.), Nov. 28, 1836. Crosbie Smith and Anne Scott, "Presbyterians at Work: A Case Study of Glasgow and Liverpool" (Paper presented at International Colloquium on Commerce and Culture, Liverpool, UK, Apr. 22, 2006), 22, n. 60.
115. Moses Taylor to R. Growing & Co., Dec. 19, 1836, Moses Taylor outgoing letterbook, vol. 2, series 1, MTP.
116. *NYH*, Dec. 10, 1836.
117. Henry Van Der Lyn to his sister, Jan. 9, 1837, BV Van Der Lyn, Henry, MS 2590, MCNYHS.
118. *NYH*, Dec. 13, 1836. Animal magnetism, also described as galvanism, was a popular theory in the 1830s. David S. Reynolds, *Waking Giant: America in the Age of Jackson* (New York: HarperCollins, 2008), 231–32. For an application of this idea to medicine, see H. H. Sherwood, *Electro-Galvanic Symptoms, and Electro-Magnetic Remedies* (New York: J. W. Bell, 1837).
119. Prime Ward & King to Baring Brothers & Co., Dec. 16, 1836, Reel 39, BBLOC.
120. *NYH*, Dec. 24, 1836.
121. William Leggett, "Thoughts on the Causes of the Present Discontents," *Plaindealer*, Dec. 10, 1837 (emphasis in original).
122. *NYH*, Dec. 31, 1836.
123. *NYH*, Jan. 9, 1837.
124. *Liverpool Courier and Commercial Advertiser*, Feb. 1, 1837.
125. *PIC*, Feb. 9, 1837.
126. *PIC*, Feb. 11, 1837.
127. *NYH*, Jan. 16, 1837.

128. Andrew Jackson, "The Annual Message," *Niles Weekly Register* (Baltimore), Dec. 10, 1836.
129. Henry Toland to Martin Van Buren, Nov. 9, 1836, Reel 21, MVBLOC.
130. JLSJ to NMRS, Oct. 31, 1836, XI/38/15, RAL.

Chapter 3

1. The following account is based on a composite of these New York City newspapers' coverage except where a specific quotation is cited: New York *Plaindealer*, *New York Evening Post*, New York *Sun*, New York *Journal of Commerce*, New York *Evening Star*, *Morning Courier and New-York Enquirer*, and *New York Herald*.
2. Diary of Philip Hone, Feb. 13, 1837, 12:377, BV Hone, Philip, MS 1549, MCNYHS. For a reading of the riot in terms of gender, see Joshua R. Greenberg, *Advocating the Man: Masculinity, Organized Labor, and the Household in New York, 1800–1840* (New York: Columbia University Press, 2008), 190–206.
3. Fitzwilliam Byrdsall, *The History of the Loco-Foco or Equal Rights Party: Its Movements, Conventions and Proceedings, with Short Characteristic Sketches of Its Prominent Men* (New York: Clement & Packard, 1842), 102.
4. "Mob Meeting – Riot and Pillage," *Journal of Commerce* (New York), Feb. 14, 1837.
5. On women stealing flour, see "Outrage and Riot," *Morning Courier and New-York Enquirer*, Feb. 14, 1837; and "Mob Meeting – Riot and Pillage."
6. "Outrage and Riot"; and "Public Meeting in the Park – Disgraceful Riots," *The Sun* (New York), Feb. 14, 1837.
7. "The Flour Rioters – Police – Tuesday," *Morning Courier and New-York Enquirer*, Feb. 15, 1837; and "The Flour Rioters," *Journal of Commerce* (New York), Feb. 18, 1837.
8. Diary of Philip Hone, Feb. 14, 1837, 12:380, BV Hone, Philip, MS 1549, MCNYHS.
9. *The Sun* (New York), Feb. 16, 1837.
10. Thompson referred to this process as "setting the price" and suggested that "the *expectation* of riot" was effective in "getting corn to market; in restraining rising prices; and in intimidating certain kinds of profiteering." He contrasted threats of riot with "the extortionate mechanisms of an unregulated market economy." E. P. Thompson, "The Moral Economy of the English Crowd in the Eighteenth Century," *Past & Present* 50 (Feb. 1971): 108, 120, 123, 134 (emphasis in original). Herbert Gutman pointed to the similarity between the 1837 flour riot and those studied by Thompson. Herbert G. Gutman, "Work, Culture, and Society in Industrializing America, 1815–1919," *American Historical Review* 78, no. 3 (June 1973): 574–75.
11. Blaug defines "historical reconstruction" as "accounting for the ideas of past thinkers in terms that these thinkers and their contemporary followers would have accepted as a correct description of what they intended to say." Blaug considers only economists, but this chapter broadens the spectrum of who counts in the history of economic thought. By doing so, it follows the lead of

Catherine Kelly, whose work has sought "to appropriate the notion of intellectual history for historical subjects who are typically excluded from the ranks of thinkers." Mark Blaug, "No History of Ideas, Please, We're Economists," *Journal of Economic Perspectives* 15, no. 1 (2001): 151; and Catherine E. Kelly, *In the New England Fashion: Reshaping Women's Lives in the Nineteenth Century* (Ithaca, NY: Cornell University Press, 1999), 6, n. 6.

12. Richard Hildreth, *Banks, Banking, and Paper Currencies* (Boston: Whipple & Damrell, 1840), 91–92; Old Fashioned Man, *The Pressure and Its Causes: Being the Old Fashioned Notions of an Old Fashioned Man* (Boston: Otis, Broader, 1837), 37–38; and *Three Degrees of Banking: Or The Romance of Trade* (Boston: Weeks, Jordan, 1838), 55–56.

13. A. P. Peabody, "Memoir," in *Sermons by Rev. Jason Whitman: With a Sketch of His Life and Character, and Extracts from His Correspondence* (Boston: Benjamin H. Greene, 1849), xviii.

14. Jason Whitman, *The Hard Times: A Discourse Delivered in the Second Unitarian Church and Also in the First Parish Church, Portland, Sunday, January 1st, 1837* (Portland, 1837), 4. For more on the rise of popular or timely subjects in sermons, see Lawrence Buell, "The Unitarian Movement and the Art of Preaching in 19th Century America," *American Quarterly* 24, no. 2 (May 1972): 171.

15. Whitman, *Hard Times*, 4.

16. John Codman, *The Signs of the Times: A Sermon, Delivered Before the Pastoral Association of Massachusetts, in the Park Street Church, Boston, May 24, 1836* (Boston: D. K. Hitchcock, 1836); and George Putnam, *The Signs of the Times: A Sermon Preached Sunday, March 6, 1836* (Boston: Charles J. Hendee, 1836).

17. Putnam, *Signs of the Times*, 6, 10–11, 20.

18. Erskine Mason, *A Rebuke to the Worldly Ambition of the Present Age: A Sermon, Preached in the Bleecker-Street Church, N.Y. July 10, 1836* (New York: West & Trow, 1836), 11, 23–24.

19. Whitman, *Hard Times*, 9, 4–5, 15. According to Howe, doctrinal differences suggested plural "awakenings" rather than a single "Second Great Awakening," but these many movements had a common effect: "[the choice of] which religion to embrace (if any) enhanced individualism." Howe, *What Hath God Wrought*, 186, 188. According to Linda Kerber, women enjoyed the personal independence that came from the idea that "one could affect the terms of one's own salvation." Linda K. Kerber, "Women and Individualism in American History," *The Massachusetts Review* 30, no. 4 (1989): 594.

20. Whitman, *Hard Times*, 8, 7, 9, 4, 6, 7.

21. Ibid., 7, 10, 11, 6. Whitman's combination of divine and human causation was not unusual. Mark Noll finds that in the 1830s, "economic reasoning remained superstructure and religion remained deep structure." Mark A. Noll, "Protestant Reasoning about Money and the Economy, 1790–1860: A Preliminary Probe," in *God and Mammon*, 277.

22. Whitman, *Hard Times*, 18, 11, 12, 14, 15, 16, 17, and 15.

23. Ibid., 17, 18.

24. Peabody, "Memoir," xi–xxix. For religious publishing networks, see David Paul Nord, *Faith in Reading: Religious Publishing and the Birth of Mass Media in America* (Oxford, UK: Oxford University Press, 2004).

25. N. L. Frothingham, *The Duties of Hard Times: A Sermon Preached to the First Church on Sunday Morning, April 23, 1837* (Boston: Munroe & Francis, 1837); George Ripley, *The Temptations of the Times: A Discourse Delivered in the Congregational Church in Purchase Street, on Sunday Morning, May 7, 1837* (Boston: Hilliard, Gray, 1837); Andrew P. Peabody, *Views of Duty Adapted to the Times: A Sermon Preached at Portsmouth, N.H., May 14, 1837* (Portsmouth: J. W. Foster, 1837); Samuel J. May, *These Bad Times the Product of Bad Morals: A Sermon Preached to the Second Church in Scituate, Mass. May 21, 1837* (Boston, 1837); Henry Colman, *The Times: A Discourse Delivered in the Hollis Street Church, Boston, on Sunday, June 11, 1837* (Boston: Weeks, Jordan, 1837); Joel Parker, *Moral Tendencies of Our Present Pecuniary Distress: A Discourse, Delivered May 14th, 1837* (New Orleans, 1837); Leonard Bacon, *The Duties Connected with the Present Commercial Distress: A Sermon, Preached in the Center Church, New Haven, May 21, 1837 and Repeated May 23* (New Haven, 1837); Orestes Augustus Brownson, *Babylon Is Falling: A Discourse Preached in the Masonic Temple to the Society for Christian Union and Progress on Sunday Morning May 26, 1837* (Boston: I. R. Butts, 1837); and Silas McKeen, *God Our Only Hope: A Discourse on the Condition and Prospects of Our Country, Delivered in Belfast, Maine, on Fast Day, April 20, 1837* (Belfast, 1837).

26. S. K. L., "Existing Commercial Embarrassments," *Christian Examiner* (July 1837): 392–406.

27. Frances H. Green, *The Housekeeper's Book: Comprising Advice on the Conduct of Household Affairs in General; and Particular Directions for the Preservation of Furniture, Bedding, &c.; for the Laying in and Preserving of Provisions: With a Complete Collection of Receipts for Economical Domestic Cookery: The Whole Carefully Prepared for the Use of American Housekeepers* (Philadelphia: William Marshall, 1837), 13, 15, 33.

28. Ibid., 13 (emphasis in original).

29. Lyman Preston, *The Book-keeper's Diploma: Or, A Full and Lucid Treatise on the Equation of Payments* (New York: F. F. Ripley, 1837); Marsh, *Science of Double-Entry Book-Keeping*; Michael Zakim "Bookkeeping as Ideology," *Common-Place* 6, no. 3 (Apr. 2006), http://www.common-place.org/vol-06/no-03/zakim/; and Michael Zakim, "The Business Clerk as Social Revolutionary; or, a Labor History of the Nonproducing Classes," *Journal of the Early Republic* 26, no. 4 (2006): 595.

30. Green, *Housekeeper's Book*, 18–19.

31. For the extensive literature on women and the market, their experiences with accounting, and the valuation of their labor, see Amy Dru Stanley, "Home Life and the Morality of the Market," in *The Market Revolution in America*, ed. Melvyn Stokes and Stephen Conway (Charlottesville: University Press of Virginia, 1996), 74–96.

32. Lydia Maria Child, *The American Frugal Housewife: Dedicated to Those Who Are Not Ashamed of Economy* (New York: Samuel S. & William Wood, 1838), 4.

33. Ibid., 5, 4.

34. Ibid., 5–6. Although this passage sounds as if it were written especially for 1837, it appears in the 1832 edition as well. Lydia Maria Child, *The American Frugal Housewife* (Boston: Carter & Hendee, 1832), 6.

35. Child, *American Frugal Housewife* (1838), 99 (emphasis in original).

36. Ibid., 6. Rosemarie Zagarri argues that by the 1830s, excepting a few radical reformers, "Women themselves became unwilling to acknowledge the political dimensions of their behavior." Child is arguing that domestic behavior can have political ramifications, but she is not explicitly urging women to be political. Rosemarie Zagarri, *Revolutionary Backlash: Women and Politics in the Early American Republic* (Philadelphia: University of Pennsylvania Press, 2007), 181.

37. Child, *American Frugal Housewife* (1838), 6, 7.

38. Lydia Maria Child, *The Family Nurse; or Companion of The Frugal Housewife* (Boston: Charles J. Hendee, 1837), 4. On Child's financial troubles, see Patricia G. Holland, "Lydia Maria Child as a Nineteenth-Century Professional Author," *Studies in the American Renaissance* (1981): 157–67.

39. Webster, *American Dictionary*, s.v. "economy."

40. "Original Literary Review," *The Ladies' Companion* (May 1837): 52. Damrell published the sales figures in his "Advertisement" at the beginning of *Elinor Fulton*. Hannah Farnham Sawyer Lee, *Elinor Fulton* (Boston: Whipple & Damrell, 1837), vii.

41. Hannah Farnham Sawyer Lee, *Three Experiments of Living* (Boston: William S. Damrell, 1837), vi.

42. "Works on Health and Economy," *The Graham Journal of Health and Longevity* (Apr. 4, 1837): 8.

43. For more on the life of Lee, see *Appleton's Cyclopaedia of American Biography*, ed. James Grant Wilson and John Fiske (New York: D. Appleton, 1888), s.v. "Lee, Hannah Farnham Sawyer," 3:662; *A Critical Dictionary of English Literature, and British and American Authors, Living and Deceased, From the Earliest Accounts to the Middle of the Nineteenth Century*, ed. Samuel Austin Allibone (Philadelphia: J. B. Lippincott, 1858), s.v. "Lee, Mrs. Hannah F.," 2:1074.

44. *Zion's Herald* (Jan. 18, 1837): 11. The Library Company of Philadelphia holds both the first and twentieth editions, both of which were published in 1837. The American Antiquarian Society holds fourteen editions or bindings that span in years from 1837 to 1849.

45. Lee, *Three Experiments*, 24, 14, 16.

46. Ibid., 69, 81, 83, 66 (emphasis in original).

47. Ibid., 83.

48. Ibid., 90, 93, 95, 102, 108, 123–24 (emphasis in original).

49. Ibid., 132, 131.

50. Ibid., 135, 137. According to Lee's theory of individual accountability for financial distress, these working-class folks ought to be independent agents responsible for their own financial fates just like the Fultons. One impoverished character argues that "the ladies are very good at getting up societies and fairs to help us, but they often seem unwilling to pay us the full price of our labor." The same character expands this line of argument by stating that when women started selling "those curious little things they sell at fairs" to raise

funds for charity, they put a fallen lady who derived her livelihood from this production out of business. "It is hard times for her," continued the character in commercial terms, "she says the market is overrun" (35). Lee's formulation of the difference between middle-class failure and working-class poverty is more fully developed in her subsequent books.

51. Ibid., 139, 140, 142, 143 (emphasis in original).
52. *Godey's Lady's Book* (Mar. 1837): 143. Reynolds would categorize Lee's fiction as a "conventional" work of didactic literature that fell into the "evangelical" half of the reform movement as opposed to the Unitarian emphasis on "rational" reform. Lee's novels are moral appeals to the senses and to emotion rather than the intellect. David S. Reynolds, *Beneath the American Renaissance: The Subversive Imagination in the Age of Emerson and Melville* (Cambridge, MA: Harvard University Press, 1988), 57.
53. Lee, *Three Experiments*, 134.
54. *Godey's Lady's Book* (Mar. 1837): 143.
55. "Three Experiments of Living," *The Knickerbocker; or New York Monthly Magazine* (Mar. 1837): 308; and "Literary Notices," *Maine Monthly Magazine* (Mar. 1837): 424.
56. *Army and Navy Chronicle* (Feb. 23, 1837): 122.
57. *Southern Rose* (Mar. 18, 1837): 119; and "Literature for the Times," *The Southern Literary Messenger* (Dec. 1837): 742.
58. "Three Experiments of Living," *Boston Medical and Surgical Journal* (Mar. 29, 1837): 126.
59. *Godey's Lady's Book* (Mar. 1837): 143 (emphasis in original).
60. Ralph Waldo Emerson, *Journals of Ralph Waldo Emerson with Annotation*, ed. Edward W. Emerson and Waldo E. Forbes (Boston: Houghton Mifflin, 1910), 4:194. Written in March 1837, this passage suggests themes of experiential learning that he would theorize more fully in his "American Scholar" address given a few months later. On Emerson, individualism, and the market revolution, see Jeffrey Sklansky, *The Soul's Economy: Market and Selfhood in American Thought, 1820–1920* (Chapel Hill: University of North Carolina Press, 2002), 38–52; and Michael T. Gilmore, *American Romanticism and the Marketplace* (Chicago: University of Chicago Press, 1988), 18–34.
61. For differing views of the effects of the Panic of 1837 on the writers of the American Renaissance, see María Carla Sánchez, *Reforming the World: Social Activism and the Problem of Fiction in Nineteenth-Century America* (Iowa City: University of Iowa Press, 2008), 28–87; William Charvat, *The Profession of Authorship in America, 1800–1870: The Papers of William Charvat*, ed. Matthew J. Bruccoli (Columbus: Ohio University Press, 1968), 49–67; and Richard F. Teichgraeber III, *Sublime Thoughts/Penny Wisdoms: Situating Emerson and Thoreau in the American Market* (Baltimore, MD: Johns Hopkins University Press, 1995), 155–221.
62. Lee, *Elinor Fulton*, vii.
63. Horatio Weld, *Fourth Experiment of Living: Living Without Means* (Boston: Otis, Broaders, 1837), xv. Reynolds would characterize Weld's book as a piece of "subversive" reform literature. Instead of focusing on hope and possibility, Weld depicted the darker, immoral side of financial interactions in graphic detail. Reynolds, *Beneath the American Renaissance*, 57–59.

64. *New Experiments: Means Without Living* (Boston: Weeks, Jordan, 1837), iii, vii, viii (emphasis in original).

65. William A. Alcott, *Ways of Living on Small Means* (Boston: Light & Stearns, 1837), 36, 48, 84 (emphasis in original).

66. Andrew Combe, *Observations on Mental Derangement: Being an Application of the Principles of Phrenology to the Elucidation of the Causes, Symptoms, Nature and Treatment of Insanity. First American Edition with notes and Bibliography by an American Physician* (Boston: Marsh, Capen & Lyon, 1834), 163.

67. Combe, *Principles of Physiology*, 206–7.

68. Edward William Tuson, *The Dissector's Guide; or Student's Companion: Illustrated by Numerous Wood Cuts, Clearly Exhibiting and Explaining the Dissection of Every Part of the Human Body*, 2nd ed. (Boston: William D. Ticknor, 1837), 190.

69. Silas Jones, *Practical Phrenology* (Boston: Russell, Shattuck, & Williams, 1836), 23, 59–62, 72, 83–84, 157–58; Andrew Combe, *Observations on Mental Derangement*, 163–64.

70. George Combe, *A System of Phrenology, Fifth American Edition* (Boston: Marsh, Capen and Lyon, 1838), 197, 238–41, 403–4, 513; *The Pressure and Its Causes*, 15; and Silas Jones, *Practical Phrenology*, frontispiece.

71. Madeleine B. Stern, *Heads & Headlines: The Phrenological Fowlers* (Norman: University of Oklahoma Press, 1971), xi.

72. Andrew Combe, *Observations on Mental Derangement*, 164.

73. *Living on Other People's Means, or The History of Simon Silver* (Boston: Weeks, Jordan, 1837), vii, 40, 54, 55. These names are puns. "Drumstick" plays on the phrase to "drum up" business; "Bubbleville" indicates a city built on an unstable and inflated market.

74. "Literary Record," *The Knickerbocker* 9, no. 5 (May 1837): 530 (emphasis in original).

75. Ibid.; and "Original Literary Review," 52. For four examples of unauthorized spin-offs by men, see *New Experiments*; Alcott, *Ways of Living on Small Means*; Weld, *Fourth Experiment of Living*; *Uncle Solomon and the Holman Family; Or, How to Live in Hard Times by a Poor Man* (Boston: Cassady and March, 1837). Templin argues that Lee's novels were part of a genre of women's narrative responses to economic crises throughout the nineteenth century. She discusses several other women writers who wrote novels following the Panic of 1837, including Emma C. Embury, *Constance Latimer; or the Blind Girl* (New York: Harper & Brothers, 1838); Catherine Sedgwick, *Live and Let Live; or, Domestic Service Illustrated* (New York: Harper & Brothers, 1837); and Elizabeth Oaks Smith, *Riches Without Wings; or, the Cleveland Family* (Boston: George W. Light, 1838). Mary Templin, "Panic Fiction: Women and Antebellum Economics" (PhD diss., University of Wisconsin, 2001). Also, see Sánchez, *Reforming the World*, 73–83.

76. Francis Wayland and H. L. Wayland, *A Memoir of the Life and Labors of Francis Wayland, D.D., LL.D.: Late President of Brown University* (New York: Sheldon, 1867), 1:389.

77. Francis Wayland, *The Elements of Political Economy*, new ed., ed. Aaron L. Chapin (New York: Sheldon, 1886). For a brief history of the transformation

from "political economy" to "economics," see Colin Wright, "Competing Conceptions of Political Economy," in *From Political Economy to Economics and Back?* ed. James H. Nichols Jr. and Colin Wright (San Francisco: Institute for Contemporary Studies Press, 1990), 57–66.

78. Jeffrey Sklansky argues that by the 1830s, romanticism created a counter-revolution to political economy because the latter subject "proved more effective in inciting rebellion than in promoting the harmony and stability of a new social order." Nevertheless, political economy became a subject taught in America's institutions of higher education at precisely this period. Sklansky, *The Soul's Economy*, 31.

79. Francis Wayland, *The Elements of Political Economy* (New York: Leavitt, Lord, 1837), 90, 172, vi.

80. Webster, *American Dictionary*, s.v. "economy."

81. "Review of *The Elements of Political Economy*," *The New York Review*, no. 2 (Oct. 1837): 384; Francis Bowen, "Review of *The Elements of Political Economy*," *Christian Examiner and General Review* 24, no. 1 (Mar. 1838): 56; and "Review of Wayland's *Political Economy*," *The American Biblical Repository* (Oct. 1, 1837): 399.

82. Preface to Lee, *Three Experiments of Living*, vii–viii.

83. "Review of *The Elements of Political Economy*," *The New York Review*, 386 (emphasis in original). Also see "Review of Wayland's *Political Economy*," *The American Biblical Repository* (Oct. 1, 1837).

84. Wayland, *Elements of Political Economy* (1837), 249.

85. Ibid., 254.

86. Ibid., 264.

87. Ibid., 268.

88. Ibid., 297.

89. Ibid., 273, 288 (emphasis in original).

90. Ibid., 261–62.

91. Ibid., 133 (emphasis in original).

92. He had been giving the lectures "for some years passed" and started writing the book in 1835 when he finished his previous textbook on moral philosophy. Ibid., vi; and Francis Wayland to his mother, Mar. 11, 1836, quoted in Wayland and Wayland, *Memoir of the Life and Labors of Francis Wayland*, 1: 370.

93. "Review of *Elements of Political Economy*," *The Christian Review* (June 1, 1837): 244–45.

94. Wayland, *Elements of Political Economy* (1837), 304–5.

95. Ibid., 306–7.

96. Ibid., 307, 301.

97. Ibid., vii

98. "Review of *The Elements of Political Economy*," *The Christian Review*, 244.

99. Joseph Holdich, "Review of *The Elements of Political Economy*," *The Methodist Magazine and Quarterly Review* 19, no. 4 (Oct. 1, 1837): 422.

100. Hildreth, *History of Banks*, 76–78. For more on Hildreth, see Arthur M. Schlesinger Jr., "The Problem of Richard Hildreth," *New England Quarterly* 13, no. 2 (1940): 223–45.

101. Wayland, *Elements of Political Economy* (1837), vii.
102. Smith H. & Co. to Smith & Co., Feb. 15, 1837, written on the blank half of the *New Orleans Commercial Letter Sheet Prices Current*, Feb. 15, 1837, AAS.
103. *New Orleans Prices Current and Shipping List*, Nov. 19, 1836, reproduced in *Commercial Bulletin* (New Orleans), Nov. 19, 1836.
104. "New-York Price Current," *Shipping and Commercial List and New-York Price Current*, Feb. 11, 1837.
105. *Commercial Bulletin* (New Orleans), Apr. 6, 1837.
106. Wayland, *Elements of Political Economy* (1837), vii.
107. Ibid., 3 (emphasis in original).
108. Francis Bowen, "Review of *The Elements of Political Economy*," *Christian Examiner and General Review* 24, no. 1 (Mar. 1838): 53. Bowen wrote two political economy textbooks: *The Principles of Political Economy Applied to the Condition, the Resources, and the Institutions of the American People* (Boston: Little, Brown, 1856); and *American Political Economy: Including Strictures on the Management of the Currency and the Finances Since 1861, with a Chart Showing the Fluctuations in the Price of Gold* (New York: C. Scribner, 1870).
109. Joseph Holdich, "Review of *The Elements of Political Economy*," *The Methodist Magazine and Quarterly Review* 19, no. 4 (Oct. 1, 1837): 407.
110. Francis Bowen, "Review of *The Elements of Political Economy*," *Christian Examiner and General Review* 24, no. 1 (Mar. 1838): 52, 54.
111. Holdich, "Review of *The Elements of Political Economy*," *The Methodist Magazine and Quarterly Review*, 411.
112. Citing the distinction between the fear of starvation and "preferring an 11 percent return to a 9 percent return on corporate bond holdings," William M. Reddy uses the term "monetary exchange asymmetry" to explain that "not all desires are alike." William M. Reddy, *Money and Liberty in Modern Europe: A Critique of Historical Understanding* (Cambridge, UK: Cambridge University Press, 1987), 200.
113. In 1837, this issue had just begun to inspire the Romantic Movement. Sklansky, *Soul's Economy*, 33–72.
114. Thompson suggests that political economy served the interests of merchants and describes the "specious air of empirical validation" of political economy's model of equilibrium in flour markets. Thompson, "Moral Economy of the English Crowd," 91. Karl Polyani dates the rise of *laissez-faire* as "a militant creed" to the 1830s. Karl Polanyi, *The Great Transformation: The Political and Economic Origins of Our Time*, 2nd ed. (1944; Boston: Beacon Press, 2001), 143.
115. For economic laws as a source of psychological relief from the uncertainties of the tumultuous financial conditions of the early nineteenth century, see Elaine Freedgood, "Banishing Panic: Harriet Martineau and the Popularization of Political Economy," *Victorian Studies* 39, no. 1 (1995): 33–53.
116. Bowen, "Review of *The Elements of Political Economy*," 55.
117. Ibid.
118. Francis Wayland, *The Elements of Political Economy: Abridged for the Use of Academies* (Boston: Gould, Kendall, and Lincoln, 1837), 79.

119. Diary of Philip Hone, Feb. 18, 1837, 12:387, BV Hone, Philip, MS 1549, MCNYHS.

Chapter 4

1. "Correspondence of Commercial Advertiser," *New-York Spectator*, Mar. 10, 1837; and "Inauguration and Ball," *NYH*, Mar. 11, 1837.
2. Petition of Thomas Fidoe Ormes, Dec. 15, 1836, fol. 57, G6/286, BOEA. Most of the records of this investigation are recorded in two places in the Bank of England Archives: in the folios of the Court of Directors (G6/286), and in the minutes of the Committee of Inspection of the Drawing Office Minute Book (M5/285). Some are also in the minutes of the Court of Directors Minute Book (G4/59). For brevity, these records will be referred to by their call numbers rather than titles.
3. On boredom of clerks, see Augst, *Clerk's Tale*, 207–16. On clerks' often unfulfilled ambition, see Luskey, *On the Make*. For the historiography of white-collar workers in Britain, see Peter Bailey, "White Collars, Gray Lives? The Lower Middle Class Revisited," *Journal of British Studies* 38 (July 1999): 273–90.
4. Report of the Committee of Inspection for the Drawing Office, Dec. 9, 1836, fol. 53, G6/286, BOEA; and Minutes, Dec. 9, 1836, M5/285, BOEA. For the architecture of the BOE, see "Plan of the Bank dated 1834," *Sir John Soane: Architect and Surveyor to the Bank of England* (London: Bank of England Museum, 2004). In 1838, stockbrokers were banned from the Rotunda. Abramson, *Building the Bank of England*, 196.
5. "Money Market and City Intelligence," *Times* (London), Dec. 9, 1836.
6. "Money Market and City Intelligence," *Times* (London), Dec. 10, 1836. This article was republished as: "Money Market," *Sun* (London), Dec. 10, 1836.
7. Ibid.
8. "Money Market and City Intelligence," *Times* (London), Dec.10, 1836.
9. Report of the Committee of Inspection for the Drawing Office, Dec. 14, 1836, fol. 52, G6/286, BOEA; minutes, Dec. 14, 1836, M5/285, BOEA; and minutes, Dec. 15, 1836, G4/59, BOEA.
10. Koenig defines gossip as "communication about people known to the persons involved in the communication" and rumor as "a proposition that is unverified and in general circulation." Frederick Koenig, *Rumor in the Marketplace: The Social Psychology of Commercial Hearsay* (Dover, MA: Auburn House, 1985), 2.
11. For the history of this transition, see Abramson, *Building the Bank of England*, 19–32, 57–58, 69–70, 156–61. Although gossip has often been associated with women, Anthony Rotundo finds "conversation" to be "the most important of pastimes in the male culture of play" of the nineteenth century. Rotundo, *American Manhood*, 201.
12. Report of the Committee of Inspection for the Drawing Office, Dec. 15, 1836, fol. 53, G6/286, BOEA; Minutes, Dec. 9, 1836, M5/285, BOEA; and Petition of John Smith, Dec. 14, 1836, fol. 81, G6/286, BOEA.
13. Report of the Committee of Inspection for the Drawing Office, Dec. 15 1836, fol. 53, G6/286, BOEA; and Minutes, Dec. 9, 1836, M5/285, BOEA. For regulation of clerks, see Abramson, *Building the Bank of England*, 165.

14. Report of the Committee of Inspection for the Drawing Office, Dec. 15 1836, fol. 52, G6/286, BOEA; Minutes, Dec. 9, 1836, M5/285, BOEA; and Minutes, Dec. 15, 1836, G4/59, BOEA.
15. Minutes, Dec. 15, 1836, G4/59, BOEA; Petition of Thomas Whitford, Dec. 12, 1836, fol. 58, G6/286, BOEA; John Smith Resignation, Dec. 16, 1836, fol. 81, G6/286, BOEA; Minutes of the Committee of Treasury recommending an allowance to John Smith late of the Bill Office, Dec. 28, 1836, fol. 105, G6/286, BOEA; and Minutes, Dec. 29, 1836, G4/59, BOEA.
16. Report of the Committee of Inspection for the Drawing Office, Dec. 15 1836, fol. 52, G6/286, BOEA; Minutes, Dec. 9, 1836, M5/285, BOEA; Minutes, Dec. 15, 1836, G4/59, BOEA; and Petition of Thomas Fidoe Ormes, Dec. 15, 1836, fol. 57, G6/286, BOEA. On City clerks' working conditions, see Kynaston, *City of London*, 146–50. For more on clerks' chances of upward mobility in an American context, see Brian Luskey, "'What Is My Prospects?': The Contours of Mercantile Apprenticeship, Ambition, and Advancement in the Early American Economy," *Business History Review* 78, no. 4 (2004): 665–702.
17. Trial of James Monds, Oct. 28, 1830, ref. no. t18301028–5, Old Bailey Proceedings Online, www.oldbaileyonline.org; and Petition of Thomas Fidoe Ormes, Dec. 15, 1836, fol. 57, G6/286, BOEA. Although a reform movement was active in 1830, forgery remained a capital offense until 1832. Phil Handler, "Forgery and the End of the 'Blood Code' in Early Nineteenth-Century England," *The Historical Journal* 48, no. 3 (Sept. 2005): 683–702.
18. Report of the Committee of Inspection for the Drawing Office, Dec. 15 1836, fol. 52, G6/286, BOEA; Minutes, Dec. 9, 1836, M5/285, BOEA; Minutes, Dec. 15, 1836, G4/59, BOEA; Petition of Thomas Fidoe Ormes, Dec. 15, 1836, fol. 57, G6/286, BOEA; Resignation of Thomas Fidoe Ormes, Dec. 16, 1836, fol. 82, G6/286, BOEA; and Minutes, Dec. 22, 1836, G4/59. For poverty in London, see David R. Green, *Pauper Capital: London and the Poor Law, 1790–1870* (Farnham: Ashgate, 2010); and Green, *From Artisans to Paupers*.
19. Minutes, Dec. 8, 1836, C5/282, BOEA; and Minutes, Dec. 8, 1836, M5/472, BOEA. The BOE's proceedings relating to the American houses are recorded in the Committee of the Treasury minute book (G8/29) and occasionally in the Court of Directors minute books (G4/59 and G4/60) or the "Private Minute Book" (M5/472), as well as in a single volume entitled "American Houses Account, 1836–1842" (C5/282). Additional sources are located in folders for each account (C5/232-C5/267), in a Letter Book (C82/81), and in various files relating to legal cases that all begin with call number F. I will refer to call numbers rather than titles.
20. "Money Market and City Intelligence," *Times* (London), Feb. 10, 1837. For failures, see "Money Market and City Intelligence," *Times* (London), Feb. 9, 1837.
21. "Money Market and City Intelligence," *Times* (London), Feb. 10, 1837; and "Money Market and City Intelligence," *Times* (London), Feb. 14, 1837.
22. Minutes, Oct. 26, 1836, G8/29, BOEA; Minutes, Oct. 26, 1836, C5/282, BOEA; Minutes, Dec. 8, 1836, C5/282, BOEA; and Minutes, Dec. 8, 1836, M5/472, BOEA.

23. For Americans sending bills instead of specie, see William Brown to the Governor and Directors of the Bank of England, Mar. 2, 1837, C5/282, BOEA; and Minutes, Mar. 2, 1837, M5/472, BOEA.

24. "Money Market," *Morning Chronicle* (London), Feb. 10, 1837.

25. "Money Market," *Morning Chronicle* (London), Feb. 14, 1837.

26. "Money Market and City Intelligence," *Times* (London), Feb. 27, 1837.

27. Diary of Joshua Bates, Feb. 11, 1837, DEP 74, vol. 3, BA. For the "key," see "1836," HC16.93, BA. For descriptions of the system, see Thomas Wren Ward to Baring Brothers, Dec. 24, 1834, HC16.74, BA; and Hidy, "Credit Rating," 85–88.

28. Minutes, Feb. 23, 1837, M5/472, BOEA; and Minutes, Feb. 23, 1837, C5/282, BOEA.

29. "Money Market and City Intelligence," *Times* (London), Feb. 27, 1837.

30. Minutes, Mar. 2, 1837, C5/282, BOEA; and Minutes, Mar. 2, 1837, M5/472, BOEA. For a survey of the historiography of British reform, see John K. Walton, *Chartism* (New York: Routledge, 1999), 1–5.

31. Minutes, Mar. 2, 1837, C5/282, BOEA; and Minutes, Mar. 2, 1837, G4/59, BOEA.

32. "Money Market and City Intelligence," *Times* (London), Mar. 3, 1837.

33. "Money Market," *Morning Chronicle* (London), Mar. 3, 1837.

34. Minutes, Mar. 2, 1837, C5/282, BOEA; and Minutes, Mar. 2, 1837, G4/59, BOEA.

35. Minutes, Mar. 4, 1837, C5/282, BOEA; and Minutes, Mar. 4, 1837, M5/472, BOEA.

36. Diary of Joshua Bates, Mar. 4, 1837, DEP 74, vol. 3, BA.

37. "Money Market and City Intelligence," *Times* (London), Mar. 3, 1837.

38. "Money Market," *Morning Chronicle* (London), Mar. 3, 1837.

39. Diary of Joshua Bates, Mar. 4, 1837, DEP 74, vol. 3, BA.

40. Minutes, Mar. 4, 1837, C5/282, BOEA; and Minutes, Mar. 4, 1837, G4/59, BOEA.

41. "Money Market and City Intelligence," *Times* (London), Mar. 8, 1837; and "Money Market and City Intelligence," *Times* (London), Mar. 6, 1837.

42. Diary of Joshua Bates, Mar. 4, 1837, DEP 74, vol. 3, BA.

43. "Money Market and City Intelligence," *Times* (London), Mar. 8, 1837.

44. Martin Van Buren, "Inaugural Address," *Washington Globe*, Mar. 6, 1837. For a physical description of the president-elect, see Wilentz, *Rise of American Democracy*, 446. For the crowd, see Ted Widmer, *Martin Van Buren* (New York: Henry Holt, 2005), 94.

45. Van Buren, "Inaugural Address."

46. U.S. Constitution, Article I, Section 10.

47. Van Buren, "Inaugural Address."

48. "Editors' Correspondence," *Daily National Intelligencer* (Washington), Mar. 8, 1837.

49. "The Inaugural," *New-York Spectator*, Mar. 10, 1837.

50. "From the *Richmond Enquirer* of Thursday: Cursory Sketches," *Washington Globe*, Mar. 13, 1837.

51. "The Inaugural – The Past Reign – The Coming Reign," *NYH*, Mar. 7, 1837.

52. Diary of Philip Hone, Mar. 6, 1837, 12:412, BV Hone, Philip, MS 1549, MCNYHS.

53. "The Farewell Address," *Daily National Intelligencer* (Washington), Mar. 6, 1837 (emphasis in original).

54. *Connecticut Courant* (Hartford), Mar. 11, 1837; and "From the *Richmond Enquirer* of Thursday: Cursory Sketches," *Washington Globe*, Mar. 13, 1837.

55. Andrew Jackson, "Farewell Address," *Washington Globe*, Mar. 6, 1837.

56. Ibid.

57. Ibid.

58. Diary of Philip Hone, Mar. 6, 1837, 12:412, BV Hone, Philip, MS 1549, MCNYHS.

59. "Editor's Correspondence," *Daily National Intelligencer* (Washington), Mar. 17, 1837.

60. Jackson, "Farewell Address."

61. "Bill to Protect the Currency," *New Orleans Bee*, Mar. 3, 1837.

62. Minutes, Mar. 4, 1837, Citizens' Bank Minute Book, vol. 1, CBLARC. For weather and setting, see *PIC*, Mar. 4, 1837; and Gibson, *Gibson's Guide*, 321–22.

63. Roeder, "New Orleans Merchants," 265–7. For more on the Hermann family and their firms, see Korn, *Early Jews of New Orleans*, 110–19. For networks of cotton factors, see John R. Killick, "The Cotton Operations of Alexander Brown and Sons in the Deep South, 1820–60," *The Journal of Southern History*, 43 (May 1997): 178–79; Kilbourne, *Debt, Investment, Slaves*; Roeder, "New Orleans Merchants," 222–69; Robert E. Roeder, "Merchants of Antebellum New Orleans," *Explorations in Entrepreneurial History*, 10 (Apr. 1958): 113–22; and Woodman, *King Cotton*.

64. For the first news of declining cotton prices, see *PIC*, Feb. 9, 1837. For fluctuations in cotton prices, see Rousseau, "Jacksonian Monetary Policy," 479. For the steamboat disaster, see *Hermann, Briggs & Co. vs. Western Marine & Fire Insurance Co.*, 13 La. 516, docket no. 3446 (May 1839) Orleans Parish, UNO.

65. Thomas Barrett & Co. to JLSJ, Mar. 9, 1837, reprinted in *New Orleans Bee*, Mar. 29, 1837; and *New Orleans Bee*, June 28, 1839.

66. Roeder, "New Orleans Merchants," 366.

67. Minutes, Mar. 5, 1837–Mar. 15, 1837, Citizens' Bank Minute Book, vol. 1, CBLARC.

68. Although the rumors floating around New Orleans are only documented in the print of newspaper articles, these word-of-mouth information networks produced real consequences. For evidence of the anxiety of everyday people, see *PIC*, Mar. 8, 1837.

69. *NYH*, Mar. 17, 1837.

70. Thomas Barrett & Co. to JLSJ, Mar. 7, 1837, as mentioned in Thomas Barrett & Co. to JLSJ Mar. 9, 1837, reprinted in *NYH*, Mar. 18, 1837, and *New Orleans Bee*, Mar. 29, 1837.

71. *NYH*, Mar. 18, 1837.

72. For evidence of JLSJ failure and bankruptcy, see JLSJ to NMRS, Mar. 19, 1837 (two letters on this date), XI/38/15, RAL; JLSJ to NMRS, Sept. 29, 1837, XI/38/15, RAL; and Case-file 1210, NARA.

73. JLSJ to NMRS, Mar. 15, 1837, XI/38/15, RAL.
74. NMRS to JLSJ, Aug. 30, 1836, II/10/1, RAL; NMRS to JLSJ, Nov. 9, 1836, II/10/1, RAL; NMRS to JLSJ, Feb. 9, 1837, II/10/1, RAL; and JLSJ to NMRS, Mar. 7, 1837, XI/38/15, RAL. For the Rothschild's requests, also see NMRS to JLSJ, Nov. 19, 1836, and Jan. 9, 1837, II/10/1, RAL.
75. Diary of Philip Hone, Mar. 14, 1837, 12:418–20, BV Hone, Philip, MS 1549, MCNYHS (pun emphasized in original).
76. *New-York Spectator*, Mar. 21, 1837; and JLSJ to NMRS, Mar. 15, 1837, XI/38/15, RAL.
77. *NYH*, Mar. 18, 1837. A few days after the Joseph failure, a rumor begun by the Rothschilds' Philadelphia correspondents asserted that the Josephs had lost the Rothschilds' backing, but by this time, the Josephs had convinced the press and the public that the Hermann failure had been the cause of their undoing. *NOTA*, Apr. 1, 1837.
78. *New-York Spectator*, Mar. 21, 1837.
79. *NYH*, Mar. 18, 1837.
80. Edward Cruft to George Newbold, Mar. 21, 1837, George Newbold Papers, MS 451, MCNYHS (emphasis in original).
81. *NOTA*, Mar. 29, 1837 (emphasis in original).
82. *Morning Courier and New-York Enquirer*, Mar. 18, 1837.
83. Diary of Philip Hone, Mar. 17, 1837, 12:426, BV Hone, Philip, MS 1549, MCNYHS.
84. JLSJ to NMRS, Mar. 19, 1837, XI/38/15, RAL.
85. Diary of Philip Hone, Mar. 18, 1837, 12:428, BV Hone, Philip, MS 1549, MCNYHS.
86. This letter was printed in many of New York City's newspapers and reprinted in papers throughout the country. For examples, see *NYH*, Mar. 18, 1837; *Morning Courier and New-York Enquirer*, Mar. 18, 1837; *NOTA*, Mar. 29, 1837; and in both English and French in the *New Orleans Bee*, Mar. 29, 1837. The letter was also used as a model of commercial letter writing in a textbook for clerks. B. F. Foster, *The Clerk's Guide, or Commercial Correspondence; Comprising Letters of Business, Forms of Bills, Invoices, Account-Sales, and an Appendix, Containing Advice to Young Tradesmen and Shopkeepers, Equation of Payments, Commercial Terms &c.* (Boston: Perkins & Marvin, 1837), 107–8.
87. "The Banking House of J. L. & S. Joseph," *New York Daily Express*, Mar. 18, 1837.
88. Canal Street was the location of all of the Hermann family's firms. Gibson, *Gibson's Guide*, 99. For the significance of Canal Street, see Tregle, *Louisiana*, 11–22.
89. *NOTA*, Apr. 1, 1837.
90. For express mail times, see Gibson, *Gibson's Guide*, 224.
91. *NOTA*, Mar. 7, 1837, reprinted in *Daily National Intelligencer* (Washington), Mar. 17, 1837; and *NYH*, Mar. 17, 1837 (emphasis in original).
92. Gibson, *Gibson's Guide*, 320–21. After a month of panic, the New Orleans *Picayune* described Bank's Arcade as a place where land speculators had formerly purchased "embryo cities" but now attracted patrons with "mint

juleps and gin slings." *PIC*, Apr. 25, 1837. For population and demo-graphics, see Winston, "Notes on the Economic History," 200, 223.

93. *NOTA*, Apr. 1, 1837; and *PIC*, Apr. 1, 1837 (emphasis in original).

94. *NOTA*, Mar. 28, 1837; *NOTA*, Mar. 7, 1837, reprinted in *Daily National Intelligencer* (Washington), Mar. 17, 1837, and *NYH*, Mar. 17, 1837. For the hope that the failure would benefit "younger enterprising merchants," see *PIC*, Mar. 9, 1837.

95. *NOTA*, Mar. 7, 1837, reprinted in *Daily National Intelligencer* (Washington), Mar. 17, 1837, and *NYH*, Mar. 17, 1837; *Enquirer* (Richmond, VA), Mar. 18, 1837; *Floridian* (Tallahassee), Mar. 18, 1837; *Vermont Patriot and State Gazette* (Montpelier), Apr. 10, 1837; *Daily Commercial Bulletin and Missouri Literary Register* (St. Louis), Mar. 22, 1837; and *North Western Gazette and Galena Advertiser* (Galena, IL), Apr. 15, 1837.

96. "Terms of the *True American*," *NOTA*, Mar. 11, 1837. For the economics of the New Orleans presses, see *PIC*, Mar. 17, 1837.

97. *NOTA*, Apr. 7, 1837.

98. *NOTA*, Apr. 15, 1837.

99. *NOTA*, Apr. 7, 1837. Democrats would later accuse Whigs of purposely starting panic to try to force President Van Buren to revoke many of the economic policies of his predecessor. The Democrats' argument may be based on Gibson's column in the *True American*, which did exaggerate and cause panic. *Daily National Intelligencer* (Washington), Apr. 27, 1837.

100. For John Gibson's "true" American stance, see A. E. Fossier, "Charles Aloysus Luzenberg, 1805–1848: A History of Medicine in New Orleans between the Years 1830–1848," *Louisiana Historical Quarterly* 26 (1943): 47–137; and C. F. Youngman, "Historic Sketch of L'Ami des Lois," Mss. no. 793, LARC. For an example of anti-Jewish statements in the *True American*, see "Very Late from New Orleans," *NI3*, May 9, 1837.

101. John Gibson to Dr. C. A. Luzenberg, June 6, 1838, printed in Fossier, "Charles Aloysus Luzenberg," 90.

102. *NOTA*, Apr. 7, 1837.

103. Fayette Copeland, *Kendall of the Picayune: Being His Adventures in New Orleans, on the Texan Santa Fe Expedition, in the Mexican War, and in the Colonization of the Texas Frontier* (Norman: University of Oklahoma Press, 1943), 24.

104. *NOTA*, Apr. 29, 1837. For more on newspaper readership, see John C. Nerone, "The Mythology of the Penny Press," *Critical Studies in Mass Communication*, 4 (Dec. 1987): 376–400.

105. *PIC*, Mar. 8, 1837. On Mar. 17, 1837, the *New York Herald* inaccurately cited this column as originally printed on Mar. 7, 1837. I have found no other reprinting of this column.

106. *PIC*, Mar. 8, 1837. For more on the origin of the *Picayune* and penny press, see Copeland, *Kendall and the Picayune*, 20–22; James L. Crouthamel, *Bennett's New York Herald and the Rise of the Popular Press* (Syracuse, NY: Syracuse University Press, 1989); John S. Kendall, "George Wilkins Kendall and the Founding of the New Orleans 'Picayune,'" Mss. no. 251, LARC; Nerone, "Mythology of the Penny Press," 383–403; and Carl

R. Osthaus, *Partisans of the Southern Press: Editorial Spokesmen of the Nineteenth Century* (Lexington: University of Kentucky Press, 1994).
107. *PIC*, Mar. 8, 1837.
108. Osthaus, *Partisans of the Southern Press*, 46–67.
109. J. I. Cohen Jr. & Brothers to NMRS, Mar. 28, 1837, XI/38/64 1837, RAL. For more on the Cohens, see W. Ray Luce, "The Cohen Brothers of Baltimore: From Lotteries to Banking," *Maryland Historical Magazine* 68 (Fall 1973): 288–308.
110. Henry Wheeling to Levi Woodbury, Mar. 21, 1837, Reel 15, Levi Woodbury Papers, LOC.
111. Andrew Jackson to Martin Van Buren, Mar. 30, 1837, Reel 22, MVBLOC.
112. Wayland, *Elements of Political Economy* (1837), 378.
113. Ibid.
114. Combe, *System of Phrenology*, 238 (emphasis in original).
115. Ibid., 513.

Chapter 5

1. *The Colored American* (New York), Mar. 4, 1837; and Lewis Tappan, *The Life of Arthur Tappan* (New York: Hurd and Houghton, 1870), 185.
2. Diary of Philip Hone, Mar. 4, 1837, 12:408, BV Hone, Philip, MS 1549, MCNYHS.
3. Diary of Philip Hone, Mar. 4, 1837, 12:408–9, BV Hone, Philip, MS 1549, MCNYHS.
4. Diary of Philip Hone, Apr. 24, 1837, 12:479, BV Hone, Philip, MS 1549, MCNYHS.
5. Diary of Philip Hone, Apr. 12, 1837, 12:463, BV Hone, Philip, MS 1549, MCNYHS.
6. Diary of Philip Hone, Mar. 20, 1837, 12:428, BV Hone, Philip, MS 1549, MCNYHS.
7. For more on shinning, see Balleisen, *Navigating Failure*, 73–75.
8. Joshua Bates to T. W. Ward, Sept. 14, 1836, LB 5c, BA.
9. A. G. Harrison to George Newbold, Mar. 29, 1837, George Newbold Papers, MS 451, MCNYHS.
10. For more on dunning and begging for leniency, see Balleisen, *Navigating Failure*, 76–77.
11. Edward Cruft to George Newbold, Mar. 27, 1837, George Newbold Papers, MS 451, MCNYHS.
12. JLSJ to NMRS, Apr. 2, 1837, XI/38/15, RAL. For more on lawsuits relating to bankruptcy, see Balleisen, *Navigating Failure*, 81–84.
13. "Suits," *Journal of Commerce* (New York), Apr. 19, 1837, reprinted in *NI3*, Apr. 22, 1837.
14. For legal costs, see Balleisen, *Navigating Failure*, 137–43.
15. Joseph Biggs, *To America in Thirty-Nine Days before Steamships Crossed the Atlantic*, 2nd ed. (Idbury, UK: Village Press, 1927), 9; and Balleisen, *Navigating Failure*, 12–13.

16. Opposition of Planters and Merchants Bank of Mobile, and Testimony of George Gale, *Andrews vs. His Creditors*, 11 La. 464, docket no. 3222 (Jan. 1838) Orleans Parish, UNO.
17. Opposition of Planters and Merchants Bank of Mobile, *Andrews vs. His Creditors*, 11 La. 464, docket no. 3222 (Jan. 1838) Orleans Parish, UNO.
18. *Andrews vs. His Creditors*, 11 La. 464; 1838 La. Lexis 4, at *4, and at *10.
19. *NOTA*, Apr. 17, 1837.
20. Testimony of Samuel Hermann Sr., *Andrews vs. His Creditors*, 11 La. 464, docket no. 3222 (Jan. 1838) Orleans Parish, UNO.
21. Testimony of Joseph Wood, *Andrews vs. His Creditors*, 11 La. 464, docket no. 3222 (Jan. 1838) Orleans Parish, UNO.
22. Testimony of George Gale, *Andrews vs. His Creditors*.
23. See also *The Planters' and Merchants' Bank of Mobile vs. Andrews*, 8 Port. 404; 1839 Ala. Lexis 6; *The Bank of Mobile, Hallett, et al. vs. Hall*, 6 Ala. 639; 1844 Ala. Lexis 475; *Hull & Leavens vs. The Planters and Merchants Bank of Mobile*, 6 Ala. 761; 1844 Ala. Lexis 514; *Andrews & Brothers vs. McCoy*, 8 Ala. 920; 1846 Ala. Lexis 228; and *Glidden vs. Doe Ex Dem. Andrews*, 10 Ala. 166; 1846 Ala. Lexis 263.
24. "General Bankrupt Law," *NYH*, Apr. 18, 1837.
25. "Suits," *Journal of Commerce*.
26. "From the Office of the *True American*," *NI3*, Apr. 13, 1837.
27. Ibid.
28. Balleisen, *Navigating Failure*, 30–31.
29. Jonathan Child to Isaac Bronson, Apr. 5, 1837, box 88: fol. 4, Bronson family papers, NYPL.
30. R. & J. Phillips to NMRS, Mar. 31, 1837, XI/38/205, RAL.
31. Moses Taylor to J. W. Welsh, Mar. 18, 1837, Moses Taylor outgoing letterbook, vol. 2, series 1, MTP. For more on Taylor's business decisions, see Daniel Hodas, *The Business Career of Moses Taylor: Merchant, Finance Capitalist, and Industrialist* (New York: New York University Press, 1976), 28–36.
32. Christmas, Livingston, Prime, & Coster to Jackson, Riddle & Co., Mar. 16, 1837, Jackson, Riddle and Co. records, Mss. no. 85, LARC.
33. Moses Taylor to Drake & Co., Mar. 21, 1837, Moses Taylor outgoing letterbook, vol. 2, series 1, MTP.
34. Philo Shelton to Moses Taylor, Apr. 3, 1837, box 3, fol. s-t (1837), MTP.
35. "An Important Caution," Apr. 13, 1837, *NI3*.
36. Moses Taylor to Chas. Drake & Co., Mar. 21, 1837, Moses Taylor outgoing letterbook, vol. 2, series 1, MTP.
37. Moses Taylor to Charles Kline Jr., Mar. 21, 1837, Moses Taylor outgoing letterbook, vol. 2, series 1, MTP.
38. Ayers P. Merrill to William Newton Mercer, Mar. 20, 1837, box 1, fol. 10, William Newton Mercer papers, Mss. no. 64, LARC.
39. Moses Taylor to Lambert Gettings, Mar. 20, 1837, Moses Taylor outgoing letterbook, vol. 2, series 1, MTP.
40. Moses Taylor to Drake & Coit, Apr. 5, 1837, Moses Taylor outgoing letterbook, vol. 2, series 1, MTP (emphasis in original).

41. Moses Taylor to Charles Drake & Co., Apr. 5, 1837, Moses Taylor outgoing letterbook, vol. 2, series 1, MTP; and Moses Taylor to Drake & Coit, Apr. 5, 1837, Moses Taylor outgoing letterbook, vol. 2, series 1, MTP.
42. Moses Taylor to Drake & Co., Mar. 23, 1837, Moses Taylor outgoing letterbook, vol. 2, series 1, MTP.
43. Ayers P. Merrill to William Newton Mercer, Mar. 29, 1837, box 1, fol. 10, William Newton Mercer papers, Mss. no. 64, LARC.
44. Moses Taylor to Drake & Coit, Apr. 7, 1837, Moses Taylor outgoing letterbook, vol. 2, series 1, MTP.
45. Moses Taylor to Drake & Coit, Apr. 20 1837, Moses Taylor outgoing letterbook, vol. 2, series 1, MTP.
46. JLSJ to NMRS, Apr. 10, 1837, X1/38/15, RAL.
47. Aaron H. Palmer to NMRS, May 8, 1837, XI/38/199, RAL.
48. *Times* (London), Apr. 4, 1837.
49. *Times* (London), Apr. 5, 1837.
50. *Times* (London), Apr. 6, 1837.
51. *Times* (London), Apr. 5, 1837.
52. Diary of Joshua Bates, Apr. 9, 1837, DEP 74, vol. 3, BA.
53. *Times* (London), Apr. 10, 1837.
54. Minutes, Apr. 6, 1837, Apr. 27, 1837, May 4, 1837, C5/282, BOEA; and Minutes, Apr. 6, 1837, Apr. 27, 1837, May 4, 1837, G4/60, BOEA.
55. Diary of Joshua Bates, Apr. 15, 1837, DEP 74, vol. 3, BA.
56. James de Rothschild to NMRS, Apr. 6, 1837, XI/109J/J/37, RAL. Gregory S. Hunter, "August Belmont," in *The Encyclopedia of American Business History and Biography: Banking & Finance to 1913*, ed. Larry Schweikart (New York: Facts on File, 1990), 37–44.
57. James de Rothschild to NMRS, Mar. 28, 1837, XI/109J/J/37, RAL.
58. NMRS to August Belmont, Apr. 22, 1837, II/10/1, RAL.
59. NMRS to August Belmont, Apr. 29, 1837, II/10/1, RAL.
60. August Belmont to NMRS, May 16, 1837, XI/62/04/1/1, and translated in T54/1, RAL.
61. James de Rothschild to NMRS, July 16, 1837, X1/109J/J/37, RAL.
62. NMRS to August Belmont, Apr. 22, 1837, II/10/1, RAL.
63. August Belmont to NMRS, May 16, 1837, XI/62/04/1/1, RAL.
64. *NYH*, Apr. 18, 1837.
65. *Journal of Commerce* (New York), Apr. 18, 1837, reprinted in *NI3*, Apr. 22, 1837.
66. *New York Express*, Apr. 20, 1837, reprinted in *NI3*, Apr. 25, 1837.
67. *NOTA*, Apr. 15, 1837. Gibson most likely meant "quondam," which Noah Webster defined as "former." Webster, *Dictionary*, s.v. "quondam."
68. August Belmont to NMRS, July 24, 1837, XI/62/04/1/57, RAL.
69. James to NMRS, July 16, 1837, X1/109j/j/37, RAL. Within three years of his arrival in New York, Belmont had earned more than $100,000. Hunter, "August Belmont," 38.
70. Biggs, *America in Thirty-Nine Days*, 1–2.
71. Diary of Philip Hone, May 18, 1837, 13:52, BV Hone, Philip, MS 1549, MCNYHS.

72. Diary of Philip Hone, May 20, 1837, 13:53, BV Hone, Philip, MS 1549, MCNYHS.

73. Biggs, *America in Thirty-Nine Days*, 3.

74. *NYH*, Apr. 18, 1837. Nick Yablon provides a case study of Cairo, a "paper city" in southern Illinois, through the lenses of Charles Dickens and the Bank War. Nick Yablon, *Untimely Ruins: An Archaeology of American Urban Modernity, 1819–1919* (Chicago: Chicago University Press, 2009), 63–106.

75. Mark E. Nackman, "Anglo-American Migrants to the West: Men of Broken Fortunes? The Case of Texas, 1821–46," *Western Historical Quarterly* 5, no. 4 (Oct., 1974): 450–51.

76. Thomas P. Copes to Doctor Joseph S. Copes, May 19, 1837, fol. 39, box 1, Joseph S. Copes papers, Mss. no. 733, LARC.

77. Philip Paxton [pseud], *A Stray Yankee in Texas* (New York, 1854), quoted in Nackman, "Anglo-American Migrants," 448, 450.

78. An 1838 magazine defined the term as a "western phrase." "A Hotel Dinner: From Notes in Pencil, on the Back of a Bill of Fare," *The Knickerbocker: or, New-York Monthly Magazine* 12, no. 3 (Sept. 1838): 230. For other examples, see Frederick Jackson, *A Week in Wall Street* (New York, 1841), 129; as "absquatulators" in *Some Comicalities* (New York: Dick & Fitzgerald, 1841); and as "absquatulation" in the 1837 setting of Dion Boucicault, *The Poor of New York: A Drama in Five Acts* (New York: Samuel French, 1857), 8.

79. Testimony of P. J. Byron, *Stinson, Curator, &c. vs. Buisson*, 17 La. 567, docket no. 3686 (Mar. 1841) Orleans Parish, UNO.

80. *Stinson, Curator, &c. vs. Buisson*, 17 La. 567; 1841 La. Lexis 221, at *2.

81. Petition for a Respite filed May 19, 1837, *Stinson, Curator, &c. vs. Buisson*, 17 La. 567, docket no. 3686 (Mar. 1841) Orleans Parish, UNO.

82. *Stinson, Curator, &c. vs. Buisson*, 17 La. 567; 1841 La. Lexis 221, at *8.

83. Probate petition, *Gravillon vs. Richard's Executor et al.*, 13 La. 293, docket no. 3555 (Apr. 1839) Orleans Parish, UNO.

84. Étienne Richard to Charles Chamberet, June 1, 1837, *Gravillon vs. Richard's Executor et al.*, 13 La. 293, docket no. 3555 (Apr. 1839) Orleans Parish, UNO.

85. Ibid.

86. Ibid.

87. *Gravillon vs. Richard's Executor et al.*, 13 La. 293; 1839 La. Lexis 138, at *8.

88. Donna T. Andrew, "The Suicide of Sir Samuel Romilly: Apotheosis or Outrage?" in *From Sin to Insanity: Suicide in Early Modern Europe*, ed. Jeffrey R. Wait (Ithaca, NY: Cornell University Press, 2004), 175–88. Suicide became a symbol of the need for individual responsibility and the need for self-regulation. Richard Bell, "The Double Guilt of Dueling: The Stain of Suicide in Anti-Dueling Rhetoric in the Early Republic," *Journal of the Early Republic* 29, no. 3 (2009): 383–410. For broader shifts in the meaning of suicide, see Richard Bell, *We Shall Be No More: Suicide and Self-Government in the Newly United States* (Cambridge, MA: Harvard University Press, 2012).

89. *New Orleans Bee*, May 4, 1837.

90. Théodore Nicolet to NMRS, Dec. 10, 1830, XI/112/96, RAL.

91. Inventory of the Property of Théodore Nicolet, Grima, Felix. V. 16, Act 425, May 12, 1837, NONA. For more on mahogany in the early American republic

and as an important element of New Orleans furnishings, see Jennifer L. Anderson, *Mahogany: The Costs of Luxury in Early America* (Cambridge, MA: Harvard University Press, 2012); and Jack D. Holden et al., *Furnishing Louisiana: Creole and Acadian Furniture, 1735 to 1835* (New Orleans: Historic New Orleans Collection, 2010).

92. I am indebted to Mary Lou Eichhorn for finding Nicolet in the records of the French Evangelical Church. Notarial records of square 97, 300–6 N. Rampart St. and 1033–35 Bienville St., Vieux Carré Survey, HNOC. For Nicolet as consul, see Jean Boze to Henri de Ste-Gême, May 3, 1837, fol. 275, Ste-Gême Family Papers, MSS 100, HNOC.

93. Testimony of Joaquin Vignier, *Saul vs. Nicolet's Executors*, 15 La 246, docket no. 3389 (Apr. 1840) Orleans Parish, UNO.

94. Testimony of Edward Salgman, *Rasch vs. Johns & Co.*, 11 La. 46, docket no. 3475 (May 1839) Orleans Parish, UNO.

95. Retrocession of Slaves, Théodore Nicolet to Jean Baptiste Colla, Grima, Felix. V. 15, Act 380, Apr. 28, 1837, NONA. For credit and slave sales, see Steven Deyle, *Carry Me Back: The Domestic Slave Trade in American Life* (Oxford, UK: Oxford University Press, 2005), 160–61, 170; and Baptist, "Toxic Debt." For seizure of slaves as payment for debts, see Judith Kelleher Shafer, *Slavery, the Civil Law, and the Supreme Court of Louisiana* (Baton Rouge: Louisiana State University Press, 1994), 168–79. By voluntarily agreeing to a private act of "retrocession," Nicolet avoided a more public case of insolvency or foreclosure.

96. Inventory of the Property of Théodore Nicolet, Grima, Felix. V. 16, Act 425, May 12, 1837, NONA.

97. Testimony of Frederick Frey, *Rasch vs. Johns & Co.*

98. Judgment rendered June 4, 1838, *Rasch vs. Johns & Co.*

99. Testimony of Theodore Blanchard, *Rasch vs. Johns & Co.*

100. Théodore Nicolet to Anthony Rasch, May 2, 1837, *Rasch vs. Johns & Co.*

101. *New Orleans Bee*, May 4, 1837; and Jean Boze to Henri de Ste-Gême, May 3, 1837, fol. 275, Ste-Gême Family Papers, MSS 100, HNOC.

102. Jean Boze to Henri de Ste-Gême, May 3, 1837, fol. 275, Ste-Gême Family Papers, MSS 100, HNOC. For Nicolet's age, see Will of Théodore Nicolet, filed May 5, 1837, mf vrd410, vol. 5, p. 456, NOCA.

103. Jean Boze to Henri de Ste-Gême, May 3, 1837, fol. 275, Ste-Gême Family Papers, MSS 100, HNOC.

104. *New Orleans Bee*, May 4, 1837.

105. Jean Boze to Henri de Ste-Gême, May 3, 1837, fol. 275, Ste-Gême Family Papers, MSS 100, HNOC.

106. The Louisiana municipal and appellate courts heard many cases related to Nicolet's insolvency. In addition to the cases previously cited, see *Nicolet's Executor vs. Moreau et al.*, 13 La. 313; 1839 La. Lexis 143; and *Thomas Bailly Blanchard, Executor vs. Henry Lockett*, 1843 La. Lexis 115; 4 Rob. 370.

107. "Money Market," NYH, May 2, 1837.

108. "The Times," *Barre Gazette* (Barre, MA), May 12, 1837.

109. "Money Market," NYH, May 2, 1837.

110. "Editor's Correspondence," *NI3*, Apr. 13, 1837.
111. *PIC*, May 10, 1837 (emphasis in original).
112. Moses Taylor to Drake & Coit, May 1, 1837, Moses Taylor outgoing letter-book, vol. 2, series 1, MTP; and Moses Taylor to Charles Drake & Co., May 1, 1837, Moses Taylor outgoing letterbook, vol. 2, series 1, MTP.
113. Diary of Philip Hone, May 2, 1837, 13:14, BV Hone, Philip, MS 1549, MCNYHS. Hone's entry on Nathan Mayer Rothschild's death provides evidence of his anti-Semitism. Diary of Philip Hone, Aug. 8, 1836, 12:74, BV Hone, Philip, MS 1549, MCNYHS.
114. Israel Clark to Charles Grandison Finney, May 1, 1837, quoted in Bertram Wyatt-Brown, *Lewis Tappan and the Evangelical War Against Slavery* (Cleveland, OH: Press of Case West Reserve University, 1969), 174. The Tappan failure undeniably influenced the spread of the abolitionist movement as this large financier of the antislavery campaign could no longer contribute. Bertram Wyatt-Brown, "Partners in Piety: Lewis and Arthur Tappan Evangelical Abolitionists, 1828–1841" (PhD diss., Johns Hopkins University, 1963), 238–41. John Stauffer argues that the experience of the panic and the depression that followed radicalized white abolitionists John Brown and Gerrit Smith, while allowing black abolitionists Fredrick Douglass and James McCune Smith to gain inclusion into the abolitionist movement. John Stauffer, *The Black Hearts of Men: Radical Abolitionists and the Transformation of Race* (Cambridge, MA: Harvard University Press, 2002), 71–133. For Finney's economic thought in the late 1830s, see Jason Matthew Yeatts, "Vision and Ethic: The Economic Thought of Charles Finney from 1836 to 1839" (MA thesis, Emmanuel School of Religion, 2009).
115. "From New York, Editor's Correspondence," *NI3*, May 6, 1837.
116. "From the *N. Y. Commercial Advertiser*," *NI3*, May 6, 1837.
117. Diary of Philip Hone, May 2, 1837, 13:14, BV Hone, Philip, MS 1549, MCNYHS.
118. "From the *N. Y. Commercial Advertiser*," *NI3*, May 6, 1837.
119. *The Colored American* (New York), Mar. 4, 1837. David Nord has argued that although Tappan's failure diminished the resources of religious publishing societies, administrative problems were more fundamental to the problem of creating a national distribution network. Nord, *Faith in Reading* (New York: Oxford University Press), 89.
120. "Arthur Tappan & Co.," *The Emancipator* (New York), May 11, 1837.
121. Others have identified uneasiness with the concept of white, male economic victimization in the 1830s. Based on an extensive review of literary sources, David Anthony has argued that "in the interval between the 1837 Panic and the 1857 Panic," a new "debtor masculinity" turned male economic victimization into a source of emotive power (106). David Anthony, *Paper Money Men: Commerce, Manhood, and the Sensational Public Sphere in Antebellum America* (Columbus: Ohio State University Press, 2009), 102–22.
122. Stauffer notes radical abolitionists' apocalyptic descriptions of the panic and their slavery-based causation. Stauffer, *Black Hearts of Men*, 114–18.
123. "The Pressure," *The Emancipator* (New York), May 11, 1837 (emphasis in original).

124. "Gloomy Picture – N. Orleans Bee, April 15th," *The Emancipator* (New York), May 11, 1837.
125. "The Trade in Blood," *The Emancipator* (New York), May 11, 1837 (emphasis in original).
126. Ibid. The article explains that this quotation is actually taken from the *New Orleans Bee* of April 1, 1837.
127. "*The New Orleans Bulletin* of April 11th," *The Emancipator* (New York), May 11, 1837.
128. "And the New Orleans Bee," *The Emancipator* (New York), May 11, 1837.
129. Ibid. The argument in the *Emancipator* linking financial crisis and slavery suggests more and more forcefully that "Slavery must be abolished before *the times* can be better." "The Times," *The Emancipator* (New York), June 1, 1837 (emphasis in original).
130. "A Statement and a Call," *The Colored American* (New York), June 17, 1837.
131. "Northern Distress Produced by Southern Slavery," *The Colored American* (New York), May 13, 1837 (emphasis in original).
132. "Northern Distress Produced by Southern Slavery," *The Colored American* (New York), May 13, 1837.
133. Charles Francis Adams, *Further Reflections upon the State of the Currency in the United States* (Boston: William D. Ticknor, 1837), 3.
134. *PIC*, May 4, 1837.
135. Frothingham, *Duties*, 11, 10, 3. Frothingham's use of history to comment on present experience reflects his interest in the Romantic Movement. Not only was he an avid reader of Heine and Walter Scott, but he also translated German Romantic poets for the American market. Stopping short of transcendentalism, Frothingham was friends with key figures in this movement to turn inward or toward nature for divine revelation. O. B. Frothingham, "Some Phases of Idealism in New England," *Atlantic Monthly* 52, no. 309 (July 1883): 13–14.
136. Frothingham, *Duties*, 7, 6.
137. Ibid., 7, 9, 10.
138. Ibid., 10, 11.
139. Ibid., 10–11.
140. Ibid., 17–18.
141. Peabody, *Views of Duty*, 3–4.
142. Ibid., 5, 6. For the interest beginning in the 1830s in the individual and the development of the idea of the moral faculties of the mind, see Lewis Perry, *Intellectual Life in America: A History* (New York: Franklin Watts, 1984), 207–13.
143. Peabody, *Views*, 15. For more on the principles of "voluntary wrong-doing," see E. Brooks Holifield, *Theology in America: Christian Thought from the Age of the Puritans to the Civil War* (New Haven, CT: Yale University Press, 2003), 205.
144. "The Gentleman in Black," *PIC*, Mar. 8, 1837.
145. "The Gentleman in Black," *PIC*, Mar. 29, 1837.
146. Thomas Ewing Dabney, *One Hundred Great Years: The Story of the Times-Picayune from Its Founding to 1940* (1944; New York: Greenwood Press, 1968), 22.

147. "The Gentleman in Black," *PIC*, Mar. 12, 1837 (emphasis in original).
148. "The Gentleman in Black," *PIC*, Mar. 8, 1837; and "The Gentleman in Black," *PIC*, Mar. 31, 1837.
149. "The Troublous Times," *PIC*, Apr. 13, 1837.
150. "The Gentleman in Black," *PIC*, Apr. 30, 1837 (emphasis in original).
151. Reynolds argues that subversive reform literature undermined the genre's original intent of encouraging upstanding behavior by focusing on sensational descriptions of sin. The *Picayune's* editors did the reverse. By satirizing reformist interpretations of the panic, they spread their moralistic message. Reynolds, *Beneath the American Renaissance*, 56–59.
152. "The Gentleman in Black," *PIC*, Apr. 30, 1837; and "The Gentleman in Black," *PIC*, Mar. 8, 1837.
153. Citizen of Massachusetts, *The Times: Or, The Pressure and Its Causes Examined; An Address to the People* (Boston, 1837), 3.
154. Ibid., 5.
155. Ibid., 23 (emphasis in original).
156. David Anthony suggests that sensational literature from the period sought "to project financial crisis – and more specifically, capitalist desire – onto figures of Otherness such as the Jew and the speculator." Anthony, *Paper Money Men*, 28–29.
157. From an economist's perspective, Green discusses the "tautological" definition of "'excessive credit,' 'overspeculation' and 'overinvestment.'" Green, *Finance and Economic Development*, 165.
158. "Cause and Effect," *NI3*, Apr. 6, 1837.
159. "Editor's Correspondence," *NI3*, Mar. 28, 1837.
160. *New York Daily Express*, reprinted in "American Enterprise," *NI3*, Mar. 28, 1837.
161. *The Pennsylvania Reporter*, reprinted in "More of the Demoniac Spirit," *NI3*, Apr. 27, 1837.
162. "Opinions of the Press," *Washington Globe*, Apr. 22, 1837.
163. "From the *National Gazette*," *NI3*, Apr. 25, 1837.
164. "More of the Demoniac Spirit," *NI3*, Apr. 27, 1837 (emphasis in original).
165. Citizen of Massachusetts, *The Times*, 3 (emphasis in original).
166. "From the *N. Y. Commercial Advertiser*," *NI3*, May 6, 1837.
167. *PIC*, May 4, 1837.
168. "Editor's Correspondence," *NI3*, May 9, 1837.
169. Ibid.
170. Caroline White to Charles White, May 1837, 1990.64.1.1.23, White Family Collection, Research Library, Old Sturbridge Village, Sturbridge, MA. Special thanks to Mary Fuhrer for finding and transcribing this source.

Chapter 6

1. Minutes, Apr. 6, 1837, G4/60, BOEA.
2. Minutes, Apr. 6, 1837, C5/282, BOEA.
3. *Times* (London), Apr. 17, 1837.
4. *Times* (London), Apr. 18, 1837.

5. Apr. 13, 1837, *NI3*.
6. The men composing the committee included James Brown, Frederick Sheldon, John W. Leavitt, James Boorman, Jakob Harvey, John A. Stevens, and Charles A. Heckscher. "Committee of Circulation and Conference," fol. Feb. 1837, box John Austin Stevens, 1809–1852, BV Stevens, John Austin, MS 2456, MCNYHS.
7. Jeffrey Sklansky, "'A Bank on Parnassus': Nicholas Biddle and the Beauty of Banking," *Common-place* 6, no. 3 (Apr. 2006), http://www.common-place. org/vol-06/no-03/sklansky/; and Yablon, *Untimely Ruins*, 89–94.
8. Govan, *Nicholas Biddle*, 283–87.
9. L. Ray Gunn, *Decline of Authority: Public Economic Policy and Political Development in New York, 1800–1860* (Ithaca, NY: Cornell University Press, 1988), 92–93; and Redlich, *Molding of American Banking*, 1: 89–95.
10. Application to the BUS, fol. Feb. 1837, box John Austin Stevens, 1809–1852, BV Stevens, John Austin, MS 2456, MCNYHS. Despite the filing of this document in the collection, the letter is actually dated Mar. 24, 1837.
11. Application to the BUS, fol. Feb. 1837, box John Austin Stevens, 1809–1852, BV Stevens, John Austin, MS 2456, MCNYHS.
12. *Plaindealer* (New York), Apr. 1, 1837.
13. "The Cat Out of the Bag," *Plaindealer* (New York), Apr. 29, 1837. Leggett argued that Biddle outsmarted the New Yorkers by convincing them that he was acting on their behalf when he was really acting on behalf of his foreign stockholders. In actuality, the BOE sent the BUS a letter proposing a very similar plan on March 22, 1837. Given the speed of transatlantic transportation, it is impossible that Biddle could have known about the BOE proposal. This is a perfect example of the parallel panics occurring in New York City and London. Hammond, *Banks and Politics*, 459–67.
14. For the complex relationship among New York State banks and between them and the BUS, see John M. McFaul, *The Politics of Jacksonian Finance* (Ithaca, NY: Cornell University Press, 1972), 48–57, 101–6; and Gatell, "Sober Second Thoughts," 19–40.
15. For New York City's rivalries, see Chap.1, n. 102.
16. Application to the BUS, fol. Feb. 1837, box John Austin Stevens, 1809–1852, BV Stevens, John Austin, MS 2456, MCNYHS.
17. Nicholas Biddle to John A. Stevens, Mar. 24, 1837, fol. Mar. 1837, box John Austin Stevens, 1809–1852, BV Stevens, John Austin, MS 2456, MCNYHS.
18. Nicholas Biddle to John A. Stevens, Mar. 25, 1837, fol. Mar. 1837, box John Austin Stevens, 1809–1852, BV Stevens, John Austin, MS 2456, MCNYHS.
19. "Commercial," *NYH*, Mar. 29, 1837.
20. "Commercial," *NYH*, Mar. 28, 1837.
21. Diary of Philip Hone, Mar. 28, 1837, 12:441, BV Hone, Philip, MS 1549, MCNYHS.
22. N. Biddle to M. Eyre, Mar. 29, 1837, reel 24, Nicholas Biddle Papers [Microfilm], LOC.
23. John Mills enunciated the idea that crises resulted from shifts in the confidence of businessmen in 1867; see John Mills, "On Credit Cycles and the Origin of Commercial Panics" (1867), in *Business Cycle Theory: Selected Texts,*

1860–1939, ed. Harald Hagemann (London: Pickering & Chatto, 2002), 1:88. Although looking at a later period, Scott Sandage argues that sentiments acted as a currency exchanged in the business world. Scott A. Sandage, "The Gaze of Success: Failed Men and the Sentimental Marketplace, 1873–1893," in *Sentimental Men: Masculinity and the Politics of Affect in American Culture*, ed. Mary Chapman and Glenn Hendler (Berkeley: University of California Press, 1999), 181–201.

24. "Commercial," *NYH*, Mar. 29, 1837.
25. Diary of Philip Hone, Mar. 28, 1837, 12:441, BV Hone, Philip, MS 1549, MCNYHS.
26. "Commercial," *NYH*, Mar. 29, 1837
27. Diary of Philip Hone, Mar. 28, 1837, 12:442, BV Hone, Philip, MS 1549, MCNYHS.
28. Howe, *What Hath God Wrought*, 393; and McFaul, *Politics of Jacksonian Finance*, 16–57.
29. Diary of Philip Hone, Mar. 28, 1837, 12:442, BV Hone, Philip, MS 1549, MCNYHS.
30. *New York Express*, Mar. 27, 1837, reprinted in *Commercial Bulletin* (New Orleans), Apr. 10, 1837.
31. Diary of Philip Hone, Mar. 28, 1837, 12:442, BV Hone, Philip, MS 1549, MCNYHS.
32. Biddle, quoted in Diary of Philip Hone, Mar. 29, 1837, 12:443, BV Hone, Philip, MS 1549, MCNYHS.
33. Nicholas Biddle to John A. Stevens, Mar. 29, 1837, fol. Mar. 1837, box John Austin Stevens, 1809–1852, BV Stevens, John Austin, MS 2456, MCNYHS.
34. Biddle, quoted in Hammond, *Banks and Politics*, 461.
35. Nicholas Biddle to John A. Stevens, Mar. 29, 1837, fol. Mar. 1837, box John Austin Stevens, 1809–1852, BV Stevens, John Austin, MS 2456, MCNYHS.
36. Biddle, quoted in Hammond, *Banks and Politics*, 462–63.
37. Minutes, May 25, 1837, C5/282, BOEA; and Minutes, May 25, 1837, G4/60, BOEA.
38. Diary of Philip Hone, Mar. 29, 1837, 12:444, BV Hone, Philip, MS 1549, MCNYHS.
39. "The Panic," *Morning Courier and New-York Enquirer*, Apr. 7, 1837.
40. Gunn, *Decline of Authority*, 131–32; Miller, *Enterprise of a Free People*, 203–5; and Barbara Oberg, "New York State and the 'Specie Crisis' of 1837," *Business and Economic History* 14 (1985): 37–51.
41. "Commercial," *NYH*, Mar. 29, 1837.
42. Dickens, quoted in Govan, *Nicholas Biddle*, 396–97; and in Yablon, *Untimely Ruins*, 89.
43. Compare Govan, *Nicholas Biddle*, 398–413 and Arthur M. Schlesinger Jr., *The Age of Jackson* (Boston: Little, Brown, 1946), 222, 252–53, 395.
44. For narratives of failure, see Sandage, *Born Losers*; and Balleisen, *Navigating Failure*.
45. For the process of reinvention in the slave pens, see Johnson, *Soul by Soul*, 162–88. For enslaved people as collateral and the process of collection, see Baptist, "Toxic Debt"; and Kilbourne, *Slave Agriculture*, 129–48.

46. Quotation in Kilbourne, *Slave Agriculture*, 134.
47. *Morning Chronicle* (London), Apr. 25, 1837.
48. Minutes, Apr. 6, 1837, C5/282, BOEA; and Minutes, Apr. 6, 1837, G4/60, BOEA.
49. For architectural analysis of the relationship between the City's structures to the structures of finance, see Black, "Spaces of Capital," 351–75; and Abramson, *Building the Bank of England*. For the image of British politics in Westminster, see Dana Arnold, *Re-presenting the Metropolis: Architecture, Urban Experience and Social Life in London 1800–1840* (Burlington, VT: Ashgate, 2000), 43–63; and M. H. Port, "Government and the Metropolitan Image: Ministers, Parliament and the Concept of a Capital City, 1840–1915," in *The Metropolis and Its Image: Constructing Identities for London, c. 1750–1950*, ed. Dana Arnold (Malden, MA: Blackwell, 1999), 101–26.
50. On Whig factionalism, see Newbould, *Whiggery and Reform*, 1–12; and Peter Mandler, *Aristocratic Government* (New York: Oxford University Press), 1–9.
51. Minutes, Apr. 6, 1837, C5/282, BOEA; and Minutes, Apr. 6, 1837, G4/60, BOEA. Although a moderate, Spring Rice expressed his partiality toward free trade as an early member of the Political Economy Club and was a protégé of Lord Lansdowne who set out "to master the new sciences of finance and administration, surrounding himself with experts – political economists, scientists, bankers, agronomists – recruited both from the country gentry and from the rising professional classes" (Mandler, *Aristocratic Government*, 29). See also Mandler, *Aristocratic Government*, 100, 113, 163. Thomas Spring Rice who is discussed in this chapter is not the same man as the T. Spring Rice who famously performed under the minstrel name of Jim Crow at the same time on the London stage.
52. Minutes, Apr. 13, 1837, C5/282, BOEA; and Minutes, Apr. 13, 1837, G4/60, BOEA. See also D. M. Williams, "Liverpool Merchants and the Cotton Trade, 1820–1850," in *Liverpool and Merseyside: Essays in the Economic and Social History of the Port and Its Hinterland*, ed. J. R. Harris (New York: Augustus M. Kelley, 1969), 183. Cotton price decline calculated by comparing the prices reported weekly in the Liverpool *Chronicle* between Jan. 7, 1837 and Apr. 15, 1837.
53. Minutes, Apr. 13, 1837, C5/282, BOEA; and Minutes, Apr. 13, 1837, G4/60, BOEA. The meeting held by the Liverpudlians before their departure for London is described in the London *Times*, Apr. 8, 1837. For more on the 1825–26 crisis, see Iain S. Black "Money, Information and Space: Banking in Early Nineteenth-Century England and Wales," *Journal of Historical Geography* 21, no. 4 (1995): 398–412; Kynaston, *City of London*, 63–72; and Jenks, *Migration of British Capital*, 52–64.
54. Minutes, Apr. 13, 1837, C5/282, BOEA; and Minutes, Apr. 13, 1837, G4/60, BOEA. The Liverpudlians expressed "regret" at the BOE's decision. Minutes, Apr. 20, 1837, C5/282, BOEA; and Minutes, Apr. 20, 1837, G4/60, BOEA.
55. "Money Market and City News," *Morning Chronicle* (London), Apr. 14, 1837. For the significance of "laws," see Mary Poovey, *Genres of the Credit Economy: Mediating Value in Eighteenth- and Nineteenth-Century Britain* (Chicago: University of Chicago Press, 2008), 200.

56. Grote, quoted in John Henry Barrow, ed., *The Mirror of Parliament for the 3rd Session of the 14th Parliament of Great Britain and Ireland in the 3rd and 4th Years of the Reign of Queen Victoria, Appointed to Meet January 16 and from Thence Continued Till August 11, 1840,* vol. 2 (London: Longman, Orme, Brown, Green, & Longmans, 1840), 1680.

57. Compare the lists of the firms that pledged security on Mar. 9, 1837, to the list of elected directors on Apr. 5, 1837. Mar. 9, 1837, G4/59, BOEA; and Apr. 5, 1837, G4/60, BOEA.

58. For the evolution of the debate about the lender of last resort responsibilities of the BOE, see Dennis O'Brien, "The Lender-of-Last-Resort Concept in Britain," *History of Political Economy* 35, no. 1 (2003): 1–19. Kindleberger interprets the BOE's deviation from standard operating procedure as evidence that it was acting as a lender of last resort. Charles P. Kindleberger, "The Lender of Last Resort: Pushing the Doctrine Too Far?" in *The World Economy and National Finance in Historical Perspective* (Ann Arbor: University of Michigan Press, 1995), 149. Lévy-Leboyer agrees that the BOE acted as a lender of last resort in the 1830s but argues that these actions resulted in the diminishment of the BOE's regulatory role. Maurice Lévy-Leboyer, "Central Banking and Foreign Trade: The Anglo-American Cycle in the 1830s," in *Financial Crises: Theory, History, and Policy,* ed. Charles P. Kindleberger and Jean-Pierre Laffargue (Cambridge, UK: Cambridge University Press, 1982), 66–110.

59. Minutes, Apr. 13, 1837, C5/282, BOEA; and Minutes, Apr. 6, 1837, G4/60, BOEA.

60. Minutes, Apr. 13, 1837, C5/282, BOEA; and Minutes, Apr. 6, 1837, G4/60, BOEA.

61. "G. Wildes & Co. Circular of Liquidation," Apr. 13, 1837, C5/238, BOEA.

62. Diary of Joshua Bates, May 7, 1837, DEP 74, vol. 3, BA.

63. Minutes, Apr. 27, 1837, May 1, 1837, May 3, 1837, May 4, 1837, May 11, 1837, May 18, 1837, C5/282, BOEA; and Minutes, Apr. 27, 1837, May 1, 1837, May 3, 1837, May 4, 1837, May 11, 1837, May 18, 1837, G4/60, BOEA.

64. Diary of Joshua Bates, Apr. 15, 1837, DEP 74, vol. 3, BA.

65. "Money Market and City Intelligence," *Times* (London), Apr. 10, 1837; and "The Bank and the American Merchants," *Courier* (London), reprinted in *Times* (London), Apr. 10, 1837.

66. For the failure of classical economists to study the business cycle, see Kim Kyun, *Equilibrium Business Cycle Theory in Historical Perspective* (New York: Cambridge University Press, 1988), 18–22. According to Poovey, John Stuart Mill gestured toward seeing panics as "(unfortunate) episodes in the natural course of trade." Poovey, *Genres of the Credit Economy,* 241.

67. "Money Market and City News," *Morning Chronicle* (London), Apr. 19, 1837.

68. "Money Market and City News," *Times* (London), Apr. 10, 1837. For more on cultural responses to uncertainty, see Stuart Blumin, "Explaining the New Metropolis: Perception, Deception, and Analysis in Mid-Nineteenth-Century New York City," *Journal of Urban History* 11, no. 1 (Nov. 1984), 9–38; Cohen, *Murder of Helen Jewett*; James W. Cook, *The Arts of Deception: Playing with Fraud in the Age of Barnum* (Cambridge, MA: Harvard University Press, 2001); Ann Fabian, *Card Sharps, Dream Books & Bucket*

Shops: Gambling in 19th-Century America (Ithaca, NY: Cornell University Press, 1990); Karen Halttunen, *Murder Most Foul: The Killer and the American Gothic Imagination* (Cambridge, MA: Harvard University Press, 1998); Karen Halttunen, *Confidence Men and Painted Women: A Study of Middle-Class Culture in America, 1830–1870* (New Haven, CT: Yale University Press, 1982); "A Cabinet of Curiosities," *Commonplace* 4, no. 2 (Jan. 2004); and "Cultures of Deception," panel, Society for Historians of the Early American Republic Annual Meeting (July 2006).

69. "Money Market and City Intelligence," *Times* (London), Apr. 10, 1837.

70. For the history of political economists advocating for the separation of politics and economics, see Emma Rothschild, *Economic Sentiments: Adam Smith, Condorcet, and the Enlightenment* (Cambridge, MA: Harvard University Press, 2001), 3, 50.

71. "Money Market and City Intelligence," *Times* (London), Apr. 11, 1837; and "Money Market and City Intelligence," *Times* (London), Apr. 12, 1837.

72. "Money Market and City Intelligence," *Times* (London), Apr. 11, 1837.

73. Hume, quoted in Barrow, *Mirror of Parliament*, 1680.

74. "Money Market and City Intelligence," *Times* (London), Apr. 11, 1837.

75. "Money Market and City Intelligence," *Times* (London), Apr. 18, 1837.

76. Smith, Hubbard & Co. to Smith & Co., Apr. 26, 1837, Smith, Hubbard and Company records, Mss. no. 73, LARC.

77. Thomas Barrett & Co. to JLSJ, Mar. 9, 1837, reprinted in *NYH*, Mar. 18, 1837, and *New Orleans Bee*, Mar. 29, 1837.

78. Minutes, Mar. 11, 1837, Citizens' Bank Minute Book, vol. 1, CBLARC. Redlich argues that there had been earlier attempts at cooperation between New Orleans banks. He finds these "truly remarkable for the time" because other financial communities did not try to work together until 1837 and, in general, banks cooperated only for specific ends or to combat specific evils. Redlich, *Molding of American Banking*, 2:256.

79. *Condition of State Banks*, 25th Cong., 2nd sess., Feb. 27, 1839, H. R. Doc. 227, serial vol. 348, sess. vol. 5., 486–567; and *Condition of the State Banks*, 26th Cong., 2nd sess., Mar. 3, 1841, H. R. Doc. 111, serial vol. 385, sess. vol. 4, 630–1081.

80. On the founding of *The Economist*, see *The Economist, 1843–1943: A Centenary Volume* (New York: Oxford University Press, 1943), 1–17.

81. Unfortunately, I did not transcribe or photograph the dissenting opinions of these two directors before Hurricane Katrina. This collection was damaged by the flood in New Orleans because it was stored in the basement of Jones Hall, the special collections building. Although the archivists at Tulane expect the minute books to survive, the preservation process had not been completed on these sources at the time of publication.

82. Forstall's Banking Act, which passed in the Louisiana House of Representatives the day before the Hermann failure, was the first attempt to regulate the state's banks. For more on this, see "Bill to Protect the Currency," *New Orleans Bee*, Mar. 3, 1837; Neu, "Edmond J. Forstall," 186–201; Redlich, *Molding of American Banking*, 2:32–44.

83. *New Orleans Bee*, Mar. 21, 1837. Throughout the month of April, as a devoted Democratic paper, the *Bee* defended the Specie Circular, Andrew

Jackson, and Martin Van Buren against charges of having caused the crisis by blaming bankers, merchants, and speculators.

84. *Commercial Bulletin* (New Orleans), Mar. 21, 1837. For an example of the *Commercial Bulletin*'s avowal of Whig politics advocating the recharter of the BUS, see Apr. 10, 1837.
85. "The Financial Crisis," *New Orleans Bee*, Mar. 31, 1837.
86. Ibid.
87. "The Money Crisis," *New Orleans Bee*, Apr. 6, 1837.
88. *NOTA*, Apr. 14, 1837.
89. *NOTA*, Apr. 19, 1837.
90. *New Orleans Bee*, Apr. 15, 1837. Naomi Lamoreaux has argued that bank directors in New England during the early American republic used banks as sources of credit for their personal investments, and that this "insider lending" was not challenged by the non-banking public until after 1837. The debates in the New Orleans press in April 1837 suggest the beginning of a challenge to this practice. Lamoreaux, *Insider Lending*, 31–51.
91. "The Crisis," *NOTA*, Mar. 28, 1837; "The All Engrossing Topic," *NOTA*, Mar. 29, 1837; and "The Banks, – The Banks," *NOTA*, Mar. 31, 1837. For an example of a response, see Freeholder, "Favoritism of the Banking Institutions in New Orleans," *New Orleans Bee*, Apr. 4 1837.
92. "By the Express Mail," *New Orleans Bee*, Apr. 6, 1837.
93. *NOTA*, Apr. 19, 1837.
94. *NOTA*, Apr. 14, 1837.
95. *PIC*, Apr. 13, 1837.
96. *PIC*, Apr. 15, 1837 (emphasis in original).
97. Ayers P. Merril to William Newton Mercer, Apr. 14, 1837, box 1, fol. 10, William Newton Mercer papers, Mss. no. 64, LARC.
98. "Union Bank of Louisiana," Gibson, *Gibson's Guide*, illustration following 324; and R. W. Hidy, "The Union Bank of Louisiana Loan, 1832: A Case Study in Marketing," *The Journal of Political Economy* 47, no. 2 (Apr. 1939): 232–53. On neo-classical architecture and banks, see Abramson, *Building the Bank of England*, 113–14; Charles Belfoure, *Monuments to Money: The Architecture of American Banks* (Jefferson, NC: McFarland, 2005), 42–69; and Sklansky, "The Bank on Parnassus."
99. "Union Bank of Louisiana," Gibson, *Guide*, 340.
100. Minutes, Apr. 12, 1837, Citizens' Bank Minute Book, vol. 1, CBLARC.
101. Minutes, Mar. 22, 1837, Mar. 29, 1837, Citizens' Bank Minute Book, vol. 1, CBLARC.
102. Minutes, Apr. 12, 1837, Apr. 13, 1837, Citizens' Bank Minute Book, vol. 1, CBLARC. For the bond sales and special praise of Forstall's leadership, see "Agreeable News," *New Orleans Bee*, Apr. 7, 1837.
103. "The Banks and the Merchants," *New Orleans Bee*, Apr. 12, 1837.
104. *NOTA*, Apr. 14, 1837.
105. "The Banks and the Merchants," *New Orleans Bee*, Apr. 12, 1837.
106. Minutes, Apr. 14, 1837, Citizens' Bank Minute Book, vol. 1, CBLARC.
107. *New Orleans Bee*, Apr. 15, 1837.
108. *New Orleans Bee*, Apr. 18, 1837.

109. *New Orleans Bee*, Apr. 15, 1837.
110. Ayers P. Merril to William Newton Mercer, May 1, 1837, box 1, fol. 10, William Newton Mercer papers, Mss. no. 64, LARC.
111. "New York Meeting," *New Orleans Bee*, May 5, 1837.
112. "Dangerous State of the Country – The Only Remedy – in immediate meeting of Congress," *NYH*, Mar. 30, 1837.
113. For Van Buren's nicknames, see Widmer, *Martin Van Buren*, 4.
114. Watson, *Liberty and Power*, 205. For the multifaceted nature of Van Buren's coalition, see Wilentz, *Rise of American Democracy*, 453. For a review of the literature on the election of 1836, see William G. Shade, "'The Most Delicate and Exciting Topics': Martin Van Buren, Slavery, and the Election of 1836," *Journal of the Early Republic* 18, no. 3 (1998): 459–84.
115. Howe, *What Hath God Wrought*, 488.
116. Gorham A. Worth to Martin Van Buren, Mar. 12, 1837, reel 22, MVBLOC.
117. Silas Wright Jr. to Martin Van Buren, Mar. 21, 1837, reel 22, MVBLOC.
118. Ibid.
119. Donald B. Cole, *Martin Van Buren and the American Political System* (Princeton, NJ: Princeton University Press, 1984), 288–89. For one example of a letter from a Democrat remarking on public opinion in favor of the repeal of the Specie Circular, see Henry Toland to Martin Van Buren, Mar. 9, 1837, reel 22, MVBLOC.
120. "Editor's Correspondence," *NI3*, Apr. 13, 1837; and *Washington Globe*, Apr. 18, 1837.
121. Martin Van Buren to Andrew Jackson, Apr. 24, 1837, reel 23, MVBLOC.
122. Whereas more than three hundred individual merchants and firms called for the meeting, at least four thousand attended it. "Meeting of Merchants," *Morning Courier and New-York Enquirer*, Apr. 25, 1837; and "Great Meeting of Merchants," *Morning Courier and New-York Enquirer*, Apr. 26, 1837.
123. "Great Meeting of Merchants," *Morning Courier and New-York Enquirer*, Apr. 26, 1837; and "From the *N. Y. Evening Post*, April 26," *Washington Globe*, Apr. 29, 1837.
124. Diary of Philip Hone, Apr. 26, 1837, 13:3, BV Hone, Philip, MS 1549, MCNYHS.
125. "True Causes of the Revolution – The Remedy," *NYH*, May 6, 1837; and "Great Meeting of Merchants," *NYH*, Apr. 26, 1837.
126. Diary of Philip Hone, Apr. 26, 1837, 13:3, BV Hone, Philip, MS 1549, MCNYHS.
127. Diary of Philip Hone, Apr. 26, 1837, 13:4, BV Hone, Philip, MS 1549, MCNYHS.
128. "From the *N. Y. Evening Post*, April 26," *Washington Globe*, Apr. 29, 1837. The use of the lower case "w" in "whig" may have been a visual pun on the undercapitalization of Whig banks.
129. "From the *N. Y. Evening Post*, April 26," *Washington Globe*, Apr. 29, 1837.
130. Diary of Philip Hone, Apr. 26, 1837, 13:5, BV Hone, Philip, MS 1549, MCNYHS.
131. Diary of Philip Hone, Apr. 28, 1837, 13:9, BV Hone, Philip, MS 1549, MCNYHS.

132. Martin Van Buren to Isaac Hone, May 3, 1837, reel 23, MVBLOC.

133. Isaac Hone et al. to Martin Van Buren, May 3, 1837, reel 23, MVBLOC.

134. Ibid. For the way nineteenth-century Americans shaped their vision of national authority, see Brian Balogh, *A Government out of Sight: The Mystery of National Authority in Nineteenth-Century America* (Cambridge, UK: Cambridge University Press, 2009).

135. Martin Van Buren to Isaac Hone [draft in hand of Benjamin Franklin Butler], May 4, 1837, reel 23, MVBLOC.

136. "Great Meeting of Citizens," *New-York Spectator*, May 11, 1837. All of the correspondence between the committee and the president is published in this number.

137. Diary of Philip Hone, May 6, 1837, 13:19, BV Hone, Philip, MS 1549, MCNYHS.

138. Diary of Philip Hone, May 8, 1837, 13:22, BV Hone, Philip, MS 1549, MCNYHS.

139. "State of the Country," *NYH*, May 5, 1837.

140. Diary of Philip Hone, May 8, 1837, 13:23–24, BV Hone, Philip, MS 1549, MCNYHS.

141. Diary of Philip Hone, May 8, 1837, 13:24–25, BV Hone, Philip, MS 1549, MCNYHS.

142. Reginald Charles McGrane, *The Panic of 1837: Some Financial Problems of the Jacksonian Era* (1924, Chicago: University of Chicago Press, 1965), v. McGrane employed metaphors of the "stage" to describe the "principal actors in the drama" (1, 69).

Chapter 7

1. "Coroner's Inquest," *NYH*, May 5, 1837.

2. Diary of Philip Hone, May 4, 1837, 13:15, BV Hone, Philip, MS 1549, MCNYHS.

3. "Coroner's Inquest," *NYH*, May 5, 1837.

4. Diary of Philip Hone, May 4, 1837, 13:15, BV Hone, Philip, MS 1549, MCNYHS.

5. "From the N. Y. *Commercial Advertiser* of Wednesday Evening, May 10," *Portsmouth Journal of Literature and Politics* (Portsmouth, NH), May 13, 1837. For the inauguration, see "Board of Aldermen," *NYH*, May 10, 1837.

6. For "Fortune's Favorite," see "Splendid Scheme," *Plaindealer* (New York), Apr. 1, 1837; and "New York Mayor," *Washington Globe*, Apr. 17, 1837.

7. *Documents of the Assembly of the State of New York*, 60th sess., 1837, vol. 4, doc. 328, 13. For the origin of the committee, see "The Legislature," *Plaindealer* (New York), Jan. 28, 1837.

8. "Mr. Flemming's Resignation," *NYH*, May 2, 1837.

9. *Documents of the Assembly of the State of New York*, 61st sess., 1838, vol. 4, doc. 318, 26.

10. Ibid., 12, 21.

11. For the firm's failure, see "Money Market" *NYH*, Apr. 21, 1837.

12. *Documents of the Assembly of the State of New York*, 61st sess., 1838, vol. 4, doc. 318, 12, 21.
13. "Editor's Correspondence," *NI3*, May 6, 1837.
14. "Friday, May 5, 1837," *New York Times*, May 9, 1837 (emphasis in original).
15. "Saturday, May 6, 1837," *New York Times*, May 9, 1837.
16. "Editor's Correspondence," *NI3*, May 6, 1837 (emphasis in original).
17. Kamensky, *Exchange Artist*, 140–41.
18. Reprinted in "The Mechanic's Bank," *New York Times*, May 9, 1837 (emphasis in original).
19. Diary of Philip Hone, May 4, 1837, 13:16, BV Hone, Philip, MS 1549, MCNYHS.
20. "Editor's Correspondence," *NI3*, May 6, 1837.
21. "From the N. Y. *Journal of Commerce*, May 5," *NI3*, May 9, 1837.
22. "Mechanic's Bank," *New York Times*, May 9, 1837.
23. "Money Market. Friday, May 5," *NYH*, May 6, 1837.
24. *Documents of the Assembly of the State of New York*, 61st sess., 1838, vol. 4, doc. 318, 14.
25. Many New York City bankers disliked the Safety Fund because they saw it as prejudiced in favor of country banks. Because the Safety Fund was sponsored by the Democratic Party, Whigs disliked the fund for partisan reasons. James Roger Sharp, *The Jacksonians Versus the Banks: Politics in the States After the Panic of 1837* (New York: Columbia University Press, 1970), 47–48.
26. "Money Market," *NYH*, May 9, 1837; and "From the New York *Express*, Saturday, 6 P.M.," *NI3*, May 11, 1837.
27. "Money Market," *NYH*, May 9, 1837; *NI3*, May 11, 1837; and *Documents of the Assembly of the State of New York*, 61st sess., 1838, vol. 4, doc. 318, 3.
28. "From the New York *Express*, Saturday, 6 P.M.," *NI3*, May 11, 1837.
29. "From the Same, Monday, 12 P.M.," *NI3*, May 11, 1837 (emphasis in original).
30. Ibid. The Dry Dock Bank's officers claimed that the bank "never suspended payment" but received an "injunction" from a state office to continue paying its bills. This expedient removed blame and possible forfeiture of the bank's charter from the directors. *Documents of the Assembly of the State of New York*, 61st sess., 1838, vol. 4, doc. 318, 2–3, 11.
31. "From the Same, Monday, 12 P.M.," *NI3*, May 11, 1837.
32. "From the *New York Commercial Advertiser*, Eve. May 8," *NI3*, May 11, 1837.
33. *NI3*, May 11, 1837.
34. "Money Market," *NYH*, May 8, 1837.
35. "Money Market," *NYH*, May 9, 1837.
36. Edward Williams Clay, "The Times," *broadside* (New York: H. R. Robinson, 1837). Hand-colored versions of this print are available at the AAS and the Library Company of Philadelphia.
37. Diary of Philip Hone, May 10, 1837, 13:29, BV Hone, Philip, MS 1549, MCNYHS.
38. E. T. Throop to Martin Van Buren, May 10, 1837, reel 23, MVBLOC.
39. "From the N. Y. *Daily Express*, The City Bank Notes," *Portsmouth Journal of Literature and Politics* (Portsmouth, NH), May 13, 1837.

40. Wayland, *Elements of Political Economy* (1837), 268 (emphasis in original).
41. "From the N. Y. *Commercial Advertiser* of Wednesday Evening, May 10, Suspension of Specie Payments," *Portsmouth Journal of Literature and Politics* (Portsmouth, NH), May 13, 1837. Rousseau suggests that this sum represented nearly 90 percent of the specie reserves. Rousseau, "Jacksonian Monetary Policy," 482.
42. "New York Banks," *New York Times*, May 12, 1837.
43. Diary of Philip Hone, May 8, 1837, 13:22, BV Hone, Philip, MS 1549, MCNYHS.
44. "From the N. Y. *Commercial Advertiser* of Wednesday Evening, May 10, Suspension of Specie Payments," *Portsmouth Journal of Literature and Politics* (Portsmouth, NH), May 13, 1837; Diary of Philip Hone, May 10, 1837, 13:28, BV Hone, Philip, MS 1549, MCNYHS; and "The Winding Up of the Crisis – General Suspension of Specie Payments by the Banks in New York," *NYH*, May 10, 1837. For the application to the legislature and the New York laws regarding banking, see Albert Gallatin to William L. Marcy, May 10, 1837, fol. 1837, BV Stevens, John Austin, MS 2456, MCNYHS; and Oberg, "New York State and the 'Specie Crisis' of 1837."
45. National Bank in the City of New York Minutes on the Specie Crisis of 1837, May 9–19, 1837, Supplement, reel 4, Albert Gallatin Papers, MS 238, MCNYHS.
46. "Suspension of Specie Payments by the Banks," *NYH*, May 9, 1837.
47. Ibid.
48. Diary of Philip Hone, May 8, 1837, 13:22, BV Hone, Philip, MS 1549, MCNYHS.
49. "Suspension of Specie Payments by the Banks," *NYH*, May 9, 1837. Bennett made this argument through an extended analogy to the murder case of the prostitute Helen Jewett. Bennett found financial success in reporting on Jewett's murder. For more on the murder of Helen Jewett, see Cohen, *Murder of Helen Jewett*. For more on the *Herald*'s sensationalism as an economic strategy, see Andie Tucher, *Froth & Scum: Truth, Beauty, and the Ax Murder in America's First Mass Medium* (Chapel Hill: University of North Carolina Press, 1994).
50. JLSJ to NMRS, May 8, 1837, XI/38/15, RAL.
51. "Liverpool Packets," *New-York Spectator*, May 1, 1837; and "Cleared," *NYH*, May 8, 1837. The newspapers transported by the *Roscoe* reported on the failure of the Dry Dock Bank and were dated May 8, 1837, so they must have been afternoon papers. This is corroborated by a letter from Aaron H. Palmer dated May 8, 10 A.M., which suggests that the Dry Dock Bank's suspension was "apprehended" but not yet confirmed. *Caledonian Mercury* (Edinburgh), June 1, 1837; and Aaron H. Palmer to NMRS, May 8, 1837, XI/38/199, RAL.
52. In 1830, the captain, Joseph C. Delano, had made the westbound voyage in sixteen days; this record held until 1846. Albion, *Square-Riggers on Schedule*, 163, 278–79, 334. For the *Roscoe* as the source of the news, see "The Latest Intelligence," *Derby Mercury* (Derby, England), May 31, 1837; "Money Market and City News," *Morning Chronicle* (London), May 31, 1837; and NMRS to Prime, Ward & King, May 31, 1837, American Letter Book, II/10/1, RAL.

53. *Caledonian Mercury* (Edinburgh), June 1, 1837; and "The Latest Intelligence," *Derby Mercury* (Derby, England), May 31, 1837.
54. "Money-Market and City Intelligence," *Times* (London), June 2, 1837.
55. Minutes, May 30, 1837, C5/282, BOEA; and Minutes, May 30, 1837, G4/60, BOEA.
56. "Money-Market and City Intelligence," *Times* (London), June 2, 1837; Minutes, May 30, 1837, May 31, 1837, C5/282, BOEA; and Minutes, May 30, 1837, May 31, 1837, G4/60, BOEA.
57. "Money-Market and City Intelligence," *Times* (London), June 1, 1837.
58. "Money-Market and City Intelligence," *Times* (London), June 2, 1837.
59. Hottinguer & Co. to Baring Brothers, June 1, 1837, HC7.1.78, BA.
60. "Money-Market and City Intelligence," *Times* (London), June 2, 1837.
61. Ibid.
62. Minutes, June 1, 1837, C5/282, BOEA; and Minutes, June 1, 1837, G4/60, BOEA.
63. "Money-Market and City Intelligence," *Times* (London), June 2, 1837.
64. Minutes, June 1, 1837, C5/282, BOEA; and Minutes, June 1, 1837, G4/60, BOEA.
65. Minutes, June 1, 1837, C5/282, BOEA; Minutes, June 1, 1837, G4/60, BOEA; and "Money-Market and City Intelligence," *Times* (London), June 3, 1837.
66. "Money-Market and City Intelligence," *Times* (London), June 3, 1837.
67. "Money Market," *Globe and Traveller* (London), June 3, 1837.
68. Eight merchant banking houses failed by June 6, 1837. NMRS to J. I. Cohen & Son, June 6, 1837, II/10/1, RAL.
69. "Money-Market and City Intelligence," *Times* (London), June 3, 1837.
70. "Money-Market and City Intelligence," *Times* (London), June 5, 1837.
71. Ibid.
72. Minutes, June 1, 1837, C5/282, BOEA; Minutes, June 1, 1837, G4/60, BOEA; and diary of Joshua Bates, June 18, 1837, DEP 74, vol. 3, BA. For a transcript of the letter to the BOE along with a great deal of other internal correspondence, see Series I, Brown Brothers Harriman Records, MS 78, MCNYHS. For the influence of these events on the firm, see Perkins, *Financing Anglo-American Trade*, 37–39, 99–101, 118–24, 143–44.
73. John Crosby Brown, *A Hundred Years of Merchant Baking: A History of Brown Brothers and Company, Brown, Shipley & Company, and the Allied Firms* (New York, 1909), 85–86.
74. John Very to his niece, Oct. 5, 1901, quoted in Brown, *A Hundred Years*, 88.
75. Diary of Joshua Bates, June 8, 1837, DEP 74, vol. 3, BA.
76. The biggest windfall for Barings was increased market share. For more on Barings' profit from the panic, see Austin, "Baring Brothers," 306–35.
77. Morrison Cryder to Alsop, June 9, 1837, quoted in Austin, "Baring Brothers," 306.
78. *Globe and Traveller* (London), June 5, 1837. For the public statement of the Ws' affairs, see "Money-Market and City Intelligence," *Times* (London), June 6, 1837.
79. "Money-Market and City Intelligence," *Times* (London), June 7, 1837.
80. The London *Times* correctly predicted that the idea that the BOE ought to "bolster up" financial institutions was "an idea only just started, but they may

be assured that it will be a long time before they hear the last of it." "Money-Market and City Intelligence," *Times* (London), June 6, 1837. For accusations and outcomes, see Austin, "Baring Brothers," 317–18; Peter Evans Austin, *Baring Brothers and the Birth of Modern Finance* (London: Pickering & Chatto, 2007), 181–90; and Clapham, *Bank of England*, 177–85.

81. Diary of Joshua Bates, June 24, 1837, DEP 74, vol. 3, BA.

82. "Money Market," *Globe and Traveller* (London), June 5, 1837.

83. "Money-Market and City Intelligence," *Times* (London), June 5, 1837.

84. "From the N. Y. *Commercial Advertiser* of Wednesday Evening, May 10. Suspension of Specie Payments," *Portsmouth Journal of Literature and Politics* (Portsmouth, NH), May 13, 1837.

85. Diary of Philip Hone, May 10, 1837, 13:35, BV Hone, Philip, MS 1549, MCNYHS.

86. For more on issues surrounding small denomination currency, see Thomas J. Sargent and François R. Velde, *The Big Problem of Small Change* (Princeton, NJ: Princeton University Press, 2002), 3–14; Roland P. Falkner, "The Private Issue of Token Coins," *Political Science Quarterly* 16, no. 2 (June 1901): 303–27; and Seth Rockman, *Scraping By: Wage Labor, Slavery, and Survival in Early Baltimore* (Baltimore, MD: Johns Hopkins University Press, 2009), 174. Some later hard-times tokens included a postage stamp encased in glass within the coin to provide a standard of value. John Hewlett, a private collector, has shown the author an example of this.

87. "To the Female Public," *NYH*, May 16, 1837.

88. Diary of Philip Hone, May 10, 1837, 13:35, BV Hone, Philip, MS 1549, MCNYHS.

89. "Suspension of Specie Payments," *New-York Spectator*, May 11, 1837.

90. Diary of Philip Hone, May 10, 1837, 13:34, BV Hone, Philip, MS 1549, MCNYHS.

91. Moses Taylor to J. W. Welsh, May 9, 1837, Moses Taylor outgoing letter-book, vol. 2, series 1, MTP.

92. Moses Taylor to A. Morales & Co., May 12, 1837, Moses Taylor outgoing letterbook, vol. 2, series 1, MTP.

93. For continued decline in cotton prices, see "Four Days Later," *NYH*, May 10, 1837.

94. *Farmer's Cabinet* (Amherst, NH), May 19, 1837.

95. "Suspension in New-York from the *New York Journal of Commerce*," *Farmer's Cabinet* (Amherst, NH), May 19, 1837.

96. "From the N.Y. *Evening Post* of May 10," *Washington Globe*, May 12, 1837.

97. "From the N.Y. *Evening Post*, 2 o'clock P.M.," *New-Hampshire Patriot and State Gazette* (Concord), May 15, 1837.

98. "The Crisis, 'Laissez nous faire,'" *Plaindealer* (New York), May 13, 1837.

99. "From the New York *Commercial Advertiser*," *Salem Gazette* (Salem, MA), May 13, 1837.

100. "The Winding Up of the Crisis – General Suspension of Specie Payments by the Banks in New York," *NYH*, May 10, 1837.

101. For stock prices, see "From the N.Y. *Evening Post*, 2 o'clock P.M.," *New-Hampshire Patriot and State Gazette* (Concord), May 15, 1837.

102. Moses Taylor to Andrew Castillo, May 17, 1837, Moses Taylor outgoing letterbook, vol. 2, series 1, MTP.
103. Diary of Philip Hone, May 10, 1837, vol. 13:36, BV Hone, Philip, MS 1549, MCNYHS.
104. Diary of Philip Hone, May 11, 1837, vol. 13:37, BV Hone, Philip, MS 1549, MCNYHS. For a history of medical language applied to economic events, see Daniele Besomi, "Crises as a Disease of the Body Politick. A Metaphor in the History of Nineteenth-Century Economics," *Journal of the History of Economic Thought* 33, no. 1 (Mar. 2011): 67–118.
105. Moses Taylor to Drake & Coit, June 19, 1837, Moses Taylor outgoing letterbook, vol. 2, series 1, MTP.
106. Moses Taylor to R. Groning & Co., July 8, 1837, Moses Taylor outgoing letterbook, vol. 2, series 1, MTP.
107. T. E. Throop to Martin Van Buren, May 10, 1837, reel 23, MVBLOC; and "Suspension of Specie Payments," *Farmer's Cabinet* (Amherst, NH), May 19, 1837.
108. "Bank Suspension," *Farmer's Cabinet* (Amherst, NH), May 19, 1837. For a detailed analysis of the spread of the news of the New York suspensions, see Pred, *Urban Growth*, 246–55.
109. Pred discovered the multiple origins of the suspension. Pred, *Urban Growth*, 249, 254.
110. Andrew Jackson to Martin Van Buren, June 6, 1837, reel 23, MVBLOC.
111. *NI3*, May 16, 1837 (emphasis in original).
112. Examiner [pseud.], *The Causes of the Present Crisis Shown by an Examiner* (Philadelphia, 1837), 23.
113. A Citizen of New-York [pseud.], *Seventeen Numbers, Under the Signature of Neckar, Upon the Causes of the Present Distress of the Country with a Proposed Remedy* (New York, 1837), 31.
114. Adams, *Further Reflections*, 4.
115. Ibid., 5.
116. *Auto-Biography of Sam Simple, Giving an Account of the Administration of the Affairs of the Simple Family from the Year 1829 to 1837, by His Aunt Deborah Crabstick, Together with a History of Some New and Important Experiments in Government Never before Tried; Being a Method of Reducing It to a "Simple Machine," with an Account of the Success Which Attended This Notable and Patriotic Undertaking: A Political Allegory* (Boston, 1837), 29.
117. Junius [pseud.], *"The Vision of Judgment; or, A Present for the Whigs of '76 & '37: In Ten Parts"* (New York: H.R. Robinson, 1838), 7–8, 31 (emphasis in original).
118. Old Fashioned Man, *Pressure and Its Causes*, 14, 5, 54, 17, 52 (emphasis in original).
119. Citizen of Massachusetts, *The Times*, 9, 10, 13.
120. M. Van Schaick to Martin Van Buren, May 12, 1837, reel 23, MVBLOC.
121. *House Journal*, 25th Cong., 1st sess., Sept. 4, 1837, 3.
122. "Great Meeting of Citizens," *New-York Spectator*, May 11, 1837.
123. Andrew Jackson to Martin Van Buren, June 6, 1837, reel 23, MVBLOC. For the reasons behind Van Buren's proclamation calling Congress, see

John Niven, *Martin Van Buren: The Romantic Age of American Politics* (New York: Oxford University Press, 1983), 415–16.

124. Pacificus [pseud.], *What Will Congress Do?* (Philadelphia, 1837); *A Practical Plan for a National and State Currency* (New York, 1837); *The Outline for a Plan for Regulating Domestic Exchanges: A Remedy for Our Sufferings and a Few Allusions to a General Banking Law* (1837); and *The Remedy* (1837). Van Buren faced both a Whig opposition united in advocacy of the BUS and a Democratic party divided between advocates of state banks and of hard money. Cole argues that the president sought a policy that would unify his party and sought advice from both factions. McFaul argues that the suspension of specie payments made Van Buren's proposal for an Independent Treasury "inevitable." Cole, *Martin Van Buren*, 298–301; and McFaul, *The Politics of Jacksonian Finance*, 216.

125. Hannah Farnham Sawyer Lee, *Rich Enough: A Tale of the Times* (Boston: Whipple and Damrell, 1837), 63, 70.

126. Ibid., 69. Besomi identifies references to cobwebs in the writings of several English political economists in the 1810s and 1820s. Cobweb metaphors for these writers suggested the interconnected fluctuations of prices. In contrast, Lee's metaphor of the spider's web illustrated how mercantile networks trapped innocent individuals. Although it is possible that Lee read these texts, she does not write about the subjects of Besomi's authors (supply, demand, prices, and cycles of crises). Daniele Besomi, "John Wade's Early Endogenous Dynamic Model: 'Commercial Cycle' and Theories of Crises," *European Journal of Economic Thought* 15, no. 4 (Dec. 2008): 611–39; and Daniele Besomi, "The Periodicity of Crises: A Survey of the Literature Before 1850," *Journal of the History of Economic Thought* 31, no. 1 (Mar. 2010): 112–19.

127. Lee, *Rich Enough*, 70–71, 63, 72.

128. Francis Wayland, *Elements of Political Economy*, 2nd ed. (New York: Robinson and Franklin, 1838), 212.

129. Wayland, *Elements of Political Economy: Abridged* (1837), iv, 172, 176.

130. Francis Wayland, *The Moral Law of Accumulation: The Substance of Two Discourses, Delivered in the First Baptist Meeting House, Providence, May 14, 1837* (Providence, RI: John E. Brown, 1837), 14. Two decades may have seemed too soon for Wayland, who had "occasion" to preach about financial crisis again in 1857. In these later sermons, he reiterated the argument he had added to the 1838 edition of his textbook: "The want of confidence has generated a panic, and fear has naturally impaired that confidence unreasonably." Again, he looked for something broader than individual action as he wrote, "I do not know that any men, or any class of men, have been particularly to blame." This change in his economic thinking was a product of the panic in 1837. Francis Wayland, *"Thoughts on the Present Distress: Two Sermons Preached in the First Baptist Church, Providence, on the 11th and 25th of October, 1857"* (Providence, RI: George H. Whitney, 1857), 5.

131. Wayland, *Moral Law of Accumulation*, 5–6, 8.

132. Ibid., 16, 21, 13, 27–28, 8, 28.

133. Ibid., 28.

134. Wilentz, *Rise of American Democracy*, 439.
135. William M. Gouge, *An Inquiry into the Expediency of Dispensing with Bank Agency and Bank Paper in the Fiscal Concerns of the United States* (Philadelphia, 1837), 16, 17, 18, 20, 18.
136. Gouge, *Inquiry*, 22, 30, 25.
137. Martin Van Buren, "Special Session Message: September 4, 1837," *The American Presidency Project* [online], ed. John T. Woolley and Gerhard Peters, http://www.presidency.ucsb.edu/ws/?pid=67234.
138. Ibid.
139. Ibid.
140. Memorials from citizens and speeches made by politicians in Congress were printed in the Senate and House Journals and in newspapers. These texts as well as letters to newspapers, all of which contained partisan accounts of events in 1837, were often reprinted as pamphlets. Examples include John Sergeant, *Speech of the Hon. Mr. Sergeant, of Pennsylvania, on the Resolution Reported from the Committee of Ways and Means, Declaring it Inexpedient to Charter a National Bank, Delivered in the House of Representatives, September 26, 1837, and During the Morning Hour of Two Other Days* (Washington, 1837); and Francis O. J. Smith, *Letters from Mr. Smith, Member of Congress from Maine, in Vindication of His Vote against the Sub-Treasury Bill* (Portland, 1837).
141. Howe, *What Hath God Wrought*, 507, 591; Hammond, *Banks and Politics in America*, 542–45; and Cole, *Martin Van Buren*, 359.
142. Although the textbooks of the 1840s and 1850s sided with one political side or another, later textbooks complained that government intervention in the economy was the cause of America's booms and busts. For examples of the partisan perspective, see Charles A. Goodrich, *A History of the United States of America* (Boston: Jenks & Palmer, 1843), 364–69; Emma Willard, *History of the United States, or, Republic of America* (New York: A. S. Barnes, 1845), 388–91; and J. Olney, *A History of the United States: For the Use of Schools and Academies* (New Haven, CT: Durrie & Peck, 1851), 257–59. For examples of the *laissez-faire* perspective, see Samuel G. Goodrich, *The American Child's Pictorial History of the United States, Illustrated by Sixty Engravings* (Philadelphia: J. H. Butler, 1879), 207; and John William Burgess, *The Middle Period, 1817–1858* (New York: Scribner, 1897), 284.
143. T. E. Throop to Martin Van Buren, May 10, 1837, reel 23, MVBLOC.
144. Diary of Philip Hone, May 10, 1837, 13:35, BV Hone, Philip, MS 1549, MCNYHS.
145. "Money Market," *Globe and Traveller* (London), June 12, 1837.
146. "Money Market," *Globe and Traveller* (London), June 14, 1837.
147. "The Crisis in America," *Globe and Traveller* (London), June 13, 1837.
148. "Money-Market and City Intelligence," *Times* (London), June 7, 1837.
149. NMRS to J. I. Cohen Jr. & Brother, June 22, 1837, II/10/1, RAL.
150. *Times* (London), June 23, 1837.
151. The periodization of British history around the reigns of monarchs may explain why the events in the spring of 1837 receive little attention in the

scholarship on nineteenth-century Britain. The Victorian Era began just as the panic in 1837 ended.

152. Diary of Joshua Bates, July 1, 1837, DEP 74, vol. 3, BA.

153. *Times* (London), June 27, 1837.

154. *Times* (London), June 3, 1837.

155. The enormous paper trail of the BOE's law firm for the three W cases remains in the Freshfields Collection at the BOEA. For an example, see "Inland Revenue," May 12, 1881, F12/8, BOEA.

156. "Money-Market and City Intelligence," *Times* (London), June 5, 1837.

157. "Money-Market and City Intelligence," *Times* (London), June 3, 1837.

158. For evidence of the international reach of Wildes's failure, see "Balances 30 April 1837," C5/238, BOEA.

159. T. W. Ward to J. A. Stevens, July 27, 1837, fol. 1837, BV Stevens, John Austin, MS 2456, MCNYHS.

160. For the depiction of a bankruptcy practice and the benefits of the 1841 Bankruptcy Act to the legal profession, see Balleisen, *Navigating Failure,* 1–2, 137–46.

161. *NYH*, May 10, 1837.

162. For more on state bankruptcy laws, see Peter Coleman, *Debtors and Creditors in America: Insolvency, Imprisonment for Debt, and Bankruptcy, 1607–1900* (Madison: University of Wisconsin Press, 1974).

163. For the politics of passing and repealing this law, see Balleisen, *Navigating Failure,* 101–8, 119–24.

164. "Schedule B," Joseph Lazarus Joseph case file, NARA. For Joseph's wife's name, see *Articles, &c. of the New Brighton Association* (New York, 1836).

165. Diary of Philip Hone, Apr. 10, 1837, 12:461, BV Hone, Philip, MS 1549, MCNYHS.

166. Petition of Robert M. K. Strong, Esq., Joseph Lazarus Joseph case file, NARA.

167. Sandage, *Born Losers,* 101.

168. I have not been able to locate any additional sources on the three partners of J. L. & S. Joseph & Co. Neither of the Joseph brothers nor their third partner, Moses Henriques, appears in the Dunn and Bradstreet records at Baker Library, Harvard University.

169. For the creation of the Commercial Court, see Richard Holcombe Kilbourne Jr., *Louisiana Commercial Law: The Antebellum Period* (Baton Rouge: Paul M. Herbert Law Center Louisiana State University, 1980), 84–90.

170. For sources on the negotiations of the BOE in New Orleans, see C5/260, BOEA.

171. Minutes, Feb. 3, 1836, Citizens' Bank Minute Book, vol. 1, CBLARC; Minutes, July 3, 1837, Citizens' Bank Minute Book, vol. 2, CBLARC; and Citizens' Bank of Louisiana Bond Certificate, fol. 4, CBLARC.

172. *Boidore vs. Citizens' Bank,* 9 La. 506, docket no. 2956 (May 1836) Orleans Parish, UNO. In this case, two free men of color sued the Citizens' Bank of Louisiana for failing to pay them their dividends. Under its 1835 charter, the Citizens' Bank had to limit shareholders to "free white citizens of the United States & domiciled in the state of Louisiana" to receive the "faith of the state" as security for their bonds. The flooding after Hurricane Katrina damaged the

papers of the CBLARC, but papers relating to the chartering process are housed in this case file.

173. "Agreeable News," Apr. 7, 1837, *New Orleans Bee*.

174. Minutes, May 22, 1837, Citizens' Bank Minute Book, vol. 2, CBLARC.

175. "Documents Relative to the Banks of Louisiana. Published by Order of the Legislature of Louisiana" (New Orleans, n.d.), LARC.

176. Minutes, May 14, 1837, Citizens' Bank Minute Book, vol. 2, CBLARC.

177. Minutes, May 20, 1837, Citizens' Bank Minute Book, vol. 2, CBLARC. After the Citizens' Bank suspended specie payments, the directors repealed the motion to print small denomination bills for the first municipality. Minutes, June 15, 1837, Citizens' Bank Minute Book, vol. 2, CBLARC.

178. Minutes, June 6, 1837, Citizens' Bank Minute Book, vol. 2, CBLARC.

179. Minutes, June 12, 1837, Citizens' Bank Minute Book, vol. 2, CBLARC.

180. For several of the key decisions surrounding the suspension of specie payments, directors read their reasons for their votes into the minutes. This suggests a great deal of disagreement among the board. Minutes, June 22, 1837, Citizens' Bank Minute Book, vol. 2, CBLARC.

181. Minutes, May 23 1837, Citizens' Bank Minute Book, vol. 2, CBLARC.

182. Minutes, July 3, 1837, Sept. 21, 1837, Nov. 27, 1837, Citizens' Bank Minute Book, vol. 2, CBLARC; Minutes, Mar. 2, 1837, C5/282, BOEA; and Minutes, Mar. 2, 1837, M5/472, BOEA. F. de Lizardi & Co. would eventually sue Thomas Wilson & Co. to reclaim the Citizens' Bank funds. As the BOE had assumed control over Wilson's assets, Lizardi and the BOE battled for almost a decade over this money. F17/13, BOEA.

183. Minutes, May 24, 1837, Citizens' Bank Minute Book, vol. 2, CBLARC.

184. Minutes, May 27, 1837, Citizens' Bank Minute Book, vol. 2, CBLARC.

185. Minutes, June 29, 1837, Citizens' Bank Minute Book, vol. 2, CBLARC.

186. Neu, "Edmond J. Forstall," 194.

187. *Condition of the State Banks*, 26th Cong., 2d sess., 1841, H. R. Doc. 111, serial 385, vol. 4, 786.

188. Ibid., 789. This is a reprinted letter that originally appears in Minutes, Sept. 5, 1838, Citizens' Bank Minute Book, vol. 2, CBLARC.

189. Ibid., 787, 786.

190. Ibid., 788.

191. "Letter to the Editor," *New Orleans Bee*, June 27, 1837 (emphasis in original). Transcribed and graciously provided to the author by Jan Bradford of the Hermann-Grima Historic House.

192. Korn, *Early Jews of New Orleans*, 118. Korn notes that Hermann's will is nowhere to be found. Perhaps he did not own enough property to necessitate a will on his death.

193. Dufour, *Women Who Cared*, 36; and Korn, *Early Jews of New Orleans*, 118.

194. For an example, see "Remise de Billet," Grima, Felix. V. 15, Act 236, March 14, 1837, NONA.

195. Evidence of Lucien's large notarial practice is preserved at NONA. After their parents died in the early 1850s, Lucien and Samuel Hermann Jr. moved to California to risk their fortunes in the gold rush. In an interview with Jan Bradford of the Hermann-Grima Historic House, I learned of a letter

describing the San Francisco firm: Stockton Strawbridge to Jane Strawbridge Ledyard, Jan. 21, 1855, http://users.erols.com/aswhite/Stockton Strawbridge to Jane Ledyard.html. The fortunes of the family are also summarized in Korn, *Early Jews of New Orleans*, 118–19.

196. Neu, "Edmond J. Forstall," 193–99; and Reginald C. McGrane, *Foreign Bondholders and American State Debts* (New York: Macmillan, 1935), 185–92.

197. Edmond J. Forstall to Baring Brothers & Co., Jan. 12, 1848, HC5.7.6, BA.

198. Edmond J. Forstall to Baring Brothers & Co., Apr. 21, 1848, HC5.7.6.47, BA.

199. Edmond J. Forstall to Baring Brothers & Co., Oct. 11, 1849, HC5.7.6.97, BA.

200. This agreement did not preclude Forstall from engaging in commercial agriculture. After an aunt left him her sugar plantation in 1845, Forstall earned a considerable income from this estate, which was operated by 130 slaves. Neu, "Edmond J. Forstall," 199; *American National Biography Online*, s.v. "Forstall, Edmond Jean," by Irene D. Neu, http://www.anb.org/articles/10/10-02148.html.

201. *Condition of the State Banks*, 26th Cong., 2d sess., 1841, H. R. Doc. 111, serial 385, vol. 4, 788.

202. The New York banks were required to resume in May 1838. Thus, these powerful bankers pushed for an early resumption of specie payments, whereas the BUS and other institutions sought a slower process to fulfill cotton speculations. McGrane, *Panic of 1837*, 183–208; and Hammond, *Banks and Politics*, 467–90.

203. Economists disagree about whether change in the bond market originated in Britain or America. Temin, *Jacksonian Economy*, 148–55; and Namsuk Kim and John Joseph Wallis, "The Market for American State Government Bonds in Britain and the United States, 1830–43," *Economic History Review* 58, no. 4 (2005): 736–64. For case studies of internal improvement projects in particular states, see Larson, *Internal Improvement*, 195–224. For banks as cotton factors, see Kilbourne, *Slave Agriculture and Financial Markets*, 84–95; and Green, *Finance and Economic Development*, 95–96.

204. Thomas P. Bancroft to F. C. Lowell, Dec. 30, 1837, letter written on blank side of *New-Orleans Wholesale Prices Current*, Dec. 30, 1837, AAS.

205. Austin, "Baring Brothers," 309; Austin, *Baring Brothers* (2007), 175; and Temin, *Jacksonian Economy*, table 3.2, 148–53.

206. Thomas P. Bancroft to F. C. Lowell, Dec. 15, 1838, letter written on blank side of *New-Orleans Wholesale Prices Current*, Dec. 15, 1838, AAS.

207. Temin, *Jacksonian Economy*, 152–55. Jenks provides a more global context to the shifting economic conditions of 1839. Jenks, *Migration of British Capital*, 95–96.

208. Larson, *Internal Improvement*, 195–224.

209. McGrane, *Foreign Bondholders*, 265–69. In early 1839, the city of Mobile, Alabama, also failed to make interest payments on its loans, earning it the distinction of being America's first municipal default. Harriet E. Amos, *Cotton City: Urban Development in Antebellum Mobile* (Tuscaloosa: University of Alabama Press, 1985), 124.

210. Kim and Wallis, "Market for American State Government Bonds," 741–45, 755–56; Austin, *Baring Brothers* (2007), 177–80; and Temin, *Jacksonian*

Economy, 153–55. For the significance of the Crisis of 1839, see John Joseph Wallis, "What Caused the Crisis of 1839?" (Apr. 2001), NBER Working Paper No. H0133, http://ssrn.com/abstract=267421. For a comparison of 1839–43 with 1929–33, see Temin, *Jacksonian Economy*, 155–164.

211. W. H. Chaloner traces the mythology of this phrase to free trade advocates in the early 1900s. He finds that the whole decade may not have been "hungry," but that real economic hardship existed for the working class from 1838 to 1842. W. H. Chaloner, "The Hungry Forties" in *Industry and Innovation: Selected Essays of W. H. Chaloner*, ed. D. A. Farnie and W. O. Henderson (London: Frank Cass, 1990), 232–42. For the politicization of hunger in the 1840s, see Peter J. Gurney, "'Rejoicing in Potatoes': The Politics of Consumption in England during the 'Hungry Forties,'" *Past & Present* 203, no. 1 (May 2009): 99–136.

212. Temin, *Jacksonian Economy*, 155–65. Havens also compared 1837–43 with the Great Depression. He discovered that the policies proposed in the 1830s and 1840s were more limited than those proposed in the 1930s because they "had to be based upon contemporary economic analyses of depressions." R. Murray Havens, "Reactions of the Federal Government to the 1837–1843 Depression," *Southern Economic Journal* 8, no. 3 (Jan. 1942): 389. The limitations of the "contemporary economic analyses" that Havens outlines not only influenced the policies of the time but also determined the types of data available to later researchers.

213. The average height of Ohio National Guardsmen did not return to pre-1837 levels until the 1920s, and the Great Depression did not create a trough in stature. Although a quantitative measure, stature is not ordinarily considered by economic historians in evaluating the severity of depressions, but it might offer a different comparison for historical events than the calculations of economic growth. Richard H. Steckel, "Stature and the Standard of Living," *Journal of Economic Literature* 33, no. 4 (Dec. 1995): 1921, figure 2.

214. Writing from the midst of the Great Depression, Samuel Rezneck found parallels in the late 1830s and early 1840s. Samuel Rezneck, "The Social History of an American Depression, 1837–1843," *American Historical Review* 40, no. 4 (July 1935): 662–87.

215. Ralph Waldo Emerson, "The American Scholar," in *The Portable Emerson*, ed. Carl Bode in collaboration with Malcolm Cowley, new ed. (New York: Penguin, 1981), 59, 55.

216. Edward L. Widmer, *Young America: The Flowering of Democracy in New York City* (Oxford, UK: Oxford University Press, 1999), 3–26; Sánchez, *Reforming the World*, 28–34; Mihm, *Nation of Counterfeiters*, 181; and Howe, *What Hath God Wrought*, 318. Although Benjamin's biographer argued that "the panic of 1837 caused fourteen banks to fail and paralyzed business, thus setting him back in his practice," the court records suggest that business was booming for the litigator, especially when he served as counsel for men associated with the Hermann family. Eli N. Evans, *Judah P. Benjamin: The Jewish Confederate* (New York: The Free Press, 1988), 28. For examples of Benjamin's work in the late 1830s, see *Wells & Co. vs.*

Hermann, Briggs & Co. and A. M. Nathan, suit record, docket no. 284, Louisiana Commercial Court (Orleans Parish), NOCA.

217. John L. O'Sullivan, quoted in Widmer, *Young America,* 3.
218. Abraham Lincoln, "Address Before the Young Men's Lyceum of Springfield, Illinois, January 27, 1838," *The Collected Works of Abraham Lincoln* (New Brunswick, NJ: Rutgers University Press, 1953–55), 1:115.
219. Goodrich, *A History of the United States of America* (1843), 362.
220. Ibid., 365, 366.
221. Olney, *History of the United States,* 257; and Samuel G. Goodrich, *A Pictorial History of the United States: With Notices of Other Portions of America North and South, a New Edition, with Numerous Developments* (Philadelphia: E. H. Butler, 1865), 488.
222. William Swinton, *A Condensed School History of the United States, Constructed for Definite Results in Recitation, and Containing a New Method of Topical Reviews* (New York: Ivison, Blakeman, Taylor, 1871), 189.
223. Henry Clews, *Twenty-Eight Years in Wall Street* (New York: Irving, 1888), 179.

Epilogue

1. The following paragraphs are based on a survey of seventeen textbooks published between 2009 and 2012.
2. David Goldfield et al., *The American Journey: A History of the United States,* 6th ed. (Upper Saddle River, NJ: Prentice Hall, 2011), 274. For a late 1836 start date, see also David M. Kennedy, Lizabeth Cohen, and Thomas A. Bailey, *The American Pageant: A History of the American People,* 14th ed., vol. 1, *To 1877* (Boston: Wadsworth, Cengage Learning, 2010), 245. For a May start date, see Mark C. Carnes and John A. Garraty, *The American Nation: A History of the United States,* 14th ed. (Upper Saddle River, NJ: Prentice Hall, 2012), 260. Many textbooks fall somewhere between these two dates. For examples, see James Oakes et al., *Of the People: A History of the United States* (New York: Oxford University Press, 2010), 437; James L. Roark et al., *The American Promise: A History of the United States,* 5th ed., vol. 1, *To 1877* (Boston: Bedford/St. Martin's, 2012), 350; John M. Murrin et al., *Liberty, Equality, Power: A History of the American People,* 6th ed., vol. 1, *To 1877* (Boston: Wadsworth, Cengage Learning, 2012), 407–8; Alan Brinkley, *The Unfinished Nation: A Concise History of the American People,* 6th ed. (New York: McGraw-Hill, 2010), 230; Mary Beth Norton et al., *A People & A Nation: A History of the United States,* 9th ed., advantage ed., vol. 1, *To 1877* (Boston: Wadsworth, Cengage Learning, 2012), 354; Carol Berkin et al., *Making America: A History of the United States,* 6th ed., vol. 1, *To 1877* (Boston: Wadsworth, Cengage Learning, 2012), 309; James West Davidson et al., *Experience History: Interpreting America's Past* (New York: McGraw-Hill, 2011), 297; and Steven M. Gillon and Cathy D. Matson, *The American Experiment: A History of the United States,* 3rd ed., vol. 1, *To 1877* (Boston: Houghton Mifflin Harcourt, 2009), 372.

3. Robert A. Divine et al., *The American Story*, 4th ed., vol. 1, *To 1877* (Upper Saddle River, NJ: Longman, 2011), 261.

4. Paul S. Boyer, *The Enduring Vision: A History of the American People*, 7th ed., Cengage Advantage ed. (Boston: Wadsworth, Cengage Learning, 2011), 299 (emphasis removed).

5. Roark et al., *American Promise*, 351.

6. Berkin et al., *Making America*, 309.

7. John Mack Faragher et al., *Out of Many: A History of the American People*, brief 6th ed. (Upper Saddle River, NJ: Prentice Hall, 2012), 271.

8. Berkin et al., *Making America*, 309; and Brinkley, *Unfinished Nation*, 230.

9. Murrin et al., *Liberty, Equality, Power*, 407; James A. Henretta, Rebecca Edwards, and Robert O. Self, *America's History*, 7th ed., vol. 1, *To 1877* (Boston: Bedford/St. Martin's, 2011), 324; and Edward L. Ayers et al., *American Passages*, brief 4th ed., vol. 1, *To 1877* (Boston: Wadsworth, Cengage Learning, 2012), 237.

10. Kennedy, Cohen, and Bailey, *American Pageant*, 244–45; Eric Foner, *Give Me Liberty! An American History*, Seagull 3rd ed., vol. 1, *To 1877* (New York: W. W. Norton, 2012), 387; Oakes et al., *Of the People*, 437; Divine et al., *American Story*, 260–61; Faragher et al., *Out of Many*, 271; Divine et al., *American Story*, 260–61; and Gillon and Matson, *American Experiment*, 371–72.

11. Goldfield et al., *American Journey* (2012), 274–75.

12. Davidson et al., *Experience History*, 272; and Carnes and Garraty, *American Nation*, 260. For an example of a text that tries to balance structural and cultural causation, see Roark et al., *American Promise*, 348–51.

13. For an explanation of the Palmer Rule, see Matthews, *Study in Trade-Cycle History*, 168. Although Palmer did not provide a date of publication for his pamphlet, Loyd dated his response "25th February, 1837." This suggests that Palmer's pamphlet was published during the first eight weeks of 1837. Samuel Jones Loyd [Lord Overstone], *Reflections Suggested by a Perusal of Mr. J. Horsley Palmer's Pamphlet on the Causes and Consequences of the Pressure on the Money Market* (London: Pelham Richardson, 1837), 3.

14. John Horsley Palmer, *The Causes and Consequences of the Pressure upon the Money-Market: With a Statement of the Action of the Bank of England from 1st October, 1833, to the 27th December, 1836* (London: P. Richardson, 1837), 42.

15. Loyd had been born above his father's London bank and spent most of his first four decades involved in the daily operations of finance. As a member of the Political Economy Club, he was the unusual banker who thought about finance in terms broader than the balancing of ledgers. *Oxford Dictionary of National Biography*, s.v. "Loyd, Samuel Jones, Baron Overstone (1796–1883)," by Michael Reed, http://www.oxforddnb.com/view/article/17115.

16. Loyd, *Reflections Suggested*, 44.

17. Harry E. Miller, "Earlier Theories of Crises and Cycles in the United States," *The Quarterly Journal of Economics* 38, no. 2 (1924): 309–11.

18. Besomi, "Periodicity of Crises," 85–132; and Daniele Besomi, "Graphical Representations of Overstone's Cycle of Trade," in *Classical Political Economy and Modern Theory: Essays in Honour of Heinz Kurz*, ed. Christian Gehrke et al. (London: Routledge, 2012), 289–312.

19. Kyun, *Equilibrium Business Cycle Theory*, 21–22; Miller, "Earlier Theories of Crises," 294; and Sandmo, *Economics Evolving*, 103. The emergence of graphical depictions of supply and demand curves dates between 1838 and 1890. Sandmo, *Economics Evolving*, 147–49, 217–20; and Thomas M. Humphrey, "Marshallian Cross Diagrams," in *Famous Figures and Diagrams in Economics*, ed. Mark Blaug and Peter Lloyd (Northampton, MA: Edward Elgar, 2010), 29–37.

20. "General glut" debates sought causality for depressions in oversupply or monetary factors but drew no conclusions about universal causes of panics. Harald Hagemann, introduction to *Business Cycle Theory*, 1:x. Mitchell provides a brief concordance of the most significant contributions. Wesley C. Mitchell, *Business Cycles: The Problem and Its Setting* (New York: National Bureau of Economic Research, 1927), 4, n. 2.

21. "The Times," *The Sun* (New York), reprinted in *Farmer's Cabinet* (Amherst, NH), May 12, 1837. For examples of explorations of past financial crises by American and English authors in the 1830s, see Gilbart, *History of Banking*; and Gouge, *A Short History of Paper-Money and Banking in the United States* (Philadelphia, 1833).

22. Engels, quoted in Simon Clarke, *Marx's Theory of Crisis* (London: St. Martin's Press, 1994), 79.

23. Karl Marx, "Ricardo's Denial of General Over-Production. Possibility of a Crisis Inherent in the Inner Contradictions of Commodity and Money," in *The Marx-Engels Reader*, 2nd ed., ed. Robert C. Tucker (New York: W. W. Norton, 1978), 443–44.

24. Clément Juglar, *Commercial Crises (1863/73)*, trans. Cécile Dangel-Hagnauer, *Research in the History of Economic Thought and Methodology* 28A (2010): 115–47. Until recently, Thom's heavily redacted translation has been the standard English translation. Clément Juglar, *Des Crises commerciales et de leur retour périodique en France, en Angleterre et aux États-Unis*, 2nd ed., trans. and ed. DeCourcy Wright Thom as *A Brief History of Panics and Their Periodic Occurrence in the United States* (1916; repr. New York: August M. Kelley, 1966). For a brief summary of the theories of Juglar, Mills, and Jevons, see Hagemann, *Business Cycle Theory*, 1:x–xiii, xv–xvi. For an evaluation of Juglar's theory of "recurring" cycles, see Daniele Besomi, "'Periodic Crises': Clément Juglar Between Theories of Crises and Theories of Business Cycles," *Research in the History of Economic Thought and Methodology* 28A (2010): 169–283.

25. John Mills, "On Credit Cycles," 1:88.

26. William Stanley Jevons, "Commercial Crises and Sun-Spots" (1884), in Hagemann, *Business Cycle Theory*, 1:177. Jevons read the paper to the British Association for the Advancement of Science in 1875; in 1878, he presented a revised version. Daniele Besomi, "'Hath Rain a Father?' Sunspots and the Periodicity of Panics: Jevons, His Critics, and an Omen from the Press," *Storia del Pensiero Economico* (2008): 169–79.

27. Members of the New-York Press, *'37 and '57: A Brief Popular Account of all the Financial Panics and Commercial Revulsions in the United States, from 1690 to 1857; with More Particular History of the Two Great Revulsions of 1837 and 1857* (New York, 1857), 1 (emphasis in original).

28. Members of the New-York Press, '*37 and* '*57*, ii.
29. Mary Poovey's study of the differentiation of the genres of economic writing during the nineteenth century argues that the rise of economic experts calmed British anxieties over panics after the people learned to disregard their skepticisms about political economy. Poovey, *Genres of the Credit Economy*, 219–283.
30. "Phenomena of the Pressure," *New York Times*, Oct. 7, 1857.
31. "The Panic: 1837 and 1857," *New York Times*, Oct. 15, 1857.
32. Samuel Hurd Walley, *The Financial Revulsion of 1857: An Address Delivered Before the American Statistical Association, at Boston, February 10, 1858* (Boston: American Statistical Association, 1858), 11. "Walley, Samuel Hurd, (1805–1877)" *Biographical Directory of the United States Congress, 1774–Present*, http://bioguide.congress.gov/scripts/biodisplay.pl?index=W000087
33. Goodrich, *Pictorial History of the United States*, 488.
34. Before the 1850s, textbooks described the financial crisis in the spring of 1837 under the heading of Van Buren's administration. In some cases, the description of the effects of the crisis appeared under the headings of the administrations of Harrison and Tyler as well as Van Buren. For examples, see Goodrich, *History of the United States of America* (1843), 364–69; Marcius Willson, *History of the United States* (New York: Caleb Bartlett, 1846), 339–40; Egbert Guernsey, *History of the United States of America*, 5th ed. (New York: Cady and Burgess, 1848), 406–12; and Salma Hale, *History of the United States, from Their First Settlement as Colonies, to the Close of Mr. Tyler's Administration, in 1845* (Cincinnati, OH: E. D. Truman, 1849), 305–7.
35. Swinton, *Condensed School History*, 189.
36. Goodrich, *American Child's Pictorial History*, 207.
37. Burgess, *Middle Period*, 284.
38. Walley, *Financial Revulsion of 1857*, 3.
39. Ann Fabian, "Speculation on Distress: The Popular Discourse of the Panics of 1837 and 1857," *Yale Journal of Criticism* 3, no. 1 (1989): 128. Historian Samuel Rezneck also explained this phenomenon, "the literature of depressions was not merely a byproduct of any incidental search for causes and remedies. It was in a real sense a part of the depression itself." Samuel Rezneck, *Business Depressions and Financial Panics: Essays in American Business and Economic History* (New York: Greenwood, 1968), 8.
40. The types of texts produced as a result of panic have varied over time and space. Poovey, *Genres of the Credit Economy*, 219–81; Sánchez, *Reforming the World*, 28–87; and Sandage, *Born Losers*, 22–98.
41. Jevons cites the work of John Allan Broun, "The Decennial Period of Magnetic Variations, and of Sun-Spot Frequency," *Nature* 16 (May 24, 1877): 62–64. Jevons, "Commercial Crises," 1:177–78.
42. Jevons, "Commercial Crises," 1:178, 182–83.
43. Contemporaries critiqued this aspect of Jevons's theory. Besomi, "Hath Rain a Father?" 170–72.
44. Jevons, "Commercial Crises," 1:182–83.
45. Burgess, *Middle Period*, 284. Margaret Schabas has argued that the economy was denaturalized in the nineteenth century based on her examination of

classical political economy theorists. Meanwhile, Ann Fabian has argued that economic texts written in other genres during the panics of 1837 and 1839 indicate the naturalization of capitalism. The different source base explains the conflicting findings of these two scholars. Schabas, *Natural Origins*, 142–58; and Fabian, "Speculation on Distress," 127–42.

46. For the rise of statistical knowledge in the nineteenth century, see Cohen, *A Calculating People*, 116–226; Theodore M. Porter, *The Rise of Statistical Thinking, 1820–1900* (Princeton, NJ: Princeton University Press, 1986); and Theodore M. Porter, *Trust in Numbers: The Pursuit of Objectivity in Science and Public Life* (Princeton, NJ: Princeton University Press, 1995). For numbers as facts in "market culture," see William M. Reddy, *The Rise of Market Culture: The Textile Trade and French Society, 1750–1900* (Cambridge, UK: Cambridge University Press, 1984), 12.

47. Mitchell, *Business Cycles*, 11.

48. Joseph A. Schumpeter, *Business Cycles: A Theoretical, Historical, and Statistical Analysis of the Capitalist Process* (New York: McGraw-Hill, 1939), 1:163 (emphasis in original).

49. Mitchell, *Business Cycles*, 2, 11, 381.

50. Ibid., 2.

51. Arthur F. Burns and Wesley C. Mitchell, *Measuring Business Cycles* (New York: National Bureau of Economic Research, 1946), 78–79. Recently, economists have expressed doubts about the reliability of historical data from the period prior to the Civil War. Calomiris and Gorton suggest that "data limitations prevent a detailed empirical analysis of the earliest panics." Calomiris and Gorton, "Origins of Banking Panics," 113. For the inaccuracy of the data in the 1830s, see Hugh Rockoff, "Monetary Statistics Before the National Banking Era," *Historical Statistics of the United States Millennial Edition Online* (2009). Milton Friedman also noted that the "specie estimates before 1873 are subject to large errors." Milton Friedman and Anna Jacobson Schwartz, *Monetary Statistics of the United States: Estimates, Sources, Methods* (New York: National Bureau of Economic Research, 1970), 210.

52. Mitchell, *Business Cycles*, ix.

53. Besomi argues that the lived experience of hard times changed during the late nineteenth century; longer periods of "depression" coincided with new theories that emphasized phases rather than turning points. Besomi, "Naming Crises," 75–78.

54. Mitchell, *Business Cycles*, ix. Historians of science debate the relationship between the fields of economics, engineering, and physics. Philip Mirowski, *More Heat Than Light: Economics as Social Physics; Physics as Nature's Economics* (New York: Cambridge University Press, 1989); Porter, *Trust in Numbers*, 48–72; and Schabas, *Natural Origins*, 156–58.

55. Thom, appendix to Juglar, *A Brief History of Panics* (1916), 180.

56. McGrane, *The Panic of 1837*, v.

57. Ibid., 1, 177, 235.

58. Jenks, *Migration of British Capital*, 1, 65, 85.

59. Matthews, *Study in Trade-Cycle History*, 1, v-vii, 202, 55–60.

60. Examples include John Kenneth Galbraith, Ben Bernanke, and Christina Romer.
61. John Kenneth Galbraith's *The Great Crash, 1929* and Murray N. Rothbard's *The Panic of 1819: Reactions and Policies* are exceptions. Even though the word "panic" appears in the title, Rothbard's research question asked whether "the crisis of 1818–9, and the depression until 1821" fit into the model of "modern business cycles as interpreted by Mitchell" (28). This suggests that the phrase "The Panic of 1819" referred to a several-year period rather than an acute crisis. John Kenneth Galbraith, *The Great Crash, 1929* (1954; New York: Houghton Mifflin, 1997); and Murray N. Rothbard, *The Panic of 1819: Reactions and Policies* (1962; Auburn, AL: Ludwig Von Mises Institute, 2007).
62. In the 1930s, social historians interested in questions of class studied non-financial panic. George Lefebvre, *The Great Fear of 1789: Rural Panic in Revolutionary France*, trans. Joan White (New York: Pantheon Books, 1973).
63. Samuel Rezneck, *Business Depressions*, 201. Scott Sandage offered an intellectual biography of Rezneck in his address "When Business Met Culture: 1837 in American History" presented at the 2007 Program in Early American Economy and Society at the Library Company of Philadelphia Annual Conference, "The Panic of 1837: Getting By and Going Under in a Decade of Crisis." For another depression-inspired historical analysis of 1837, see Havens, "Reactions of the Federal Government," 380–90.
64. Samuel Rezneck, *Business Depressions*, 201. Charles P. Kindleberger confirmed Rezneck's conclusion, citing the many books on business cycles written in the 1930s and the relative lack of books that appeared in the postwar period "presumably because the recessions from the 1940s to the 1960s were mild." Charles P. Kindleberger and Robert Z. Aliber, *Manias, Panics, and Crashes: A History of Financial Crises*, 5th ed. (Hoboken, NJ: John Wiley & Sons, 2005), 8. Jerry Z. Muller provides a brief summary of the postwar relationship between markets and government in *The Mind and the Market: Capitalism in Western Thought* (New York: Anchor Books, 2003), 322–26.
65. Schlesinger, *Age of Jackson*, 217, 218, 225, 43.
66. Hammond, *Banks and Politics*, 483, 467, 451. Hammond expressed this goal through sentences that provided guidance for central bankers. For example, he wrote, "No central banker should be endowed with such an unfailing eye for the bright side of things only" (465). Fritz Redlich had already associated the BUS with the functions of a central bank. Redlich, *The Molding of American Banking*. The Panic of 1837 has also served as a lesson to private bankers. Austin, "Baring Brothers"; Ralph W. Hidy, *The House of Baring in American Trade and Finance: English Merchant Bankers at Work, 1763–1861* (Cambridge, MA: Harvard University Press, 1949); and Perkins, *Financing Anglo-American Trade*.
67. Political historians challenged Hammond by reexamining his arguments on the state and local levels. For examples, see McFaul, *Politics of Jacksonian Finance*; Edward Pessen, *Jacksonian America: Society, Personality, and Politics* (Homewood, IL: Dorsey Press, 1969); and Sharp, *Jacksonians Versus the Banks*. Sean Wilentz countered Hammond's emphasis on bankers with an emphasis on workers in his rereading of the panic as social history. Sean Wilentz, *Chants Democratic: New York City and the Rise of the American Working*

Class, 1788–1850 (New York: Oxford University Press, 1984), 294. Economic historians with economics backgrounds also challenged Hammond by using the 1830s to evaluate central, state, and "free" banking. For examples, see Green, *Finance and Economic Development*, 165; J. Van Fernstermaker, *The Development of American Commercial Banking, 1782–1837* (Kent, OH: Kent State University Press, 1965); Hugh Rockoff, *The Free Banking Era: A Re-examination* (New York: Arno Press, 1975); Schweikart, *Banking in the American South*; Bodenhorn, *A History of Banking*; White, *Free Banking in Britain*; Lamoreaux, *Insider Lending*; and Wahl, "He Broke the Bank," 188–220. For the divide between history and economic history, see Cathy Matson, "A House of Many Mansions: Some Thoughts on the Field of Economic History," in *The Economy of Early America: Historical Perspectives & New Directions*, ed. Cathy Matson (University Park: Pennsylvania State University Press, 2006), 1–70.

68. Temin, *Jacksonian Economy*, 11. For Temin's synthesis of "the traditional story" that focused on political causation, see his *Jacksonian Economy*, 17–22.

69. Ibid., 23, 26, 17.

70. Ibid., 23. This argument has recently been challenged by another econometric study. Wallis, "What Caused the Crisis of 1839?"

71. Temin, *Jacksonian Economy*, 113. This definition of panic had become standard in economics. Green, for example, defined the Panic of 1837 as the suspension of specie payments and the period between March and May as a "sharp financial contraction." Green, *Finance and Economic Development*, 99, 26.

72. Temin, *Jacksonian Economy*, 116.

73. Marvin Meyers's non-quantitative study of Jacksonian economic culture recasts the issues of anticipation, confidence, and doubt in a term he invented to describe Americans of the 1830s: "venturous conservatives." Marvin Meyers, *The Jacksonian Persuasion: Politics and Beliefs* (1957; Stanford, CA: Stanford University Press, 1968), 55.

74. Rousseau, "Jacksonian Monetary Policy," 457–88; Richard H. Timberlake Jr., "The Specie Circular and Distribution of the Surplus," *Journal of Political Economy* 68, no. 2 (1960): 109–17; Richard H. Timberlake Jr., "The Specie Circular and the Sale of Public Lands: A Comment," *Journal of Economic History* 25, no. 3 (1965): 414–16; and Knodell, "Rethinking the Jacksonian Economy," 541–74.

75. Robert M. Solow, foreword to *Manias, Panics, and Crashes*, by Kindleberger and Aliber, viii. Only the posthumous edition includes Aliber as a coauthor.

76. Kindleberger and Aliber, *Manias, Panics, and Crashes*, 297.

77. Ibid., 24, 32.

78. "All Prizes in Economic Sciences," Nobelprize.org, http://nobelprize.org/nobel_prizes/economics/laureates/.

79. Kindleberger and Aliber, *Manias, Panics, and Crashes*, 38–54. The death of *homo economicus* has been a much-discussed topic in economic theory. For an overview of the debate, see O'Boyle, "Requiem for *Homo Economicus*," 321–37.

80. Kindleberger and Aliber, *Manias, Panics, and Crashes*, 32.

81. Jessica M. Lepler, "Pictures of Panic: Constructing Hard Times in Words and Images," *Common-Place* 10, no. 3 (Apr. 2010), http://www.common-place.org/vol-10/no-03/lepler/.

82. Charles W. Calomiris and Larry Schweikart, "The Panic of 1857: Origins, Transmission, and Containment," *Journal of Economic History* 51, no. 4 (Dec. 1991): 807–34; and Charles W. Calomiris and Joseph R. Mason, "Contagion and Bank Failures during the Great Depression: The June 1932 Chicago Banking Panic," *American Economic Review* 87, no. 5 (Dec. 1997): 863–83. Frederic Mishkin argues that the definition of financial crisis as bank panic limits the "financial disturbances that can have serious adverse effects on the aggregate economy"; he advocates, instead, the "asymmetric information approach." Mishkin, "Asymmetric Information and Financial Crises," 104. For a criticism of the equation of bank runs with panic from a sociological perspective, see Leon Mann, Trevor Nagel, and Peter Dowling, "A Study of Economic Panic: The 'Run' on the Hindmarsh Building Society," *Sociometry* 39, no. 3 (1976): 223–35.

83. Charles W. Calomiris and Joseph R. Mason, "Fundamentals, Panics, and Bank Distress during the Depression," *American Economic Review* 93, no. 5 (2003): 1615. Calomiris and Gorton equate "bank runs" and "bank panics" as long as the runs are not limited to a single institution. Calomiris and Gorton, "Origins of Banking Panics," 109–73, 112.

84. Behavioral economists have begun looking at non-quantitative approaches to studying irrationality – especially in terms of economic narratives. For a popular-audience summary of recent findings, see Akerlof and Shiller, *Animal Spirits*. For studies of narratives of economics, see Donald N. McCloskey, *The Rhetoric of Economics* (Madison: University of Wisconsin Press, 1985); Donald N. McCloskey, *If You're So Smart: The Narrative of Economic Expertise* (Chicago: University of Chicago Press, 1990); and Donald N. McCloskey, "The Problem of Audience in Historical Economics: Rhetorical Thoughts on a Text by Robert Fogel," *History and Theory* 24, no. 1 (1985): 1–22.

85. Akerlof and Shiller, *Animal Spirits*, 4, 177, n. 7.

86. Wilentz's *Chants Democratic* is an important exception within the subfield of social history that employed the panic as a turning point in the history of labor organization. In 1991, Charles Seller's *The Market Revolution* stoked controversy over the history of capitalism in America. Charles Sellers, *The Market Revolution: Jacksonian America, 1815–1846* (Oxford, UK: Oxford University Press, 1991); Melvyn Stokes and Stephen Conway, eds., *The Market Revolution in America: Social, Political, and Religious Expressions, 1800– 1880* (Charlottesville: University Press of Virginia, 1996); "A Symposium on Charles Sellers, 'The Market Revolution: Jacksonian America, 1815–1846,'" *Journal of the Early Republic* 12 (Winter 1992): 445–76; Daniel Feller, "Review: The Market Revolution Ate My Homework," *Reviews in American History* 25, no. 3 (Sept. 1997): 408–15; and Larson, *The Market Revolution in America*. Fueled in part by this debate, interest in the cultural history of capitalism has exploded in the last decade. Examples include Kamensky, *Exchange Artist*; Luskey, *On the Make*; Mihm, *Nation of Counterfeiters*; Opal, *Beyond the Farm*; and Sandage, *Born Losers*. For the culture of capitalism in Britain, see Margot C. Finn, *The Character of Credit: Personal Debt in English Culture, 1740–1914* (Cambridge, UK: Cambridge University Press, 2003); Patrick Brantlinger, *Fictions of State: Culture and*

Credit in Britain, 1694–1994 (Ithaca, NY: Cornell University Press, 1996); Green, *Pauper Capital*; and Abramson, *Building the Bank of England*.

87. Nineteenth-century history has only recently been reconceived in light of scholarship on the colonial period's "Atlantic World" and the twentieth-century's "Internationalization of American History." Reflecting this timing, Thomas Bender's synthesis skips most of the period between the Revolution and the Civil War. Thomas Bender, *A Nation Among Nations: America's Place in World History* (New York: Hill and Wang, 2006).

88. Howe, *What Hath God Wrought*, 502, 373–95, 498–508; and Wilentz, *Rise of American Democracy*, 360–74, 392–403, 436–46.

89. Some of the publications that inspired this project include: Balleisen, *Navigating Failure*; Cohen, *Murder of Helen Jewett*; Dupre, *Transforming the Cotton Frontier*; Bruce H. Mann, *Republic of Debtors: Bankruptcy in the Age of American Independence* (Cambridge, MA: Harvard University Press, 2002); Johnson, *Soul By Soul*; and Scott A. Sandage, "Deadbeats, Drunkards, and Dreamers: A Cultural History of Failure in America, 1819–1893" (PhD diss., Rutgers University, 1995). For a historiographical survey of recent cultural history, see James W. Cook, "The Kids Are All Right: On the 'Turning' of Cultural History," *American Historical Review* 117, no. 3 (June 2012): 746–71. For an analysis of intergenerational influences in cultural history, see Nathan Perl-Rosenthal, "Comment: Generational Turns," *American Historical Review* 117, no. 3 (June 2012): 804–13.

90. Baptist, "Toxic Debt"; Alasdair Roberts, *America's First Great Depression: Economic Crisis and Political Disorder after the Panic of 1837* (Ithaca, NY: Cornell University Press, 2012), 42–43; Larson, *Market Revolution*, 92; and Nelson, *Nation of Deadbeats*, 119–21.

91. *Wikipedia*, s.v. "Panic of 1837," modified May 12, 2003, http://en.wikipedia.org/w/index.php?title=Panic_of_1837&oldid=911890 (emphasis removed). The "Panic of 1837" entry was created by Daniel Mayer, a biologist and geographic information science specialist, during a period when he "went a bit wikicrazy by racking-up an insane number of edits," allowing him to claim to be the "most active non-bot-using contributor from early 2002 to early 2004." *Wikipedia*, s.v. "User:Mav," modified January 22, 2012, http://en.wikipedia.org/w/index.php?title=User:Mav&oldid=472703157

92. *Wikipedia*, s.v. "Panic of 1837," modified August 9, 2012, http://en.wikipedia.org/w/index.php?title=Panic_of_1837&oldid=506513352

93. Mitchell, *Business Cycles*, 11.

94. For studies that have looked at panics and the business cycle as cultural constructions, see Fabian, "Speculations on Distress"; and Roger Backhouse, "Misunderstanding the History of the Business Cycle," *History of Political Economy* 37, no. 2(2005): 179–84.

95. Mitchell, *Business Cycles*, 11.

96. Clay, "The Times." For more on Edward Williams Clay, his lithographs, and nineteenth-century political cartoons, see Nancy Reynolds Davison, "E. W. Clay: American Political Caricaturist of the Jacksonian Era" (PhD diss., University of Michigan, 1980); Frank Weitenkampf, *Political Caricature*

in the United States (New York: New York Public Library, 1953); and Bernard F. Reilly Jr., *American Political Prints, 1776–1876* (Boston: G. K. Hall, 1991).

97. Clay, "The Times."
98. Newspaper headlines started to hint at a crisis in subprime mortgages in January 2007, but the phrase "the subprime mortgage crisis" (without hyphenation and with a definite article) did not appear until March when Reuters quoted the term from a Standard and Poor's report. Although the phrase "the Panic of 2008" appeared in July 2008, it wore scare quotes as late as September 2009. By May 2010, however, it appeared on the front page of the *New York Times* as a noun that required no explanation. In August 2008, an Associated Press reporter covered economists' debates over conflicting indicators and highlighted one financial consulting firm's creation of "The Great Recession Game of '08." By March 2010, the Great Recession had clearly become a proper noun in popular culture when the *New York Times Magazine*'s cover included the headline "How to Prevent the Next Great Recession"; the corresponding article had a different and more generic title. These names suggest different solutions. Lingling Wei, "Subprime Lenders May Face Funding Crisis," *Wall Street Journal*, Jan. 10, 2007; "Morgan Stanley to Sell Subprime Lender's Loans," *New York Times*, Mar. 27, 2007; E. J. Dionne Jr., "Capitalism's Reality Check," *The Washington Post*, July 11, 2008; Kevin M. Warsh, "The Fed's Job Is Only Half Over," *Wall Street Journal*, Sept. 25, 2009; Graham Bowley, "Dow Falls 1,000, Then Rebounds, Shaking Market," *New York Times*, May 7, 2010; Ellen Simon, "Gimme a 'V'! Or would that be a 'W' or 'U'?: People of Numbers Turning to Letters to Describe the Downturn," *Chicago Tribune*, Aug. 26, 2008; and "Heading Off the Next Financial Crisis: The Case for More – and More Nuanced – Regulation," *New York Times Magazine*, Mar. 28, 2010.
99. Landon Thomas Jr., "To Some, the Widening Crisis Seems Driven by Fear, Not Facts," *New York Times*, Jan. 22, 2008.
100. Peter S. Goodman, "Economy Fitful, Americans Start to Pay as They Go: Living Within Means; Easy Credit Era Over, Some See a Trend Back to Thrift," *New York Times*, Feb. 5, 2008.
101. *Time*, Oct. 13, 2008; *Vanity Fair*, Apr. 2009; and *The New Yorker*, May 18, 2009.
102. *The Economist*, Jan. 26, 2008, and July 19, 2008.
103. "French Church," *Louisiana Advertiser* (New Orleans, LA), Apr. 12, 1827.
104. "Religious Intelligence," *The Christian Advocate* 6 (1828): 515, 566.
105. Herman Cope Duncan, *The Diocese of Louisiana: Some of Its History, 1838–1888* (New Orleans, 1888), 79.
106. *Eastern Argus* (Portland, ME), May 16, 1837.

Index

Note: Page numbers with 'n' refer to notes in the text

18677838R00201

Printed in Poland
by Amazon Fulfillment
Poland Sp. z o.o., Wrocław